Away3D 3.6 Essentials

Take Flash to the next dimension by creating detailed, animated, and interactive 3D worlds with Away3D

Matthew Casperson

[PACKT] open source *
PUBLISHING   community experience distilled

BIRMINGHAM - MUMBAI

Away3D 3.6 Essentials

Copyright © 2011 Packt Publishing

All rights reserved. No part of this book may be reproduced, stored in a retrieval system, or transmitted in any form or by any means, without the prior written permission of the publisher, except in the case of brief quotations embedded in critical articles or reviews.

Every effort has been made in the preparation of this book to ensure the accuracy of the information presented. However, the information contained in this book is sold without warranty, either express or implied. Neither the author, nor Packt Publishing, and its dealers and distributors will be held liable for any damages caused or alleged to be caused directly or indirectly by this book.

Packt Publishing has endeavored to provide trademark information about all of the companies and products mentioned in this book by the appropriate use of capitals. However, Packt Publishing cannot guarantee the accuracy of this information.

First published: January 2011

Production Reference: 1190111

Published by Packt Publishing Ltd
32 Lincoln Road
Olton
Birmingham, B27 6PA, UK.

ISBN 978-1-849512-06-0

www.packtpub.com

Cover Image by John M. Quick (john.m.quick@gmail.com)

Credits

Author
Matthew Casperson

Reviewers
Todsaporn Banjerdkit
Tony Lukasavage
Jerome Maurey-Delaunay

Acquisition Editor
Eleanor Duffy

Development Editor
Maitreya Bhakal

Technical Editor
Manasi Poonthottam

Indexer
Hemangini Bari

Editorial Team Leader
Mithun Sehgal

Project Team Leader
Lata Basantani

Project Coordinator
Leena Purkait

Proofreader
Ting Baker

Graphics
Nilesh Mohite

Production Coordinator
Aparna Bhagat

Cover Work
Aparna Bhagat

About the Author

Matthew Casperson has worked in IT for nearly a decade in a variety of roles, including development and support. In his spare time, he loves nothing more than to experiment with the latest Web and multimedia technologies. Many of these experiments can be found on Matthew's personal website at `http://goo.gl/2Hgr`.

Away3D 3.6 Essentials is Matthew's first book, but hopefully won't be the last!

> Credit has to be given to the amazing team behind Away3D. They have produced an incredible library, and I'm continually amazed at how they push the boundaries of the Flash platform.

About the Reviewers

Todsaporn Banjerdkit, also known as "Katopz", started with Flash ActionScript in 1999 and it was love at first sight. His hobby as an ActionScript coder turned into a full-time job at a worldwide advertising company in Thailand.

He enjoys building Web experiences and casual Flash games. He also joined Away3D and JigLibFlash as a core developer member, mainly handling Away3DLite. Joining an open source community brought him great opportunities. He has met developers and made lots of friends around the world because of to it.

When not coding, he enjoys designing 3D model characters as a hobby.

> Thanks to my mom (Germgai), my girlfriend (Faiiz), and my cats (Pignoom and Kabmoo)!

Tony Lukasavage graduated with a Computer Science and Engineering degree from Bucknell University in 2002, and since then has become a coding Swiss Army knife, constantly engaging in exciting projects. Ranging from journeyman to expert in an array of computer languages, he avoided becoming a single language zealot and prefers to choose the right tool for the job. Language-agnostic concepts and object-oriented design are his specialties.

Tony is currently developing health system applications, including medical imaging and transfer in AS3 and service-oriented architecture in C#. In addition, he regularly submits demos and code for Away3D, ActionScript3, graphics, Android mobile development, and anything else that catches his eye. See his developer's blog: `http://savagelook.com/blog`.

www.PacktPub.com

Support files, eBooks, discount offers, and more

You might want to visit www.PacktPub.com for support files and downloads related to your book.

Did you know that Packt offers eBook versions of every book published, with PDF and ePub files available? You can upgrade to the eBook version at www.PacktPub.com and as a print book customer, you are entitled to a discount on the eBook copy. Get in touch with us at service@packtpub.com for more details.

At www.PacktPub.com, you can also read a collection of free technical articles, sign up for a range of free newsletters and receive exclusive discounts and offers on Packt books and eBooks.

PACKTLIB®

http://PacktLib.PacktPub.com

Do you need instant solutions to your IT questions? PacktLib is Packt's online digital book library. Here, you can access, read and search across Packt's entire library of books.

Why Subscribe?

- Fully searchable across every book published by Packt
- Copy and paste, print and bookmark content
- On demand and accessible via web browser

Free Access for Packt account holders

If you have an account with Packt at www.PacktPub.com, you can use this to access PacktLib today and view nine entirely free books. Simply use your login credentials for immediate access.

Table of Contents

Preface	**1**
Chapter 1: Building Your First Away3D Application	**7**
Choosing between Away3D for Flash Player 9 or Flash Player 10	**7**
Downloading Away3D	**8**
Downloading the source ZIP file	8
Downloading the source using SVN	9
Using TortoiseSVN	9
Creating an empty project for Away3D	**10**
Adobe Flex Builder or Flash Builder	10
FlashDevelop	10
Adobe Flash CS4	11
Targeting the Flash Player 10 runtime	**13**
Adobe Flex Builder and Adobe Flash Builder	13
FlashDevelop	15
Adobe Flash CS4	17
Creating the initial application	**18**
Running Away3DTemplate	**21**
Adobe Flex Builder and Adobe Flash Builder	21
FlashDevelop	22
Adobe Flash CS4	23
The end result	24
Positioning objects in a 3D scene	**25**
Extending Away3DTemplate to populate the scene	**26**
Running SphereDemo	**28**
Adobe Flex and Adobe Flash Builder	28
FlashDevelop	28
Adobe Flash CS4	28
The end result	29
Summary	**29**

Table of Contents

Chapter 2: Creating and Displaying Primitives — 31
The basic elements of a 3D object — 31
Vertices — 32
Triangle faces — 32
Sprite3D — 35
Segments — 38
UV coordinates — 38
Creating primitive 3D objects — 39
Common init object properties — 45
Cone — 46
Cube — 47
Cylinder — 51
Geodesic sphere — 52
Grid plane — 54
LineSegment — 56
Plane — 57
RegularPolygon — 58
RoundedCube — 59
SeaTurtle — 60
Skybox — 62
Skybox6 — 63
Sphere — 64
Torus — 66
Triangle — 67
Trident — 68
Summary — 69

Chapter 3: Moving Objects — 71
Global, parent, and local coordinate systems — 71
World space — 72
Parent space — 73
Local space — 75
Transformation functions / properties and their coordinate systems — 78
Modifying position — 79
The x, y, and z properties — 79
The position property — 80
The move functions — 80
The moveTo() function — 81
Modifying rotation — 82
The rotation init object parameters — 82
The rotation properties — 83

[ii]

The rotateTo() function	83
The eulers property	84
The rotate() function	84
The lookAt() function	84
The pivotPoint property	85
The movePivot() function	86
The scenePivotPoint property	87
The pitch(), roll(), and yaw() functions	87
Modifying scale	**88**
The scale init object parameter	88
The scale() function	88
The scaleX, scaleY, and scaleZ properties	88
Modifying the transform	**89**
Tweening	**89**
Nesting	**92**
Summary	**97**
Chapter 4: Z-Sorting	**99**
The painter's algorithm	**100**
Sorting the scene	**100**
Adjusting the sorting order	**103**
The pushfront and pushback properties	103
The screenZOffset property	104
The ownCanvas property	106
A note about Z-Sorting	**107**
Additional renderers	**108**
Summary	**116**
Chapter 5: Materials	**117**
The difference between textures and materials	**117**
Resource management	**118**
Defining colors in Away3D	**119**
By integer	119
By string	120
Pixel Bender	**121**
Lights and materials	**122**
Shading techniques	**123**
Texture mapping	123
Normal mapping	124
Environment mapping	125
Flat shading	126
Phong shading	126

Table of Contents

Applying materials	**127**
Basic materials	137
WireColorMaterial	137
WireframeMaterial	139
ColorMaterial	140
Bitmap materials	141
BitmapMaterial	141
TransformBitmapMaterial	143
Animated materials	145
MovieMaterial	145
AnimatedBitmapMaterial	146
Interactive MovieMaterial	148
Composite materials	149
DepthBitmapMaterial	149
EnviroBitmapMaterial	151
EnviroColorMaterial	153
Light materials	154
WhiteShadingBitmapMaterial	154
ShadingColorMaterial	155
PhongBitmapMaterial	157
PhongColorMaterial	158
PhongMovieMaterial	159
Dot3BitmapMaterial	160
Pixel Bender materials	161
Dot3BitmapMaterialF10	161
PhongPBMaterial	162
PhongMultiPassMaterial	164
FresnelPBMaterial	165
CubicEnvMapPBMaterial	167
Loading textures from external files	**168**
BitmapFileMaterial	169
Using the TextureLoadQueue	169
Summary	**172**
Chapter 6: Models and Animations	**173**
3D formats supported by Away3D	**174**
Exporting 3D models	174
Exporting from 3ds Max	175
Exporting from MilkShape	176
Exporting from Sketch-Up	176
Exporting from Blender	177
A note about the Collada exporters	178
Loading a 3D model	**179**
Animated models	180
MD2—Loading an embedded file	180
Static models	190

[iv]

The problem with init and Init objects	202
Converting a loaded model to an ActionScript class	204
Summary	206

Chapter 7: Cameras — 207

The properties of a camera	**208**
Camera lenses	**209**
ZoomFocusLens and PerspectiveLens classes	210
SphericalLens class	210
OrthogonalLens class	212
Camera classes	**212**
Target camera	219
Hover camera	220
Spring camera	223
Summary	**224**

Chapter 8: Mouse Interactivity — 225

Away3D mouse events	**225**
The difference between ROLL_OVER / ROLL_OUT and MOUSE_OVER / MOUSE_OUT	**227**
Projecting the mouse position into the scene	**231**
Summary	**240**

Chapter 9: Special Effects with Sprites — 241

Using the Sprite3D class	**242**
Using the DirectionalSprite class	**245**
Using the DepthOfFieldSprite class	**251**
Using a particle system	**255**
Creating the Away3D Stardust initializer	256
Creating the Away3D Stardust particle renderer	258
Creating the Stardust emitter	261
Putting it all together	265
Summary	**267**

Chapter 10: Creating 3D Text — 269

Embedding fonts	**270**
Displaying text in the scene	**271**
3D Text materials	**273**
Extruding 3D text	**274**
Warping 3D text	**277**
Summary	**285**

Table of Contents

Chapter 11: Extrusions and Modifiers — 287
Creating a flag with the PathExtrusion class — 288
Creating walls with the LinearExtrusion class — 291
Creating a vase with the LatheExtrusion class — 293
Creating terrain with the SkinExtrusion class — 297
Reading the height of a terrain surface with the ElevationReader class — 302
HeightMapModifier — 306
Summary — 310

Chapter 12: Filters and Postprocessing Effects — 311
Flash and Away3D filters — 312
The Flash filters — 312
Applying filters — 312
Applying the BlurFilter — 317
Applying the DisplacementMapFilter — 318
Applying the GlowFilter — 319
Applying Pixel Bender shaders — 320
Applying filters to the view — 321
Away3D filters — 322
Render Sessions — 326
Postprocessing with the BitmapRenderSession — 327
Summary — 333

Chapter 13: Performance Tips — 335
Determining the current frame rate — 335
Setting the maximum frame rate — 337
Setting Flash quality to low — 338
Reducing the size of the viewport — 339
Scaling the viewport output — 340
Triangle caching — 341
Level of detail models — 345
Away3D filters — 348
ZDepthFilter — 348
MaxPolyFilter — 348
Offscreen rendering — 349
Model formats — 360
Summary — 368

Index — 369

Preface

Away3D is one of the most popular real-time 3D engines available for Flash, allowing for the creation of a wide range of 3D applications, including visualizing detailed 3D environments, displaying animated 3D models, creating 3D text, and showing off a huge variety of special effects. With Away3D, a little ActionScript, and a big imagination the possibilities are endless.

This book will guide you through the various features available in Away3D, demonstrating the possibilities it opens up for the Flash platform. With practical examples and some real-world tips, you will be up and running with Away3D in no time.

Starting with the very basics, this book will walk you through creating your first Away3D application by downloading the Away3D source code and using it from within a number of authoring tools like Flex Builder, Flash Builder, FlashDevelop, and Flash CS4. Next, you ease your way through creating your first primitive 3D objects from scratch, then move on to creating stunning 3D environments with incredibly detailed textures and animations. You will learn how to make your applications react to the user, learn ways to focus your camera and view your 3D scene from any angle, and then take your Away3D application to the next level with a number of optimization techniques that allow you to obtain the best performance from Away3D, without compromising on visual appeal.

From displaying a simple sphere through to creating entire 3D cities, this book will show you the steps you need to follow, with plenty of tips to help you avoid common pitfalls.

Preface

What this book covers

Chapter 1, Building Your First Away3D Application, which will show you how to create your first Away3D application using a variety of IDEs, including Flex Builder, Flash Builder, FlashDevelop, and Flash CS4.

Chapter 2, Creating and Displaying Primitives, where you will explore the various primitive 3D objects available in Away3D.

Chapter 3, Moving Objects, which shows you how to move, rotate, and scale 3D objects within the scene, either directly or through the TweenLite library.

Chapter 4, Z-Sorting, which explores the tricks that can be employed to solve sorting and rendering issues that can arise in Away3D applications.

Chapter 5, Materials, which takes a look at the various materials that are included in Away3D, from basic materials that display a single color, right through to those materials that make use of the advanced Pixel Bender platform. Lighting is also covered in this chapter.

Chapter 6, Models and Animations, where you will learn how to load and display both static and animated 3D models created in external 3D modeling applications.

Chapter 7, Cameras, which explores the various properties that affect how the scene is viewed, as well as demonstrating the camera classes available in Away3D that allow you to easily track and view the 3D objects in your scene.

Chapter 8, Mouse Interactivity, where you will learn how to respond to the mouse in order to create interactive 3D applications that are easy and natural to use.

Chapter 9, Special Effects with Sprites, where a number of special effects are demonstrated, including integration with the Stardust particle engine.

Chapter 10, Creating 3D Text, which shows you how to create and manipulate 3D text.

Chapter 11, Extrusions and Modifiers, which explores how complex 3D objects can be created directly by Away3D without the aid of an external 3D modeling application.

Chapter 12, Filters and Postprocessing Effects, which will show you how to add exciting visual effects to your Away3D applications.

Chapter 13, Performance Tips, where you will learn how to optimize your Away3D applications, which will allow you to create spectacular 3D environments while maintaining a high level of performance.

What you need for this book

Anyone looking to build engaging, interactive, and eye-catching websites or addictive 3D games will appreciate the power of Away3D, and this book will provide all the information that is needed to harness that power. All you need is an Internet connection to download Away3D, and an ActionScript IDE such as Flex/Flash Builder, Flash CS4, or Flash Develop, which is free to download and use.

Who this book is for

This book is meant for beginners as well as experienced Flash developers who are looking to create 3D applications in Flash using the Away3D engine. Whether you are using Away3D for the first time or are a seasoned developer, this book will provide you with a solid foundation in taking Flash to the next dimension. It can also be used as a reference guide by Flash developers who are already familiar with Away3D.

Conventions

In this book, you will find a number of styles of text that distinguish between different kinds of information. Here are some examples of these styles, and an explanation of their meaning.

Code words in text are shown as follows: "By extending the Away3DTemplate class, we have created a simple 3D application with the SphereDemo class using only a few lines of code."

A block of code is set as follows:

```
import away3d.core.base.Object3D;
import away3d.primitives.Cone;
import away3d.primitives.Cube;
import away3d.primitives.Cylinder;
import away3d.primitives.GeodesicSphere;
```

New terms and **important words** are shown in bold. Words that you see on the screen, in menus or dialog boxes for example, appear in the text like this: "In order to use the TweenLite library it has to be added to the **Source path** in Flex/Flash Builder and Flash CS4, or the **Project Classpaths** in FlashDevelop".

> Warnings or important notes appear in a box like this.

> Tips and tricks appear like this.

Reader feedback

Feedback from our readers is always welcome. Let us know what you think about this book—what you liked or may have disliked. Reader feedback is important for us to develop titles that you really get the most out of.

To send us general feedback, simply send an e-mail to feedback@packtpub.com, and mention the book title via the subject of your message.

If there is a book that you need and would like to see us publish, please send us a note in the **SUGGEST A TITLE** form on www.packtpub.com or e-mail suggest@packtpub.com.

If there is a topic that you have expertise in and you are interested in either writing or contributing to a book, see our author guide on www.packtpub.com/authors.

Customer support

Now that you are the proud owner of a Packt book, we have a number of things to help you to get the most from your purchase.

> **Downloading the example code for the book**
>
> You can download the example code files for all Packt books you have purchased from your account at http://www.PacktPub.com. If you purchased this book elsewhere, you can visit http://www.PacktPub.com/support and register to have the files e-mailed directly to you.

Errata

Although we have taken every care to ensure the accuracy of our content, mistakes do happen. If you find a mistake in one of our books—maybe a mistake in the text or the code—we would be grateful if you would report this to us. By doing so, you can save other readers from frustration and help us improve subsequent versions of this book. If you find any errata, please report them by visiting http://www.packtpub.com/support, selecting your book, clicking on the **errata submission form** link, and entering the details of your errata. Once your errata are verified, your submission will be accepted and the errata will be uploaded on our website, or added to any list of existing errata, under the Errata section of that title. Any existing errata can be viewed by selecting your title from http://www.packtpub.com/support.

Piracy

Piracy of copyright material on the Internet is an ongoing problem across all media. At Packt, we take the protection of our copyright and licenses very seriously. If you come across any illegal copies of our works, in any form, on the Internet, please provide us with the location address or website name immediately so that we can pursue a remedy.

Please contact us at copyright@packtpub.com with a link to the suspected pirated material.

We appreciate your help in protecting our authors, and our ability to bring you valuable content.

Questions

You can contact us at questions@packtpub.com if you are having a problem with any aspect of the book, and we will do our best to address it.

Building Your First Away3D Application

Creating your first Away3D application can be a daunting task due to the number of steps that have to be completed before even a single line of code is written. This chapter will walk you through the steps required to get your first Away3D application up and running.

This chapter covers the following topics:

- The different Away3D versions
- Downloading Away3D
- Configuring your development environment
- An overview of the concepts used by Away3D
- Creating a simple application
- Compiling the application with your chosen authoring tool

Choosing between Away3D for Flash Player 9 or Flash Player 10

Flash Player 10 was released by Adobe in 2008, and it brought with it a number of performance improvements and additional features that greatly benefit 3D engines like Away3D. However, these features are not backwards compatible, which means that a Flash application that targets Flash Player 10 will not run on Flash Player 9. To accommodate both Flash Player 9 and 10, Away3D maintains two versions of the engine: Away3D version 2.x, which targets Flash Player 9, and Away3D version 3.x, which targets Flash Player 10.

Building Your First Away3D Application

When Flash Player 10 was initially released, developers had good reason to support the older version Flash Player 9, because the percentage of devices with Flash Player 10 installed was relatively small. At the time of writing though Flash Player 10 is installed on over 90% of internet-enabled devices. You can view the current statistics on the Adobe website at `http://www.adobe.com/products/player_census/flashplayer/version_penetration.html`.

Given the significant market penetration of Flash Player 10, and the additional performance and features provided by the Flash Player 10 version of Away3D, this book will focus on Away3D version 3.x.

Downloading Away3D

Away3D can be downloaded from two different locations. The first location is the download page on the Away3D website at `http://away3d.com/downloads`. Here you will find links to ZIP files for the stable releases of the Away3D engine. These releases have been tested and are deemed to be of a high enough quality to be used in production.

The second location that Away3D can be downloaded from is the SVN repository hosted on Google Code at `http://code.google.com/p/away3d/`. The code in the SVN repository represents the current, up-to-the-minute state of Away3D. Using this code gives you access to the latest features and bug fixes that have not yet made their way into a stable release. However, this code is still in the process of being tested, so is generally not recommended for everyday use.

Downloading the source ZIP file

Unless otherwise stated, all the examples in this book have been compiled against Away3D version 3.6, which is the latest stable release at the time of writing. This file can be downloaded from the Away3D website at `http://away3d.com/downloads` or by using the direct link `http://away3d.com/download/away3d_3_6_0.zip`. If you are downloading the ZIP file from the download page, click on the **Flash 10** link under the heading **Version 2.6.0 / 3.6.0**.

> Away3D is a very active project, with new releases made every few months. It is possible that by the time you are reading this, the download page or direct link has been changed from what has been described above. If that is the case you can download `away3d_3_6_0.zip` from the Packt website.
>
> The examples presented in this book may work with later versions of the Away3D engine, but using version 3.6 will guarantee compatibility.

Once you have downloaded the ZIP file, you will need to extract it to a convenient location somewhere on your computer. Remember this location, because you will reference it later when you set up your development environment.

Downloading the source using SVN

SVN provides a convenient way to get access to the very latest version of Away3D, and tools, such as TortoiseSVN, make accessing the Away3D SVN repository a straightforward process.

Using TortoiseSVN

TortoiseSVN is a popular and free SVN client that integrates with Windows Explorer to provide easy access to SVN repositories. Use the following steps to download and install TortoiseSVN, and then use it to download the Away3D source code:

1. Download TortoiseSVN from `http://tortoisesvn.net/downloads`.
2. Install TortoiseSVN using the default settings, and reboot your computer.
3. Once your computer has booted back up, create a new folder in a convenient location that will be used to contain the Away3D source code. For simplicity, you may want to consider creating a folder called `Away3D` in the root folder of drive C.
4. Right-click on your new folder and click on the **SVN Checkout** option.
5. You will be presented with the **Checkout** dialog box. Enter `http://away3d.googlecode.com/svn/trunk/fp10/Away3D/src` into the **URL of repository** textbox.

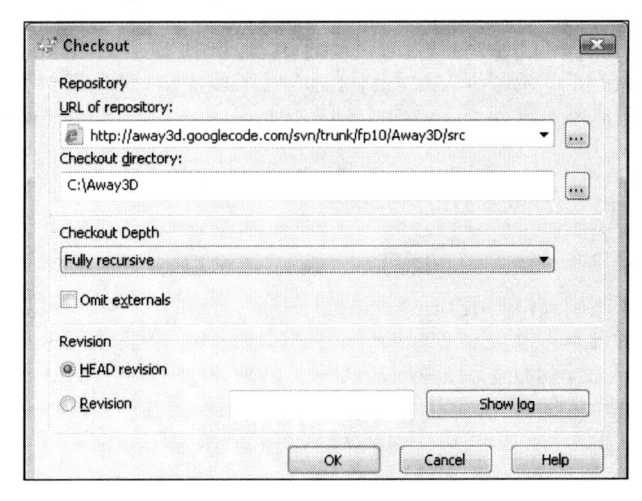

6. Click on the **OK** button to download the Away3D files.

Building Your First Away3D Application

Creating an empty project for Away3D

In order to create an Away3D application, you first need to create and configure a project within your authoring tool. In addition, to make use of Away3D engine the new project will have to be configured so that it can access the Away3D source code.

Adobe Flex Builder or Flash Builder

The following steps show you how to create a new project in Flash and Flex Builder that uses the Away3D library:

1. Open up Adobe Flex and click **File | New | ActionScript project**.
2. You will now be asked to **Specify the location of the files in the new project**. Type the name of the project in the **Project name** textbox and click on the **Next** button.
3. You will now be asked to **Set the build paths for the new ActionScript Project**. Under the **Source Path** tab, click on the **Add Folder** button.
4. Click on the **Browse** button to select to the location where you saved the Away3D source code, or type it directly into the textbox.
5. With the Away3D source code folder selected, click on the **OK** button.
6. The Away3D source code directory is now listed in the **Source Path** list. Click on the **Finish** button to create the project.

FlashDevelop

FlashDevelop is a free Integrated Development Environment, or IDE, that can be used to create Flash applications. When used in conjunction with the Flex SDK, which is also free, FlashDevelop can be used to write and compile Flash applications. FlashDevelop can be found on its website at http://www.flashdevelop.org.

The following steps show you how to create a new project in FlashDevelop that uses the Away3D library:

1. Open FlashDevelop and click **Project | New Project…**.
2. Select **AS3 Project** from the **ActionScript 3** group in the **Installed Templates** list. Type a name for the project in the **Name** textbox, and specify a location for the project in the **Location** textbox. Enabling the **Create directory for project** checkbox will create a subdirectory for the project in the **Location** directory. Click on the **OK** button to create the project.

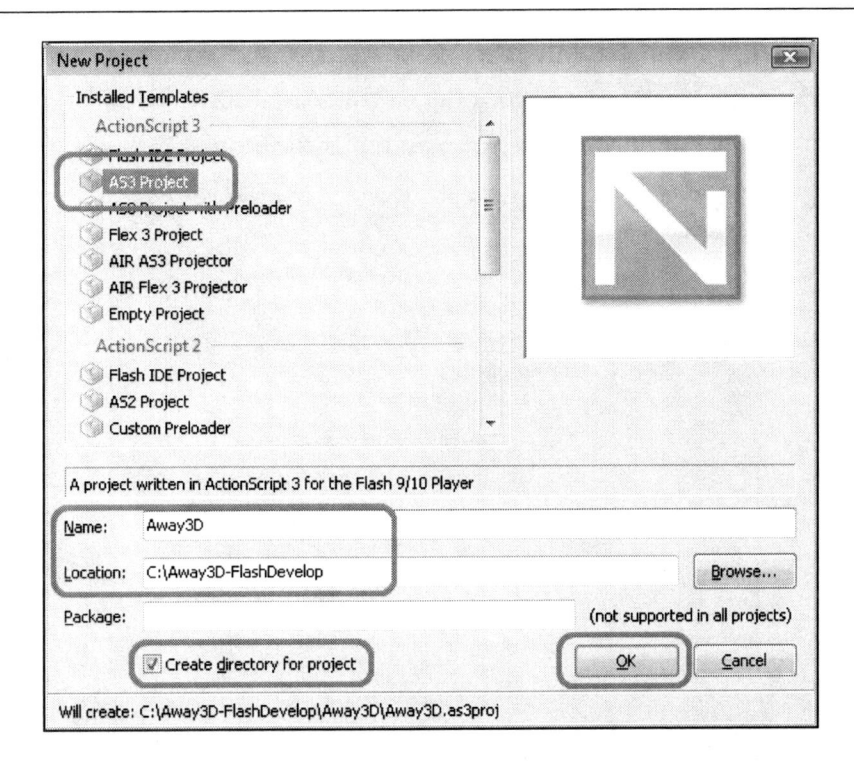

3. Click **Project | Properties...**.
4. Click on the **Classpaths** tab, and click the **Add Classpath...** button.
5. Browse to the location where you saved the Away3D source code and click on the **OK** button.
6. The Away3D source code directory is now listed in the **Project Classpaths** list (note that FlashDevelop uses relative paths for the classpath entries that exist on the same drive as the project). Click on the **OK** button to save the changes.

Adobe Flash CS4

Adobe Flash is the original Flash authoring tool. Adobe Flash places a large emphasis on providing a visual environment in which to create Flash animations, but it can also be used to create Flash applications using only ActionScript. The following steps show you how to create a new project in Adobe Flash CS4 that uses the Away3D library:

1. Open up Adobe Flash CS4 and click **File | New...**.
2. Select **Flash File (ActionScript 3.0)** from the **General** tab and click on the **OK** button.

3. Click **File | Publish Settings…**.
4. Click on the **Flash** tab, and click the **Settings…** button.
5. Click on the button with the plus icon under the **Source Path** tab.

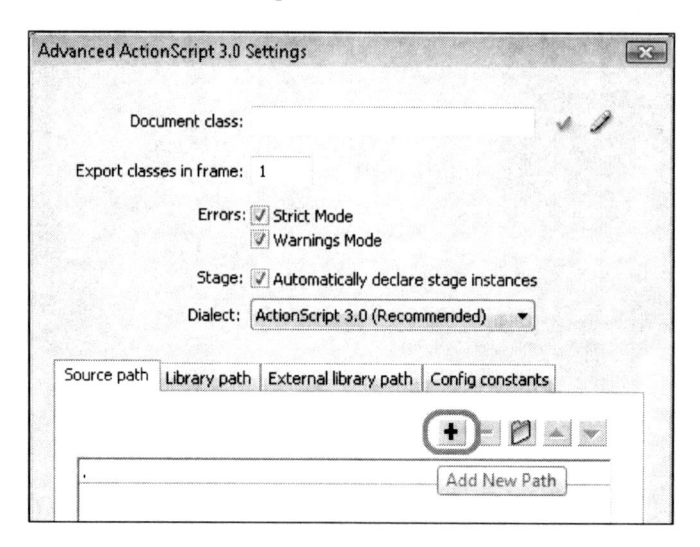

6. Click on the button with the folder icon.

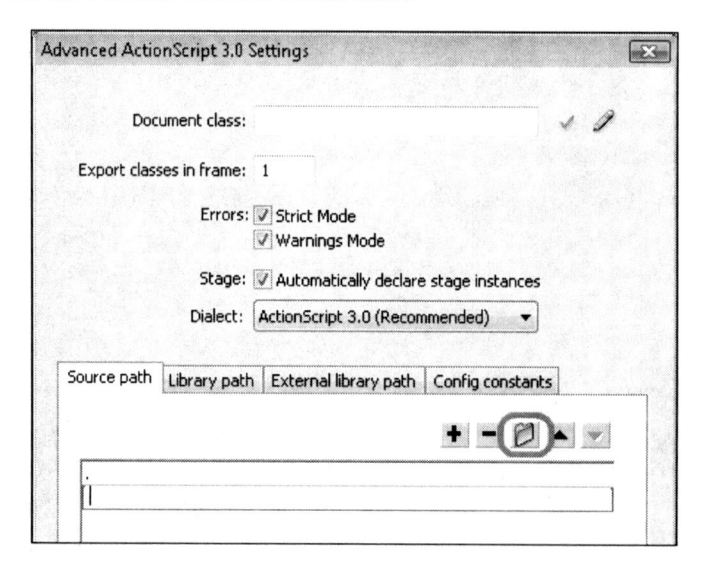

7. Browse to the Away3D source code directory, or type it directly into the list, and click on the **OK** button to save the changes.
8. Click on the **OK** button to close the **Advanced ActionScript 3.0 Settings** window.

9. Click on the **OK** button to close the **Publish Settings** window.
10. Click **File | Save** and save the FLA file to a directory of your choice.

Targeting the Flash Player 10 runtime

As we mentioned at the beginning of this chapter, Away3D 3.x targets the Flash Player 10 runtime. In order to compile an application using Away3D 3.x, your authoring tool needs to be configured to use a version of the Flex SDK 3.2 or above.

The Flex SDK can be freely downloaded from `http://opensource.adobe.com/wiki/display/flexsdk/Download+Flex+3`. It is best to download the latest milestone release of the Adobe Flex SDK listed on the page. Once downloaded, extract the ZIP file to a convenient location.

Adobe Flex Builder and Adobe Flash Builder

These steps are only required in Flex Builder 3. In Flash Builder 4, the default Flex SDK is version 4.0, and the default target Flash Player version is 10.

1. With your ActionScript project open, click **Project | Properties**.
2. Select the **ActionScript Compiler** option from the left-hand pane. Make sure the **Require Flash Player version** checkbox is enabled, and enter **10.0.0** as the version. Now click on the **Configure Flex SDKs** link.

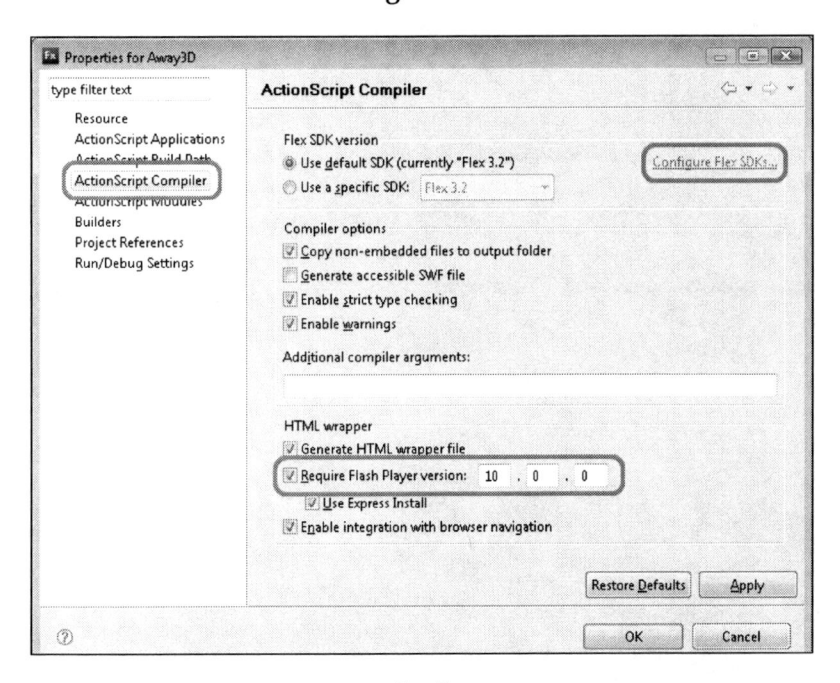

Building Your First Away3D Application

3. Click on the **Add** button.

4. In the **Add Flex SDK** dialog box, type in the location where the Flex SDK was extracted to in the **Flex SDK location** textbox, or click on the **Browse** button to search for the directory.

5. The **Flex SDK name** textbox should now show the name of the selected Flex SDK. Click on the **OK** button in the **Add Flex SDK** dialog box to return to the **Preferences** window.

6. Enabling the checkbox next to the new SDK instructs Flex to use that SDK by default. Click on the **OK** button to return to the project properties window.

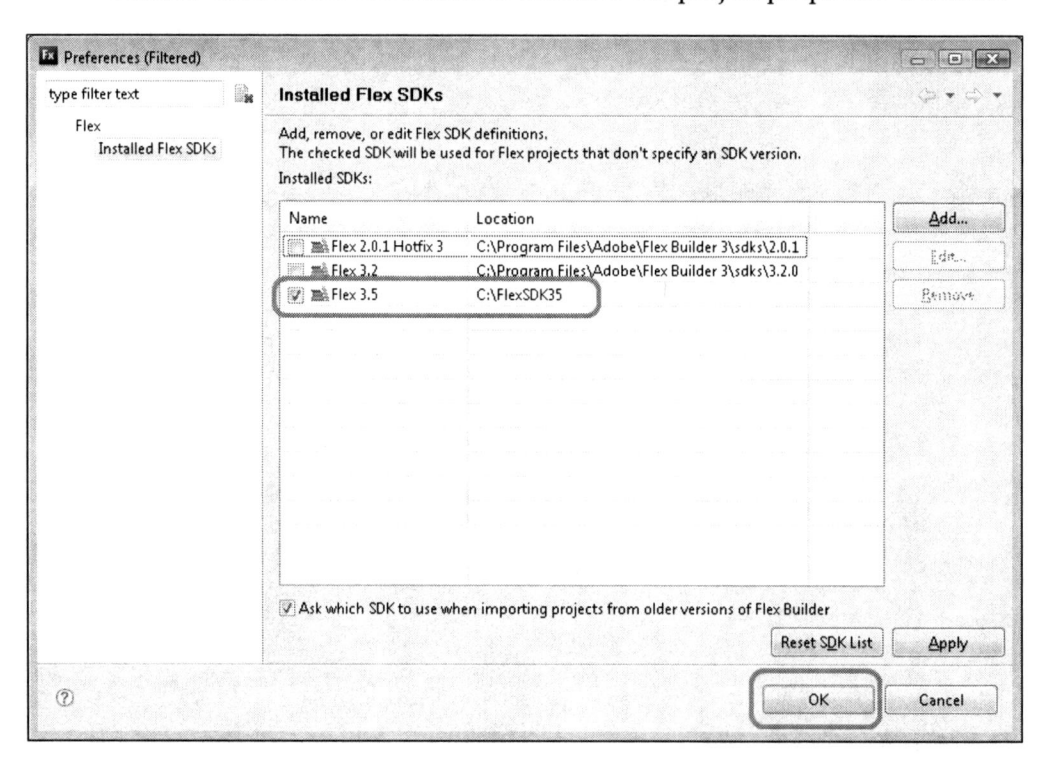

7. The version number shown next to the **Use default SDK** radio button in the **Flex SDK version** group box should be that of the new Flex SDK. Click on the **OK** button to close down the properties window.

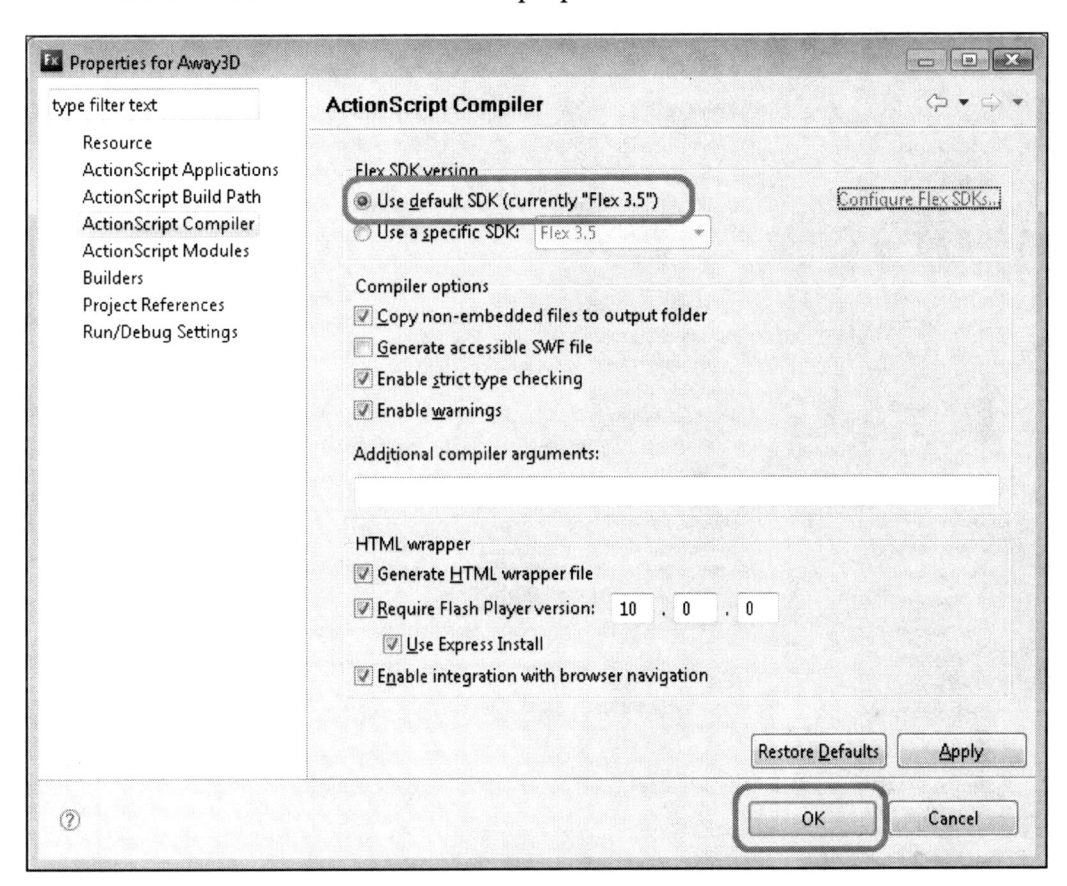

FlashDevelop

When you install FlashDevelop for the first time you do have the option of also downloading a copy of the Flex SDK that already supports Flash Player 10. Or you can use the following steps to manually specify the location of a suitable Flex SDK:

1. Click **Tools | Program Settings...**.

Building Your First Away3D Application

2. Select the **AS3Context** option in the left-hand pane, and click on the button with the three ellipses next to **Flex SDK Location**, which can be found in the group of options labeled **Language**.

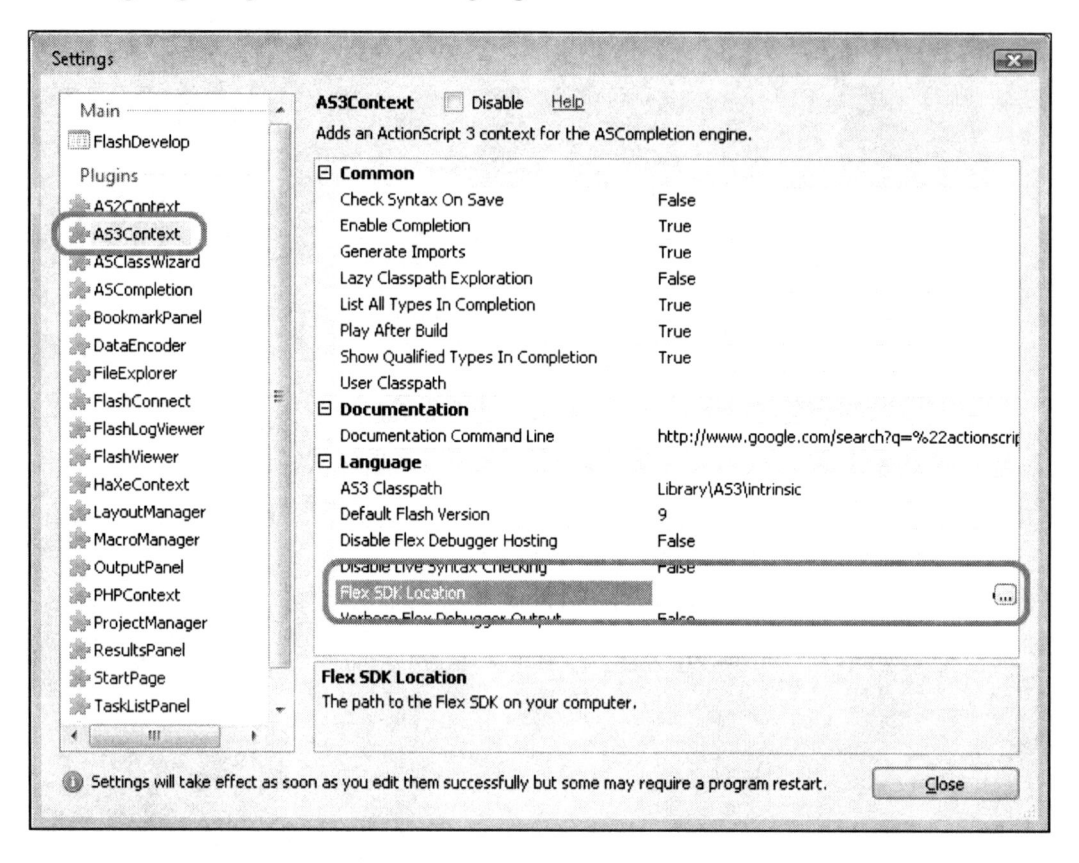

3. Browse to the location where the Flex SDK has been extracted and click on the **OK** button.

4. The **Flex SDK Location** should now show the updated location. Click on the **Close** button.

5. With a FlashDevelop project open, click **Project | Properties**.

6. Under the **Output** tab select **Flash Player 10** from the **Target** drop-down list. Click on the **OK** button to save the changes.

Adobe Flash CS4

The following steps show you how to use the Flex SDK in Adobe Flash CS4:

1. Click **Edit | Preferences**.
2. Select the **ActionScript** option in the left-hand **Category** pane. Then click on the **ActionScript 3.0 Settings...** button.
3. Type in the location where the Flex SDK was extracted to in the **Flex SDK Path** textbox, or browse to the folder location by clicking on the button with the folder icon at the end of the textbox.
4. Click on the **OK** button to save the changes.

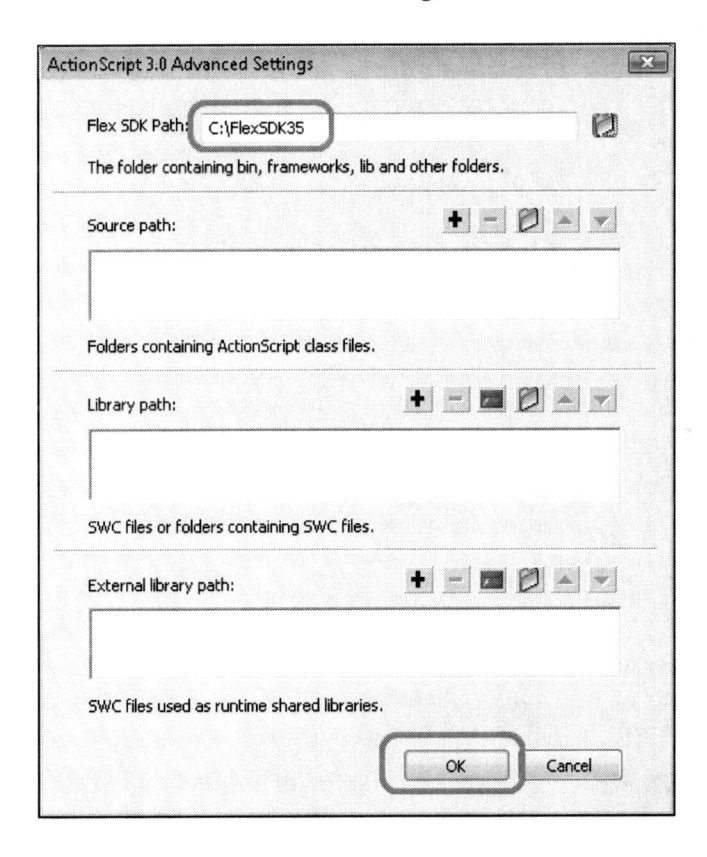

5. Click on the **OK** button to close the **Preferences** window.

Building Your First Away3D Application

Creating the initial application

At this point, your authoring tool is configured and a new project has been created and configured to use the Away3D library and a version of the Flex SDK that targets Flash Player 10. It's now time to create your first Away3D application.

Away3D includes a large number of features, but there are a few basic classes that need to be set up before these features can be used. These classes are:

- `Scene3D`, which represents the 3D space that holds the 3D objects that are to be displayed on the screen. This is commonly referred to as the scene.
- `Camera3D`, which provides an object through which the scene is viewed. This is commonly referred to as the camera.
- `View3D`, which is a container `Sprite` added to the stage that displays the scene as it is viewed by the camera. This is commonly referred to as the view.

> The term **3D object** used throughout this book is a general term that refers to any 3D model or primitive shape that is placed in the scene. 3D objects are represented by the `Object3D` class, from the `away3d.core.base` package, or classes that extend the `Object3D` class.

The `Away3DTemplate` class will include the basic logic required to create and initialize the scene, camera, and view objects. Let's take a look at the code that makes up the `Away3DTemplate` class.

```
package
{
```

The scene, camera, and view, which are represented by classes called `Scene3D`, `Camera3D`, and `View3D`, are imported to make them available within the class.

```
import away3d.cameras.Camera3D;
import away3d.containers.Scene3D;
import away3d.containers.View3D;
```

We also import the Flash `Sprite` class, which will be extended by the `Away3DTemplate` class, and the Flash `Event` class, used by the Flash event system.

```
import flash.display.Sprite;
import flash.events.Event;
```

By extending the Sprite class, the Away3DTemplate class can be added to the Flash stage just like any other visual element.

```
public class Away3DTemplate extends Sprite
{
```

We define properties for the scene, camera, and view, using the classes that were imported above.

```
protected var scene:Scene3D;
protected var camera:Camera3D;
protected var view:View3D;
```

The constructor goes on to call a number of functions, each of which is used to set up an aspect of the 3D application.

```
public function Away3DTemplate():void
{
```

First user interface elements are created by the initUI() function.

```
initUI();
```

Those properties that make up the core elements of the Away3D engine (that is, the scene, camera, and view) are initialized by calling the initEngine() function.

```
initEngine();
```

The scene is populated by the initScene() function.

```
initScene();
```

Event listeners are configured by the initListeners() function.

```
initListeners();
}
```

The initEngine() function is where the core elements of the Away3D engine are created.

```
protected function initEngine():void
{
```

The only object we need to explicitly create is the View3D class.

```
view = new View3D();
```

While we could also manually create the scene and camera, these objects are created by the View3D class by default. Here we simply get a reference to these two objects for convenience.

> By default, the camera is positioned 1,000 units towards the negative end of the Z-axis (so its position is (0, 0, -1000)), looking back at the scene origin. See the section *Positioning objects in a 3D scene* for more information on positioning within a 3D scene.

```
scene = view.scene;
camera = view.camera;
```

Just like our own `Away3DTemplate` class, the `View3D` class extends the Flash `Sprite` class. In order for the `View3D` object to be visible on the screen we need to add it as a child.

```
addChild(view);
```

Finally, the `View3D` object is repositioned so it is in the centre of the screen. Note that the X and Y coordinates assigned here position the `View3D` object within the Flash stage, and are not related to a position within the 3D scene.

```
view.x = stage.stageWidth / 2;
view.y = stage.stageHeight / 2;
}
```

The `initListeners()` function is used to register event handlers.

```
protected function initListeners():void
{
```

We have registered the `onEnterFrame()` function to be called once per frame in response to the `Event.ENTER_FRAME` event.

```
addEventListener(Event.ENTER_FRAME, onEnterFrame);
}
```

In the `onEnterFrame()` function we render a single frame to the screen by calling the `View3D` `render()` function. Remember that the `onEnterFrame()` function is called continuously in response to the `Event.ENTER_FRAME` event. By continuously rendering frames in this manner, we can create the impression of movement or animation within a 3D scene, just like the frames of a film strip being projected onto a screen.

```
protected function onEnterFrame(event:Event):void
{
   view.render();
}
```

The `initScene()` function is where we populate the scene, giving us something to look at when the application is run. Because the `Away3DTemplate` class is designed to be generic, this function is empty. It is expected that additional classes will extend the `Away3DTemplate` class and implement the `initScene()` function.

```
protected function initScene():void {}
```

The `initUI()` function is where we create any user interface elements. Just like the `initScene()` function, the `initUI()` function is empty, and is expected to be implemented by classes that extend the `Away3DTemplate` class.

```
        protected function initUI():void {}
    }
}
```

> It is common to create and initialize the three classes referenced by the `initEngine()` function regardless of the type of 3D application you are trying to create, be it a game, a 3D user interface, or a simple banner. Away3D does include a class called `SimpleView`, contained in the `away3d.test` package, that allows you to get up and running quickly by initializing these classes. The `Away3DTemplate`, while achieving much the same end result, has been designed to be easily used as the base for all the applications that will be created throughout the rest of the book.

Running Away3DTemplate

The instructions under the heading *Creating an empty project for Away3D* stepped you through the process of creating an empty project ready to accept code that uses the Away3D engine. In order to run the `Away3DTemplate` class, we now need to add that class to the empty project. We also need to specify the class as the application entry point, meaning it will be executed when the application is first run.

Adobe Flex Builder and Adobe Flash Builder

The following steps show you how to add the `Away3DTemplate` class to the Flex and Flash Builder projects we created earlier:

1. When using the previous instructions to create an empty project, Flex/Flash Builder will create a default ActionScript file for you with the same name as the project, for example, `Away3D.as`. This file needs to be deleted, so right-click on the file in the **Project Explorer | Flex Navigator** pane and click on the **Delete** option.
2. Click on the **Yes** button to confirm the deletion of the file.

Building Your First Away3D Application

3. Click **File | New | ActionScript Class**.
4. In the **New ActionScript Class** dialog box, type `Away3DTemplate` in the **Name** textbox and click on the **Finish** button.
5. Paste the code for the `Away3DTemplate` class into the new `Away3DTemplate.as` file, overwriting any default code that may be present.
6. Right-click on the `Away3DTemplate.as` file in the **Project Explorer | Flex Navigator** pane and click on the **Set as Default Application** option. The icon for the file should include a green triangle and a blue sphere.

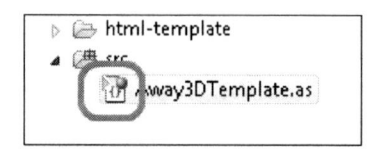

7. To compile and run the application click **Run | Run | Away3DTemplate**.

FlashDevelop

The following steps show you how to add the `Away3DTemplate` class to the FlashDevelop project we created earlier:

1. Using the previous instructions to create an empty project, FlashDevelop will create a default file called `Main.as` in the `src` directory. This needs to be deleted. Right-click on the file in the **Project** pane and click on the **Delete** option.
2. Press the **OK** button to confirm the deletion of the file.
3. Click **File | New | AS3 Document**.
4. Paste the code for the `Away3DTemplate` class into the new file, overwriting any default code that may be present.
5. Click **File | Save**. Save the new file as `Away3DTemplate.as` under the project `src` directory by clicking the **Save** button.

Chapter 1

6. Right-click on the `Away3DTemplate.as` file in the **Project** pane and click on the **Always Compile** option. The icon for the file should change to include a green arrow pointing down.

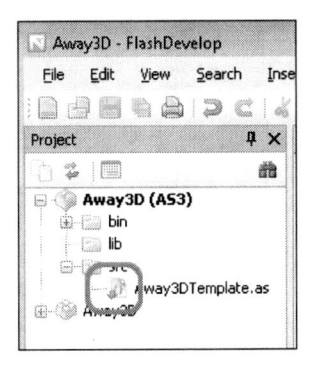

7. To compile and run the application click **Project | Test Movie**.

Adobe Flash CS4

The following steps show you how to add the `Away3DTemplate` class to the Adobe Flash CS4 project we created earlier:

1. Click **File | New…**.
2. Select **ActionScript File** from the **General** tab and click on the **OK** button.
3. Paste the code for the `Away3DTemplate` class into the new file.
4. Click **File | Save**.
5. Save the file as `Away3DTemplate.as` in the same directory as the FLA file from the previous instructions.
6. Go back to the FLA file and click **File | Publish Settings…**.
7. Click on the **Flash** tab, and click on the **Settings…** button.

Building Your First Away3D Application

8. Type in **Away3DTemplate** into the **Document Class** textbox, and click on the **OK** button to save the changes.

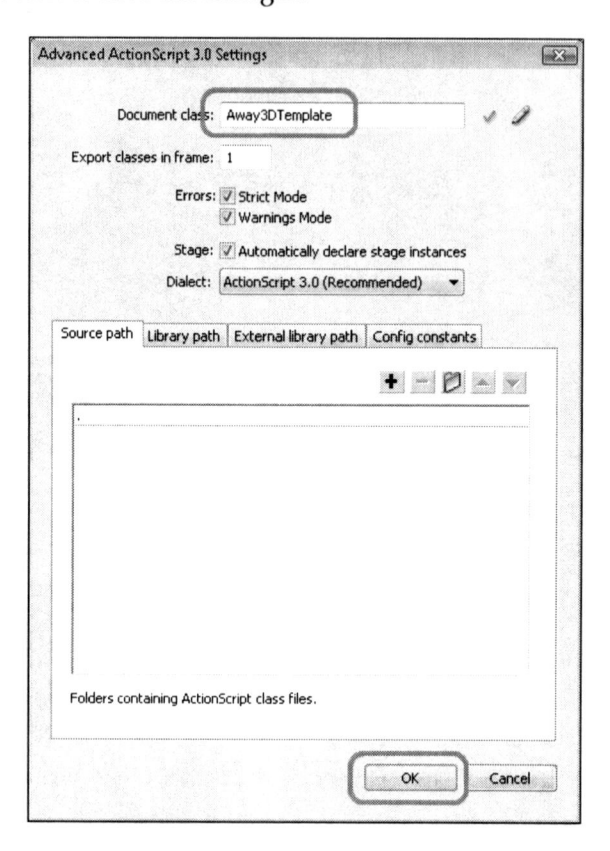

9. Click on the **OK** button to close the **Publish Settings** window.
10. To compile and run the application click **Control | Test Movie**.

> If you see the ActionScript Class Warning dialog box when clicking the **OK** button in step 8, go back to step 5 and make sure that you saved the `Away3DTemplate.as` file in the same directory as the FLA file.

The end result

When you compile and run the application you will see, well, nothing. However, this is fine, because it is the expected result. The `Away3DTemplate` class has provided a foundation that takes care of the initialization and updating of the Away3D engine, but does not create any visible objects that will be shown on the screen.

Positioning objects in a 3D scene

Before we start adding objects to the scene, it is important to know how objects are positioned in a 3D environment.

Traditional 2D Flash applications place objects on the screen along the X (or horizontal) and Y (or vertical) axes. These Cartesian coordinates uniquely define a position in 2D space.

Away3D extends the 2D coordinate system by adding a third Z-axis to allow the depth of an object to be defined.

3D coordinate systems are generally referred to as left or right handed. Away3D uses a left-handed coordinate system. To visualize the left-handed coordinate system, hold your left hand up with your palm facing away from you. Point your middle finger away from you in the same direction as the palm of your hand. Point your index finger straight up in the air, and point your thumb to the right. With your fingers and thumb pointing like this imagine that your middle finger is the Z-axis, your index finger is the Y-axis, and your thumb is the X-axis, with each finger or thumb pointing towards the positive ends of the axes.

While pointing your fingers in the air might seem like an amusing exercise, it is an easy way to work out which way is up in 3D.

The following image shows the three axes that make up a left-handed 3D coordinate system. Notice that the Y-axis in the coordinate system is inverted compared to the traditional 2D coordinate system used by Flash. In Flash, placing an object lower on the screen means assigning it a higher position on the Y-axis. In Away3D, objects with higher Y values will move up along the Y-axis.

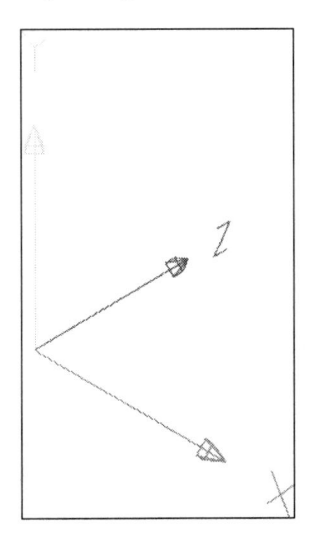

Building Your First Away3D Application

Extending Away3DTemplate to populate the scene

To actually display a 3D object on the screen, we will need to create another class called `SphereDemo`. Let's take a look at the code for the `SphereDemo` class.

```
package
{
```

Away3D includes a number of primitive shapes that can be easily added to the scene. These primitives are covered in more detail in *Chapter 2, Creating and Displaying Primitives*. We will be adding the sphere primitive to the scene, which is represented by the `Sphere` class.

```
import away3d.primitives.Sphere;
```

The `SphereDemo` class will extend `Away3DTemplate`, allowing us to initialize and update the Away3D engine with a minimum amount of code.

```
public class SphereDemo extends Away3DTemplate
{
```

In the `SphereDemo` constructor, we simply call the `Away3DTemplate` constructor with the `super()` statement, which will in turn initialize the Away3D engine by calling the `initUI()`, `initEngine()`, `initScene()`, and `initListeners()` functions.

```
public function SphereDemo()
{
  super();
}
```

The `initScene()` function was deliberately left empty in the `Away3DTemplate` class. The `SphereDemo` class overrides this function to add a sphere to the scene.

```
protected override function initScene():void
{
```

First, we call the `initScene()` function from the base class.

> In truth, calling the `initScene()` function from the base class will do nothing, as this function was deliberately left empty in the `Away3DTemplate` class. However, calling the base class functions is a good habit to get into, as it is required by other functions like `initEngine()` and `initListeners()`.

```
super.initScene();
```

[26]

Chapter 1

We then create a new `Sphere` 3D object. The `Sphere` 3D object will be placed at the origin of the scene, by default. If you remember from the `Away3DTemplate` class, the camera is placed at (0, 0, -1000), and is oriented to look back at the scene origin. This means the `Sphere` 3D object will be in front of the camera when we run the application.

> A number of Away3D classes accept an instance of the `Object` class, called an init object, as a constructor parameter. This init object is created using object literal notation. The following code would create a `Sphere` object, and place it at (0, 0, 500).
>
> ```
> var sphere:Sphere = new Sphere(
> {
>     x: 0,
>     y: 0,
>     z: 500
> }
> );
> ```
>
> Object literal notation is a short-hand way of creating associative arrays, which are instances of the `Object` class that maps properties to values. The following code has the same effect as the previous code:
>
> ```
> var obj:Object = new Object();
> obj.x = 0;
> obj.y = 0;
> obj.z = 500;
> sphere = new Sphere(obj);
> ```
>
> The properties of the `Sphere` object could also have been set after it was instantiated.
>
> ```
> var sphere:Sphere = new Sphere();
> sphere.x = 0;
> sphere.y = 0;
> sphere.z = 500;
> ```
>
> Although we don't use an init object here, they will be used extensively throughout the rest of the book.

```
           var sphere:Sphere = new Sphere ();
```

Finally, in order for the sphere to be visible it needs to be added as a child of the scene.

```
            scene.addChild(sphere);
          }
        }
      }
```

[27]

Building Your First Away3D Application

Running SphereDemo

For all authoring tools creating an application that builds off the `Away3DTemplate` class involves creating a new ActionScript AS file, writing the new class to the AS file, and specifying the new class as being the one that should be run when the application is executed.

The process of running the `SphereDemo` class can be used to run any of the example classes that will subsequently be presented throughout the book. As you will see, the process is very similar to creating the original `Away3DTemplate` class, with a few name changes.

Adobe Flex and Adobe Flash Builder

Follow steps 3 to 7 from the instructions under the preceding heading *Running Away3DTemplate in Adobe Flex*, substituting the name `Away3DTemplate` for `SphereDemo`, where appropriate. This will result in your project including both the `SphereDemo` and `Away3DTemplate` classes and **AS** files, with the `SphereDemo` class being set as the default application.

FlashDevelop

Follow steps 3 to 7 from the instructions under the preceding heading *Running Away3DTemplate in FlashDevelop*, substituting the name `Away3DTemplate` for `SphereDemo`, where appropriate. This will result in your project including both the `SphereDemo` and `Away3DTemplate` classes and **AS** files, with the `SphereDemo` class being set to always compile.

Adobe Flash CS4

Follow steps 1 to 10 from the instructions under the preceding heading *Running Away3DTemplate in Adobe Flash CS4*, substituting the name `Away3DTemplate` for `SphereDemo` where appropriate. This will result in the two files, `SphereDemo.as` and `Away3DTemplate.as`, residing in the same directory as the FLA file, with the `SphereDemo` class being used as the entry point to (or `Document` class) for application.

The end result

Now when you compile and run the application, you will see a sphere displayed on the screen. By extending the Away3DTemplate class, we have created a simple 3D application with the SphereDemo class using only a few lines of code. This example demonstrates how the Away3DTemplate class can be used as a foundation to quickly create new Away3D applications. All the examples presented throughout this book will build on the Away3DTemplate class in much the same way as we have done here with SphereDemo.

Summary

We have discussed the two versions of Away3D, with version 2.x targeting Flash Player 9, and version 3.x targeting Flash Player 10. The reasons for using one version or the other were highlighted, along with the reason why this book will focus on Away3D version 3.x.

We saw the steps required to download the Away3D source code, either as a ZIP file or from the SVN repository. The process of configuring the authoring tools Flex Builder, Flash Builder, FlashDevelop, and Flash CS4 was described, allowing each of these tools to create Away3D applications.

With the authoring tools configured we could create the Away3DTemplate class, which was then built upon by the SphereDemo class to show off the process of compiling and running a simple Away3D application.

Now that we have seen how to configure the authoring tools and created the Away3DTemplate class as a base for future Away3D applications, we can start to explore the features provided by the Away3D engine. In the next chapter, we will see how to create the primitive 3D objects supplied with Away3D.

2
Creating and Displaying Primitives

In the last chapter, we saw how to get a simple Away3D application up and running by creating a class that added a sphere to the scene. The sphere is just one of many primitive 3D objects that are included with Away3D. This includes some common shapes like cubes, planes, and cones, and some not so common shapes, such as a sea turtle. In this chapter, we will look at a number of classes that can be used to create primitive 3D objects by creating a sample application that adds each of them to the scene in response to input via the keyboard.

But before diving into these primitive classes, we will first learn about the basic elements; vertices, triangle faces, `Sprite3D` objects, and segments; that are used as the building blocks for more complex 3D shapes. In addition, we will explore the UV coordinate system, which defines how texture maps are applied to the surface of a 3D object.

This chapter covers the following:

- A look at the basic elements that make up a 3D object
- The UV coordinate system
- Creating and displaying the primitive 3D objects included in Away3D

The basic elements of a 3D object

Each 3D object displayed by Away3D is actually a collection of a number of base elements that have been combined to create the shape you see on the screen. There are four base elements that are used to construct more complex 3D objects:

- Vertices
- Triangle faces

- Sprite3D objects
- Segments

While some of these elements cannot be seen directly, they still play a vital role in creating the end result. Let's take a look at these basic elements, and how they work together to create a 3D object.

Vertices

A **vertex** is a point in 3D space defined by its position along the X, Y, and Z axes. An individual vertex does not have any volume or shape, and is not visible in the scene, but they can be used in combination to represent the corners of 3D shapes.

Vertices are represented by the Vertex class from the away3d.core.base package.

Triangle faces

A group of three vertices are used to define the corners of a triangle, otherwise known as a **triangle face**, or just a **face**.

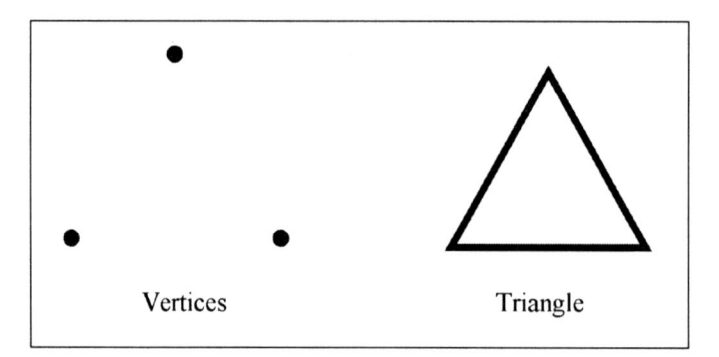

The triangle face is one of the three elements used by Away3D that can be added directly to a **mesh** to create more complex shapes. A mesh can be thought of as a container used to hold a collection of these basic elements, allowing them to be displayed as a group to visualize more recognizable 3D objects. Meshes are represented by the Mesh class from the away3d.core.base package.

Chapter 2

Simple meshes can be made up using a small number of triangle faces. This cube mesh is made up of 12 triangles: 2 triangles for each side.

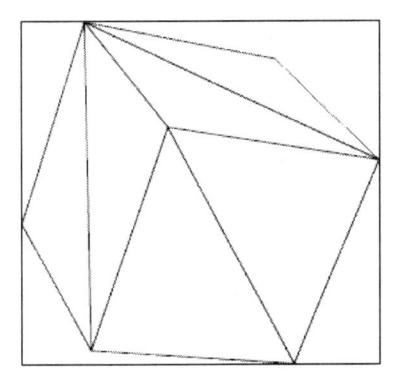

More complex meshes, such as this car, can comprise several thousand triangle faces.

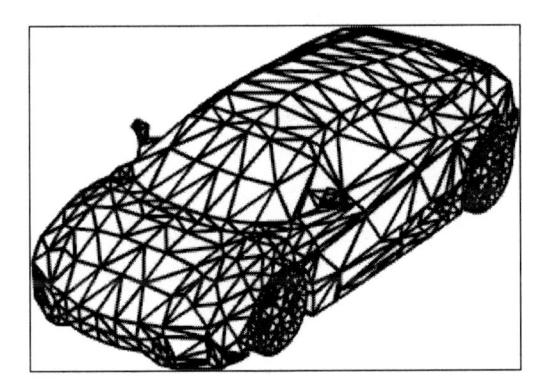

> Generally speaking, the more complex the 3D object, the more time it takes Away3D to process it. So in a real world application, you would want to limit the number of complex meshes that are visible at any one time in order to maintain an acceptable level of performance.

Triangle faces are represented by the `Face` class from the `away3d.core.base` package. Here is some example code that creates a mesh containing a single triangle face.

First, we need to create a new instance of the `Mesh` class. This will hold the triangle face element.

```
var mesh:Mesh = new Mesh();
```

[33]

Creating and Displaying Primitives

Next, we create a new instance of the `Face` class. This represents the triangle face element that will be added to the mesh.

```
var face:Face = new Face(
```

The first three parameters passed to the `Face` constructor define the three vertices that make up the corners of the triangle.

```
new Vertex(0, 10, 0),
new Vertex(-10, -10, 0),
new Vertex(10, -10, 0),
```

The fourth parameter can be used to define a material that is applied to this element. *Chapter 5, Materials,* looks at materials in more detail. We have passed in `null` here, which means the triangle face will use the default mesh material.

> The default material applied to a mesh is an instance of the `WireColorMaterial` class, which displays a color that is randomly assigned each time a `WireColorMaterial` object is constructed. This means that the triangle face being created here will display a different color each time the application is run.

```
null,
```

The last three parameters define the UV coordinates to be applied to the triangle face, which in turn define how a material will be applied. The following UV coordinates section discusses these coordinates in more detail.

```
    new UV(0, 0),
    new UV(0, 1),
    new UV(1, 0)
);
```

Finally, the triangle face is added as part of the mesh.

```
mesh.addFace(face);
```

The resulting `Mesh` object can then be added to the scene.

The order in which the vertices are defined in a triangle face determine which side of the triangle is considered the front, and which side is the back. The distinction is important because the back of a triangle face is not visible, by default.

The side whose vertices are arranged in counterclockwise order is the front of the triangle face. The following image shows how the order of the `Vertex` objects passed in as the first three parameters to the `Face` constructor, and the counterclockwise direction that they make, define the front and back sides of the triangle face.

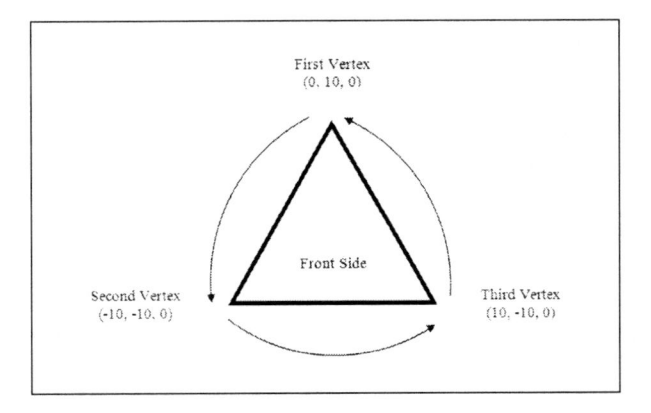

This process of creating a triangle face and adding it to a mesh is essentially how most of the primitive shapes included in Away3D are constructed, although some of the primitive classes, such as the `Cube` class, extend the `AbstractPrimitive` class from the `away3d.primitives` package to utilize the number of utility functions that the `AbstractPrimitive` class provides to aid in the creation of primitive shapes.

Sprite3D

Meshes can also contain `Sprite3D` objects, which are 2D rectangular shapes that are always oriented so they face the camera. While a `Sprite3D` object has no depth, because it is never viewed from the side, this lack of depth is never perceived by the camera.

The `Sprite3D` class exists in the `away3d.sprites` package. Here is an example that creates a `Mesh` object containing a single `Sprite3D` object that sits at the meshes origin.

```
var mesh:Mesh = new Mesh();
```

The first parameter of the `Sprite3D` constructor is the material that it will display. It is an optional parameter that defaults to `null`. Without a material a Sprite3D object simply displays a rectangle. To make this example more interesting we supply a new instance of the `BitmapMaterial` class, which is set to display an embedded image file called `MyEmbeddedTexture`. Materials, the `Cast` class, and embedding resources are covered in more detail in *Chapter 5, Materials*.

```
var sprite:Sprite3D = new Sprite3D(
  new BitmapMaterial(Cast.bitmap(MyEmbeddedTexture))
);
```

The `Sprite3D` object is then added to its parent mesh using the `addSprite()` function.

```
mesh.addSprite(sprite);
```

`Sprite3D` objects can be utilized to display details that appear the same from any direction, like snowflakes or ball decorations on a Christmas tree. `Sprite3D` objects are very simple elements, and therefore fast to render. Using `Sprite3D` objects in place of a group of triangle faces can lead to significant gains in performance.

Take the mesh representing the Earth in the following figure. This might be a part of an astronomical application designed to show off the solar system, and would be typically created from a sphere primitive. The wireframe image on the left shows the triangle faces that make up the sphere, and the image on the right shows the sphere with a texture of the Earth applied to it.

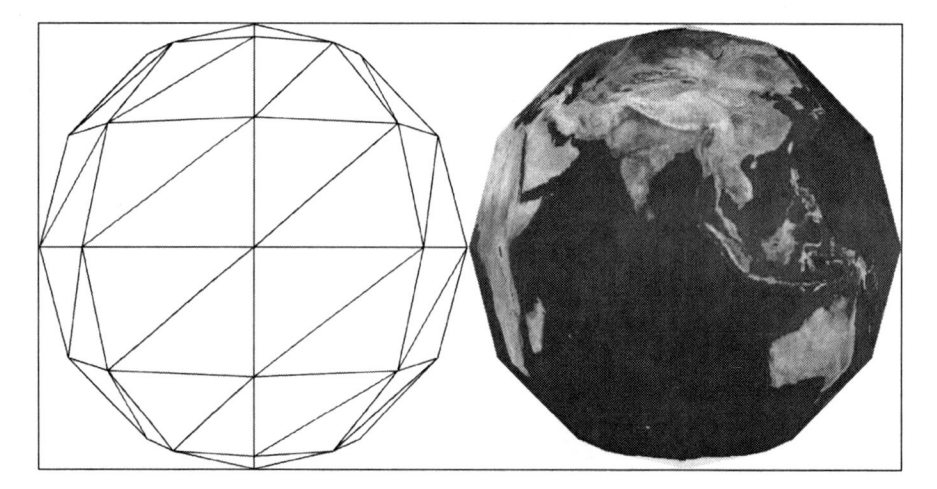

This sphere is built up from a relatively small number of triangle faces, which means that the sphere appears to have a number of sharp, angular edges. Because of the low triangle count, you could expect an Away3D application displaying this one sphere to perform well. But what if you are displaying all the planets? Maybe you also want to display all the moons around all the planets as well. Rendering the triangle faces for all those additional spheres does add up.

Now take a look at a mesh that contains a single `Sprite3D` object.

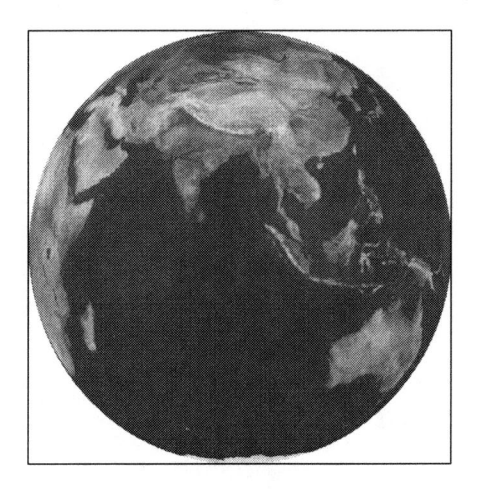

The `Sprite3D` object is displaying a material that shows the Earth from a single angle. The texture used by this material has been pre-rendered from a sphere made up of many thousands of triangles, which eliminates the sharp edges seen in the previous triangle mesh. Away3D can render this `Sprite3D` object, displaying the pre-rendered texture, much faster than it can display the lower-quality sphere from the first two images. An application displaying all the planets and moons in the solar system will run at a much higher level or performance if they were displayed as meshes made up of a single `Sprite3D` object, as opposed to being displayed as meshes made up of a number of triangle faces.

The downside to `Sprite3D` objects is that, unlike regular 3D objects, they appear the same when viewed from different angles. Even if we were to view the mesh built using a `Sprite3D` object representing the Earth from the other side, it would still show the Indian Ocean. You can see this effect in action with the `CompareSprite3DTriMesh` application from the Packt website.

> Away3D includes a class called `DirectionalSprite` that allows different images to be displayed by a flat object as the angle that it is viewed from changes. This class is covered in more detail in *Chapter 9, Special Effects with Sprites*.

Segments

Segments are used to display 2D lines. Strictly speaking, a 2D line has no volume, and should therefore be invisible. However, there are many situations where being able to view a line within the scene is useful.

Segments are represented by the Segment class from the away3d.core.base package. The geometry of a segment is defined between two vertices. Here is an example that creates a Mesh object containing a single Segment object stretching 50 units either side along the X-axis of the meshes origin:

```
var mesh:Mesh = new Mesh();
var segment:Segment = new Segment(
    new Vertex(-50, 0, 0),
    new Vertex(50, 0, 0)
);
```

Segments are added to their parent mesh using the addSegment() function.

```
mesh.addSegment(segment);
```

UV coordinates

Bitmap materials are used to display a texture map, usually from a JPG, PNG, or GIF image file, on the surface of a 3D object. The alignment of the texture map on a triangle face is determined using what are known as UV coordinates. The name comes from the axes that make up the coordinate space. These 2D coordinates have a range of 0 to 1, and are used to map a triangle face vertex to a relative position on a texture map.

The following image shows the UV coordinates for the vertices used to define the triangle face we created earlier mapped onto a checkerboard texture map.

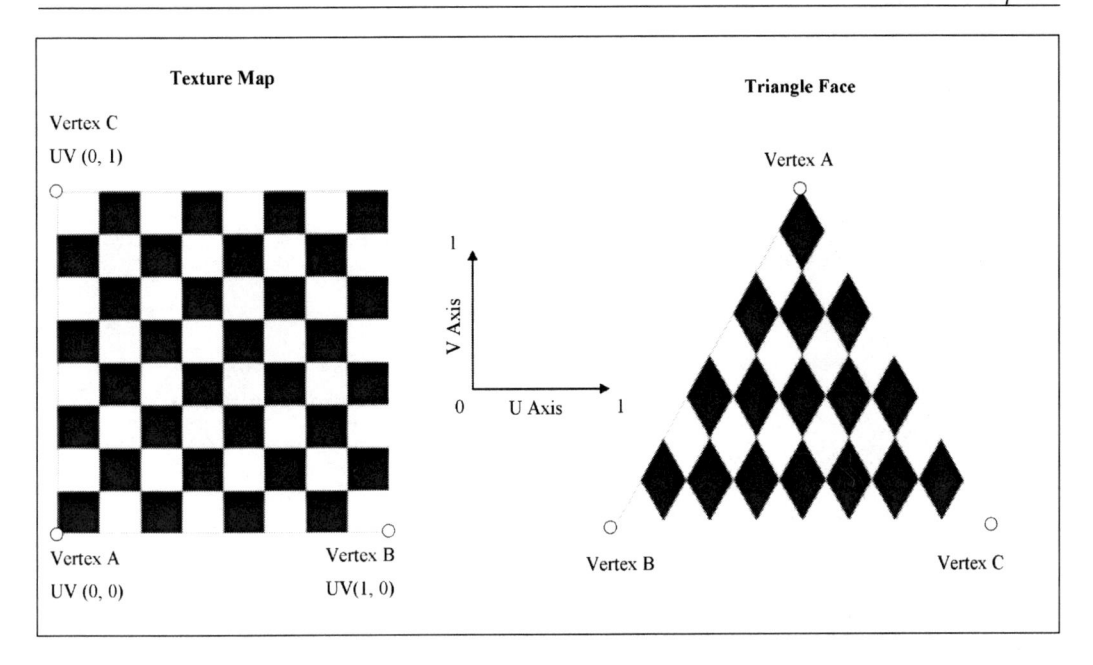

The U and V axes work in much the same way as the standard X and Y axes used by Flash. The axis naming is distinct between the coordinate systems to distinguish UV coordinates, which plot points on texture maps, to XY coordinates, which plot points within a space or on the stage. Also, keep in mind that the V axis, which increases as it moves up, is the reverse of the Y axis used by the Flash stage and the Flash drawing routines, which increases as it moves down.

Creating primitive 3D objects

We have seen how complex shapes can be built up from vertices, triangle faces, `Sprite3D` objects, and segments. In practice, it would be a tedious and error-prone task to have to create each of these shapes manually from their base elements every time we wanted to use them. Fortunately, Away3D includes a number of classes that can be used to create a wide range of primitive shapes with ease.

To demonstrate the primitive shapes included in Away3D, we will create an application that will display a selection of them on the screen. This will be implemented by a class called `PrimitivesDemo`, which will extend the `Away3DTemplate` class that was introduced in *Chapter 1, Building Your First Away3D Application*.

Creating and Displaying Primitives

The `PrimitivesDemo` class is quite large, but its function is quite simple. Let's break down the code to see how it works.

```
package
{
```

The `Object3D` class has been imported. `Object3D` is the base class for all 3D objects that can be added to the scene.

```
import away3d.core.base.Object3D;
```

A number of classes have been imported from the `away3d.primitives` package. Each of these classes represents a primitive shape that is included with the Away3D library.

```
import away3d.primitives.Cone;
import away3d.primitives.Cube;
import away3d.primitives.Cylinder;
import away3d.primitives.GeodesicSphere;
import away3d.primitives.GridPlane;
import away3d.primitives.LineSegment;
import away3d.primitives.Plane;
import away3d.primitives.RegularPolygon;
import away3d.primitives.RoundedCube;
import away3d.primitives.SeaTurtle;
import away3d.primitives.Skybox;
import away3d.primitives.Skybox6;
import away3d.primitives.Sphere;
import away3d.primitives.Torus;
import away3d.primitives.Triangle;
import away3d.primitives.Trident;
```

The application will respond to two Flash events. The first event will be triggered once per frame, which, as we saw from *Chapter 1, Building Your First Away3D Application*, is used to redraw and animate the scene. The second will be triggered when a keyboard key has been released, and will be used to change the primitive that is displayed on the screen. Responding to these events requires that we import the `Event` and `KeyboardEvent` classes from the `flash.events` package.

```
import flash.events.Event;
import flash.events.KeyboardEvent;
```

Some of the primitives have unique ways of applying materials. To demonstrate this, we will use the `BitmapFileMaterial` class. Materials are covered in more detail in *Chapter 5, Materials*.

```
import away3d.materials.BitmapFileMaterial;
```

Just like the `SphereDemo` class from *Chapter 1, Building Your First Away3D Application*, the `PrimitivesDemo` class extends the `Away3DTemplate` class, allowing it to easily initialize the Away3D engine.

```
public class PrimitivesDemo extends Away3DTemplate
```

The `PrimitivesDemo` class has one property called `currentPrimitive`, which will reference an `Object3D` object. Since all the primitive classes extend the `Object3D` class, either directly or indirectly, we can use this property to reference any of the primitive 3D objects that will be created.

```
protected var currentPrimitive:Object3D;
```

The constructor does nothing more than call the `Away3DTemplate` constructor, which in turn will call the `initUI()`, `initEngine()`, `initScene()`, and `initListeners()` functions.

```
public function PrimitivesDemo():void
{
   super();
}
```

The `initEngine()` function has been overridden to set the initial position of the camera to be 500 units down towards the negative end of the Z-axis. This will give the camera a good view of the primitive 3D objects, which will be positioned at the origin.

```
protected override function initEngine():void
{
   super.initEngine();
   camera.z = -500;
}
```

The `initScene()` function has been overridden to call the `initSphere()` function, which will cause the sphere primitive to be displayed on the screen first.

```
protected override function initScene():void
{
   super.initScene();
   initSphere();
}
```

Creating and Displaying Primitives

The `initListeners()` function is overridden to register the `onKeyUp()` function to be called when the `KeyboardEvent.KEY_UP` event is dispatched by the stage, in response to a key on the keyboard being released.

```
protected override function initListeners():void
{
  super.initListeners();
  stage.addEventListener(KeyboardEvent.KEY_UP, onKeyUp);
}
```

The `onEnterFrame()` function is called once per frame, and it is where we animate the scene.

```
protected override function onEnterFrame(event:Event):void
{
  super.onEnterFrame(event);
```

In order to see the primitive shapes from a good range of angles, we will rotate them slowly within the scene. This is done by modifying the `rotationX`, `rotationY`, and `rotationZ` properties from the `Object3D` class. Animating 3D objects in this way is covered in more detail in *Chapter 3, Moving Objects*.

The speed at which the 3D object will rotate in this example is dependent on the frame rate of the application. The more frames that are rendered per second, the faster the rotation properties will increase, and therefore the faster the 3D object will rotate.

> *Chapter 3, Moving Objects*, shows you how to use the TweenLite library to implement movement and rotation in a frame rate independent manner, while *Chapter 13, Performance Tips*, shows you how to modify the maximum frame rate.

```
  currentPrimitive.rotationX += 1;
  currentPrimitive.rotationY += 1;
  currentPrimitive.rotationZ += 1;
}
```

The `onKeyUp()` function is called when the `KeyboardEvent.KEY_UP` event has been dispatched by the stage, in response to a key on the keyboard being released.

```
protected function onKeyUp(event:KeyboardEvent):void
{
```

Before a new primitive is created and displayed, the primitive that is currently being displayed has to be removed from the scene. This is done by calling the `removeCurrentPrimitive()` function.

```
removeCurrentPrimitive();
```

We now respond to the particular key that was just released. Each key on the keyboard is identified by a numeric code. These codes can be found at: http://www.adobe.com/livedocs/flash/9.0/main/wwhelp/wwhimpl/common/html/wwhelp.htm?context=LiveDocs_Parts&file=00001136.html. The comments against the `case` statements note the key that the code relates to.

Inside each `case` statement, a function is called that will create a new primitive 3D object.

```
switch (event.keyCode)
{
  case 49:  // 1
    initCone();
    break;
  case 50: // 2
    initCube();
    break;
  case 51: // 3
    initCylinder();
    break;
  case 52: // 4
    initGeodesicSphere();
    break;
  case 53: // 5
    initGridPlane();
    break;
  case 54: // 6
    initLineSegment();
    break;
  case 55: // 7
    initPlane();
    break;
  case 56: // 8
    initRegularPolygon();
    break;
  case 57: // 9
    initRoundedCube();
    break;
  case 48: // 0
```

Creating and Displaying Primitives

```
        initTorus();
        break;
      case 81: // Q
        initTriangle();
        break;
      case 87: // W
        initSeaTurtle();
        break;
      case 69: // E
        initSphere();
        break;
      case 82: // R
        initTrident();
        break;
      case 84: // T
        initSkybox();
        break;
      case 89: // Y
        initSkybox6();
        break;
      default:
        initSphere();
        break;
    }
  }
```

Just as a 3D object has to be added to the scene using the `addChild()` function from the `scene` object for it to be visible, to remove it from the scene we call the `removeChild()` function.

The `removeCurrentPrimitive()` function, which is called by the `onKeyUp()` function before a new primitive 3D object is created, will remove the currently displayed 3D object.

```
    protected function removeCurrentPrimitive():void
    {
      scene.removeChild(currentPrimitive);
      currentPrimitive = null;
    }
```

The remainder of the `PrimitivesDemo` class is made up of the functions that create and display the various primitive 3D objects demonstrated by the application. These functions are shown in detail in the coming sections. In addition, a list of the parameters that can be supplied to the primitive class constructors is provided.

As we saw in *Chapter 1, Building Your First Away3D Application*, it is common for classes included in the Away3D library to accept an init object as a constructor parameter. This init object is usually created using object literal notation. While this practice is common, it is not universal, as you will see with the `Trident`, `Skybox`, and `SkyBox6` classes.

Unless otherwise noted, the parameters listed in the following tables relate to the properties of the init object.

Where appropriate, an accompanying image is also provided showing the primitive as a wireframe model, and with a bitmap material applied to it. Note that these images are for illustrative purposes only, as they do not reflect the output of the example code, which produces primitive 3D objects that use the default `WireColorMaterial` class as their material.

Common init object properties

All of the primitive shapes demonstrated below, with the exception of the trident, extend the `Mesh` class. Shapes like the triangle, sea turtle, line segment, and skybox extend the `Mesh` class directly, while the rest extend the `AbstractPrimitive` class, which in turn extends the `Mesh` class.

The init object supplied to the constructors of the primitive classes is passed along to the `Mesh` constructor. This means that there are a number of init object parameters that are common to all the primitive shapes (excluding the trident because it does not extend the Mesh class, and skyboxes, because they do not pass the init object down to the underlying Mesh class).

The majority of these parameters deal with how materials are applied. Materials are covered in more detail in *Chapter 5, Materials*.

Most of the init object parameters shown in these tables are also properties that can be set or accessed on the object once it has been instantiated. So

```
var plane = new Plane({bothsides: true});
```

could also be written as:

```
var plane = new Plane();
plane.bothsides = true;
```

Creating and Displaying Primitives

Parameter	Data Type	Default Value	Description
`outline`	Material	`null`	Defines a segment material to be used for outlining the 3D object.
`material`	Material	`null`	Defines the material displayed by the base elements that make up the mesh.
`back`	Material	`null`	Defines a material to be used for the back face of the base elements that make up the mesh.
`bothsides`	Boolean	`false`	Indicates whether both the front and back sides of a face should be rendered. Setting this to true disables back face culling.

Cone

Creating a new instance of a primitive class is very straightforward. Once the appropriate class has been imported from the `away3d.primitives` package, a new instance of the class can be created and added to the scene directly. This is unlike the triangle face, `Sprite3D`, and segment objects, which first had to be added to a mesh.

In truth, the process we followed to create a triangle face manually is much the same as the process used by the primitive classes. The big difference is that the primitive classes, which all extend the `Mesh` class (except for the `Trident`, `Skybox`, add `SkyBox6` classes), add the triangle faces to themselves instead of adding them to a separate instance of the `Mesh` class.

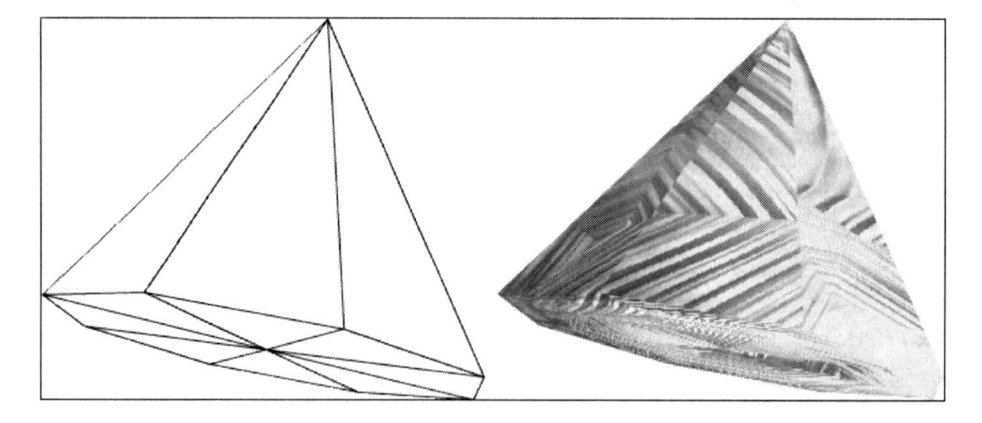

The `initCone()` function is used to create and display an instance of the Cone class.

```
protected function initCone():void
{
  currentPrimitive = new Cone(
  {
     height: 150
  }
  );
  scene.addChild(currentPrimitive);
}
```

The following table lists the init object parameters accepted by the Cone class:

Parameter	Data Type	Default Value	Description
radius	Number	100	Defines the radius of the cone base.
height	Number	200	Defines the height of the cone.
segmentsW	int	8	Defines the number of horizontal segments that make up the cone.
segmentsH	int	1	Defines the number of vertical segments that make up the cone.
openEnded	Boolean	false	Defines whether the end of the cone is left open or is closed.
yUp	Boolean	true	Determines if the cone should be oriented to point up along the Y axis.

Cube

The Cube class creates a standard six-sided cube. By default, the sides are oriented so that they are visible from outside. If you want to place the camera inside the cube and see the sides, you can set the `flip` init object parameter to `true`, which will reverse the orientation of the triangle faces that make up the sides of the cube.

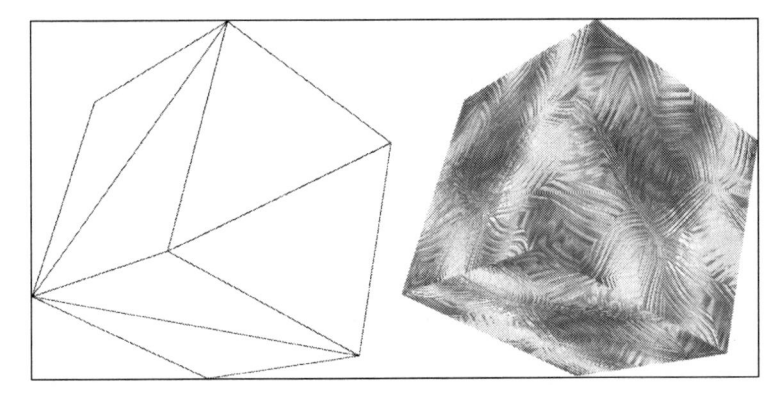

Creating and Displaying Primitives

The `initCube()` function is used to create and display an instance of the `Cube` class.

```
protected function initCube():void
{
  currentPrimitive = new Cube();
  scene.addChild(currentPrimitive);
}
```

The following table lists the init object parameters accepted by the `Cube` class:

Parameter	Data Type	Default Value	Description
width	Number	100	Defines the width of the cube.
height	Number	100	Defines the height of the cube.
depth	Number	100	Defines the depth of the cube.
flip	Boolean	false	Flips the orientation of the sides of the cube. This is used to make a cube that is visible from the inside.
segmentsW	int	1	Defines the number of segments that make up the cube along its width.
segmentsH	int	1	Defines the number of segments that make up the cube along its height.
segmentsD	int	1	Defines the number of segments that make up the cube along its depth.
mappingType	String	CubeMappingType.NORMAL / "normal"	Defines how the UV coordinates are applied to the cube. Valid values are `normal` and `map6`. These strings are also defined in the `CubeMappingType` class as the constants NORMAL and MAP6.

Parameter	Data Type	Default Value	Description
faces	CubeMaterialsData	null	A data structure that holds six materials, one for each face of the cube.
cubeMaterials	CubeMaterialsData	null	The same as the faces property. If the faces property has been set, the cubeMaterials property is ignored.

Most of the primitive classes are designed to have a single material applied to them. The Cube class is a little different. Using the cubeMaterials or faces parameters, which both accept a CubeMaterialsData object, you can specify six individual materials to be applied to each side of the cube separately. The CubeMaterialsData class resides in the away3d.primitives.data package.

The CubeMaterialsData constructor takes a number of init object parameters itself: front, back, left, right, top, and bottom. Each of these parameters accepts a material, which will be applied to the appropriate side of the cube.

```
new Cube(
{
  cubeMaterials: new CubeMaterialsData(
    {
      left: new BitmapFileMaterial("one.jpg"),
      front: new BitmapFileMaterial("two.jpg"),
      right: new BitmapFileMaterial("three.jpg"),
      back: new BitmapFileMaterial("four.jpg"),
      top: new BitmapFileMaterial("five.jpg"),
      bottom: new BitmapFileMaterial("six.jpg")
    }
  )
}
);
```

In addition, by setting the mappingType init object parameter to map6 or CubeMappingType.MAP6, it is possible to display a texture that has been split up into two rows and three columns, with each of the six divisions being applied to one of the sides of the cube.

Creating and Displaying Primitives

An example of such a texture is shown in the following figure:

This texture can then be applied to the cube like so.

```
new Cube(
{
  mappingType: CubeMappingType.MAP6,
  material: new BitmapFileMaterial("map6.jpg")
}
);
```

The following image shows the results of both the examples:

Cylinder

The Cylinder class creates either a solid or open-ended cylindrical 3D object.

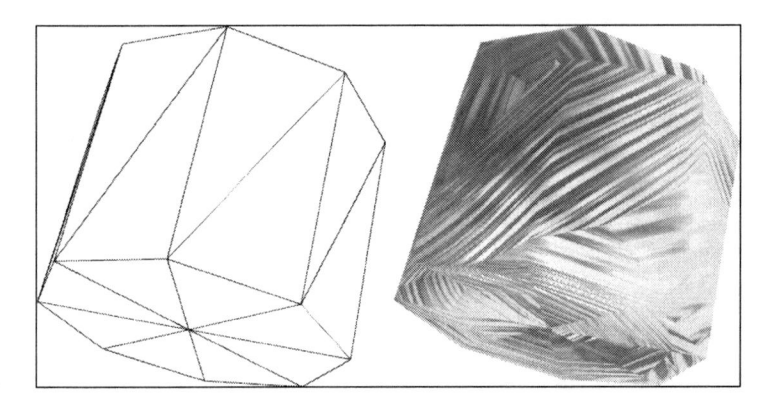

The initCylinder() function is used to create and display an instance of the Cylinder.

```
class protected function initCylinder():void
{
   currentPrimitive = new Cylinder(
     {
        height: 150
     }
   );
   scene.addChild(currentPrimitive);
}
```

The following table lists the init object parameters accepted by the Cylinder class:

Parameter	Data Type	Default Value	Description
radius	Number	100	Defines the radius of the cylinder.
height	Number	200	Defines the height of the cylinder.
segmentsW	int	8	Defines the number of horizontal segments that make up the cylinder. Increasing this number produces a more rounded cylinder.

Creating and Displaying Primitives

Parameter	Data Type	Default Value	Description
`segmentsH`	`int`	`1`	Defines the number of vertical segments that make up the cylinder.
`openEnded`	`Boolean`	`false`	Defines whether the ends of the cylinder are left open or closed.
`yUp`	`Boolean`	`true`	Determines if the cylinder should be oriented to point up along the Y-axis.

Geodesic sphere

Away3D has two sphere primitives. The geodesic sphere, being constructed with triangle faces of roughly equal size, is the more uniform of the two. This is unlike the regular sphere primitive, where the triangle faces that make up the sphere are smaller towards the top and bottom.

The following image is of a geodesic sphere primitive:

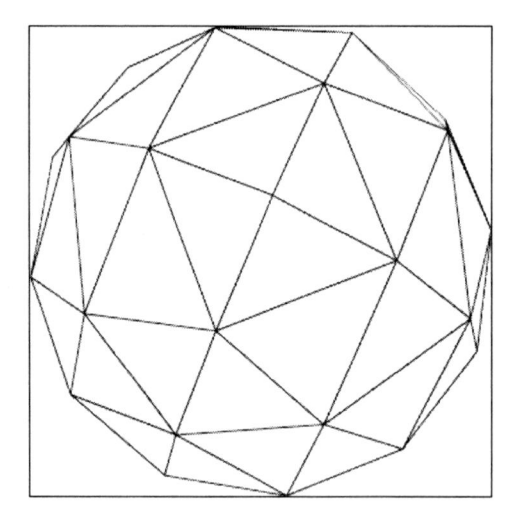

Compare the geodesic sphere with the following image, which is of a regular sphere primitive. Notice how the triangles that make up the regular sphere are much smaller towards the bottom than they are around the middle.

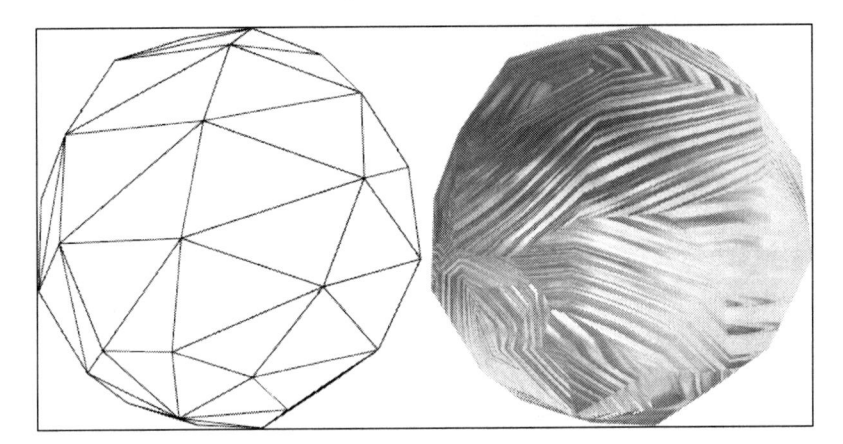

The geodesic sphere will produce a more rounded shape compared with the standard sphere using the same number of triangle faces.

> Because of the way in which the UV coordinates are assigned to the geodesic sphere, it is not useful for displaying bitmap materials. See the following section on the sphere primitive for more information.

The `initGeodesicSphere()` function is used to create and display an instance of the `GeodesicSphere` class.

```
protected function initGeodesicSphere():void
{
   currentPrimitive = new GeodesicSphere();
   scene.addChild(currentPrimitive);
}
```

Creating and Displaying Primitives

The following table lists the init object parameters accepted by the `GeodesicSphere` class:

Parameter	Data Type	Default Value	Description
radius	Number	100	Defines the radius of the sphere.
fractures	int	2	Defines the level of triangulation, with higher numbers produce smoother, more detailed spheres.

Grid plane

The grid plane is a grid of rectangles, and it is a handy primitive for judging the position of other 3D objects in the scene. Combined with the trident primitive (which is covered in the following section) to show the scene axes, it is very easy to replicate the look of a simple 3D modeling application. As you can see in the following screenshot, grid planes allow you to instantly see a 3D object's position relative to the origin (or any other point in space), which can be invaluable when debugging.

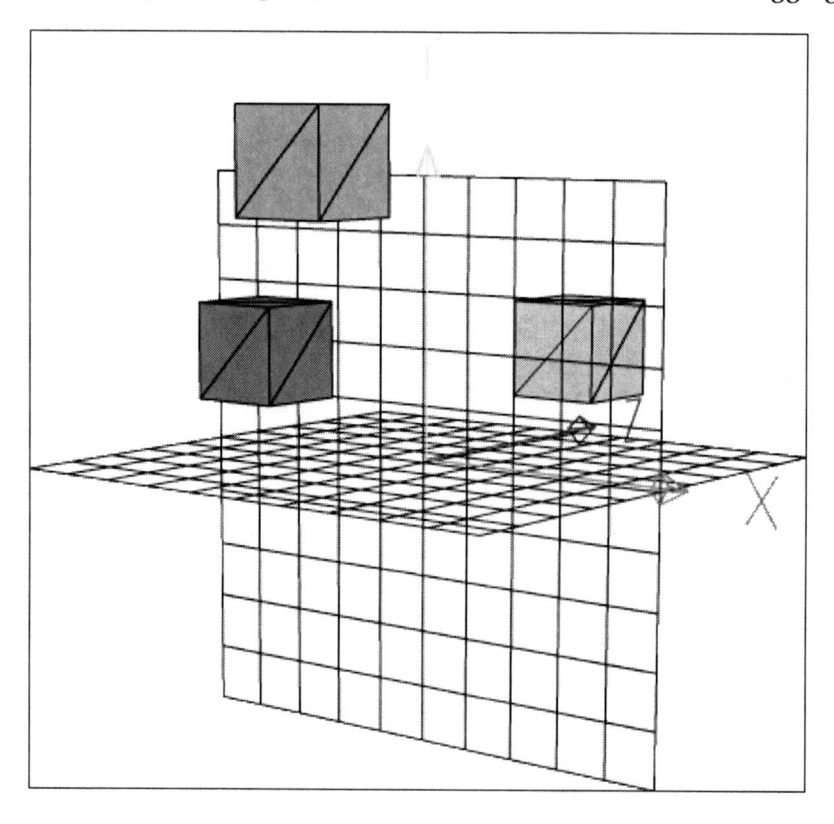

Chapter 2

The grid plane is constructed using segments rather than triangle faces. This allows it to display rectangles rather than triangles, which is how the plane primitive (which is constructed using triangle faces) is shown when it has a wire frame material applied to it.

The `initGridPlane()` function is used to create and display an instance of the `GridPlane` class.

```
protected function initGridPlane():void
{
   currentPrimitive = new GridPlane(
      {
         segments: 4
      }
   );
   scene.addChild(currentPrimitive);
}
```

The following table lists the init object parameters accepted by the `GridPlane` class:

Parameter	Data Type	Default Value	Description
width	Number	100	Defines the width of the grid.
height	Number	100	Defines the height of the grid.
segments	int	1	Sets the number of grid divisions per side, so a value of 2 would create 4 rectangles in the grid.
segmentsW	int	1	Defines the number of horizontal segments that make up the grid. This property defaults to the value assigned the segments property.
segmentsH	int	1	Defines the number of vertical segments that make up the grid. This property defaults to the value assigned the segments property.
yUp	Boolean	true	Determines if the grid plane should be oriented to point up along the Y axis.

LineSegment

The `LineSegment` class is another example of a primitive that is built using segments rather than triangle faces. It can be used to display a line between two points in space. For convenience, you would probably use the `LineSegment` class rather than build a mesh and then manually add a segment to it as we did in the section *The basic elements of a 3D object*.

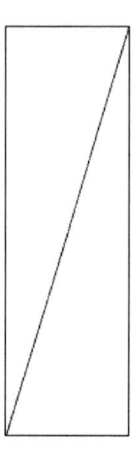

The `initLineSegment()` function is used to create and display an instance of the `LineSegment` class.

```
protected function initLineSegment():void
{
   currentPrimitive = new LineSegment(
     {
        edge: 500
     }
   );
   scene.addChild(currentPrimitive);
}
```

The following table lists the init object parameters accepted by the `LineSegment` class:

Parameter	Data Type	Default Value	Description
edge	Number	100	Sets the default line segment start and end points to be edge/2 units either side of the origin along the X axis. A value of 100 will create a line segment that starts at (-50, 0, 0) and ends at (50, 0, 0).

Parameter	Data Type	Default Value	Description
start	Vector3D	(-edge/2, 0, 0)	Sets the start point of the line segment. If specified, this parameter will override the default start point defined by the edge parameter.
end	Vector3D	(edge/2, 0, 0)	Sets the end point of the line segment. If specified, this parameter will override the default end point defined by the edge parameter.
segments	Number	1	Sets the number of segments.

Plane

The plane is a flat, rectangular shape that is only visible from one side, by default. When it is viewed from behind, the back-face culling process (which is used to improve the performance of an Away3D application by not rendering the back side of a triangle face) will prevent the primitive from being drawn. Setting the bothsides init object parameter to true will override this behavior, and ensure that the plane is visible from behind as well as from the front.

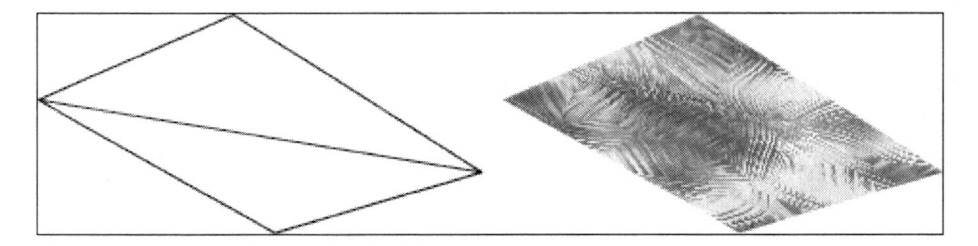

The initPlane() function is used to create and display an instance of the Plane class.

```
protected function initPlane():void
{
  currentPrimitive = new Plane(
    {
      bothsides: true
    }
  );
  scene.addChild(currentPrimitive);
}
```

Creating and Displaying Primitives

The following table lists the init object parameters accepted by the `Plane` class:

Parameter	Data Type	Default Value	Description
width	Number	100	Defines the width of the plane.
height	Number	100	Defines the height of the plane.
segments	int	1	Sets the number of segments per side, so a value of 2 would create a plane with 4 segments.
segmentsW	int	1	Defines the number of horizontal segments that make up the plane. This property defaults to the value assigned the segments property.
segmentsH	int	1	Defines the number of vertical segments that make up the plane. This property defaults to the value assigned to the segments property.
yUp	Boolean	true	Determines if the plane should be oriented to point up along the Y axis.

RegularPolygon

The `Triangle` class creates a three-sided primitive, and the `Plane` class creates one with four sides. The `RegularPolygon` class is a little more flexible, and can be used to create regular shapes with any number of sides (as long as it is more than three).

Just like the `Plane` class, an instance of the `RegularPolygon` class will not be visible from the back unless the `bothsides` init object parameter is set to `true`.

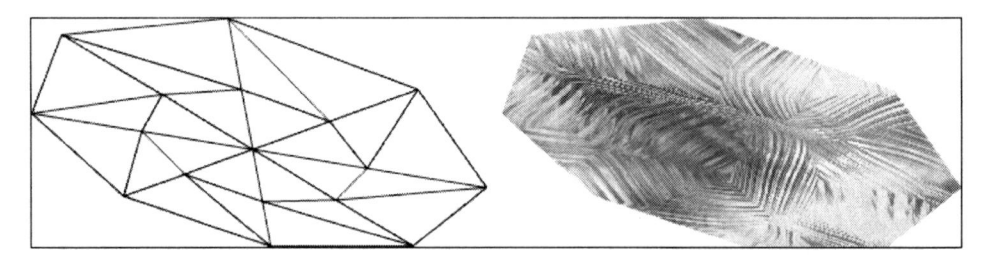

The `initRegularPolygon()` function is used to create and display an instance of the `RegularPolygon` class.

```
protected function initRegularPolygon():void
{
  currentPrimitive = new RegularPolygon(
    {
```

```
          bothsides: true
      }
   );
   scene.addChild(currentPrimitive);
}
```

The following table lists the init object parameters accepted by the `RegularPolygon` class:

Parameter	Data Type	Default Value	Description
radius	Number	100	Defines the radius of the polygon.
sides	int	8	Defines the number of sides of the polygon.
subdivision	int	1	Defines the subdivision of the polygon. Larger numbers increase the triangle count of the polygon.
yUp	Boolean	true	If true, the polygon will be created lying on the X/Z plane. If false, it will be created lying on the X/Y plane.

RoundedCube

The `RoundedCube` class produces a cube that has rounded edges. It uses significantly more triangles than the `Cube` class, so care should be taken to use the `RoundedCube` class only in situations where the rounded edges can be seen. A rounded and a regular cube off in the distance will look much the same, but the additional triangles used to construct the rounded cube will still take an additional power to process.

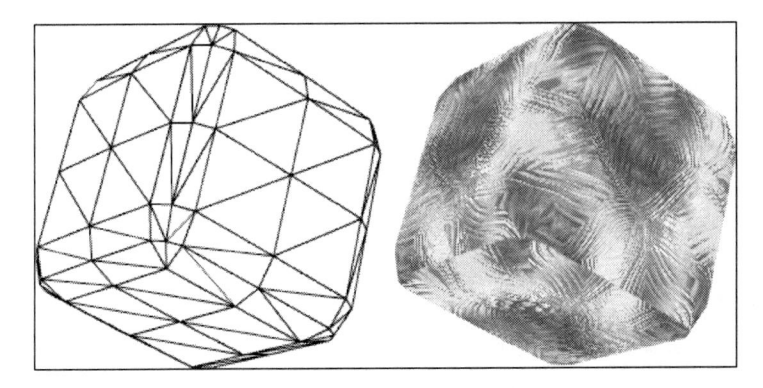

Creating and Displaying Primitives

The `initRoundedCube()` function is used to create and display an instance of the `RoundedCube` class.

```
protected function initRoundedCube():void
{
  currentPrimitive = new RoundedCube();
  scene.addChild(currentPrimitive);
}
```

The following table lists the init object parameters accepted by the `RoundedCube` class:

Parameter	Data Type	Default Value	Description
`width`	Number	100	Defines the width of the cube.
`height`	Number	100	Defines the height of the cube.
`depth`	Number	100	Defines the depth of the cube.
`radius`	Number	height / 3	Defines the radius of the corners of the cube.
`subdivision`	int	2	Defines the geometrical subdivision of the rounded cube.
`cubicmapping`	Boolean	false	Defines if the textures are projected considering the whole cube or adjusting per sides depending on radius.
`faces`	CubeMaterialsData	null	A data structure that holds six materials, one for each face of the cube.
`cubeMaterials`	CubeMaterialsData	null	The same as the faces parameter (if the faces parameter is specified this parameter is ignored).

SeaTurtle

The sea turtle can't really be considered a primitive shape, but can be created and used just like any other primitive. The sea turtle features heavily in demos created by Rob Bateman, one of the core Away3D developers, whose personal website is http://www.infiniteturtles.co.uk/blog/ (no doubt there is a correlation between the URL and the inclusion of the sea turtle as a primitive with Away3D).

Unlike the other primitives, which have shapes that lend themselves to being generated programmatically, the `SeaTurtle` class is an example of a complex 3D model that has been exported into an `ActionScript` file. *Chapter 6, Models and Animations*, will cover the model formats supported by Away3D, and how they can be exported into `ActionScript` classes, in more detail.

> The texture used in the following screenshot can be found in the example download package on the Away3D website. It has the file name `seaturtle.jpg`.

The `initSeaTurtle()` function is used to create and display an instance of the `SeaTurtle` class.

```
protected function initSeaTurtle():void
{
   currentPrimitive = new SeaTurtle(
      {
         scale: 0.3
      }
   );
   scene.addChild(currentPrimitive);
}
```

The `SeaTurtle` class has no init object parameters.

> The `scale` init object parameter, used here to uniformly scale down the size of the 3D object, is interpreted by the `Object3D` class, which is inherited by the `SeaTurtle` class. *Chapter 3, Moving Objects*, covers scaling in more detail.

Skybox

The Skybox class creates a massive cube whose sides face inwards. The dimensions of the skybox are 800,000 x 800,000 x 800,000 units. This compares with the default dimensions of the Cube class, which are 100 x 100 x 100 units. A skybox is designed to enclose the entire scene, including the camera, and usually has a material applied to it that displays a panoramic view displaying the world beyond the scene.

The following image shows two shots of the skybox from the outside, looking through the back of the cube. Usually the camera and all the other 3D objects in the scene will be enclosed by the skybox, but from the outside you can get a sense of how the six sides of the cube can be used to enclose the scene.

The skybox on the left has had some simple numbered bitmap materials applied to each of its sides. This makes it easy to see how the materials passed into the Skybox constructor map to the final result. The skybox on the right has had some specially formatted skybox textures applied to it. This is how a skybox would look in an actual Away3D application.

The initSkybox() function is used to create and display an instance of the Skybox class.

```
protected function initSkybox():void
{
  currentPrimitive = new Skybox(
    new BitmapFileMaterial("two.jpg"),
    new BitmapFileMaterial("one.jpg"),
    new BitmapFileMaterial("four.jpg"),
    new BitmapFileMaterial("three.jpg"),
    new BitmapFileMaterial("five.jpg"),
    new BitmapFileMaterial("six.jpg")
  );
  scene.addChild(currentPrimitive);
}
```

The `SkyBox` class does not take an init object. Instead, it takes six parameters, each one defining a material to be displayed on each of the six sides of the cube. These parameters are listed in the following table:

Parameter	Data Type	Default Value	Description
front	Material		The material to use for the front side of the skybox.
left	Material		The material to use for the left side of the skybox.
back	Material		The material to use for the back side of the skybox.
right	Material		The material to use for the right side of the skybox.
up	Material		The material to use for the top side of the skybox.
down	Material		The material to use for the bottom side of the skybox.

Skybox6

The `Skybox6` class is used to create a skybox, just like the `SkyBox` class. The only difference is that it takes one material divided into two rows and three columns (much like the `Cube` class when the `mappingType` parameter is set to `map6`), with each of the six segments then being applied to one of the six sides of the cube.

The following figure is a sample of a texture that can be used with the `SkyBox6` class:

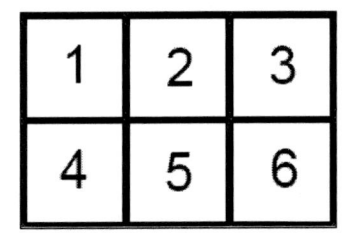

1	2	3
4	5	6

The `initSkybox6()` function is used to create and display an instance of the `Skybox6` class.

```
protected function initSkybox6():void
{
   currentPrimitive = new Skybox6(
     new BitmapFileMaterial("map6.jpg")
```

Creating and Displaying Primitives

```
    );
    scene.addChild(currentPrimitive);
}
```

The `SkyBox6` class does not take an init object. Instead, it takes a single parameter defining the material to be displayed on the cube.

Parameter	Data Type	Default Value	Description
material	Material		The material to use for the skybox.

Sphere

The `Sphere` class is the second class that can be used to create a spherical 3D object.

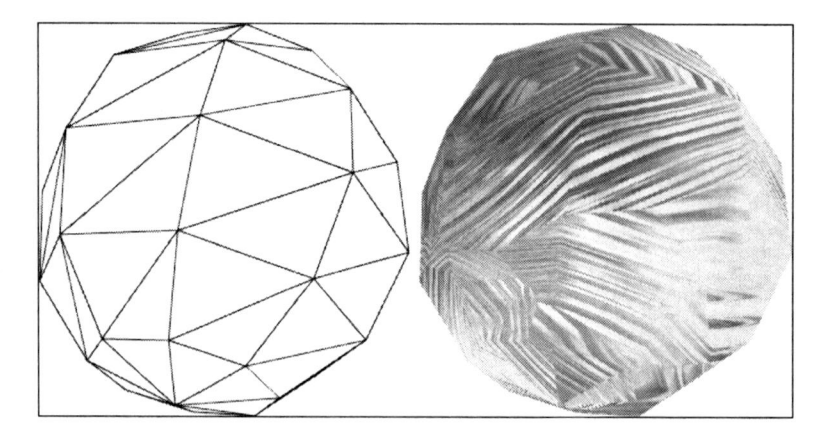

The `initSphere()` function is used to create and display an instance of the `Sphere` class.

```
protected function initSphere():void
{
   currentPrimitive = new Sphere();
   scene.addChild(currentPrimitive);
}
```

The following table lists the init object parameters accepted by the `Sphere` class:

Parameter	Data Type	Default Value	Description
`radius`	`Number`	`100`	Defines the radius of the sphere.
`segmentsW`	`int`	`8`	Defines the number of horizontal segments that make up the sphere.
`segmentsH`	`int`	`6`	Defines the number of vertical segments that make up the sphere.
`yUp`	`Boolean`	`true`	Determines if the triangle should be oriented to point up along the Y-axis.

It has already been noted that the `GeodesicSphere` class produces a more uniform sphere than the `Sphere` class. So why would you use the `Sphere` class? The answer become apparent when you apply a bitmap material to 3D objects created using both classes. The following is a screenshot of a 3D object created by the `Sphere` class. As you can see, the material is neatly applied across the surface of the sphere.

Creating and Displaying Primitives

Compare this with how the same material is applied to a 3D object created with the `GeodesicSphere` class.

It's clear that while the `GeodesicSphere` class may produce a higher quality mesh, the UV coordinates are a bit of a mess. On the other hand, the `Sphere` class will apply a material in a much more consistent and usable fashion.

However, this is only an issue when using bitmap materials. When using simple materials like `WireframeMaterial`, `WireColorMaterial`, or `ColorMaterial`, the `GeodesicSphere` class may be the better choice.

Torus

The `Torus` class creates a doughnut-shaped 3D object.

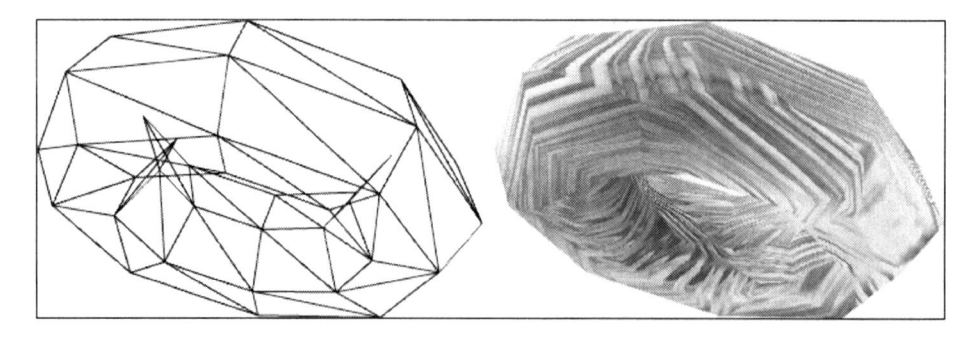

The `initTorus()` function is used to create and display an instance of the
Torus class.

```
protected function initTorus():void
{
   currentPrimitive = new Torus(
      {
         radius: 75,
         tube: 30
      }
   );
   scene.addChild(currentPrimitive);
}
```

The following table lists the init object parameters accepted by the Torus class:

Parameter	Data Type	Default Value	Description
radius	Number	100	Defines the overall radius of the torus.
tube	Number	40	Defines the tube radius of the torus. This parameter cannot be larger than the radius parameter.
segmentsR	int	8	Defines the number of radial segments that make up the torus.
segmentsT	int	6	Defines the number of tubular segments that make up the torus.
yUp	Boolean	true	If true, the torus will be created lying on the X/Z plane. If false, it will be created lying on the X/Y plane.

Triangle

The Triangle class is built from a single triangle face. Like the Plane and
RegularPolygon classes, instance of the Triangle class will not be visible from the
rear unless the bothsides init object parameter is set to true.

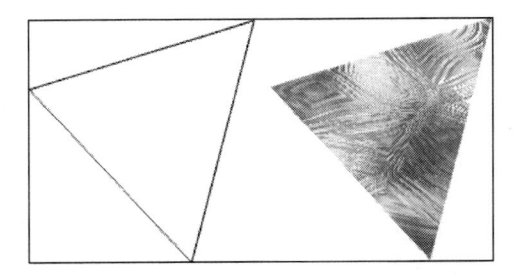

The `initTriangle()` function is used to create and display an instance of the `Triangle` class.

```
protected function initTriangle():void
{
  currentPrimitive = new Triangle(
    {
      bothsides: true
    }
  );
  scene.addChild(currentPrimitive);
}
```

The following table lists the init object parameters accepted by the `Triangle` class:

Parameter	Data Type	Default Value	Description
edge	Number	100	Sets the size of the triangle.
yUp	Boolean	true	If true, the triangle will be created lying on the X/Z plane. If false, it will be created lying on the X/Y plane.

Trident

The `Trident` class creates three-colored arrows that represent the X, Y, and Z axes. If the `showLetters` parameter is set to `true` each of these axes will also be labeled. It is very useful for debugging, as it can be used to show the orientation of a 3D object. *Chapter 3, Moving Objects*, explains how the orientation of a 3D object can affect the results of certain functions.

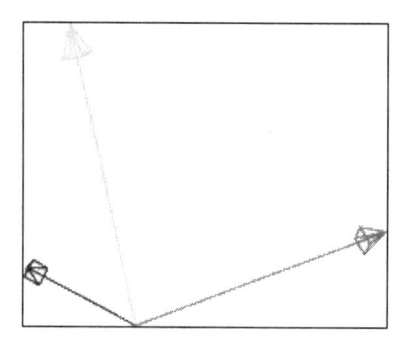

The `initTrident()` function is used to create and display an instance of the Trident class.

```
protected function initTrident():void
{
  currentPrimitive = new Trident(100);
  scene.addChild(currentPrimitive);
}
}
```

The `Trident` class constructor does not take an init object. The following two parameters in the table are passed directly to the constructor as regular parameters.

Parameter	Data Type	Default Value	Description
len	Number	1000	The length of the trident axes.
showLetters	Boolean	false	Defines whether the trident should display the letters X Y and Z.

Summary

All 3D objects are constructed using a number of basic elements: vertices, triangle faces, `Sprite3D` objects, and segments. These elements are then combined and added to a `Mesh` object to create more complex shapes, and we saw some example code that demonstrated how this can be done manually.

Texture maps are applied to the surface of a 3D object using UV coordinates, which define how a texture map is displayed by a triangle face.

Away3D includes a number of classes that allow primitive shapes like cubes, cones, spheres, and planes to be easily created without having to manually construct them from their basic elements. A sample application was presented that demonstrated how these primitive 3D objects can be created and added to the scene. The differences between similar primitives, like the sphere and geodesic sphere, were highlighted.

We also touched on some additional topics that will be covered in more detail in later chapters. The cube and skybox classes have some unique ways of applying materials, and the sphere classes showed some significant differences in the way they applied materials. For these classes, we used the `BitmapFileMaterial` class, which will be covered in more detail in *Chapter 5, Materials*.

The sample application also made use of the `rotationX`, `rotationY`, and `rotationZ` properties from the `Object3D` class to modify the orientation of the primitive 3D objects. These parameters are explored in the next chapter, in which we will learn how to move, rotate, and scale 3D objects within the scene.

3
Moving Objects

3D objects within a scene can be animated in a number of ways. We touched on this topic in *Chapter 2, Creating and Displaying Primitives*, where the primitive 3D objects created by the `PrimitivesDemo` application were rotated by modifying their `rotationX`, `rotationY`, and `rotationZ` properties. Moving, scaling, and/or rotating a 3D object can also be referred to as **transforming** a 3D object. This chapter will explore in greater detail how 3D objects can be transformed within a scene.

This chapter covers the following topics:

- The different coordinate systems
- Transforming 3D objects by modifying their position, rotation, and scale
- Transforming 3D objects using the TweenLite library
- Nesting 3D objects

Global, parent, and local coordinate systems

In *Chapter 1, Building Your First Away3D Application*, we saw how 3D objects are positioned in the scene using coordinates along the X, Y, and Z axes. In Away3D, these coordinates can be described from three points of reference: global, parent, and local coordinates. Understanding the difference between them is important because all movement, rotation, and scaling operations in Away3D work relative to one of these three coordinate systems.

World space

The **global coordinate system** represents points or vectors relative to the origin of the scene. This coordinate system can also be referred to as **world space**. The following image shows the sphere from the example application presented in *Chapter 1, Building Your First Away3D Application*.

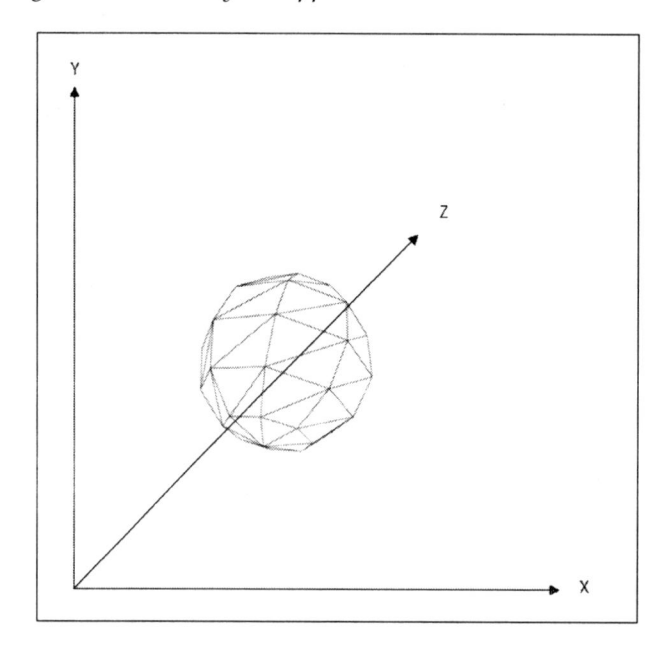

The following is the code that was used to create the sphere:

```
var sphere:Sphere = new Sphere (
{
        x: 0,
        y: 0,
        z: 500
    }
);
```

The init object supplied to the `Sphere` class constructor has set the initial position of the sphere to be at (0, 0, 500). This position is relative to the position of the 3D object's parent container. In this case, the sphere has been added as a child of the scene.

```
scene.addChild(sphere);
```

Because the sphere was added as a child of the scene, the position of the sphere will be relative to the scene. This means that the position of the sphere in world space is (0, 0, 500).

Parent space

The **parent coordinate system** is used to represent points or vectors that are relative to the position and orientation of a 3D objects parent container. This coordinate system is also known as **parent space**.

It was noted in the previous section that the position assigned to a 3D object via the x, y, and z properties is relative to the position of its parent container. When the parent of a 3D object is the scene (as has been the case with the examples presented to this point), parent space and world space are the same. However, the scene is not the only container that can hold 3D objects as children. The Scene3D class extends the ObjectContainer3D class, and it is the ObjectContainer3D class that defines the addChild() function that we have been using to add 3D objects to the scene. So, just as we have used the Scene3D object as a container for our 3D objects, so too can we use the ObjectContainer3D object.

Let's create a new application called GroupingExample, which extends the Away3DTemplate class from *Chapter 1, Building Your First Away3D Application*.

```
package
{
```

The ObjectContainer3D class is imported, making it available in the class.

```
    import away3d.containers.ObjectContainer3D;
    import away3d.primitives.Sphere;

    public class GroupingExample extends Away3DTemplate
    {
        public function GroupingExample()
        {
            super();
        }
```

We override the initScene() function to create an ObjectContainer3D object with a position of (0, 0, 500), and add it as a child of the scene. The container itself has no visual representation, so even though we have added it to the scene, the container will not be visible.

```
        protected override function initScene():void
        {
            super.initScene();

            var container:ObjectContainer3D = new ObjectContainer3D(
                {
                    x: 0,
```

```
            y: 0,
            z: 500
        }
    );
    scene.addChild(container);
```

Next, we create a new `Sphere` object, but this time we set the position to be (0, 0, 0). This will position the sphere at the origin of its parent.

```
        var sphere:Sphere = new Sphere(
            {
                x: 0,
                y: 0,
                z: 0
            }
        );
```

Now, instead of adding the sphere as a child of the scene, we add it as a child of the container.

```
        container.addChild(sphere);
        }
    }
}
```

The following image shows how the sphere is now positioned within the scene. The position of the container in parent space is (0, 0, 500). Since the parent of the container is the scene, the position of the container in world space is also (0, 0, 500).

The position of the sphere in parent space is (0, 0, 0). Given that the global position of the sphere's parent container is (0, 0, 500), and the sphere sits at the origin of its parent container, the global position of the sphere is (0, 0, 500).

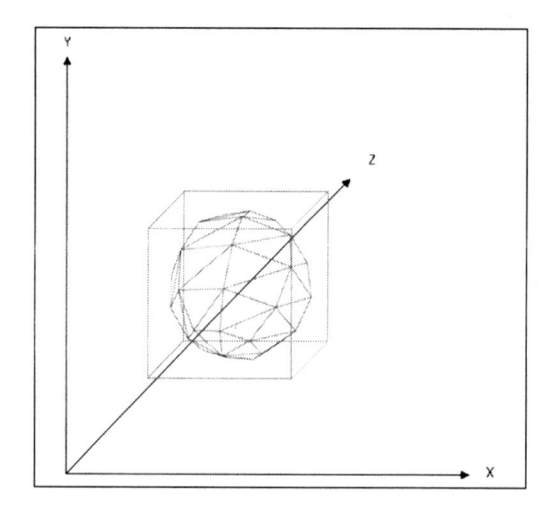

[74]

Local space

The **local coordinate system** is used to represent points and vectors relative to the orientation of an individual 3D object. This coordinate system is also known as **local space**. A number of functions to move, rotate, and scale a 3D object operate in local space.

To demonstrate this let's create a new example called `LocalAxisMovement`.

```
package
{
  import away3d.primitives.Sphere;

  public class LocalAxisMovement extends Away3DTemplate
  {
    public function LocalAxisMovement()
    {
      super();
    }

    protected override function initScene():void
    {
      super.initScene();
```

A new sphere primitive is created, positioned, and added to the scene.

```
      var sphere:Sphere = new Sphere(
        {
          x: 0,
          y: 0,
          z: 500
        }
      );
      scene.addChild(sphere);
```

At this point, the sphere is sitting 500 units along the global Z axis, as shown in the following image:

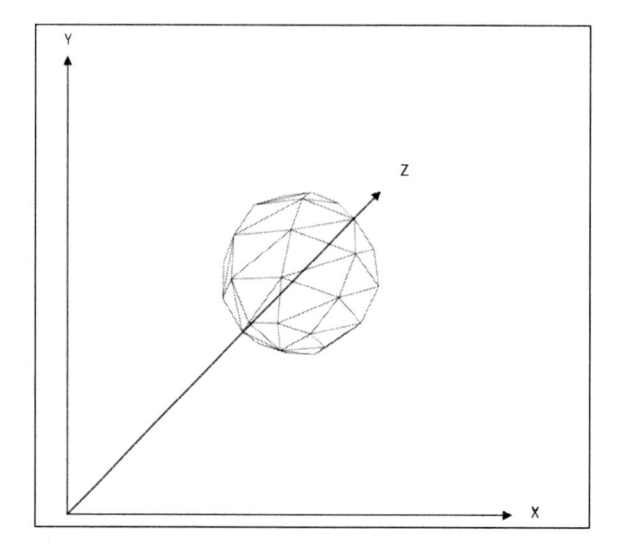

We will rotate the sphere around the Y axis by negative 90 degrees. This has the effect of modifying the orientation of the sphere's local axes.

```
sphere.rotationY = -90;
```

The following image shows how the sphere's local axes are now oriented compared to the global axes:

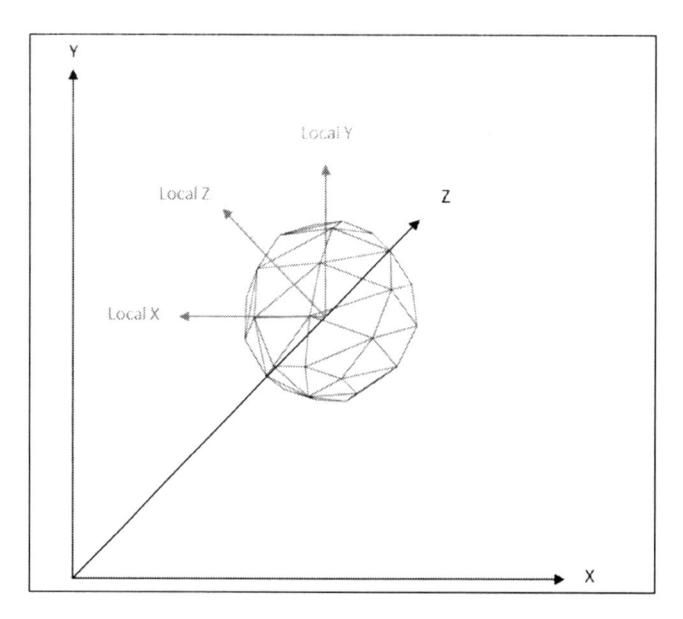

The `moveForward()` function will move the sphere along its local Z axis.

```
        sphere.moveForward(50);
    }

}
```

The final position of the sphere is shown in the following image. Note the movement of the sphere along its local Z axis (indicated by the red arrow) — the positive end of the Z axis is generally considered to be the forward direction in Away3D.

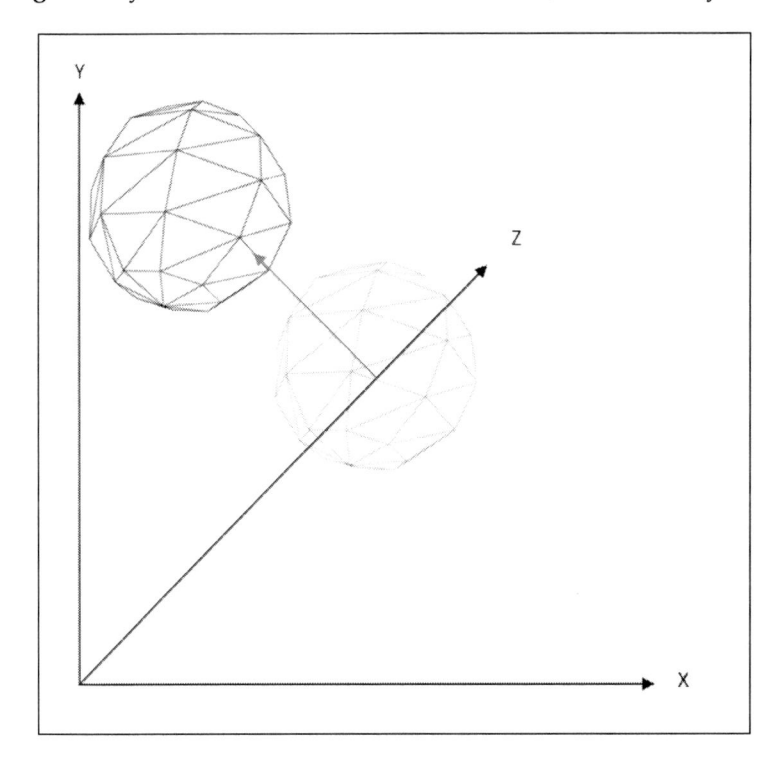

Transformation functions / properties and their coordinate systems

The following table shows the coordinate systems used by each of the functions and properties defined in the `Object3D` class that can be used to transform a 3D object:

Function / Property	World Space	Parent Space	Local Space
POSITION			
scenePosition	*		
x		*	
y		*	
z		*	
position		*	
moveForward			*
moveBackward			*
moveLeft			*
moveRight			*
moveUp			*
moveDown			*
translate			*
moveTo		*	
ROTATION			
scenePivotPoint	*		
pivotPoint			*
movePivot			*
rotationX		*	
rotationY		*	
rotationZ		*	
rotateTo		*	
lookAt		*	
eulers		*	
pitch			*
roll			*
yaw			*
rotate			*

Function / Property	World Space	Parent Space	Local Space
SCALE			
scaleX			*
scaleY			*
scaleZ			*
scale			*
TRANSFORM			
sceneTransform	*		
transform		*	

Modifying position

We have already seen how to set the position of a 3D object via the x, y, and z properties. Away3D includes a number of additional properties and functions that can also be used to move a 3D object within the scene.

The x, y, and z properties

The initial position of a 3D object can quite often be specified with the x, y, and z properties of the init object. This method has already been used in previous examples presented in the book. This method sets the position properties once when 3D object is created, rather than letting them be set to a default value and then later modifying them, making this the most efficient, and therefore preferred, way to define the initial position of a 3D object.

```
var sphere:Sphere = new Sphere(
   {
      x: 10,
      y: 20,
      z: 30
   }
);
```

> While a number of Away3D classes accept an init object, as we saw with the `Trident` class in *Chapter 2, Creating and Displaying Primitives*, this is not always the case.

The position of a 3D object can also be specified by setting x, y, and z properties of the object itself once it is created.

```
var sphere:Sphere = new Sphere();
sphere.x = 10;
sphere.y = 20;
sphere.z = 30;
```

The position of a 3D object is always set relative to the position of its parent. This is true for the x, y and z properties, and the position property. It is possible to find the position of a 3D object within the scene (or the world position) by accessing the scenePosition property, however this is a read-only property.

The position property

The position property can be set with a Vector3D object, which specifies the position of the 3D object relative to its parent on the X, Y, and Z axes all at once.

```
var sphere:Sphere = new Sphere();
sphere.position = new Vector3D(10, 20, 30);
```

The move functions

The moveForward(), moveBackward(), moveLeft(), moveRight(), moveUp(), and moveDown() functions can all be used to move a 3D object by a specified distance, relative to the 3D object's local axes. The following image shows how these directions relate to the local X, Y, and Z axes.

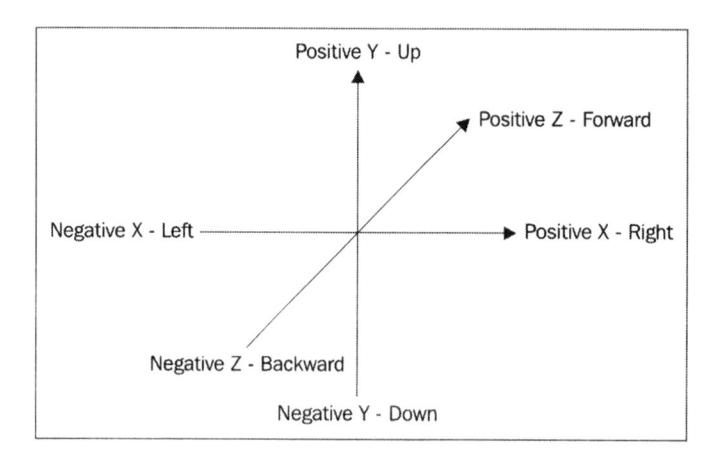

The following code moves a primitive cube 3D object 10 units forward, 20 units to the right, and then 30 units down:

```
var cube:Cube = new Cube();
cube.moveForward(10);
cube.moveRight(20);
cube.moveDown(30);
```

The individual movements are shown in the following image:

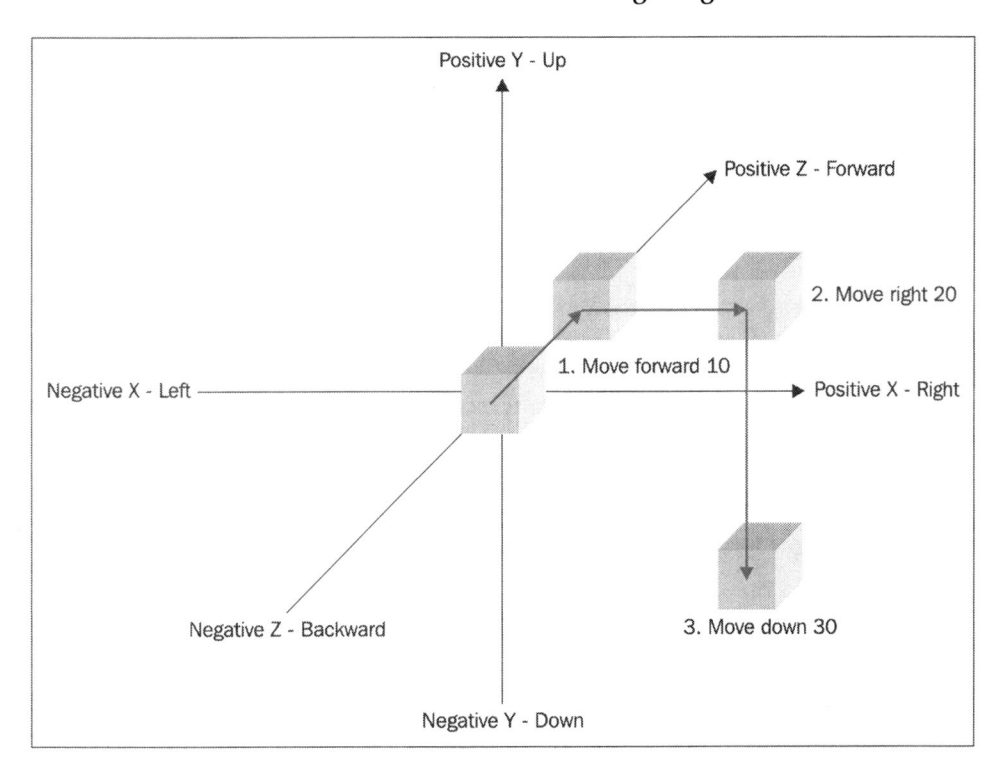

The moveTo() function

The `moveTo()` function works in much the same way as the `position` property in that it can be used to set the position of a 3D object relative to its parent along all three axes at once.

The call to the `moveTo()` function in the following example achieves the same result as assigning a `Vector3D` object with the values (20, -30, 10) to the `position` property.

```
var cube:Cube = new Cube();
cube.moveTo(20, -30, 10);
```

The translate() function

The `translate()` function is used to move a 3D object along an arbitrary vector in local space.

The first parameter, `axis`, defines the direction to move. The length of the vector is not used when calculating the distance to move (it is normalized, or modified so it has a length of one unit, by the `translate()` function). It is the second parameter, `distance`, which defines how far along the vector the 3D object will move.

The following example would move the cube to the same position as the other move functions shown previously. We know that the `axis` vector will result in the cube moving the same direction as it was moved in the other examples because we have constructed it using the same values for the X, Y, and Z axes (that is, 20, -30, and 10). We constructed it using these values for convenience; remember that, because it is normalized, it is only the direction that these vector points count. If we had specified a vector of (2, -3, 1) or (2/3, -1, 1/3), the end result would be exactly the same.

So we know that the axis vector only defines the direction in which to move, and not how far to move. Therefore, to move the cube to the same final position as the other move examples, we need to know the length of the vector (20, -30, 10). We can calculate this using Pythagoras' theorem, which states that the length of a vector can be calculated as the square root of the sum of the squared lengths of its component axes. From this we can calculate the length using the code `Math.sqrt(20*20 + -30*-30 + 10*10)` (or simply `Math.sqrt(1400)`).

```
var cube:Cube = new Cube ();
cube.translate(new Vector3D(20, -30, 10), Math.sqrt(1400));
```

Modifying rotation

Away3D includes over a dozen functions and properties that can be used to rotate a 3D object.

The rotation init object parameters

The initial rotation of a 3D object can quite often be specified using the `rotationX`, `rotationY`, and `rotationZ` init object parameters. These values represent the rotation of a 3D object around the X, Y, and Z parent space axes, and are measured in degrees.

> Away3D functions that accept an angle will usually use degrees. Flash functions like `Math.sin`, `Math.cos`, and `Math.tan` all work with radians. Be mindful of how angles are measured when using different functions.

> You can convert radians to degrees using the formula:
>
> degrees = radians * 180 / pi
>
> And degrees into radians using the formula:
>
> radians = degrees / 180 * pi

```
var sphere:Sphere = new Sphere(
  {
    rotationX: 10,
    rotationY: 20,
    rotationZ: 30
  }
);
```

The rotation properties

The rotation of a 3D object can also be specified by setting the `rotationX`, `rotationY`, and `rotationZ` properties of the object itself once it is created.

```
var sphere:Sphere = new Sphere();
sphere.rotationX = 10;
sphere.rotationY = 20;
sphere.rotationZ = 30;
```

The rotateTo() function

The `rotateTo()` function can be used to set the rotation around the parent X, Y, and Z axes with one function call. The following example code achieves the same end result as setting the `rotationX`, `rotationY`, and `rotationZ` properties individually as described previously.

```
var sphere:Sphere = new Sphere();
sphere.rotateTo(10, 20, 30);
```

The eulers property

The `eulers` property is much the same as the `rotateTo()` function, except that it takes a single `Vector3D` object instead of three individual `Numbers`.

```
var sphere:Sphere = new Sphere();
sphere.eulers = new Vector3D(10, 20, 30);
```

The rotate() function

The preceding rotation functions all work by rotating a 3D object around the parent X, Y, and Z axes. By combining rotations around these fixed axes you can rotate a 3D object to any desired position. However, in some situations it is easier and quicker to rotate a 3D object around a single arbitrary axis. The `rotate()` function can be used to do just this.

The following code will rotate the sphere 90 degrees around the local space vector (1, 0, 1).

```
var sphere:Sphere = new Sphere();
sphere.rotate(new Vector3D(1, 0, 1), 90);
```

The lookAt() function

The `lookAt()` function can be used to point the local Z axis of a 3D object towards a position in parent space, defined by the first parameter called `target`, while optionally defining the roll of the 3D object once it has been rotated to face the desired position with the second parameter.

This second parameter is called `upAxis`. This vector, in parent space, is used in conjunction with the local Z axis of the 3D object once it has been rotated to face the target position to define a plane. The 3D object is then oriented so its local Y axis lies on this plane, while also being at right angles to the local Z axis.

If the `upAxis` parameter is not supplied, a default value of `Vector3D(0, -1, 0)` will be used.

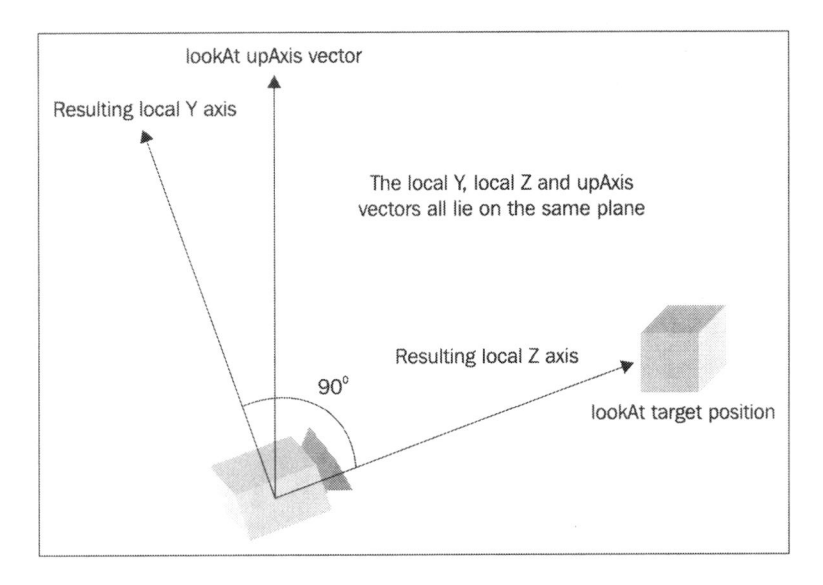

The following code will rotate the camera so that it is looking at a position (10, 20, 30) units from the origin of the camera's parent container.

```
camera.lookAt(new Vector3D(10, 20, 30));
```

The pivotPoint property

By default, the rotation functions and properties detailed so far will rotate a 3D object around the axes of its parent container, or a vector in parent space, as if the 3D object were sitting at the origin of that parent container. The cube in the following image, seen from above, has been rotated 45 degrees around the Y axis.

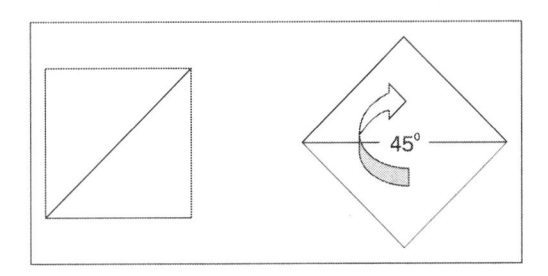

Moving Objects

It is also possible to rotate a 3D object around an external point, known as the **pivot point**, much like the pendulum in an old grandfather clock. The position of the pivot point can be defined by assigning a Vector3D object to the pivotPoint property. The position of the pivot point is defined in local space. Here we have set the pivot point 200 units to the right of the cube.

```
var cube:Cube = new Cube();
cube.pivotPoint = new Vector3D(200, 0, 0);
cube.rotationY = 45;
scene.addChild(cube);
```

Now instead of rotating "in place" when the cube is rotated 45 degrees around the Y axis, it will rotate around the new pivot point to the right.

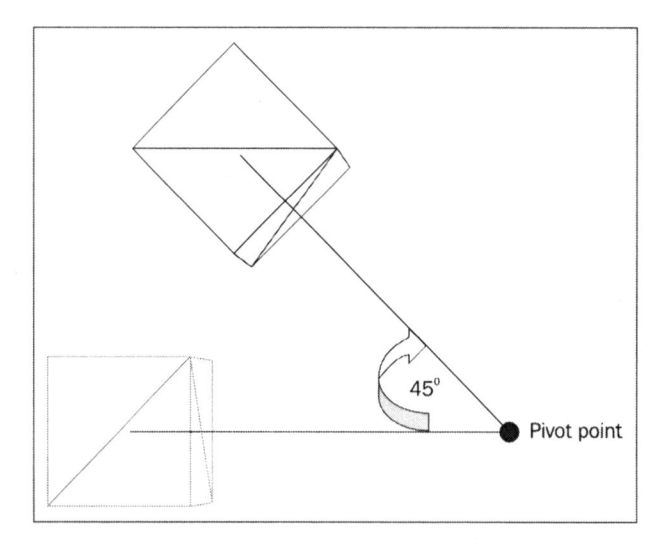

The movePivot() function

The movePivot() function can also be used to set the position of the pivot point. The difference between the pivotPoint property and the movePivot() function is that you do not have to create an intermediary Vector3D object when using the movePivot() function.

The following code has the same effect as setting the pivotPoint property at a position of (200, 0, 0).

```
var cube:Cube = new Cube();
cube.movePivot(200, 0, 0);
cube.rotationY = 45;
scene.addChild(cube);
```

The scenePivotPoint property

The `scenePivotPoint` property provides a way to find the position of the pivot point in world space. The `scenePivotPoint` property is read-only, so you can not assign a new position for the pivot point through it.

```
var cube:Cube = new Cube();
cube.movePivot(200, 0, 0);
var scenePivot:Vector3D = cube.scenePivotPoint;
```

The pitch(), roll(), and yaw() functions

The `pitch()`, `yaw()`, and `roll()` functions rotate the 3D object around the local X, Y, and Z axes respectively. These concepts are easy to visualize if you apply them to a camera. Modifying the pitch will make the camera look left and right. Modifying the yaw will make the camera look up and down. Modifying the roll would be like turning the camera upside down.

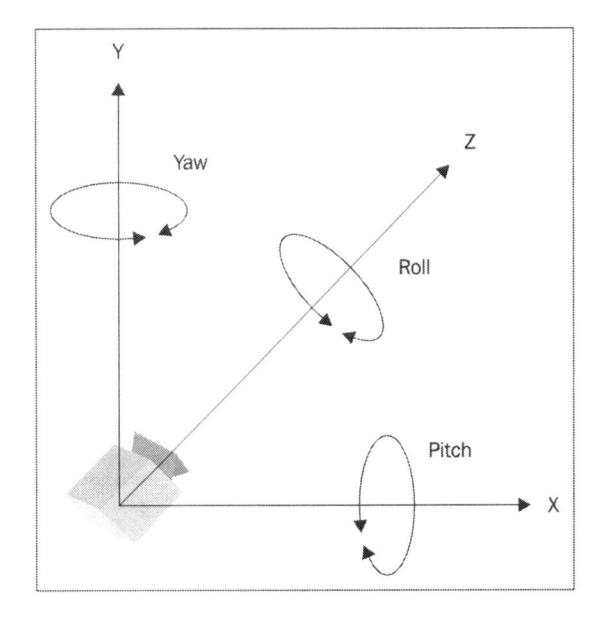

```
var sphere:Sphere = new Sphere();
sphere.pitch(90);
sphere.yaw(90);
sphere.roll(180);
```

Modifying scale

Scaling a 3D object involves modifying its dimensions along its local axes. A 3D object can be scaled uniformly along all three local axes, or along the local X, Y, or Z axis individually.

The scale init object parameter

The initial scale of a 3D object along all its local axes can quite often be specified with the `scale` init object parameter. This scales the 3D object uniformly along all three axes. In this example, we have scaled the sphere to twice its default size.

> You can also supply negative numbers to these scale functions and properties, which has the effect of turning a 3D object "inside out".

```
var sphere:Sphere = new Sphere(
  {
    scale: 2
  }
);
```

The scale() function

The `scale()` function will apply a uniform scale to all the local axes at once. This achieves the same result as the `scale` init object parameter, and can be used on those 3D objects that do not implement init objects.

```
var sphere:Sphere = new Sphere();
sphere.scale(2);
```

The scaleX, scaleY, and scaleZ properties

The scale of a 3D object along its individual local axes can be specified by setting `scaleX`, `scaleY`, and `scaleZ` properties. Here we have used these three properties to scale a 3D object by a factor of two along the X axis, by a factor of 3 along the Y axis, and by a factor of 4 along the Z axes.

```
var sphere:Sphere = new Sphere();
sphere.scaleX = 2;
sphere.scaleY = 3;
sphere.scaleZ = 4;
```

Modifying the transform

The end result of the positioning, rotating, and scaling a 3D object can be described as a single 4x4 matrix called the **transform matrix**.

> Even though we only work in three dimensions, a 4x4 matrix is required to contain the information used by all the transformations supported by Away3D, including scaling, rotations, and translations, in a single matrix.

Matrices are represented by the `Matrix3D` class in the `flash.geom` package. It is possible to manipulate a transform matrix directly, and then pass it to a 3D object via the `transform` property defined in the `Object3D` class. However, it is generally more convenient to use the listed functions to transform a 3D object rather than modifying the transform matrix directly.

Tweening

In a number of the applications presented so far, the 3D objects in the scene have been transformed slightly each frame inside the `onEnterFrame()` function. Another common method for modifying the properties of an object over time, including those properties that define the transformation of 3D objects, is called **tweening**. There are a number of free libraries that can perform tweening operations, one of which is the GreenSock TweenLite library. TweenLite can be downloaded from http://www.greensock.com/tweenlite/.

> Although it can be freely downloaded, TweenLite does have some licensing restrictions, which you can view at http://www.greensock.com/licensing/.

In order to use the TweenLite library it has to be added to the **Source path** in Flex/Flash Builder and Flash CS4, or the **Project Classpaths** in FlashDevelop, just as we did with the Away3D library in Chapter 1, *Building Your First Away3D Application*.

Moving Objects

Tweening libraries have a lot of functionality (and too much to cover in this book), but implementing a simple tweening operation is fairly straightforward. To demonstrate how TweenLite can be used with a 3D object we will create an application called `TweeningDemo`.

```
package
{
   import flash.geom.Vector3D;
   import away3d.primitives.Sphere;
```

The `TweenLite` class is imported to make it available in the `TweeningDemo` class.

```
   import com.greensock.TweenLite;

   public class TweeningExample extends Away3DTemplate
   {
      protected var sphere:Sphere;

      public function TweeningExample()
      {
         super();
      }

      protected override function initScene():void
      {
         super.initScene();
```

The camera is positioned 2,000 units up along the positive end of the Y axis, and 2,000 units down the negative end of the Z axis. We then call the `lookAt()` function to orient the camera so it is looking at the origin of the scene. Positioning and orienting the camera in this allows us to view the X/Z plane from above at a slight angle. This is perfect for viewing the sphere, which will be moving across the X/Z plane.

```
         camera.position = new Vector3D(0, 2000, -2000);
         camera.lookAt(new Vector3D(0, 0, 0));
```

A sphere primitive is created and added to the scene. Because we did not specify a position in the constructor, the sphere will initially be positioned at the scenes origin.

```
         sphere = new Sphere();
         scene.addChild(sphere);
```

The `tweenToRandomPosition()` function is then called to initialize the first tweening operation.

```
        tweenToRandomPosition();
    }

    protected function tweenToRandomPosition():void
    {
```

In the `tweenToRandomPosition()` function we make a call to the static `to()` function defined by the `TweenLite` class. The `to()` function is used to progressively modify the properties of an object over time.

The first parameter, `target`, is the object that will be modified by the tweening operation. In this case that object is our sphere.

The second parameter, `duration`, defines how long the tweening operation will take in seconds. By supplying a value of `1` here the properties of the sphere will be progressively modified from their current values to new values that we define over a period of one second.

```
        TweenLite.to(sphere, 1,
            {
```

The third parameter, `vars`, is an object that has been created with object literal notation. This is the same way that the init objects used by Away3D are created. In this object we assign the values that we want the 3D object to have once the tweening operation is complete. The properties `x`, `z`, `scaleX`, `scaleY`, `scaleZ`, and `rotationY` relate to properties that are exposed by the `Sphere` class. In this example, we have assigned random values to these properties.

The final property of the `vars` object, `onComplete`, is a special property that is recognized by the `TweenLite` class. Any function assigned to this property will be called once the tweening operation is complete. Here, we have assigned the `tweenToRandomPosition()` function. Since this tweening operation is created in the `tweenToRandomPosition()` function, this has the effect of creating an endless sequence of tweening operations. As one tweening operation is completed, the `tweenToRandomPosition()` function is called and a new one is started.

Sequencing a number of tweening operations using the `onComplete` property can create some very complex movements or scripted operations.

```
                x: Math.random() * 1000 - 500,
                z: Math.random() * 1000 - 500,
                scaleX: Math.random() * 1.5 + 0.5,
                scaleY: Math.random() * 1.5 + 0.5,
                scaleZ: Math.random() * 1.5 + 0.5,
                rotationY: Math.random() * 180,
                onComplete: tweenToRandomPosition
            }
        );
    }
  }
}
```

When this application is run, the sphere will move around the scene to random positions within -500 to 500 units along the X and Z axes. The scale of the sphere is modified to be within 0.5 to 2 times its original size, while its rotation around its local Y axis is set anywhere between 0 and 180 degrees.

One of the best things about tweening operations is that they tend to be "fire and forget". You don't have to keep a track of how much time has passed and manually modify the properties every frame, as has been done in previous applications in the `onEnterFrame()` function. In fact, you will notice that we have not used the `onEnterFrame()` function at all in this example.

> TweenLite includes a lot more functionality than has been covered by this book, and indeed the TweenMax library, also from GreenSock, includes more functionality still. To explore these additional features, you can use the interactive demos found on the GreenSock website (http://www.greensock.com), which allow you to modify the position, scale, rotation, and more of a 2D object on the screen. Just remember that tweening libraries generally have no inherent concept of 2D or 3D—they just modify the values of given properties over time. The only difference between tweening a 2D object and a 3D object is the modification of properties relating to the third dimension along the Z axis.

Nesting

As we saw with the parent coordinate system, it is possible to add 3D objects to a parent container other than the scene. Adding 3D objects to parent containers in this way is referred to as **nesting**. Nesting is used to transform a group of 3D objects simultaneously. A parent container can be moved, scaled, or rotated, which in turn will transform its children 3D objects.

Chapter 3

Let's see a practical example of nesting in action. Imagine you were creating a shoot 'em up style of game where each space ship can be matched with a variety of guns, with each gun represented by a distinct 3D object. While this could be achieved by providing a separate model for combination of ship and gun, such an approach would quickly become unworkable as the number of combinations increased. If you had five ships, and each ship should be matched with six guns, you would need to supply 30 individual models.

A better solution would be to model each of the ships and the guns separately, and combine them at runtime to form the necessary combinations.

Here is a screenshot of the gun:

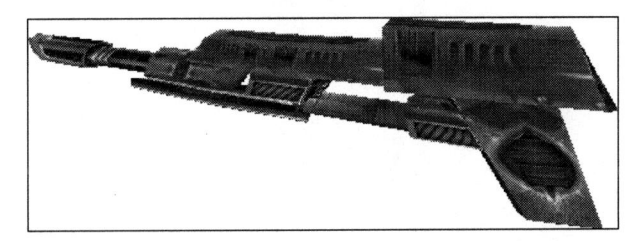

Here is a screenshot of the ship:

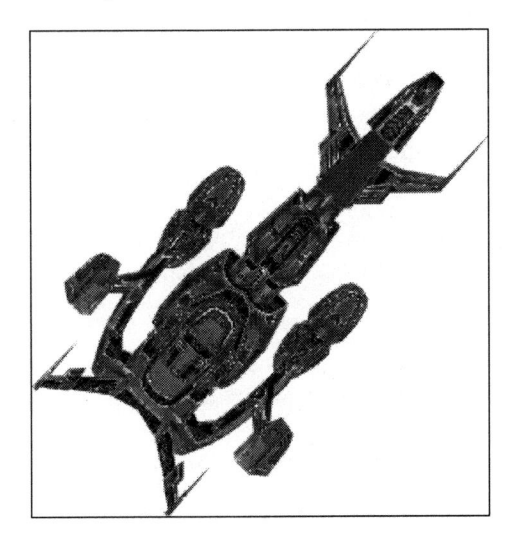

Moving Objects

And here is a screenshot of the ship and the guns combined:

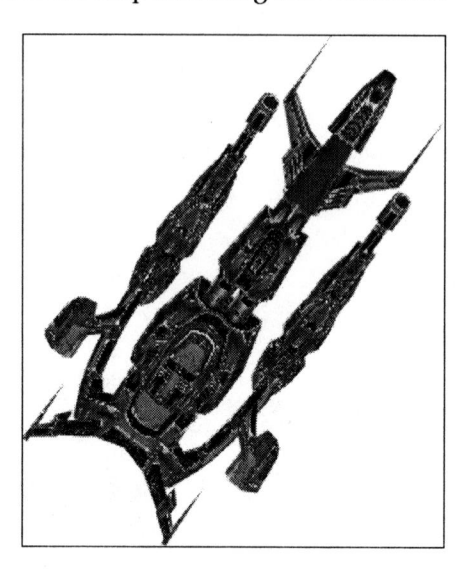

The following `NestingDemo` class demonstrates how the ship and gun 3D objects shown in the screenshots can be added to a container so they can be transformed as a single group.

```
package
{
   import away3d.containers.ObjectContainer3D;
   import away3d.core.base.Mesh;
```

The `Cast` class provides a convenient way to cast objects between types. In this example, it is used in conjunction with the `BitmapMaterial` class, which will be used to apply a material the 3D objects that we will be adding to the scene. Materials are covered in more detail in *Chapter 5, Materials*.

```
   import away3d.core.utils.Cast;
   import away3d.materials.BitmapMaterial;

   import flash.events.Event;

   public class NestingDemo extends Away3DTemplate
   {
```

The `texture.jpg` file has been embedded, and can be accessed via the `Texture` class.

```
      [Embed(source="texture.jpg")]
      protected var Texture:Class;
```

The `container` property will reference the parent container that the ship and gun models will be added to.

```
protected var container:ObjectContainer3D;

public function NestingDemo()
{
  super();
}

protected override function initScene():void
{
  super.initScene();
```

In the `initScene()` function, we create a new `BitmapMaterial` object. This will then be applied to the ship and gun 3D objects.

```
var material:BitmapMaterial =
    new BitmapMaterial(Cast.bitmap(Texture));
```

The `Fighter` class is a complex 3D object that has been exported to an `ActionScript` class. This is similar to the `SeaTurtle` class that was covered in *Chapter 2, Creating and Displaying Primitives*. It will be referenced by the `fighter` variable, and is used to represent the space ship. Exporting models to `ActionScript` classes is covered in *Chapter 6, Models and Animations*.

```
var fighter:Mesh = new Fighter();
```

The material is then applied to the 3D object.

```
fighter.material = material;
```

The gun 3D objects are created in much the same way as the ship. We create a new instance of the `Gun` class, and apply the material to it.

```
var gun1:Mesh = new Gun();
gun1.material = material;
```

In this case, the tool used to export the `Gun` class created it in such a way that the init object is not passed to the base `Mesh` class. This means the position of the 3D object cannot be set using an init object, so the position is instead set via the x, y, and z properties after the object has been created.

```
gun1.x = -150;
gun1.y = 75;
gun1.z = -115;
```

Moving Objects

The ship has two guns, so we create a second instance of the Gun class. This second gun is positioned on the opposite side of the X axis.

```
var gun2:Mesh = new Gun();
gun2.material = material;
gun2.x = 150;
gun2.y = 75;
gun2.z = -115;
```

At this point, we have three 3D objects: one ship and two guns. We want to be able to work with these three 3D objects as if they were a single item. This is where nesting is useful. First we create a new container, and add the separate 3D objects as children by supplying them as the first three parameters of the ObjectContainer3D constructor.

```
container = new ObjectContainer3D(
   fighter, gun1, gun2,
```

> You could also add each of the 3D objects to the ObjectContainer3D object once the container has been created using code like the following:
>
> container.addChild(fighter);
>
> container.addChild(gun1);
>
> container.addChild(gun2);

The final parameter is an init object, which will set the position of the container 2,000 units along the positive end of the Z axis.

```
   {
      z: 2000
   }
);

   scene.addChild(container);
}

protected override function onEnterFrame(event:Event):void
{
   super.onEnterFrame(event);
```

[96]

By nesting the ship and gun 3D objects in a container, they can now be transformed as a single group. In fact, we have already moved the 3D objects as a group by specifying the initial position of the container when it was constructed. The `onEnterFrame()` function also transforms the 3D objects as a group by modifying the rotation of the container.

```
      ++container.rotationX;
      ++container.rotationZ;
    }
  }
}
```

When you run the application, you will see that the ship and gun 3D models maintain their position relative to each other within the parent container while the parent container is moved and rotated.

Summary

The transformation of a 3D object takes place within three distinct coordinate systems or spaces. Coordinates in world space are defined relative to the scene, coordinates in parent space are defined relative to a 3D object's parent container, while coordinates in local space are defined relative to an individual 3D object.

Away3D includes over a dozen functions and properties that can be used to modify the position, rotation, and scale of 3D objects. Each of these functions transforms a 3D object within one of the three coordinate systems.

Tweening can be used to modify the properties of an object over time, and we saw an example of how the TweenLite library can be used to transform a 3D object without having to manually transform it every frame using the `onEnterFrame()` function.

Finally, we saw how nesting can be used to transform a group of 3D objects simultaneously by placing them in a container, like the `ObjectContainer3D` class, and then transforming the container.

4
Z-Sorting

Correctly sorting 3D objects within a scene is critical to being able to draw the scene on the screen correctly. Away3D uses what is known as the painter's algorithm to draw the elements that make up the scene to the screen, and it is very easy to take this process for granted, as most of the time Away3D will draw these elements in the correct order. However, there are certain situations where it is necessary to tweak the order in which Away3D sorts the 3D objects within the scene. This chapter demonstrates one such situation, and presents the methods that are available to manually correct the sorting process.

Away3D also includes some additional renderers that can be used to automatically correct the sorting order of the 3D objects within the scene. These renderers are demonstrated, and their implications on the performance of an Away3D application are explored.

This chapter covers the following:

- The painter's algorithm
- How the scene is sorted
- How to influence or force the sorting order of 3D objects
- The additional renderers

The painter's algorithm

The **painter's algorithm** refers to a technique employed by many painters in which the most distant parts of a scene are painted first, with the closer parts of the scene then being progressively painted over the top. The following image, from the Wikipedia article on the subject, shows the steps that are taken to paint an outdoor scene.

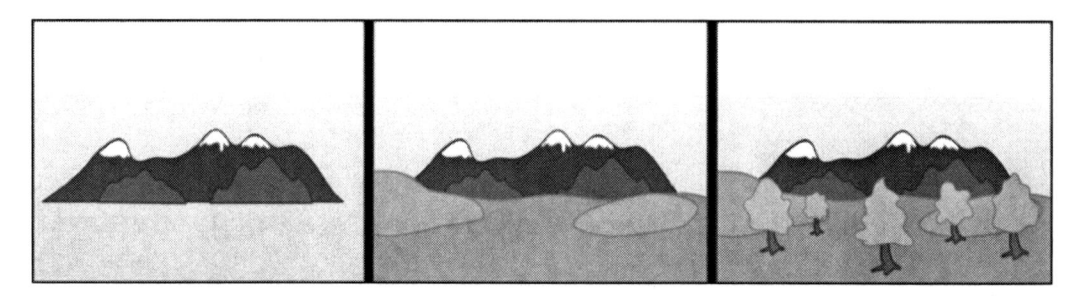

The mountains, being furthest back in the scene, are painted first. The ground and shrubs are then painted, and finally the trees are painted over both.

Z-Sorting, or **depth sorting**, is a technique that is used to sort the elements that make up a 3D object based on how far away they are when viewed by the camera. This then allows these 3D object elements to be rendered to the screen using the painter's algorithm, in order from those furthest back in the scene to those that are the closest.

For the most part, this algorithm works fine and there are no additional steps that need to be taken to render the 3D object elements in the correct order. However, there are situations where this algorithm fails. To understand how the painter's algorithm can fail, we first need to look at how the elements that make up a 3D object are sorted within the scene.

Sorting the scene

The distance of each element within the scene is determined by a single value, known as the **z depth**. The z depth value is calculated using the average position of each vertex that makes up an element along the camera's local coordinate Z-axis. An easy way to visualize the camera's local space is to imagine that the camera is sitting at the origin, and is looking directly towards the positive end of the Z-axis. This is illustrated in the following image:

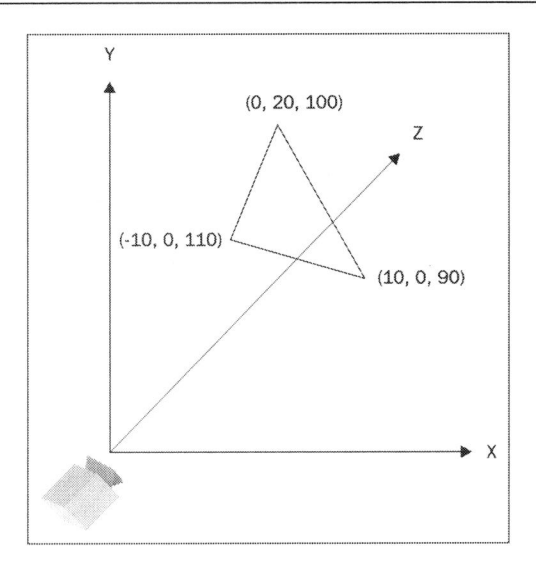

The coordinates of the vertices that make up the triangle have been noted in the image. These coordinates are in the camera's local space. To calculate the z depth, we take the Z components of these coordinates (which are 110, 100, and 90), and average them to give a final value of 100.

This single value of 100 is then used as the z depth the 2D representation of the triangle, even though the depth of the individual vertices ranges from 90 to 110. Sorting the 3D object elements by their z depths can lead to inconsistencies when the single averaged z depth value does not accurately represent a drawing primitive's relative position within the scene.

To demonstrate a situation where the 3D object elements are not sorted correctly, let's create a new example called ZSorting. In the initScene() function we will create two triangles, angled so that one appears to overlap the other from the camera's viewpoint.

```
package
{
   import away3d.primitives.Triangle;

   public class ZSorting extends Away3DTemplate
   {
      public function ZSorting()
      {
         super();
      }

      protected override function initScene():void
```

Z-Sorting

```
   {
     super.initScene();
        camera.z = 0;
     var triangleA:Triangle = new Triangle(
        {
          x: -30,
          y: 0,
          z: 500,
          rotationY: -5,
          yUp: false,
          bothsides: true
        }
     );

     var triangleB:Triangle = new Triangle(
        {
          x: 30,
          y: 0,
          z: 499,
          rotationY: 60,
          yUp: false,
          bothsides: true
        }
     );

     scene.addChild(triangleA);
     scene.addChild(triangleB);

   }
  }
}
```

The following image is a top-down view of the scene. Triangle B has a slightly smaller z depth than Triangle A, and the triangles do not intersect.

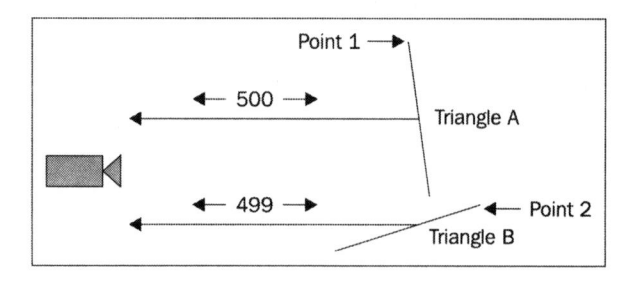

The following image shows how the two triangles are drawn when the application is run:

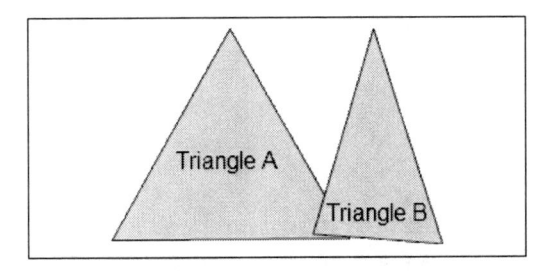

From the top-down view of the scene, it is clear that the triangle on the right (Triangle B) should appear behind the one on the left (Triangle A). But because Triangle B has a smaller z depth than Triangle A, Triangle B is considered to be in front of Triangle A. This results in Triangle B being drawn last, over the top of Triangle A. Here is a perfect example of where a single average z depth does not accurately reflect the actual depth of the 3D objects in the scene.

Adjusting the sorting order

Away3D includes a number of methods that can be employed to adjust the order in which the drawing primitives are rendered. In the example provided, the rendering order can be fixed by either bringing Triangle A to the front of the scene, or by forcing Triangle B to the back.

> The `ZSortingExtended` application available from the Packt website provides an example that implements the following procedures for correcting the sorting order of 3D objects in a single demo.

The pushfront and pushback properties

The `pushfront` property forces a drawing primitive to be sorted based on the point that is closest to the camera. For Triangle A, the closest point to the camera is Point 1. Because Point 1 is closer to the camera than the z depth of Triangle B, setting `pushfront` to `true` for Triangle A will bring it to the front of the scene, meaning it will be rendered last.

```
var triangleA:Object3D = new Triangle(
  {
    x: -30,
```

Z-Sorting

```
      y: 0,
      z: 500,
      rotationY: -5,
      yUp: false,
      bothsides: true,
      pushfront: true
   }
);
```

The `pushback` property does the opposite of `pushfront`, and forces a drawing primitive to be sorted based on the point that is furthest away from the camera. For Triangle B, the furthest point from the camera is Point 2. Because Point 2 is further away than the z depth of Triangle A, setting `pushback` to `true` for Triangle B will push it to the back of the scene, meaning it will be rendered first.

```
var triangleB:Object3D = new Triangle(
   {
      x: 30,
      y: 0,
      z: 499,
      rotationY: 60,
      yUp: false,
      bothsides: true,
      pushback: true
   }
);
```

The screenZOffset property

The `screenZOffset` property can also be used to force one triangle to be considered further away from the camera than the other. Away3D will add the `screenZOffset` value to the z depth, which allows you to adjust the relative depth of a 3D object within the scene.

A positive `screenZOffset` increases the z depth, forcing a 3D object to be considered to be more towards the back of the scene. A negative value will decrease the z depth, forcing a 3D object to be considered to be closer to the front of the scene. Note that setting the `screenZOffset` value will not change the position of the 3D object within the scene, only the order in which it is drawn.

To force Triangle A to be drawn on top of Triangle B we can specify a negative value for the `screenZOffset` parameter. In the following example, Triangle A will have a z depth of 490, placing it in front of Triangle B, which has a z depth of 499.

```
var triangleA:Object3D = new Triangle(
   {
      x: -30,
      y: 0,
      z: 500,
      rotationY: -5,
      yUp: false,
      bothsides: true,
      screenZOffset: -10
   }
);
```

To force Triangle B to be drawn on top of Triangle A, we can specify a positive value for the `screenZOffset` parameter. In the following example, Triangle B will have a z depth of 509, placing it behind Triangle A, which has a z depth of 500.

```
var triangleB:Object3D = new Triangle(
   {
      x: 30,
      y: 0,
      z: 499,
      rotationY: 60,
      yUp: false,
      bothsides: true,
      ownCanvas: true,
      screenZOffset: 10
   }
);
```

> The Away3D documentation states that the `screenZOffset` value will only have an effect on a 3D object if its `ownCanvas` property is set to `true`. With Away3D version 3.6 this is incorrect. The `screenZOffset` will be applied regardless of whether the `ownCanvas` property is `true` or `false`.

Z-Sorting

The ownCanvas property

The final way to force the sorting of 3D objects is to render them in their own canvas, which is done by setting the `ownCanvas` property to `true`, and then forcing the depth of that canvas.

A canvas is a layer into which 3D objects are drawn. They work in much the same way as layers in image-editing software packages like Photoshop. 3D objects can be rendered into a canvas, and the canvas is then drawn alongside any other 3D objects that are in the scene.

First, we set the `ownCanvas` property to `true`.

```
var triangleB:Object3D = new Triangle(
{
    x: 30,
    y: 0,
    z: 499,
    rotationY: 60,
    yUp: false,
    bothsides: true,
    ownCanvas: true
}
);
```

Then, we set the screen depth of the canvas through the `ownSession screenZ` property. Because Triangle A is 500 units away from the camera, we can specify the z depth of the canvas that will display Triangle B to be slightly more at 510. This will mean that Triangle A is considered to be closer to the camera.

```
triangleB.ownSession.screenZ = 510;
```

The following image shows how the canvas is positioned. By giving the canvas onto which Triangle B is drawn a larger `screenZ` value that the z depth of Triangle A, we have forced it to be drawn in the background.

> Be careful when setting the depth of a canvas via the `screenZ` property, because unlike the other methods of correcting the depth of a 3D object, the `screenZ` property is an absolute value and does not take into account the relative position of the camera. If the camera were at a position of (0, 0, -1000), as it is by default, the preceding code would draw the canvas that holds Triangle B in front of Triangle A, because the z depth of Triangle A would be 1500, and the z depth of the canvas would be set to the absolute value of 510.

Chapter 4

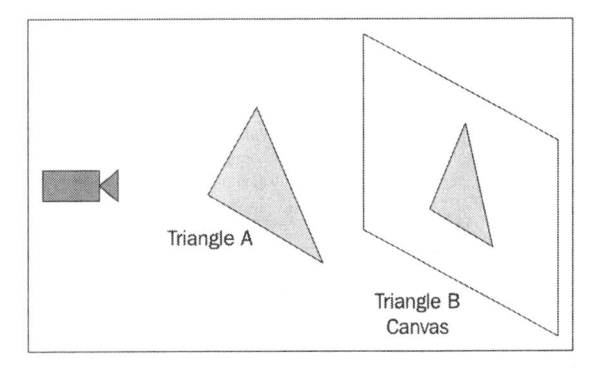

> If no screenZ value is specified, a canvas is ordered in the scene based on the z depths of the 3D objects that will be drawn into it. This means that the order of a canvas in the scene can be modified by using the pushfront, pushback, and screenZOffset properties on the 3D objects that will be drawn into it.

A note about Z-Sorting

All of the methods described above work by modifying the z depth of a 3D object relative to the other 3D objects that are in the scene. It is important to realize that the desired relative depth of these 3D objects will change depending on the position of the camera. Consider the same scene created by the ZSorting application, but now viewed from the opposite side.

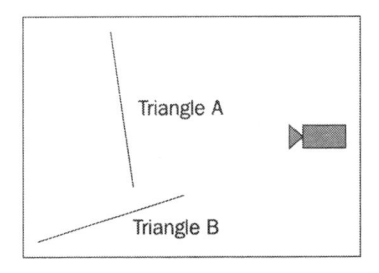

In this situation, if we were to set the pushback property to true for Triangle B, as we did to fix the rendering order when the camera was on the left, we would in fact be introducing a z-sorting error rather than fixing it. This is because from the camera's new position, Triangle B should be drawn in front of Triangle A, not behind it.

Z-Sorting

So keep in mind that the values assigned to the `pushback`, `pushfront`, `screenZOffset`, and `screenZ` properties may need to be modified as the position and orientation of the 3D objects within the scene are changed relative to the position of the camera.

> An example of where it is necessary to adjust the value of the `screenZOffset` property for a 3D object, as its position relative to the camera changes, is given in *Chapter 10, Creating 3D Text*, with the `FontExtrusionDemo` application.

Additional renderers

All the applications shown in this book have made use of the default renderer. Away3D includes three different types of renderers, each returned by static properties in the `Render` class from the `away3d.core.render` package.

The default renderer is created by the `BASIC` property. The other two renderers, created by the `CORRECT_Z_ORDER` and `INTERSECTING_OBJECTS` properties, are quadtree renderers, which are more advanced than the default `BASIC` renderer.

The `CORRECT_Z_ORDER` renderer uses a more sophisticated algorithm for sorting 3D objects in the scene, which can solve some (but not all) z-sorting issues that arise when using the default renderer. The renderer returned by the `INTERSECTING_OBJECTS` property goes one step further by additionally splitting intersecting triangles.

Using these renderers is quite simple. First the `Renderer` class is imported.

```
import away3d.core.render.Renderer;
```

Then in the `initEngine()` function we pass the object returned from the `Renderer` `CORRECT_Z_ORDER` or `INTERSECTING_OBJECTS` properties to the `View3D` constructor via the `renderer` init object parameter.

```
protected function initEngine():void
{
  scene = new Scene3D();
  camera = new Camera3D();
  view = new View3D(
    {
      renderer: Renderer.INTERSECTING_OBJECTS
    }
```

```
            );

            scene = view.scene;
            camera = view.camera;

            addChild(view);

            view.x = stage.stageWidth / 2;
            view.y = stage.stageHeight / 2;
        }
```

The active renderer can also be changed at runtime by modifying the `View3D` `renderer` property.

```
            view.renderer = Renderer.CORRECT_Z_ORDER;
```

The `RenderersDemo` application allows you to change between the three renderers at runtime by pressing 1, 2, or 3 on the keyboard, providing an opportunity to compare how they deal with intersecting 3D objects.

```
    package
    {
        import away3d.cameras.Camera3D;
        import away3d.containers.Scene3D;
        import away3d.containers.View3D;
        import away3d.core.render.Renderer;
        import away3d.materials.WireColorMaterial;
        import away3d.primitives.Cube;
        import away3d.primitives.Triangle;

        import flash.display.Sprite;
        import flash.events.Event;
        import flash.events.KeyboardEvent;
        import flash.text.TextField;

        public class RenderersDemo extends Away3DTemplate
        {
            private var triangle:Triangle;
            private var box:Cube;

            public function RenderersDemo():void
            {
```

Z-Sorting

```
      super();
   }

   protected override function initScene():void
   {
      super.initScene();
      triangle = new Triangle(
        {
          edge: 150,
          bothsides: true,
          yUp: false,
          material: new WireColorMaterial(0x224488),
          z: 500
        }
      );
      scene.addChild(triangle);

      box = new Cube(
        {
          z: 500,
          width: 50,
          height: 75,
          depth: 50,
          material: new WireColorMaterial(0x228844)
        }
      );
      scene.addChild(box);
   }

   protected override function initListeners():void
   {
      super.initListeners();
      stage.addEventListener(KeyboardEvent.KEY_UP, onKeyUp);
   }

   protected override function initUI():void
   {
      super.initUI();
      var text:TextField = new TextField();
      text.text = "Press 1 to enbale the BASIC renderer.\n" +
        "Press 2 to enable the CORRECT_Z_ORDER renderer.\n" +
```

```
            "Press 3 to enable the INTERSECTING_OBJECTS renderer.\n" +
            "Press 4 to make the box transparent.\n" +
            "Press 5 to make the box opaque.";
        text.x = 10;
        text.y = 10;
        text.width = 300;
        this.addChild(text);
    }

    protected override function onEnterFrame(event:Event):void
    {
        super.onEnterFrame(event);
        triangle.rotationY += 3;
        box.rotationY -= 1;
    }

    protected function onKeyUp(event:KeyboardEvent):void
    {
        switch (event.keyCode)
        {
            case 49:
                view.renderer = Renderer.BASIC;
                break;
            case 50:
                view.renderer = Renderer.CORRECT_Z_ORDER;
                break;
            case 51:
                view.renderer = Renderer.INTERSECTING_OBJECTS;
                break;
            case 52:
                (box.material as WireColorMaterial).alpha = 0.5;
                break;
            case 53:
                (box.material as WireColorMaterial).alpha = 1;
                break;
        }
    }
  }
}
```

Z-Sorting

In the following image, you can see the difference that the `INTERSECTING_OBJECTS` renderer makes. With the default `BASIC` renderer, shown on the left, the triangle appears to be behind the cube, despite the fact that the two 3D objects are actually intersecting. The `INTERSECTING_OBJECTS` renderer, shown on the right, will split the individual triangle faces that make up the 3D objects in order to correctly render the scene.

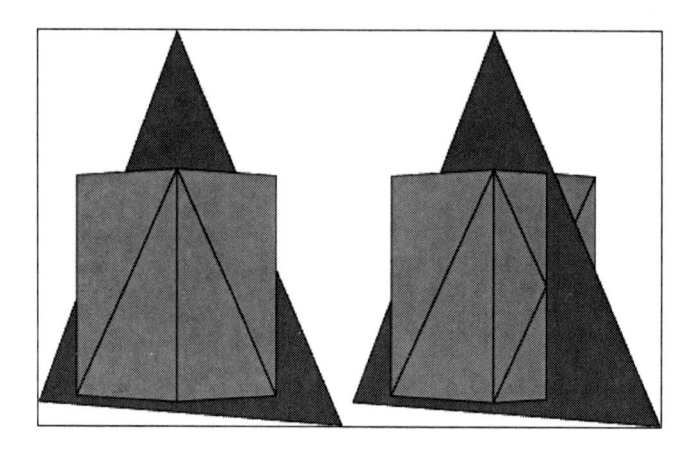

The scene created by the `RenderersDemo` application is trivial, involving only a single cube primitive and a single triangle primitive. In this case, switching between the three renderers probably won't have a great deal of impact on the performance of the application. But what happens in a more complex scene?

The `RenderersPerformanceDemo` application creates a number of spheres that bounce around inside an invisible box. Just like the `RenderersDemo` application, you can switch between the three renderers at runtime.

```
package
{
  import away3d.core.render.Renderer;
  import away3d.primitives.Sphere;
  import flash.geom.Vector3D;

  import flash.events.Event;
  import flash.events.KeyboardEvent;
  import flash.text.TextField;

  public class RenderersPerformanceDemo extends Away3DTemplate
  {
    protected static const SPEED:Number = 0.5;
    protected static const BOXSIZE:Number = 20;
```

Chapter 4

```
    protected static const NUMBERSPHERS:Number = 10;
    protected var spheres:Vector.<Sphere> = new Vector.<Sphere>();
    protected var directions:Vector.<Vector3D> = new
Vector.<Vector3D>();

    public function RenderersPerformanceDemo()
    {
      super();
    }

    protected override function initScene():void
    {
      super.initScene();
      this.camera.z = 50;
      for (var i:int = 0; i < NUMBERSPHERS; ++i)
      {
        var sphere:Sphere = new Sphere(
          {
            x: Math.random() * BOXSIZE - BOXSIZE/2,
            y: Math.random() * BOXSIZE - BOXSIZE/2,
            z: Math.random() * BOXSIZE - BOXSIZE/2,
            radius: 2
          }
        );
        spheres.push(sphere);
        this.scene.addChild(sphere);

        directions.push(new Vector3D(
          Math.random() - 0.5,
          Math.random() - 0.5,
          Math.random() - 0.5)
        );
        directions[i].normalize();
        directions[i].scaleBy(SPEED);
      }
    }

    protected override function initListeners():void
    {
      super.initListeners();
      stage.addEventListener(Event.ENTER_FRAME, onEnterFrame);
      stage.addEventListener(KeyboardEvent.KEY_UP, onKeyUp);
    }
```

Z-Sorting

```
protected override function initUI():void
{
  super.initUI();
  var text:TextField = new TextField();
  text.text = "Press 1 to enbale the BASIC renderer.\n" +
    "Press 2 to enable the CORRECT_Z_ORDER renderer.\n" +
    "Press 3 to enable the INTERSECTING_OBJECTS renderer.";
  text.x = 10;
  text.y = 10;
  text.width = 300;
  this.addChild(text);
}

protected function onKeyUp(event:KeyboardEvent):void
{
  switch (event.keyCode)
  {
    case 49:
      view.renderer = Renderer.BASIC;
      break;
    case 50:
      view.renderer = Renderer.CORRECT_Z_ORDER;
      break;
    case 51:
      view.renderer = Renderer.INTERSECTING_OBJECTS;
      break;
  }
}

protected override function onEnterFrame(event:Event):void
{
  super.onEnterFrame(event);
  for (var i:int = 0; i < 10; ++i)
  {
    var newPosition:Vector3D = new Vector3D();
    newPosition = spheres[i].position.add(directions[i]);

    for each (var property:String in ["x", "y", "z"])
    {
      if (newPosition[property] < -BOXSIZE/2)
      {
        newPosition[property] = -BOXSIZE/2;
        directions[i][property] *= -1;
      }
```

```
            if (newPosition[property] > BOXSIZE/2)
            {
              newPosition[property] = BOXSIZE/2;
              directions[i][property] *= -1;
            }
          }

          spheres[i].position = newPosition;
        }
      }
    }
  }
```

A scene made up of ten spheres is still quite simple by most standards, but note what happens when you switch to the `CORRECT_Z_ORDER` or `INTERSECTING_OBJECTS` renderers from the default `BASIC` renderer. Chances are, the application went from being smooth and fluid to quite jerky. And that's if it doesn't just throw an error about the script time out.

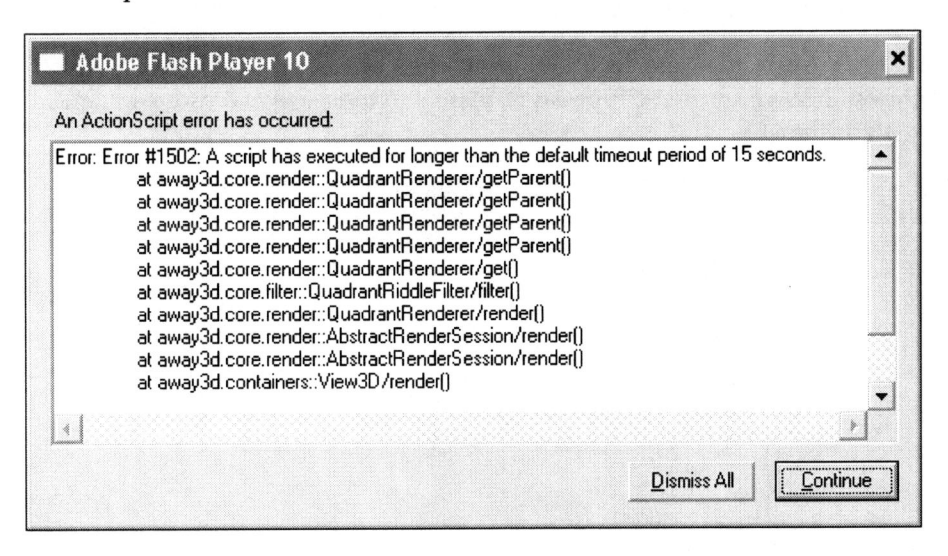

The `RenderersPerformanceDemo` application demonstrates the performance limitations of the more advanced renderers. For all but the most simple of scenes it is generally best to try and correct the sorting order of 3D objects manually in order to maintain a reasonable frame rate.

Summary

This chapter gave an overview of the painter's algorithm, which is used by Away3D to draw a scene, starting with those 3D objects that are furthest from the camera and working its way forward. We then saw the method in which Away3D determines the distance of a 3D object from the camera, which then defines the sorting order of the 3D objects. We also saw some of the limitations of the algorithms used to calculate these distances.

While the default algorithms implemented by Away3D will correctly sort the 3D objects within a scene most of the time, these limitations can lead to situations where a scene is not rendered correctly. One such situation was demonstrated, and a number of solutions were then provided that allow us to control the way in which Away3D sorts the scene including:

- The `pushback` and `pushfront` properties
- The `screenZOffset` property
- The `ownCanvas` property

In addition, we looked at the additional renderers provided by Away3D, which can be used to solve some sorting issues, thanks to their use of a more advanced sorting algorithm.

In the next chapter, we will explore the various materials that can be applied to 3D objects.

5
Materials

We have seen how 3D objects can be created and displayed within the scene, and until now they have been displayed using the default material, `WireColorMaterial`, which displays as a solid color with black outline. While this does allow us to view our 3D objects, it is a little boring. Thankfully, Away3D includes over a dozen material types that can be used to display 3D objects with a huge variety of effects, with some of the materials using the Pixel Bender technology new to Flash Player 10 to create a level of detail that has not previously been seen in Flash applications.

This chapter covers the following:

- Managing resources by embedding them, or loading them from external files
- Defining colors
- Pixel Bender
- The various shading techniques used by Away3D materials
- The different materials that can be created in Away3D
- Illuminating materials with lights

The difference between textures and materials

Throughout this chapter, a number of references will be made to materials and textures. A **texture** is simply an image, like you would create in an image editing application like Photoshop or view in a web page. Textures are then used by materials, which in Away3D are classes that can be applied to the surface of a 3D object.

Materials

Resource management

Quite a number of the materials included in Away3D rely on textures that exist in external image like a PNG, JPG, or GIF file. There are two ways of dealing with external files: embedding them or accessing them at runtime.

ActionScript includes the `Embed` keyword, which can be used to embed external files directly inside a compiled SWF file. There are a number of benefits to embedded resources:

- The Flash application can be distributed as a single file
- There is no wait when accessing the resources at runtime
- The security issues associated with accessing remote resources are avoided
- There is no additional network traffic once the SWF is downloaded
- The SWF file can be run offline
- The embedded files can have additional compression applied

The downside to embedding resources is that the size of the final SWF is increased, resulting in a longer initial download time.

Alternatively, the external files can be saved separately and accessed at runtime, which has the following advantages:

- The SWF file is smaller, resulting in shorter initial download times
- Resources are only downloaded when they are needed, and cached for future access
- Resources can be updated or modified without recompiling the SWF file

There are several downsides to accessing resources at runtime:

- Permissions on the server hosting the resources may need to be configured before the external files can be accessed
- Distribution of the final Flash application is more difficult due to the increased number of individual files
- There will be a delay when the application is run as the remote resources are downloaded

Away3D supports the use of both embedded and external resources, and both methods will be demonstrated below.

> Embedding the resources is usually the best option when managing resources. It prevents a number of possible errors due to unreliable networks and security restrictions, and produces a SWF file that is much simpler to distribute and publish.
>
> However, for applications where it is not possible to know what resources will be required beforehand, like a 3D image gallery, loading external resources is the only option. You may also want to load external resources for applications where there is a large volume of data that does not need to be downloaded immediately, like a large game with levels that the player won't necessarily see in a single sitting.

Defining colors in Away3D

The appearance of a number of materials can be modified by supplying a color. A good example is the `WireColorMaterial` material (the same one that is applied to a 3D object when no material is specified), the fill and outline colors of which can be defined via the `color` and `wirecolor` init object parameters.

Colors can be defined in Away3D in a number of different formats. Common to all the formats is the idea that a color is made up of red, green, and blue component. For example, the color purple is made up of red and blue, while yellow is made up of red and green.

By integer

Colors can be defined as an integer. These `int` values are usually defined in their hexadecimal form, which looks like `0x12CD56`. The characters that make up the `int` can be digits between 0 and 9, and characters between A and F. You can think of the characters A through to F as representing the numbers 10 to 15, allowing each character to represent 16 different values. For each color component, 00 is the lowest value, and FF is the highest. The first two characters define the red components of the color, the next two define the green component, and the final two define the blue component.

It is sometimes necessary to define the transparency of a color. This is done by adding two additional characters to the beginning of the hexadecimal notation, such as `0xFF12CD56`. In this form, the two leading characters define the transparency, or alpha, of the color. The last six characters represent the red, green, and blue components. Smaller alpha values make a color more transparent, while higher alpha values make a color more opaque.

Materials

You can see an example of a color being defined as an `int` in the `applyWireframeMaterial()` function from the `MaterialsDemo` class that is discussed later in the chapter.

By string

The same hexadecimal format used by integers can also be represented as a `String`. The only difference is that the prefix `0x` is left off. An example would be `"12CD56"`, or `"FF12CD56"`. The `MaterialsDemo applyColorMaterial()` function demonstrates the use of this color format.

Away3D also recognizes a number of colors by name. These are listed in the following table. The `MaterialsDemo applyWireColorMaterial()` function demonstrates the use of colors defined by name.

random	steelblue	royalblue	cornflowerblue
lightsteelblue	mediumslateblue	slateblue	darkslateblue
midnightblue	navy	darkblue	mediumblue
blue	dodgerblue	deepskyblue	lightskyblue
skyblue	lightblue	powderblue	azure
lightcyan	paleturquoise	mediumturquoise	lightseagreen
darkcyan	teal	cadetblue	darkturquoise
aqua	cyan	turquoise	aquamarine
mediumaquamarine	darkseagreen	mediumseagreen	seagreen
darkgreen	green	forestgreen	limegreen
lime	chartreuse	lawngreen	greenyellow
yellowgreen	palegreen	lightgreen	springgreen
mediumspringgreen	darkolivegreen	olivedrab	olive
darkkhaki	darkgoldenrod	goldenrod	gold
yellow	khaki	palegoldenrod	blanchedalmond
moccasin	wheat	navajowhite	burlywood
tan	rosybrown	sienna	saddlebrown
chocolate	peru	sandybrown	darkred
maroon	brown	firebrick	indianred
lightcoral	salmon	darksalmon	lightsalmon
coral	tomato	darkorange	orange
orangered	crimson	red	deeppink
fuchsia	magenta	hotpink	lightpink

Chapter 5

pink	palevioletred	mediumvioletred	purple
darkmagenta	mediumpurple	blueviolet	indigo
darkviolet	darkorchid	mediumorchid	orchid
violet	plum	thistle	lavender
ghostwhite	aliceblue	mintcream	honeydew
lightgoldenrodyellow	lemonchiffon	cornsilk	lightyellow
ivory	floralwhite	linen	oldlace
antiquewhite	bisque	peachpuff	papayawhip
beige	seashell	lavenderblush	mistyrose
snow	white	whitesmoke	gainsboro
lightgrey	silver	darkgrey	grey
lightslategrey	slategrey	dimgrey	darkslategrey
black	transparent		

Pixel Bender

Pixel Bender is a technology, new to Flash Player 10, that implements generalized graphics processing in the Pixel Bender language. The programs written using Pixel Bender are known as **kernels** or **shaders**. Shaders have the advantage of being able to be run across multiple CPUs and CPU cores, unlike the graphics processing done via the Flash graphics API. This gives shaders the potential to be much faster.

> The term shader and kernel can be used interchangeably with respect to Pixel Bender.

One of the advantages of using Away3D version 3.x over version 2.x is the ability to use Pixel Bender shaders. The implementation of these shaders is largely hidden by the material classes that utilize them, meaning that they can be used much like the regular material classes, while at the same time offering a much higher level of detail.

A common misconception is that Flash Player 10 uses the Graphics Processing Unit (GPU), which is common to most video chipsets these days, to execute shaders. This is incorrect. Unlike some other Adobe products that also make use of Pixel Bender shaders, Flash Player 10 does not utilize the GPU when executing shaders.

> Adobe has indicated that GPU rendering support for Pixel Bender may be included in future releases of Flash Player.

Lights and materials

Lights and materials are two sides of the same coin in Away3D. The effect of a light can only be seen on a material, and materials that can be illuminated will generally show up completely black without a light source.

Away3D includes three classes, all from the `away3d.lights` package, with each one representing a different type of light:

- Point lights, represented by the `PointLight3D` class, emit light in all directions from a point in space. The intensity of the point light is calculated using the inverse square law of attenuation (light intensity = 1 / distance^2).

- Directional lights, represented by the `DirectionalLight3D` class, emit light along a vector, like a flash light. Unlike the point light, the intensity of the directional light does not diminish with distance. The intensity does decrease as the angle between the vector along which the directional light is shining and the surface it is shining on increases.

- Ambient lights, represented by the `AmbientLight3D` class, shine on all surfaces equally. Ambient lights can be used to add a minimum amount of light to those materials that implement them.

Only a subset of the materials available in Away3D can be illuminated, and those materials may only support a subset of the different types of lights. The following table lists those materials that can be lit, which types of lights they support, and whether the material can be illuminated by multiple light sources. The material classes themselves will be covered in more detail later on in this chapter.

Material	Ambient	Directional	Point	Multiple Lights
`Dot3BitmapMaterial`	*	*		*
`Dot3BitmapMaterialF10`		*		
`PhongBitmapMaterial`	*	*		*
`PhongColorMaterial`	*	*		
`PhongMovieMaterial`	*	*		*
`PhongPBMaterial`			*	
`PhongMultipassMaterial`		*	*	*
`ShadingColorMaterial`		*	*	*
`WhiteShadingBitmapMaterial`		*	*	*

> There does not appear to be any overall design when determining which types of lights are supported by which materials. The phong shading materials are a good example. `PhongMultipassMaterial` supports both point and directional lights, while `PhongPBMaterial` only supports point lights. Neither supports the ambient light type, unlike the `PhongBitmapMaterial`, `PhongColorMaterial`, and `PhongMovieMaterial` classes.
>
> The choice of what type of light source to use in your Away3D applications will usually be determined by your choice of material, and not the other way around.

Shading techniques

Away3D materials use a number of shading techniques, sometimes in combination, to achieve their end result. These techniques can be used to apply a texture to the surface of a 3D object, illuminate a 3D object using an external light source, display a reflection of the surrounding environment, or simulate the appearance of a bumpy surface.

Texture mapping

Texture mapping is used to apply an image, usually from a PNG, JPG, or GIF file, to the surface of a 3D object. It is used on its own to display a single texture, or it can be used in conjunction with the other shading techniques.

The following image shows a sphere that uses texture mapping to display a single texture representing the Earth:

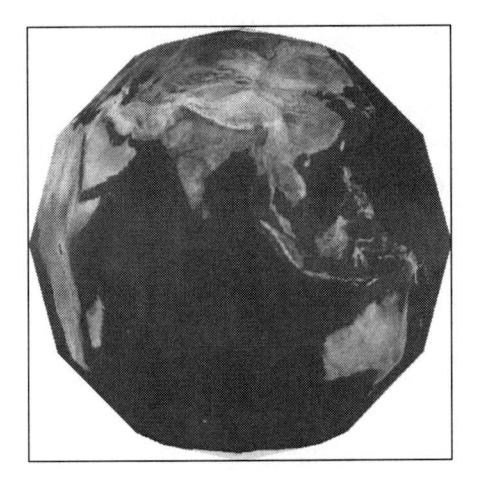

Normal mapping

Normal mapping is a technique that is used to add the appearance of depth to a 3D object. This is done by using the information stored in an image called a normal map to calculate how each part of the material should be shaded. This shading gives the impression of a bumpy surface.

Normal mapping has the benefit of adding depth detail without using additional polygons. A normal mapped low-polygon 3D object will generally be rendered faster than a high-polygon 3D object with a standard material, while maintaining much of the visual quality of the high-polygon 3D object.

> A useful utility for creating normal maps can be found at `http://www.tartiflop.com/disp2norm/`. This tool will create normal maps from a grayscale displacement map that can be applied to flat or spherical 3D objects.

The following image is an example of a normal map that can be applied to a sphere:

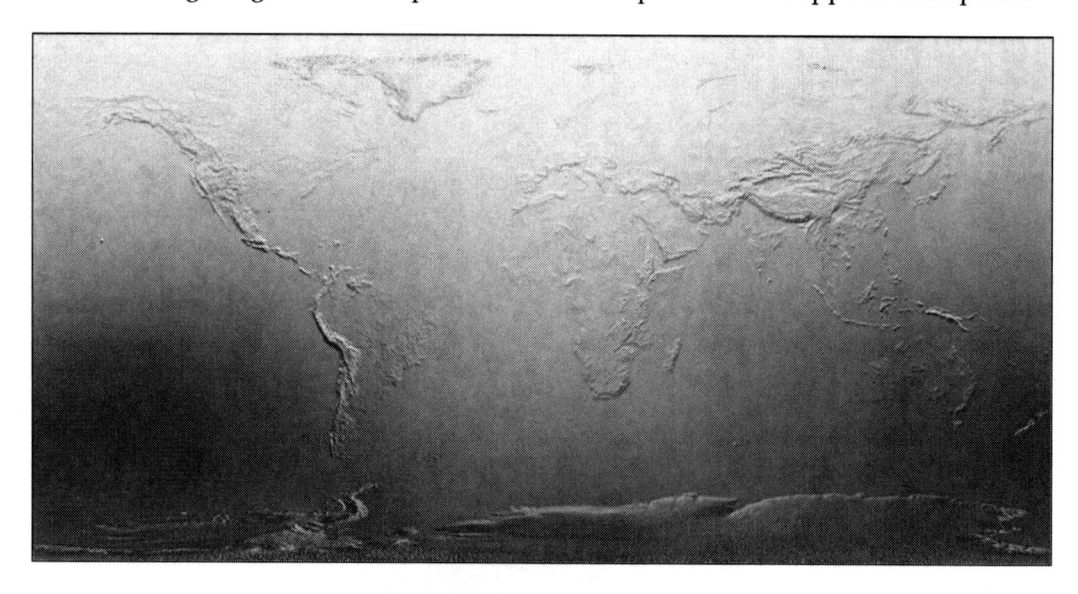

This effect is shown in the following image, where you can see how the sphere appears to have a rough surface. From the angle in the screenshot, this roughness is especially apparent over the African continent.

Chapter 5

Environment mapping

Environment mapping is used to draw a 3D object's surroundings as a reflection. Reflecting the true surroundings of a 3D object on its surface is far too computationally expensive, but the effect can be approximated using a single texture, or a collection of textures that form a cube that appears to surround the 3D object.

Environment mapping is useful for creating the appearance of shiny 3D objects, like those with a polished or metallic surface. In the following image, the first two 3D objects have had a material applied that implements environment mapping (reflecting a marble texture). The torus on the left has applied an environment map over a base texture map, while the one in the middle has applied the environment map over a solid color. As a comparison the torus on the right has had a material applied to it that uses only texture mapping.

The effect that is produced by environment mapping can be difficult to appreciate in a static screenshot, but it is immediately apparent as the 3D object moves relative to the camera.

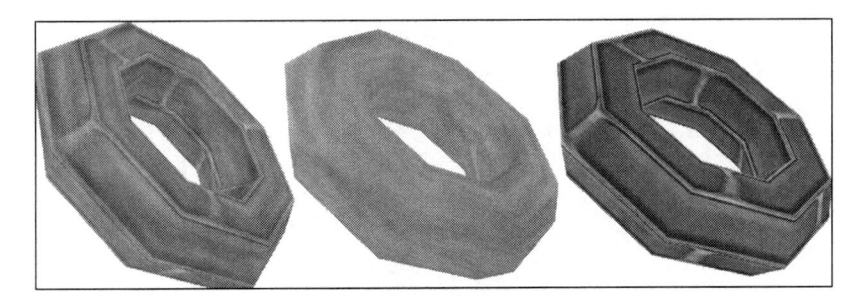

[125]

Flat shading

Flat shading is used to illuminate each polygon against a light source. It is very quick to calculate, but since each triangle face is shaded as a whole it does tend to highlight the edges of a low-polygon 3D object.

The following sphere has been illuminated using flat shading. As you can see it is easy to discern each of the triangle faces that make up the sphere.

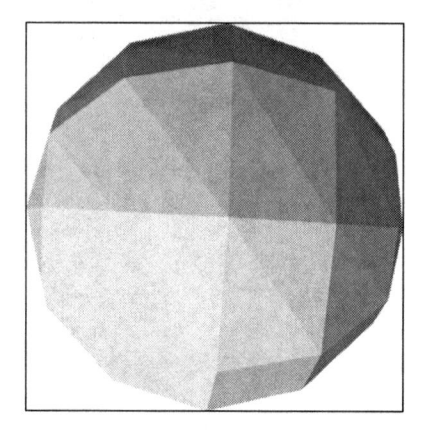

Phong shading

Phong shading will calculate the illumination of each pixel on the surface of a 3D object against a light source. This eliminates the sharp edges that can be produced by flat shading, but does so with a performance cost.

The following sphere has been illuminated using phong shading. Because each pixel is lit independently of the triangle faces, the end result is much smoother than the flat shading technique discussed previously.

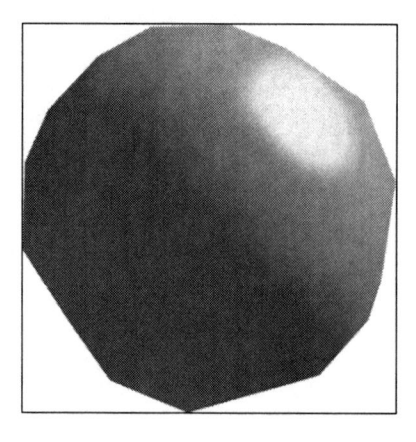

Applying materials

To demonstrate the basic materials available in Away3D, we will create a new demo called `MaterialsDemo`.

```
package
{
```

Some primitives show off a material better than others. To accommodate this, we will apply the various materials to the sphere, torus, cube, and plane primitive 3D objects in this demo. All primitives extend the `Mesh` class, which makes it the logical choice for the type of the variable that will reference instances of all four primitives.

```
import away3d.core.base.Mesh;
```

The `Cast` class provides a number of handy functions that deal with the casting of objects between types.

```
import away3d.core.utils.Cast;
```

As we saw previously, those materials that can be illuminated support point or directional light sources (and sometimes both). To show off materials that can be illuminated, one of these types of lights will be added to the scene.

```
import away3d.lights.DirectionalLight3D;
import away3d.lights.PointLight3D;
```

In order to load textures from external image files, we need to import the `TextureLoadQueue` and `TextureLoader` classes.

```
import away3d.loaders.utils.TextureLoadQueue;
import away3d.loaders.utils.TextureLoader;
```

The various material classes demonstrated by the `MaterialsDemo` class are imported from the `away3d.materials` package.

```
import away3d.materials.AnimatedBitmapMaterial;
import away3d.materials.BitmapFileMaterial;
import away3d.materials.BitmapMaterial;
import away3d.materials.ColorMaterial;
import away3d.materials.CubicEnvMapPBMaterial;
import away3d.materials.DepthBitmapMaterial;
import away3d.materials.Dot3BitmapMaterial;
import away3d.materials.Dot3BitmapMaterialF10;
import away3d.materials.EnviroBitmapMaterial;
import away3d.materials.EnviroColorMaterial;
import away3d.materials.FresnelPBMaterial;
import away3d.materials.MovieMaterial;
```

Materials

```
import away3d.materials.PhongBitmapMaterial;
import away3d.materials.PhongColorMaterial;
import away3d.materials.PhongMovieMaterial;
import away3d.materials.PhongMultiPassMaterial;
import away3d.materials.PhongPBMaterial;
import away3d.materials.ShadingColorMaterial;
import away3d.materials.TransformBitmapMaterial;
import away3d.materials.WhiteShadingBitmapMaterial;
import away3d.materials.WireColorMaterial;
import away3d.materials.WireframeMaterial;
```

These materials will all be applied to a number of primitive types, which are all imported from the `away3d.primitives` package.

```
import away3d.primitives.Cube;
import away3d.primitives.Plane;
import away3d.primitives.Sphere;
import away3d.primitives.Torus;
```

The `CubFaces` class defines a number of constants that identify each of the six sides of a cube.

```
import away3d.primitives.utils.CubeFaces;
```

The following Flash classes are used when loading textures from external image files, to handle events, to display a textfield on the screen, and to define a position or vector within the scene.

```
import flash.geom.Vector3D;
import flash.net.URLRequest;
import flash.display.BitmapData;
import flash.events.Event;
import flash.events.KeyboardEvent;
import flash.text.TextField;
```

The `MaterialsDemo` class extends the `Away3DTemplate` class that was presented in *Chapter 1, Building Your First Away3D Application*.

```
public class MaterialsDemo extends Away3DTemplate
{
```

One of the ways to manage resources that was discussed in the *Resource management* section was to embed them. Here, we see how an external JPG image file, referenced by the `source` parameter, has been embedded using the `Embed` keyword. Embedding an image file in this way means that instantiating the `EarthDiffuse` class will result in a `Bitmap` object populated with the image data contained in the `earth_diffuse.jpg` file.

```
[Embed(source = "earth_diffuse.jpg")]
protected var EarthDiffuse:Class;
```

A number of additional images have been embedded in the same way.

```
[Embed(source = "earth_normal.jpg")]
protected var EarthNormal:Class;
[Embed(source = "earth_specular.jpg")]
protected var EarthSpecular:Class;
[Embed(source = "checkerboard.jpg")]
protected var Checkerboard:Class;
[Embed(source = "bricks.jpg")]
protected var Bricks:Class;
[Embed(source = "marble.jpg")]
protected var Marble:Class;
[Embed(source = "water.jpg")]
protected var Water:Class;
[Embed(source = "waternormal.jpg")]
protected var WaterNormal:Class;
[Embed(source = "spheremap.gif")]
protected var SphereMap:Class;
[Embed(source = "skyleft.jpg")]
protected var Skyleft:Class;
[Embed(source = "skyfront.jpg")]
protected var Skyfront:Class;
[Embed(source = "skyright.jpg")]
protected var Skyright:Class;
[Embed(source = "skyback.jpg")]
protected var Skyback:Class;
[Embed(source = "skyup.jpg")]
protected var Skyup:Class;
[Embed(source = "skydown.jpg")]
protected var Skydown:Class;
```

Here we are embedding three SWF files. These are embedded just like the preceding images.

```
[Embed(source = "Butterfly.swf")]
protected var Butterfly:Class;
[Embed(source = "InteractiveTexture.swf")]
private var InteractiveTexture:Class;
[Embed(source = "Bear.swf")]
private var Bear:Class;
```

Materials

A `TextField` object is used to display the name of the current material on the screen.

```
protected var materialText:TextField;
```

The `currentPrimitive` property is used to reference the primitive to which we will apply the various materials.

```
protected var currentPrimitive:Mesh;
```

The `directionalLight` and `pointLight` properties each reference a light that is added to the scene to illuminate certain materials.

```
protected var directionalLight:DirectionalLight3D;
protected var pointLight:PointLight3D;
```

The `bounce` property is set to `true` when we want the sphere to bounce along the Z-axis. This bouncing motion will be used to show off the effect of the `DepthBitmapMaterial` class.

```
protected var bounce:Boolean;
```

The `frameCount` property maintains a count of the frames that have been rendered while `bounce` property is set to `true`.

```
protected var frameCount:int;
```

The constructor calls the `Away3DTemplate` constructor, which will initialize the Away3D engine.

```
public function MaterialsDemo()
{
  super();
}
```

The `removePrimitive()` function removes the current primitive 3D object from the scene, in preparation for a new primitive to be created.

```
protected function removePrimitive():void
{
  if (currentPrimitive != null)
  {
    scene.removeChild(currentPrimitive);
    currentPrimitive = null;
  }
}
```

The `initSphere()` function first removes the existing primitive from the scene by calling the `removePrimitive()` function, and then creates a new sphere primitive and adds it to the scene. Optionally, it can set the `bounce` property to `true`, which indicates that the primitive should bounce along the Z-axis.

```
protected function initSphere(bounce:Boolean = false):void
{
   removePrimitive();
   currentPrimitive = new Sphere();
   scene.addChild(currentPrimitive);
   this.bounce = bounce;
}
```

The `initTorus()`, `initCube()`, and `initPlane()` functions all work like the `initSphere()` function to add a specific type of primitive to the scene. These functions all set the `bounce` property to `false`, as none of the materials that will be applied to these primitives gain anything by having the primitive bounce within the scene.

```
protected function initTorus():void
{
   removePrimitive();
   currentPrimitive = new Torus();
   scene.addChild(currentPrimitive);
   this.bounce = false;
}

protected function initCube():void
{
   removePrimitive();
   currentPrimitive = new Cube(
     {
       width: 200,
       height: 200,
       depth: 200
     }
   );
   scene.addChild(currentPrimitive);
   this.bounce = false;
}

protected function initPlane():void
{
        removePrimitive();
```

Materials

```
currentPrimitive = new Plane(
    {
      bothsides: true,
      width: 200,
      height: 200,
      yUp: false
    }
  );
  scene.addChild(currentPrimitive);
  this.bounce = false;
}
```

The `removeLights()` function will remove any lights that have been added to the scene in preparation for a new light to be created.

```
protected function removeLights():void
{
  if (directionalLight != null)
  {
    scene.removeLight(directionalLight);
    directionalLight = null;
  }

  if (pointLight != null)
  {
    scene.removeLight(pointLight);
    pointLight = null;
  }
}
```

The `initPointLight()` and `initDirectionalLight()` functions each remove any existing lights in the scene by calling the `removeLights()` function, and then add their specific type of light to the scene.

```
protected function initPointLight():void
{
  removeLights();

  pointLight = new PointLight3D(
    {
      x: -300,
      y: -300,
      radius: 1000
    }
```

```
        );
        scene.addLight(pointLight);
    }

    protected function initDirectionalLight():void
    {
        removeLights();

        directionalLight = new DirectionalLight3D(
            {
                x: 300,
                y: 300,
```

The direction that the light is pointing is set to (0, 0, 0) by default, which effectively means the light is not pointing anywhere. If you have a directional light that is not being reflected off the surface of a lit material, leaving the direction property to this default value may be the cause. Here we override the default to make the light point back to the origin.

```
                direction: new Vector3D(-1, -1, 0)
            }
        );
        scene.addLight(directionalLight);
    }
```

The `initScene()` function has been overridden to call the `applyWireColorMaterial()` function, which will display a sphere with the `WireColorMaterial` material applied to it. We also set the position of the camera back to the origin.

```
    protected override function initScene():void
    {
        super.initScene();
        this.camera.z = 0;
        applyWireColorMaterial();
    }
```

The `initUI()` function adds a textfield to the stage. This textfield will be used to display the name of the currently applied material.

Materials

> The TextField object is added as a child of the main Sprite class (from which the Away3DTemplate class extends), and has no direct association with the Away3D engine. As such the x and y coordinates shown below relate to a 2D position on the screen, and not a 3D position within the Away3D scene.

```
protected override function initUI():void
{
  materialText = new TextField();
  materialText.x = 10;
  materialText.y = 10;
  materialText.width = 300;
  this.addChild(materialText);
}
```

The initListeners() function has been overridden to register the onKeyUp() function to be called when a key on the keyboard has been released.

```
protected override function initListeners():void
{
  super.initListeners();
  stage.addEventListener(KeyboardEvent.KEY_UP, onKeyUp);
}
```

The onEnterFrame() function is overridden to animate the current primitive.

```
protected override function onEnterFrame(event:Event):void
{
  super.onEnterFrame(event);
```

If bounce property is true the current primitive will bounce along the Z-axis between 400 and 600 units from the origin. This is used to show off the effect produced by the DepthBitmapMaterial class.

```
  if (bounce)
  {
    ++frameCount;
    currentPrimitive.z =
    500 + Math.sin(frameCount / 10) * 100;
  }
```

[134]

If `bounce` is `false`, the current primitive will be fixed at a position of 500 units along the Z-axis.

```
else
{
   frameCount = 0;
   currentPrimitive.z = 500;
}
```

The current primitive will also be slowly rotated around the X and Y axes.

```
   currentPrimitive.rotationX += 1;
   currentPrimitive.rotationY += 1;
}
```

The `onKeyUp()` function uses a switch statement to call a function in response to certain keyboard keys being released. The comment next to each `case` statement shows the key that the `keyCode` property relates to.

```
protected function onKeyUp(event:KeyboardEvent):void
{
   switch (event.keyCode)
   {
      case 49: // 1
         applyWireColorMaterial();
         break;
      case 50: // 2
         applyWireframeMaterial();
         break;
      case 51: // 3
         applyColorMaterial();
         break;
      case 52: // 4
         applyBitmapMaterial();
         break;
      case 53: // 5
         applyDepthBitmapMaterial();
         break;
      case 54: // 6
         applyMovieMaterial();
         break;
      case 55: // 7
         applyInteractiveMovieMaterial();
         break;
      case 56: // 8
```

Materials

```
        applyAnimatedBitmapMaterial();
        break;
    case 57: // 9
        applyDot3BitmapMaterialF10();
        break;
    case 48: // 0
        applyDot3BitmapMaterial();
        break;
    case 81: // Q
        applyEnviroBitmapMaterial();
        break;
    case 87: // W
        applyEnviroColorMaterial();
        break;
    case 69: // E
        applyFresnelPBMaterial();
        break;
    case 82: // R
        applyPhongBitmapMaterial();
        break;
    case 84: // T
        applyPhongColorMaterial();
        break;
    case 89: // Y
        applyPhongMovieMaterial();
        break;
    case 85: // U
        applyPhongPBMaterial();
        break;
    case 73: // I
        applyPhongMultiPassMaterial();
        break;
    case 79: // O
        applyShadingColorMaterial();
        break;
    case 80: // P
        applyWhiteShadingBitmapMaterial();
        break;
    case 65: // A
        applyTransformBitmapMaterial();
        break;
    case 83: // S
```

```
            applyCubicEnvMapPBMaterial();
            break;
        case 68: // D
            applyBitmapFileMaterial();
            break;
        case 70: // F
            applyExternalDot3BitmapMaterial();
            break;
    }
}
```

The remainder of the `MaterialsDemo` class is made up of the functions called by the `onKeyUp()` function that create a primitive 3D object, apply a material to it, and create a light if one is needed. The materials that are applied by these functions, the function itself, and a table showing the parameters that the materials accept are listed in the coming sections.

> Unlike the classes used to create the primitive 3D objects in *Chapter 2, Creating and Displaying Primitives*, which usually accepted a single init object as the constructor parameter, the Away3D material classes have constructors that accept a combination of regular parameters and an init object. To distinguish between the two, the regular parameters will be shown in bold in the following tables.

Basic materials

The basic materials don't rely on a texture, and so can be used without having to load or embed any external resources. This makes them easy to use, and they are great for quickly prototyping an application.

WireColorMaterial

For most of the previous demos, we have not specifically applied any particular material to the 3D objects. When no material is specified, Away3D will apply the `WireColorMaterial` material, which shades the 3D object with a solid color (this color is randomly selected at runtime unless a specific color is supplied) and draws the outline of the 3D objects triangle faces.

Here we will specifically create a new instance of the `WireColorMaterial` class and apply it to the 3D object. The color of the material has been specified by a `String` representing the color's name.

```
protected function applyWireColorMaterial():void
{
```

Materials

The `initSphere()` function is called to add a sphere primitive to the scene.

```
initSphere();
```

The name of the material is assigned to the `TextField text` property, which will display the material name on the screen.

```
materialText.text = "WireColorMaterial";
```

The material itself is then created and assigned to the local `newMaterial` variable. Here we have defined the solid color to be `dodgerblue` (using a `String` to define the color), while the color of the wireframe will be white (defined by the `int` `0xFFFFFF`) with a width of two pixels.

```
var newMaterial:WireColorMaterial =
  new WireColorMaterial("dodgerblue",
  {
    wirecolor: 0xFFFFFF,
    width: 2
  }
);
```

The new material is then assigned to the primitive via the `Mesh material` property.

```
currentPrimitive.material = newMaterial;
}
```

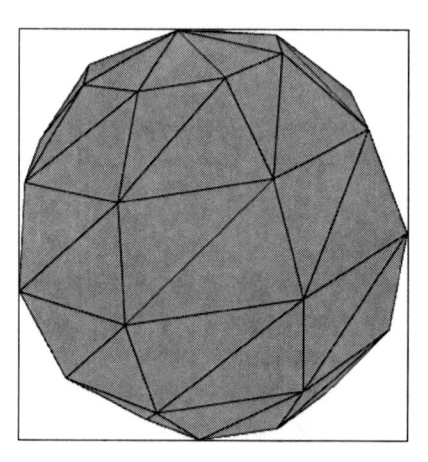

The following table lists the parameters accepted by the `WireColorMaterial` constructor. Those in bold are passed directly to the constructor, while the remaining parameters are passed in via an init object.

The `WireColorMaterial` class extends the `WireframeMaterial` class, which means the init object parameters listed for the `WireframeMaterial` class also apply to the `WireColorMaterial` class.

Parameter	Data Type	Default Value	Description
color	int / String	null / random	**Defines the solid shading color.**
alpha	Number	1	Defines the transparency of the material.
wirecolor	int / String	0x000000	Defines the color of the wireframe lines.

WireframeMaterial

The `WireframeMaterial` only draws the outline of the triangle faces that make up the 3D object. In this example, the wireframe color has been specified using an `int`. This `int` value is equivalent to the `dodgerblue` color used in the `applyWireColorMaterial()` function.

```
protected function applyWireframeMaterial():void
{
  initSphere();
  materialText.text = "WireframeMaterial";
  var newMaterial:WireframeMaterial =
    new WireframeMaterial(0x1E90FF,
    {
      width: 2
    }
  );
  currentPrimitive.material = newMaterial;
}
```

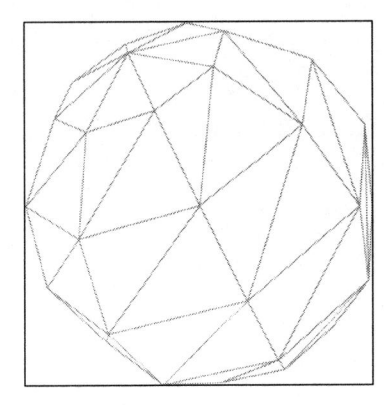

Materials

Parameter	Data Type	Default Value	Description
wireColor	int / String	null / random	**Defines the wireframe color.**
wireAlpha	Number	1	Defines the transparency of the material.
thickness	Number	1	Defines the width of the wireframe lines.

ColorMaterial

The `ColorMaterial` applies a solid color to the surface of a 3D object. This example shows the color being supplied as the string version of the `dodgerblue` hexadecimal representation.

```
protected function applyColorMaterial():void
{
  initSphere();
  materialText.text = "ColorMaterial";
  var newMaterial:ColorMaterial =
    new ColorMaterial("1E90FF");

  currentPrimitive.material = newMaterial;
}
```

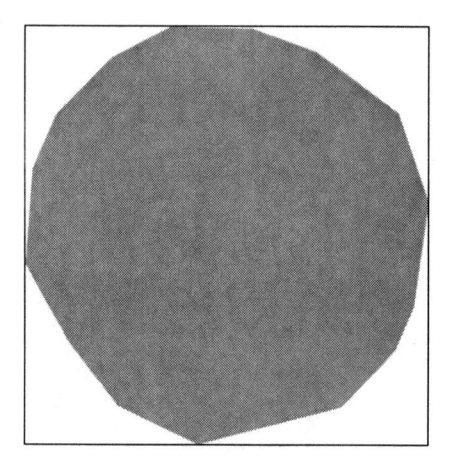

The `ColorMaterial` class extends the `WireColorMaterial` class, which means the init object parameters listed for the `WireColorMaterial` class also apply to the `ColorMaterial` class.

If the `debug` init object parameter is set to `true`, an instance of the `ColorMaterial` class will be drawn just like the `WireColorMaterial` class.

Parameter	Data Type	Default Value	Description
color	int / String	null / random	Defines the solid shading color.
debug	Boolean	false	When set to true, the material will be drawn as a WireColorMaterial.

Bitmap materials

Bitmap materials display a texture on the surface of a 3D object. These textures are usually defined in external PNG, JPG, or GIF files created with an image editing application like Photoshop.

BitmapMaterial

The `BitmapMaterial` class applies a bitmap texture to the surface of a 3D object. In this example, the bitmap is created from the embedded image contained in the `EarthDiffuse` class.

```
protected function applyBitmapMaterial():void
{
  initSphere();
  materialText.text = "BitmapMaterial";
```

Here we use the static `bitmap()` function from the `Cast` class to cast the `EarthDiffuse` class into a `BitmapData` object as required by the `BitmapMaterial` constructor.

```
  var newMaterial:BitmapMaterial =
    new BitmapMaterial(Cast.bitmap(EarthDiffuse));
  currentPrimitive.material = newMaterial;
}
```

Materials

> The `Cast` class offers a number of convenient functions to cast between types, but using these functions is not a requirement. A new instance of the `BitmapMaterial` class could also have been created using the following code:
>
> ```
> var newMaterial:BitmapMaterial = new
> BitmapMaterial(new EarthDiffuse().bitmapData);
> ```

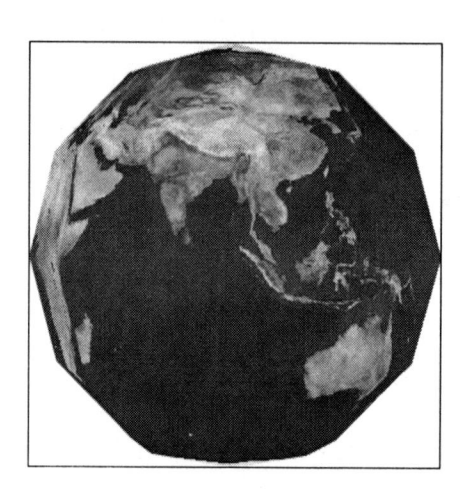

Parameter	Data Type	Default Value	Description
bitmap	BitmapData		The bitmapData object to be used as the material's texture.
wireColor	int / String	0x0000FF	Defines the color used to outline the triangles when debug is set to true.
smooth	Boolean	false	Determines if texture bitmap is smoothed (bilinearly filtered) when drawn to screen.
debug	Boolean	false	If set to true, textured triangles are drawn with white outlines. Precision correction triangles are drawn with blue outlines.
repeat	Boolean	false	Determines if texture bitmap will tile in uv-space.
blendMode	String	BlendMode.NORMAL	Defines a blendMode value for the texture bitmap. The BlendMode class, from the flash.display package, defines the blend modes that can be used.

Parameter	Data Type	Default Value	Description
colorTransform	ColorTransform	null	Defines a ColorTransform for the texture bitmap.
showNormals	Boolean	false	Displays the normals per face in pink lines.
color	int / String	0xFFFFFF	Defines a color to be applied over the base bitmap texture.

TransformBitmapMaterial

A bitmap material is usually applied to the surface of a 3D object based on its UV coordinates. The `TransformBitmapMaterial` material has a number of properties that allow its appearance to be scaled, offset, and rotated within the UV coordinates space.

Here we have used the `rotation` init object parameter to rotate the material by 45 degrees. This rotation shows up quite clearly on the cube, thanks to the checkerboard texture.

When transforming the material you will most likely want to set the `repeat` init object parameter to `true`. This ensures that the texture is repeated across the surface of the 3D object. If `repeat` is set to `false` (which it is, by default), the texture will be transformed and applied once, with the edge of the transformed texture then stretched across any remaining surface area. The screenshot on the left shows the result, if `repeat` is set to `true`. The screenshot on the right shows the result if `repeat` is set to `false`.

```
protected function applyTransformBitmapMaterial():void
{
    initCube();
    materialText.text = "TransformBitmapMaterial";
```

Materials

```
        var newMaterial:TransformBitmapMaterial =
          new TransformBitmapMaterial(Cast.bitmap(Checkerboard),
          {
            repeat: true,
            rotation: 45
          }
            );

        currentPrimitive.material = newMaterial;
      }
```

The `TransformBitmapMaterial` class extends the `BitmapMaterial` class. This means that in addition to those parameters in the following list, the init object parameters listed for the `BitmapMaterial` class are also valid for the `TransformBitmapMaterial` class.

Parameter	Data Type	Default Value	Description
bitmap	BitmapData		The bitmapData object to be used as the material's texture.
transform	Matrix	null	Transforms the texture in uv-space.
scaleX	Number	1	Scales the x coordinates of the texture in uv-space.
scaleY	Number	1	Scales the y coordinates of the texture in uv-space.
offsetX	Number	0	Offsets the x coordinates of the texture in uv-space.
offsetY	Number	0	Offsets the y coordinates of the texture in uv-space.
rotation	Number	0	Rotates the texture in uv-space.
projectionVector	Number3D	null	Projects the texture in object space, ignoring the uv coordinates of the vertex objects. Texture renders normally when set to null.
throughProjection	Boolean	true	Determines whether a projected texture is visble on the faces pointing away from the projection.
globalProjection	Boolean	false	Determines whether a projected texture uses offsetX, offsetY, and projectionVector values relative to scene coordinates.

Animated materials

A number of materials can be used to display animations on the surface of a 3D object. These animations are usually movies that have been encoded into a SWF file. You can also display an interactive SWF file, like a form, on the surface of a 3D object.

MovieMaterial

The `MovieMaterial` displays the output of a `Sprite` object, which can be animated. The sprite usually originates from another SWF file, which in this case we have embedded and referenced via the `Bear` class. A new instance of the `Bear` class is then passed to the `MovieMaterial` constructor.

```
protected function applyMovieMaterial():void
{
  initCube();
  materialText.text = "MovieMaterial";
  var newMaterial:MovieMaterial =
  new MovieMaterial(new Bear());
  currentPrimitive.material = newMaterial;
}
```

Materials

The `MovieMaterial` class extends the `TransformBitmapMaterial` class. This means that in addition to those parameters in the following list, the init object parameters listed for the `TransformBitmapMaterial` are also valid for the `MovieMaterial`.

Parameter	Data Type	Default Value	Description
movie	Sprite		The sprite object to be used as the material's texture.
transparent	Boolean	true	Defines the transparent property of the texture bitmap created from the movie.
autoUpdate	Boolean	true	Indicates whether the texture bitmap is updated on every frame.
interactive	Boolean	false	Indicates whether the material will pass mouse interaction through to the movie.
lockW	int	movie.width	A number to lock the width of the draw region other than the source movieclip source.
lockH	int	movie.height	A number to lock the height of the draw region other than the source movieclip source.

AnimatedBitmapMaterial

The `AnimatedBitmapMaterial` class displays the frames from a `MovieClip` object. In order to increase performance, it will first render each frame of the supplied `MovieClip` into a bitmap. These bitmaps are stored in a cache, which increases playback performance at the cost of using additional memory.

Because of the memory overhead resulting from this cache, the `AnimatedBitmapMaterial` cannot be used to display movie clips longer than two seconds. If you pass a movie clip longer than two seconds an exception will be thrown.

The `MovieClip` object, passed to the `AnimatedBitmapMaterial` constructor, usually originates from another SWF file. This source SWF file needs to be implemented in the ActionScript Virtual Machine 2 (AVM2) format, which is the format used by Flash Player 9 and above. This is an important point, because a large number of video conversion tools will output AVM1 SWF files.

[If you need to display a SWF movie in AVM1 format, use `MovieMaterial` class instead.]

If you try to use an AVM1 SWF file with the `AnimatedBitmapMaterial` class, an exception similar to the following will be thrown:

TypeError: Error #1034: Type Coercion failed: cannot convert flash.display::AVM1Movie@51e8e51 to flash.display.MovieClip.

> **FFmapeg** is a free, cross-platform tool that can be used to convert video files into AVM2 SWF files. It can be downloaded from `http://ffmpeg.org/`, and precompiled Windows binaries can be downloaded from `http://sourceforge.net/projects/mplayer-win32/files/FFmpeg/`. The following command will convert a WMV video into a two second AVM2 SWF file with a resolution of 320 x 240 without any audio.
>
> **ffmpeg -i Butterfly.wmv -t 2 -s 320x240 -an -f avm2 Butterfly.SWF**

```
protected function applyAnimatedBitmapMaterial():void
{
  initCube();
  materialText.text = "AnimatedBitmapMaterial";
  var newMaterial:AnimatedBitmapMaterial =
    new AnimatedBitmapMaterial(new Butterfly());
  currentPrimitive.material = newMaterial;
}
```

The `AnimatedBitmapMaterial` class extends the `TransformBitmapMaterial` class. This means that in addition to those parameters in the following list, the init object parameters listed for the `TransformBitmapMaterial` are also valid for the `AnimatedBitmapMaterial`.

Parameter	Data Type	Default Value	Description
movie	MovieClip		The movieclip to be bitmap cached for use in the material.
loop	Boolean	true	Indicates whether the animation will loop.
autoplay	Boolean	true	Indicates whether the animation will start playing on initialization.
_index	int	0	Sets the frame index of the animation.

Interactive MovieMaterial

By setting the `interactive` parameter to `true`, a `MovieMaterial` object can pass mouse events to the `Sprite` object it is displaying. This allows you to interact with the material as if it were added directly to the Flash stage while it is wrapped around a 3D object.

```
protected function applyInteractiveMovieMaterial():void
{
  initCube();
  materialText.text = "MovieMaterial - Interactive";
  var newMaterial:MovieMaterial =
    new MovieMaterial(new InteractiveTexture(),
    {
      interactive: true,
      smooth: true
    }
  );
  currentPrimitive.material = newMaterial;
}
```

Refer to the previous table for the `MovieMaterial` class for the list of constructor parameters.

Composite materials

Composite materials combine two or more base materials to achieve their final appearance. Composite materials are used to display a number of effects like shading, bump mapping, environment mapping, and lighting.

DepthBitmapMaterial

The `DepthBitmapMaterial` is similar to the `BitmapMaterial` in that it applies a bitmap texture to the surface of a 3D object. In addition, the `DepthBitmapMaterial` will shade the surface according to its distance from the camera. This can be used to apply a fog-like effect.

```
protected function applyDepthBitmapMaterial():void
{
```

The effect produced by the `DepthBitmapMaterial` class is best demonstrated on a 3D object that is moving relative to the camera. Setting the `bounce` parameter to `true` for the `initShpere()` function will cause the `onEnterFrame()` function to bounce the sphere along the Z-axis.

```
initSphere(true);
materialText.text = "DepthBitmapMaterial";
var newMaterial:DepthBitmapMaterial =
  new DepthBitmapMaterial(Cast.bitmap(EarthDiffuse),
  {
```

Here, we define the distances from the camera over which the base bitmap texture is shaded. When the material is closer to the camera than the `minZ` parameter, it takes on the color defined by the `minColor` parameter. When it is further from the camera than the `maxZ` parameter, it should take on the color defined by the `maxColor` parameter.

Materials

> There is a bug in Away3D 3.6 that causes the `DepthBitmapMaterial` class to interpret the `maxColor` parameter incorrectly. As it stands, supplying any color other than 0 to the `maxColor` parameter is required for the `DepthBitmapMaterial` object to apply a shade of black to its underlying bitmap material as it moves further from the camera. Leaving the `maxColor` parameter as its default value of 0x000000 (which is the same as 0) will cause the `DepthBitmapMaterial` object to completely ignore the base bitmap texture and only display the black shading.
>
> As you can see in the following example, we supply a black color with the alpha component defined. This value does not equal zero, and so it is sufficient to work around this bug.
>
> The actual value assigned to the `maxColor` parameter is incorrectly consumed by one of the classes contained in the `DepthBitmapMaterial` class. See the topic *The problem with init and Init objects* in *Chapter 6, Models and Animations*, for a more in depth explanation of this process.
>
> The fix for this is quite simple. Change line 122 in the `DepthBitmapMaterial.as` file from:
>
> `_depthShader = new DepthShader({minZ:_minZ, maxZ:_maxZ, color:_maxColor});`
>
> to:
>
> `_depthShader = new DepthShader({minZ:_minZ, maxZ:_maxZ, shadingColor:_maxColor});`
>
> Also change line 208 of the `DepthShader.as` file from:
>
> `color = ini.getNumber("color", 0x000000);`
>
> to:
>
> `color = ini.getNumber("shadingColor", 0x000000);`

```
      minZ: 400,
      maxZ: 500,
      maxColor: 0xFF000000
    }
  );
  currentPrimitive.material = newMaterial;
}
```

`DepthBitmapMaterial` is a composite material, meaning it uses two or more base materials to achieve its final appearance. One of the base materials is the `BitmapMaterial`, and the init object supplied to the `DepthBitmapMaterial` is also passed along to the `BitmapMaterial` constructor. This means that in addition to those parameters in the following list, the init object parameters listed for the `BitmapMaterial` are also valid for the `DepthBitmapMaterial`.

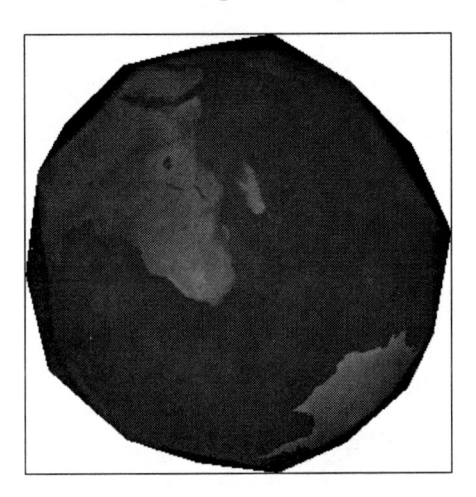

Parameter	Data Type	Default Value	Description
bitmap	BitmapData		The bitmapData object to be used as the material's texture.
minZ	Number	500	Coefficient for the minimum Z of the depth map.
maxZ	Number	2000	Coefficient for the maximum Z of the depth map.
minColor	int	0xFFFFFF	Coefficient for the color shading at minZ.
maxColor	int	0x000000	Coefficient for the color shading at maxZ.

EnviroBitmapMaterial

The `EnviroBitmapMaterial` class achieves the appearance of a reflective surface by applying a second bitmap as an environment map over a base `BitmapMaterial`.

```
protected function applyEnviroBitmapMaterial():void
{
   initTorus();
   materialText.text = "EnviroBitmapMaterial";
```

Materials

```
        var newMaterial:EnviroBitmapMaterial =
          new EnviroBitmapMaterial(
            Cast.bitmap(Bricks),
            Cast.bitmap(Marble)
          );
        currentPrimitive.material = newMaterial;
}
```

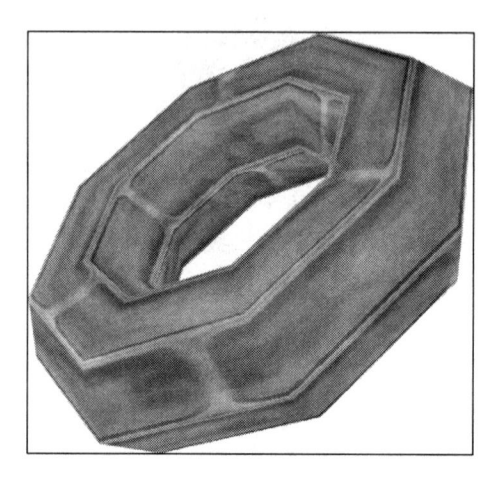

Like the `DepthBitmapMaterial` material, `EnviroBitmapMaterial` is a composite material that passes the init object to a contained instance of the `BitmapMaterial` class. This means that in addition to those parameters in the following list, the init object parameters listed for the `BitmapMaterial` are also valid for the `DepthBitmapMaterial`.

Parameter	Data Type	Default Value	Description
bitmap	BitmapData		The BitmapData object to be used as the material's texture.
enviroMap	BitmapData		The BitmapData object to be used as the material's normal map.
mode	String	linear	Setting for possible mapping methods. This parameter has no effect for the EnviroBitmapMaterial class.
reflectiveness	Number	0.5	Coefficient for the reflectiveness of the material.

EnviroColorMaterial

The `EnviroColorMaterial` is similar to `EnviroBitmapMaterial`, with the exception that it uses a solid color instead of a bitmap as the base texture.

```
protected function applyEnviroColorMaterial():void
{
   initTorus();
   materialText.text = "EnviroColorMaterial";
   var newMaterial:EnviroColorMaterial =
     new EnviroColorMaterial(
       "sandybrown",
       Cast.bitmap(Marble)
     );
   currentPrimitive.material = newMaterial;
}
```

The `EnviroColorMaterial` class indirectly extends the `ColorMaterial` class, which means the init object parameters listed for the `ColorMaterial` class also apply to the `EnviroColorMaterial` class.

Materials

Parameter	Data Type	Default Value	Description
color	int / String	random	A string, hex value, or color name representing the color of the material.
enviroMap	BitmapData		The bitmapData object to be used as the material's environment map.
mode	String	linear	Setting for possible mapping methods. This value has no effect for EnviroColorMaterial.
reflectiveness	Number	0.5	Coefficient for the reflectiveness of the environment map.
smooth	Boolean	false	Determines if the shader bitmap is smoothed (bilinearly filtered) when drawn to screen.
color	int / String	0xFFFFFF	Defines a color to be applied over the base bitmap texture.
blendMode	String	BlendMode.NORMAL	Defines a blendMode value for the shader bitmap.

Light materials

Light materials can be illuminated by an external light source. As was mentioned earlier, there are three different types of lights that can be applied to these materials: ambient, point, and directional. Also, remember that these materials will not necessarily recognize each type of light, or more than one light source. The table under the *Lights and materials* section lists which light sources can be applied to which materials.

WhiteShadingBitmapMaterial

The `WhiteShadingBitmapMaterial` class uses flat shading to apply lighting over a bitmap texture. As the class name suggests, the lighting is always white in color, ignoring the color of the source light.

```
protected function applyWhiteShadingBitmapMaterial():void
{
  initSphere();
  initPointLight();
  materialText.text = "WhiteShadingBitmapMaterial";
  var newMaterial:WhiteShadingBitmapMaterial =
    new WhiteShadingBitmapMaterial(
```

```
            Cast.bitmap(EarthDiffuse)
        );
    currentPrimitive.material = newMaterial;
}
```

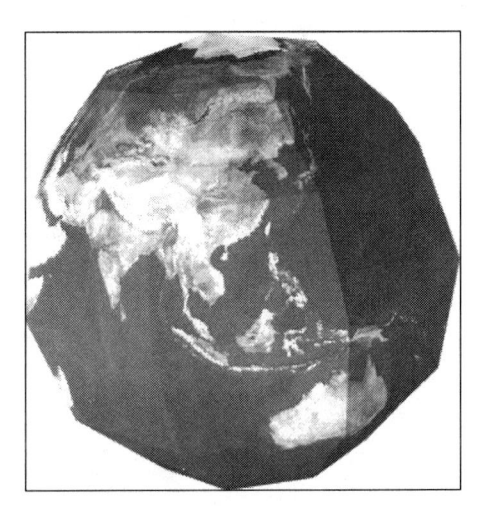

The `WhiteShadingBitmapMaterial` class extends the `BitmapMaterial` class. This means that in addition to those parameters in the following list, the init object parameters listed for the `BitmapMaterial` are also valid for the `WhiteShadingBitmapMaterial`.

Parameter	Data Type	Default Value	Description
bitmap	BitmapData		The bitmapData object to be used as the material's texture.
shininess	Number	20	Coefficient for shininess level.

ShadingColorMaterial

The `ShadingColorMaterial` class uses flat shading to apply lighting over a solid base color.

```
        protected function applyShadingColorMaterial():void
        {
            initSphere();
            initPointLight();
            materialText.text = "ShadingColorMaterial";
```

Materials

```
    var newMaterial:ShadingColorMaterial =
      new ShadingColorMaterial(
        Cast.trycolor("deepskyblue")
      );
    currentPrimitive.material = newMaterial;
}
```

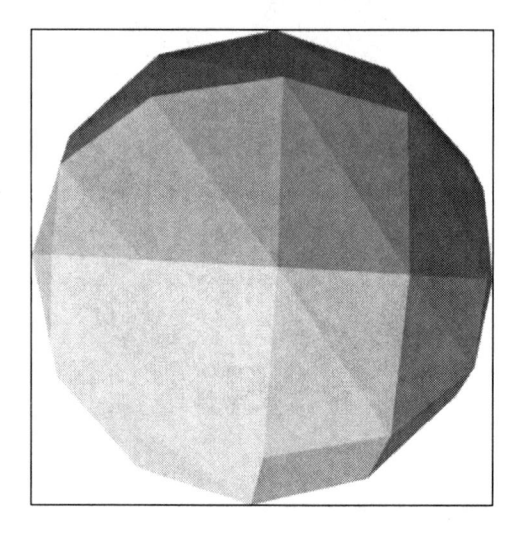

The `ShadingColorMaterial` class extends the `ColorMaterial` class. This means that in addition to those parameters in the following list, the init object parameters listed for the `ColorMaterial` class are also valid for the `ShadingColorMaterial` class.

> The `color` parameter can accept an `int` or `String` value. However, due to a bug in the `ColorMaterial` class, only an `int` value will work correctly. In the previous example, we have manually converted the color represented by the string `deepskyblue` into an `int` with the `trycolor()` function from the `Cast` class.

Parameter	Data Type	Default Value	Description
color	int / String	random	A string, hex value, or color name representing the color of the material.
ambient	int / String	colorvalue	Defines a color value for ambient light.
diffuse	int / String	colorvalue	Defines a color value for diffuse light.

Parameter	Data Type	Default Value	Description
specular	int / Strint	colorvalue	Defines a color value for specular light.
alpha	Number	1	Defines an alpha value for the material.
cache	Boolean	false	Defines whether the resulting shaded color of the surface should be cached.

PhongBitmapMaterial

The `PhongBitmapMaterial` uses phong shading to apply lighting over a `TransformBitmapMaterial` base material.

```
protected function applyPhongBitmapMaterial():void
{
  initSphere();
  initDirectionalLight();
  materialText.text = "PhongBitmapMaterial";
  var newMaterial:PhongBitmapMaterial =
    new PhongBitmapMaterial(Cast.bitmap(EarthDiffuse));
  currentPrimitive.material = newMaterial;
}
```

Materials

`PhongBitmapMaterial` is a composite material that passes the init object to a contained instance of the `TransformBitmapMaterial` class. This means that in addition to those parameters in the following list, the init object parameters listed for the `TransformBitmapMaterial` are also valid for the `PhongBitmapMaterial`.

Parameter	Data Type	Default Value	Description
bitmap	BitmapData		The bitmapData object to be used as the material's texture.
shininess	Number	20	The exponential dropoff value used for specular highlights.
specular	Number	0.7	Coefficient for specular light level.

PhongColorMaterial

The `PhongColorMaterial` uses phong shading to apply lighting over a solid color base material.

```
protected function applyPhongColorMaterial():void
{
   initSphere();
   initDirectionalLight();
   materialText.text = "PhongColorMaterial";
   var newMaterial:PhongColorMaterial =
   new PhongColorMaterial("deepskyblue");
   currentPrimitive.material = newMaterial;
}
```

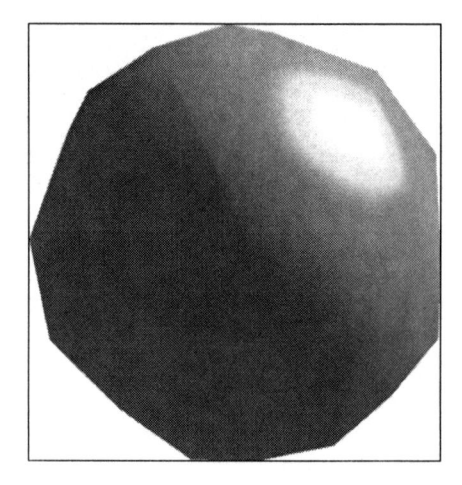

Parameter	Data Type	Default Value	Description
color	int / String	0xFFFFFF	A string, hex value or color name representing the color of the material.
shininess	Number	20	The exponential dropoff value used for specular highlights.
specular	Number	0.7	Coefficient for specular light level.

PhongMovieMaterial

The `PhongMovieMaterial` uses phong shading to apply lighting over an animated `MovieMaterial` base material.

```
protected function applyPhongMovieMaterial():void
{
   initSphere();
   initDirectionalLight();
   materialText.text = "PhongMovieMaterial";
   var newMaterial:PhongMovieMaterial =
     new PhongMovieMaterial(new Bear());
   currentPrimitive.material = newMaterial;
}
```

Materials

`PhongMovieMaterial` is a composite material that passes the init object to a contained instance of the `MovieMaterial` class. This means that in addition to those parameters in the following list, the init object parameters listed for the `PhongMovieMaterial` are also valid for the `MovieMaterial`.

Parameter	Data Type	Default Value	Description
movie	Sprite		The movie clip to be used as the material's texture.
shininess	Number	20	The exponential dropoff value used for specular highlights.
specular	Number	0.7	Coefficient for specular light level.

Dot3BitmapMaterial

The `Dot3BitmapMaterial` uses normal mapping to add depth to a 3D object.

```
protected function applyDot3BitmapMaterial():void
{
  initSphere();
  initDirectionalLight();
  materialText.text = "Dot3BitmapMaterial";
  var newMaterial:Dot3BitmapMaterial =
    new Dot3BitmapMaterial(
      Cast.bitmap(EarthDiffuse),
      Cast.bitmap(EarthNormal)
    );
  currentPrimitive.material = newMaterial;
}
```

`Dot3BitmapMaterial` is a composite material that passes the init object to a contained instance of the `BitmapMaterial` class. This means that in addition to those parameters in the following list, the init object parameters listed for the `BitmapMaterial` are also valid for the `Dot3BitmapMaterial`.

Parameter	Data Type	Default Value	Description
bitmap	BitmapData		The bitmapData object to be used as the material's texture.
normalMap	BitmapData		The bitmapData object to be used as the material's DOT3 map.
shininess	Number	20	The exponential dropoff value used for specular highlights.
specular	Number	0.5	Coefficient for specular light level.

Pixel Bender materials

Away3D includes a number of materials that make use of Pixel Bender shaders. These materials will quite often produce effects of a much higher detail than is possible with the materials listed so far. The ability to use Pixel Bender shaders is one of the advantages Away3D version 3.x has over Away3D version 2.x. This is due to the fact that Away3D 3.x targets Flash Player 10, whereas Away3D 2.x targets Flash Player 9.

Dot3BitmapMaterialF10

The `Dot3BitmapMaterialF10` class is a Pixel Bender version of the `Dot3BitmapMaterial` class.

```
protected function applyDot3BitmapMaterialF10():void
{
  initSphere();
  initDirectionalLight();
  materialText.text = "Dot3BitmapMaterialF10";
  var newMaterial:Dot3BitmapMaterialF10 =
    new Dot3BitmapMaterialF10(
      Cast.bitmap(EarthDiffuse),
      Cast.bitmap(EarthNormal)
    );
  currentPrimitive.material = newMaterial;
}
```

Materials

The `Dot3BitmapMaterialF10` class extends the `BitmapMaterial` class, which means the init object parameters listed for the `BitmapMaterial` class also apply to the `Dot3BitmapMaterialF10` class.

[💡 The textures used for the `bitmap` and `normalMap` parameters must have the same dimensions.]

Parameter	Data Type	Default Value	Description
bitmap	BitmapData		The bitmapData object to be used as the material's texture.
normalMap	BitmapData		The bitmapData object to be used as the material's DOT3 map.
shininess	Number	20	The exponential dropoff value used for specular highlights.
specular	Number	0.7	Coefficient for specular light level.

PhongPBMaterial

The `PhongPBMaterial` class uses phong shading and normal mapping to add depth and illuminate a 3D object. In addition, it uses a specular map to define the strength of the reflected light, with brighter areas reflecting more light than darker areas.

In the following image, which is embedded in the application as the class `EarthSpecular`, the oceans are shown in white, meaning that light will be reflected off those areas. The land masses are shown in black, which prevents light from being reflected off those areas.

Chapter 5

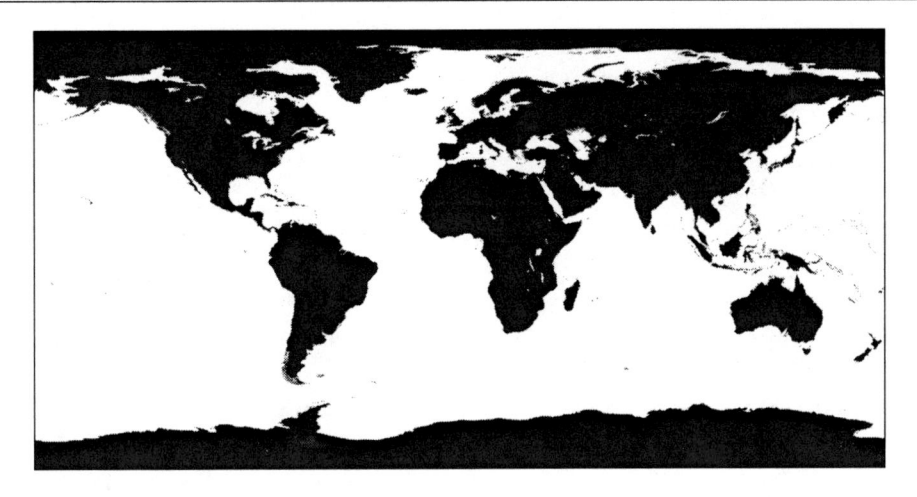

```
protected function applyPhongPBMaterial():void
{
  initSphere();
  initPointLight();
  materialText.text = "PhongPBMaterial";
  var newMaterial:PhongPBMaterial = new PhongPBMaterial(
    Cast.bitmap(EarthDiffuse),
    Cast.bitmap(EarthNormal),
    currentPrimitive,
    Cast.bitmap(EarthSpecular));
  currentPrimitive.material = newMaterial;
}
```

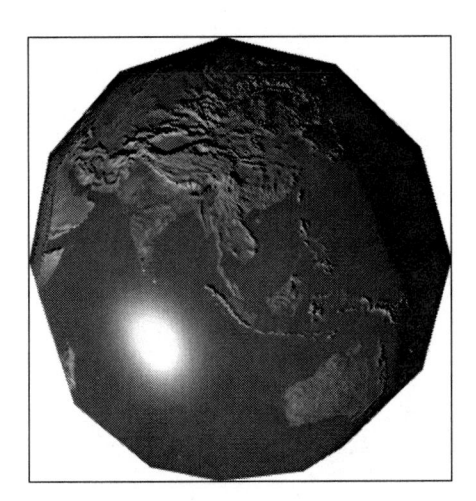

Materials

The `PhongPBMaterial` class indirectly extends the `TransformBitmapMaterial` class, which means the init object parameters listed for the `TransformBitmapMaterial` class also apply to the `PhongPBMaterial` class.

Parameter	Data Type	Default Value	Description
bitmap	BitmapData		The texture to be used for the diffuse shading.
normalMap	BitmapData		An object-space normal map.
targetModel	Mesh		The target mesh for which this shader is applied
specularMap	BitmapData	null	An optional specular map BitmapData, which modulates the specular reflections.
gloss	Number	10	The gloss component of the specular highlight. Higher numbers will result in a smaller and sharper highlight.
specular	Number	1	The strength of the specular highlight.

PhongMultiPassMaterial

The `PhongMultiPassMaterial` class is like the `PhongPBMaterial` class, except that it can be illuminated from multiple light sources.

```
protected function applyPhongMultiPassMaterial():void
{
  initSphere();
  initPointLight();
  materialText.text = "PhongMultiPassMaterial";
  var newMaterial:PhongMultiPassMaterial =
    new PhongMultiPassMaterial(
      Cast.bitmap(EarthDiffuse),
      Cast.bitmap(EarthNormal),
      currentPrimitive,
      Cast.bitmap(EarthSpecular)
    );
  currentPrimitive.material = newMaterial;
}
```

The `PhongMultiPassMaterial` class indirectly extends the `TransformBitmapMaterial` class, which means the init object parameters listed for the `TransformBitmapMaterial` class also apply to the `PhongMultiPassMaterial` class.

Parameter	Data Type	Default Value	Description
bitmap	BitmapData		The texture to be used for the diffuse shading.
normalMap	BitmapData		An object-space normal map.
targetModel	Mesh		The target mesh for which this shader is applied
specularMap	BitmapData	null	An optional specular map BitmapData, which modulates the specular reflections.
gloss	Number	10	The gloss component of the specular highlight. Higher numbers will result in a smaller and sharper highlight.
specular	Number	1	The strength of the specular highlight.

FresnelPBMaterial

The Fresnel effect refers to the phenomenon where the amount of reflectance seen on a surface depends on the viewing angle. The most common example of this is seen on the surface of a body of water. If you look down directly at a pool of water you will be able to see down through the water without much reflected light. But if you look at the water's surface from an angle you will see much more reflected light.

The `FresnelPBMaterial` class replicates this effect by reflecting a sphere map that represents the surrounding environment by a varying degree according to the viewing angle of the surface.

```
protected function applyFresnelPBMaterial():void
{
   initPlane();
   materialText.text = "FresnelPBMaterial";
```

The reflected image comes from a sphere map, which is a texture that displays the surroundings of an object as if it were reflected off the surface of a sphere. This texture has been embedded as the `SphereMap` class.

```
   var newMaterial:FresnelPBMaterial = new FresnelPBMaterial(
     Cast.bitmap(Water),
     Cast.bitmap(WaterNormal),
     Cast.bitmap(SphereMap),
     currentPrimitive,
       {
          smooth: true
       }
   );
   currentPrimitive.material = newMaterial;
}
```

Materials

You can see how the Fresnel reflection works in the following images. In the image on the left, the flat areas reflect the base blue water material. When looking at the surface from a more side on angle, the orange environment material is now reflected.

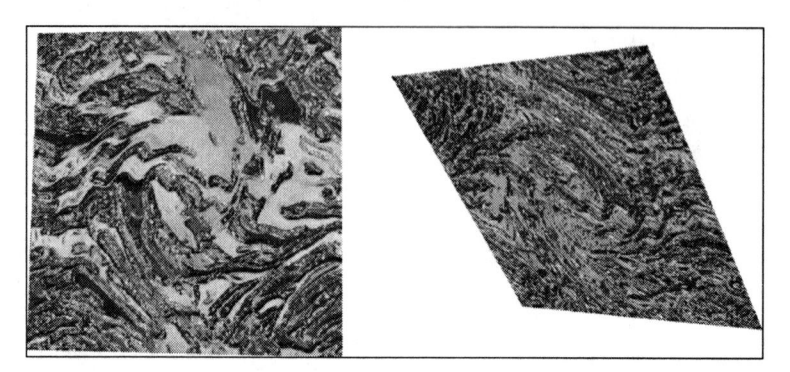

The `FresnelPBMaterial` class indirectly extends the `TransformBitmapMaterial` class, which means that the init object parameters listed for the `TransformBitmapMaterial` class also apply to the `FresnelPBMaterial` class.

Parameter	Data Type	Default Value	Description
bitmap	BitmapData		The texture to be used for the diffuse shading.
normalMap	BitmapData		An object-space normal map.
faces	Array		An array of equally sized square textures for each face of the cube map.
targetModel	Mesh		The target mesh for which this shader is applied.
envMapAlpha	Number	1	The opacity of the environment map, that is: how reflective the surface is. 1 is a perfect mirror.
outerRefraction	Number	1.0008	The refractive index of the surroundings.
innerRefraction	Number	1.330	The refractive index of the material.
refractionStrength	Number	1	The maximum amount of refraction to be performed on the diffuse texture, used to simulate water.

CubicEnvMapPBMaterial

The `CubicEnvMapPBMaterial` uses environment mapping to add the reflection of a cube of textures to a base-normal mapped texture.

```
protected function applyCubicEnvMapPBMaterial():void
{
  initSphere();
  materialText.text = "CubicEnvMapPBMaterial";
```

The reflections shown by the `CubicEnvMapPBMaterial` class come from six textures that form a cube that appears to surround the 3D object. These six textures are placed into the `sky` Array.

```
var sky:Array = new Array();
sky[CubeFaces.LEFT] = Cast.bitmap(Skyleft);
sky[CubeFaces.FRONT] = Cast.bitmap(Skyfront);
sky[CubeFaces.RIGHT] = Cast.bitmap(Skyright);
sky[CubeFaces.BACK] = Cast.bitmap(Skyback);
sky[CubeFaces.TOP] = Cast.bitmap(Skyup);
sky[CubeFaces.BOTTOM] = Cast.bitmap(Skydown);

var newMaterial:CubicEnvMapPBMaterial =
new CubicEnvMapPBMaterial(
    Cast.bitmap(EarthDiffuse),
    Cast.bitmap(EarthNormal),
    sky,
    currentPrimitive,
      {
        envMapAlpha: 0.5
      }
    );

currentPrimitive.material = newMaterial;
}
```

Materials

The `CubicEnvMapPBMaterial` class indirectly extends the `TransformBitmapMaterial` class, which means the init object parameters listed for the `TransformBitmapMaterial` class also apply to the `CubicEnvMapPBMaterial` class.

Parameter	Data Type	Default Value	Description
bitmap	BitmapData		The texture to be used for the diffuse shading.
normalMap	BitmapData		An object-space normal map.
faces	Array		An array of equally sized square textures for each face of the cube map.
targetModel	Mesh		The target mesh for which this shader is applied.
envMapAlpha	Number	1	The opacity of the environment map, i.e. how reflective the surface is. 1 is a perfect mirror.

Loading textures from external files

Although it is quite often and more convenient to embed resources into the SWF file, there are times when this is not desirable. Away3D includes a number of classes to aid in loading external resources.

There are some considerations to be aware of when accessing external resources. One of the issues is that the loading process is asynchronous, which means that the actual process of downloading an external resource is done in the background. Normally, you would deal with the data once it has been retrieved by way of a call-back function, which is called when the `Event.COMPLETE` event is dispatched.

For a simple bitmap material, the `BitmapFileMaterial` class deals with this background loading for you. You supply the URL of the external texture image, and the `BitmapFileMaterial` class takes care of all the asynchronous loading process.

Other material types don't have an equivalent of the `BitmapFileMaterial` to handle loading of external textures. For this Away3D supplies the `TextureLoadQueue` class, which will load a number of external resources as a group and notify you when they are all ready.

BitmapFileMaterial

As you can see, the `BitmapFileMaterial` is very straightforward to use. By hiding the details of the asynchronous loading process, the `BitmapFileMaterial` class allows us to simply apply it like any other material. All we need to do is supply the location of the texture file to load.

```
protected function applyBitmapFileMaterial():void
{
  initSphere();
  materialText.text = "BitmapFileMaterial";
  var newMaterial:BitmapFileMaterial =
    new BitmapFileMaterial("earth_diffuse.jpg");
  currentPrimitive.material = newMaterial;
}
```

The `BitmapFileMaterial` class extends the `BitmapMaterial` class, which means the init object parameters listed for the `BitmapMaterial` class also apply to the `BitmapFileMaterial` class.

Parameter	Data Type	Default Value	Description
url	String		Specifies the location of the texture image file to load.
checkPolicyFile	Boolean	false	Specifies the value for the `checkPolicyFile` property of the `LoaderContext` object used to load the file.

Using the TextureLoadQueue

The process becomes a little more complicated when you need to load several textures to create one material. Take the `Dot3BitmapMaterial` class as an example. It requires both diffuse texture and normal map.

The `TextureLoadQueue` can be used to load multiple external resources as a group. This allows us to initiate the loading of all the textures required by a class like `Dot3BitmapMaterial`, and then create a new instance of the class when all are loaded.

```
protected function applyExternalDot3BitmapMaterial():void
{
  initSphere();
  initDirectionalLight();
  materialText.text = "External Dot3BitmapMaterial";
```

Materials

First, we create a new instance of the `TextureLoadQueue` class.

```
var textureLoadQueue:TextureLoadQueue =
  new TextureLoadQueue();
```

We then need to create two additional objects for each file to be loaded. The first is a `URLRequest` object, whose constructor takes the URL of the external file as the first parameter.

```
var req:URLRequest =
  new URLRequest("earth_diffuse.jpg");
```

The second is a `TextureLoader` object.

```
var loader:TextureLoader = new TextureLoader();
```

We then pass both of these objects to the `TextureLoadQueue addItem()` function.

```
textureLoadQueue.addItem(loader, req);
```

This process is repeated for the normal map texture file.

```
req = new URLRequest("earth_normal.jpg")
loader = new TextureLoader();
textureLoadQueue.addItem(loader, req);
```

The `Event.COMPLETE` event will be dispatched by the `TextureLoaderQueue` object once all of the external files have been loaded. Once this event has been dispatched, we can get access to the bitmap data required to create the material. For convenience, we will create an anonymous function to respond to this event.

```
textureLoadQueue.addEventListener(
  Event.COMPLETE,
  function(event:Event):void
  {
```

We create two `BitmapData` variables, which will be assigned to the data contained in the two external files we have just loaded.

```
var diffuse:BitmapData;
var normal:BitmapData;
```

Unfortunately, the `TextureLoaderQueue` does not index the loaded images in a way that is easy to access. Instead, it provides an array of `TextureLoader` objects, and each individual `TextureLoader` object can then be identified and then processed. This involves iterating over the whole array to find out which `TextureLoader` objects relate to which external files.

```
                for each (var image:TextureLoader in textureLoadQueue.
    images)
                {
```

Regardless of which external file the current `TextureLoader` object obtained its data from, we first create a new `BitmapData` object and draw the contents of the `TextureLoader` into it.

```
                var bitmapData:BitmapData =
                    new BitmapData(image.width, image.height);
                bitmapData.draw(image);
```

Using the `filename` property of the current `TextureLoader` object, we can work out which external file it obtained its data from. This allows us to reference the new `BitmapData` object we just created with either the `diffuse` or `normal` variable.

```
                if (image.filename == "earth_diffuse.jpg")
                    diffuse = bitmapData;
                else if (image.filename == "earth_normal.jpg")
                    normal = bitmapData;
                }
```

Now that we have a reference to the diffuse and normal-map bitmaps, we can go ahead and create the `Dot3BitmapMaterial` object.

```
                currentPrimitive.material =
                    new Dot3BitmapMaterial(diffuse, normal);
            }
        );
```

Finally, with the anonymous call back function in place we can now request that the `TextureLoaderQueue` start loading the files by calling its `start()` function.

```
        textureLoadQueue.start();
        }
    }
}
```

> While we have used the `TextureLoaderQueue` class to load two external image files here, the same logic applies to loading just one file or dozens of files. You can also use the Flash / Flex Loader class directly to load external resources.

Summary

Away3D includes a large selection of materials. The various shading techniques that can be used by these materials were covered, which allows for a selection of materials ranging from those that display a simple texture map to those more advanced materials, which produce more interesting detailed results like reflections, lighting, and shadowing. We have covered Pixel Bender, and seen how it has been used by Away3D to create some of these advanced materials.

Those materials that can be lit from an external light source were listed, along with a table that breaks down the types of light sources that affect these materials.

We have seen how resources, like textures, can be embedded into the final SWF, or loaded from external resources. Embedding resources is generally the best solution as it avoids a number of potential issues like security restrictions and network failures, but for those situations where loading external resources is required, we saw how the `BitmapFileMaterial` and `LoaderQueue` classes can be used.

In the next chapter, we will learn how to load and display more complex 3D objects, which can be used in place of the primitive 3D objects that we have been using since *Chapter 1, Building Your First Away3D Application*.

6
Models and Animations

As we saw in *Chapter 2, Creating and Displaying Primitives*, it is possible to create a 3D object from the ground up using basic elements like vertices, triangle faces, Sprite3D objects, and segments. However, creating each element manually in code is not practical for more complex models. While the classes from the `away3d.primitives` package offer a solution by providing a way to quickly create some standard shapes, advanced applications will need to display more complex shapes. For those situations where these standard primitive shapes do not provide enough flexibility, Away3D can load and display
3D models created by external **3D modeling applications**.

3D modeling applications are specifically designed to provide a visual environment in which 3D models can be manipulated. It is certainly much more convenient to create or edit a 3D mesh in one of these applications than it is to build up a mesh in code using ActionScript.

Away3D can directly load a wide range of 3D formats. The process of exporting a 3D mesh into a file that can be used with Away3D will be covered for the following 3D modeling applications:

- **3ds Max**: A popular commercial modeling, animation, and rendering application which runs on Windows.
- **Blender**: A free and open source modeling application, which is available on a number of platforms, including Windows, Linux, and MacOS.
- **Milkshape**: A commercial low-polygon modeler which runs on Windows that was originally designed for the game Half-Life.
- **Sketch-up**: A free 3D modeling application provided by Google. A commercial version is also available that includes a number of additional features. Sketch-up runs on Windows and MacOS.

Actually creating a model in these 3D modeling applications is outside the scope of this book. However, 3D models are provided that can be loaded and then exported from these applications, which will allow you run through the procedure without having to know how to make a 3D model from scratch.

This chapter covers the following:

- Exporting a model from a number of 3D modeling applications
- Loading a model file in Away3D, both from an embedded resource and from an external file
- Converting 3D models into ActionScript classes

3D formats supported by Away3D

Away3D includes classes that can load a wide range of 3D model file formats. All the supported formats can be used to load a static 3D model, while a smaller number can be used to load animated models. The following table lists the 3D model formats supported by Away3D, their common extensions, whether they can load animated 3D models, and the Away3D class that is used to load and parse them.

Format	Extension	Static	Animated	Away3D Class
Collada	DAE	*	*	`Collada`
Quake II	MD2	*	*	`Md2`
3DS MAX Ascii	ASE	*		`Ase`
Away3D	AWD	*		`AWData`
Google Earth	KMZ	*		`Kmz`
3DS Max	3DS	*		`Max3DS`
Wavefront	OBJ	*		`Obj`
ActionScript	AS	*	*	

Exporting 3D models

The following instructions show you how to export a Collada file from a number of different 3D modeling applications. Collada is an open, XML-based format that has been designed to provide a way to exchange data between 3D applications. Away3D supports loading both static and animated 3D models from the Collada format.

Exporting from 3ds Max

3ds Max is a commercial 3D modeling application. At the time of writing, the latest version of the **ColladaMax** plugin, which is the plugin that we will use to export the 3D model, was 3.05C. This version supports 3ds Max 2008, 3ds Max 9, 3ds Max 8 SP3, or 3ds Max 7 SP1. Note that this version does not support 3ds Max 2010 or 2011.

A trial version of 3ds Max 9 is available, although it can be difficult to find. You should be able to find a copy if you search the Internet for `Autodesk3dsMax2009_ENU_TrialDownload.exe`, which is the name of file that will install the trial version of 3ds Max 9.

1. Download and install the ColladaMax plugin from `http://sourceforge.net/projects/colladamaya/files/`.
2. Open 3ds Max.
3. Click **File | Open**. Select the MAX file you wish to open and click on the **Open** button.
4. Click **File | Export** from within 3ds Max.
5. Select **COLLADA (*.DAE)** from the **Save as type** drop-down list.
6. Select the same directory where the original MAX file was located.
7. Type a file name for the exported file in the **File name** textbox, and click on the **Save** button.
8. In the ColladaMax **Export** dialog box make sure the following checkboxes are enabled:
    - **Relative Paths**
    - **Normals**
    - **Triangulate**
9. If you want to export animations, enable the **Enable export** checkbox.
10. If you want to export a specific range of frames, enable the **Sample animation** checkbox and enter the required values in the **Start** and **End** textboxes.

Models and Animations

11. Click on the **OK** button to export the file.

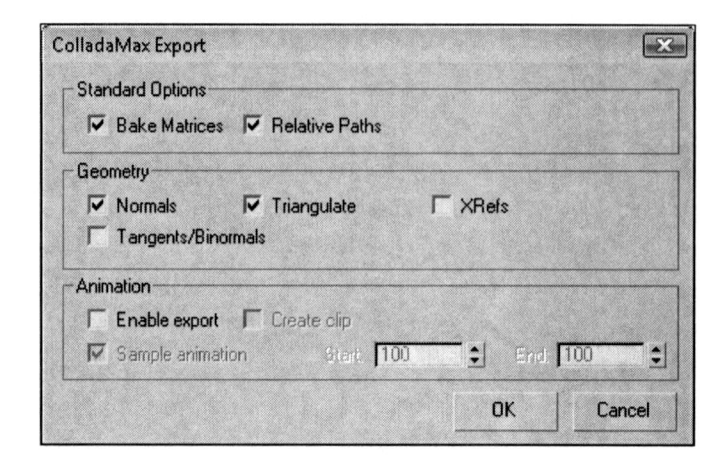

Exporting from MilkShape

The Collada exporter supplied with MilkShape does not export animations. So even if the MilkShape `MS3D` file we are loading contains an animated model, the exported Collada `DAE` file will be a static mesh. A trial version of MilkShape can be downloaded and installed from its website at `http://chumbalum.swissquake.ch/`.

1. Click **File | Open**. Select the `MS3D` file you wish to open and click on the **Open** button.
2. Click **File | Export | COLLADA…**.
3. Select the same directory where the original `MS3D` file was located.
4. Type a filename for the exported file in the **File name** textbox and click the **Save** button.

Exporting from Sketch-Up

Like Milkshape, Sketch-up does not support exporting animated Collada files. Sketch-Up can be downloaded for free from `http://sketchup.google.com/`.

1. Click **File | Open**. Select the `SKP` file you wish to open and click on the **Open** button.
2. Click **File | Export | 3D Model…**.
3. Select **Collada File (*.dae)** from the **Export type** combobox.
4. Select an appropriate directory, and type a filename for the exported file in the **File name** textbox.

5. Click on the **Options...** button.
6. Make sure the **Triangulate All Faces** checkbox is enabled.
7. If the **Export Texture Maps** option is enabled, Sketch-Up will export the textures along with the DAE file.
8. Click on the **OK** button to save the options.
9. Click on the **Export** button to export the file.

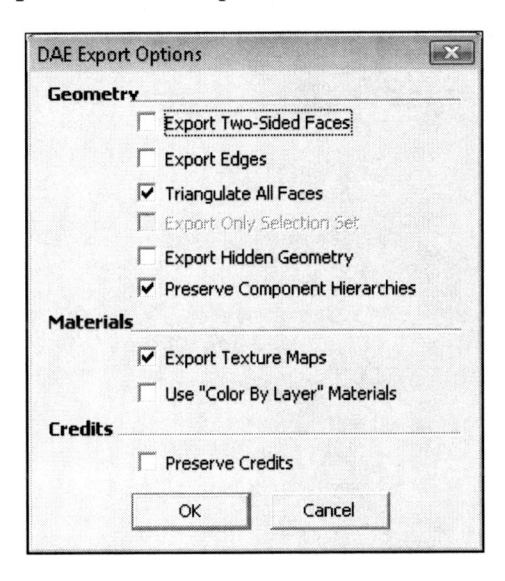

Exporting from Blender

The latest version of the Collada exporter for Blender, which is version 0.3.162 at the time of writing, does support exporting animations. However, in most cases Away3D will not load these animations correctly. It is recommended that only static meshes be exported from Blender to a Collada file.

1. Click **File | Open....** Select the BLEND file you wish to open and click on the **Open** button.
2. Click **File | Export | COLLADA1.4 (*.dae) ....**
3. Type a filename for the exported file in the directory where the original BLEND file was located in the **Export File** textbox.
4. Make sure the **Triangles** and **Use Relative Paths** buttons are pressed.

5. Click on the **Export and Close** button.

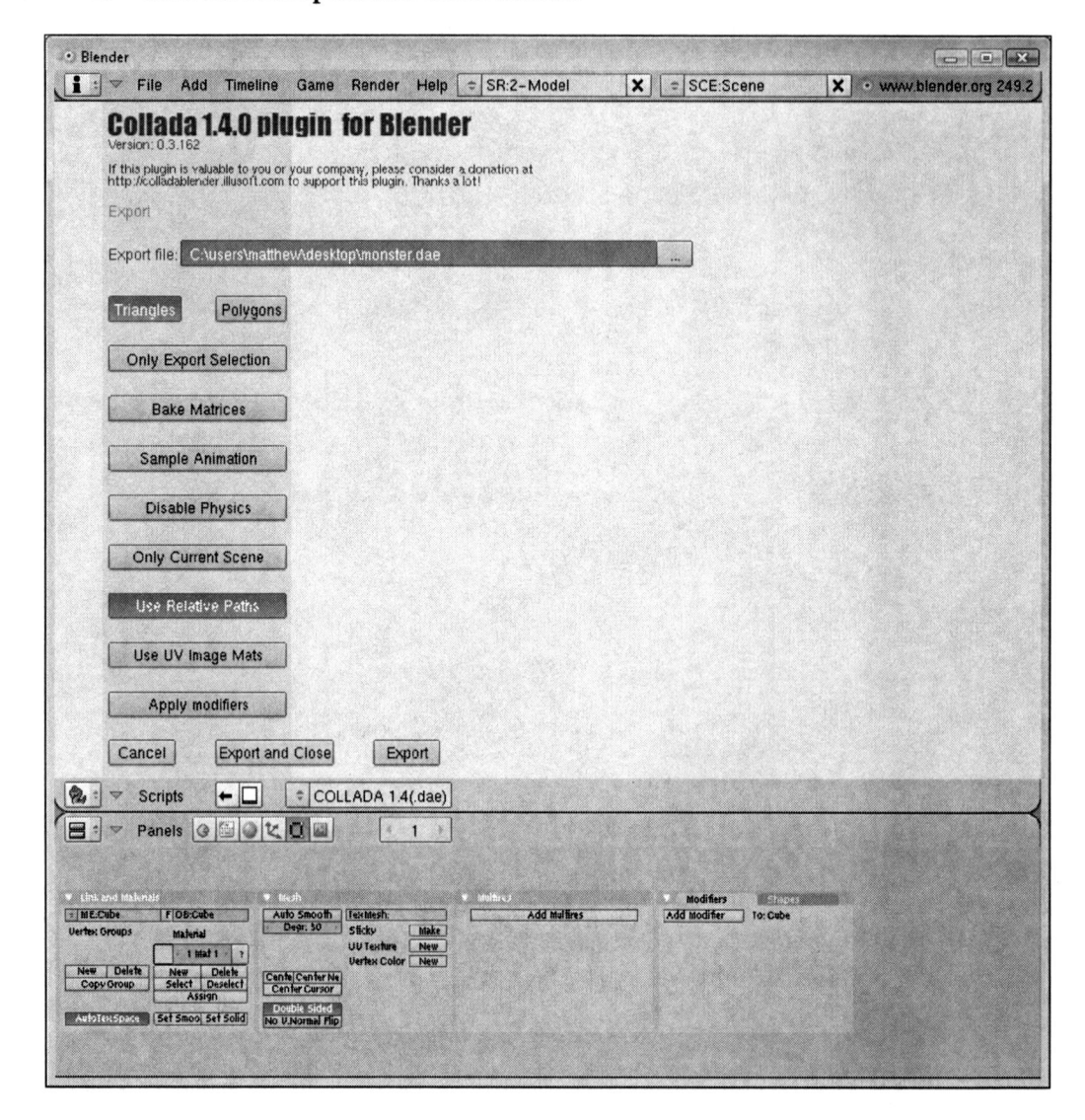

A note about the Collada exporters

Despite being free and open standard, exporting to a Collada file that can be correctly parsed by Away3D can be a hit-and-miss affair. The Collada exporters for 3ds Max are a good example. During testing, neither the built-in Collada exporter included with 3ds Max, nor the third-party **OpenCollada** exporter from http://opencollada.org (version 1.2.5 was the latest version at the time of writing) would export an animated Collada file that Away3D could read. At best

Away3D would display a static mesh, and at worst it would throw an exception when reading the DAE file. Likewise, neither of the Collada exporters that come with Blender (which was at version 2.49b at the time of writing) would consistently export an animated Collada mesh that was compatible with Away3D.

It is important to be aware that just because a 3D modeling application says that it can export to a Collada file, this is no guarantee that the resulting file can be read correctly by Away3D.

Loading a 3D model

The general steps involved in loading an embedded model are as follows:

1. Import the necessary classes.
2. Create a class that extends the Away3DTemplate class from *Chapter 1, Building Your First Away3D Application*.
3. Embed the model file and the texture file.
4. Create a constructor that calls the Away3DTemplate constructor.
5. Override the initScene() function.
   - Create a material from the embedded texture resource
   - Use the parse() function from the respective model loading class to create an Object3D, Mesh or ObjectConatiner3D object
   - Assign the material to the loaded 3D object
   - Add the 3D object to the scene
   - Play the desired animation for those models that support animations

The general steps to load an external model file are similar:

1. Import the necessary classes.
2. Create a class that extends the Away3DTemplate class from *Chapter 1, Building Your First Away3D Application*.
3. Create a constructor that calls the Away3DTemplate constructor.
4. Override the initScene() function.
   - Use the load() function from the respective model loading class to create a Loader3D object
   - Add the Loader3D object to the scene

5. Assign a function to respond to the `Loader3DEvent.LOAD_SUCCESS` event
   - Manually apply a material if needed
   - Play the desired animation for those models that support animations

Animated models

The Collada DAE, Quake 2 MD2, and ActionScript AS model formats are unique in that they can be used to load animated 3D objects. But there are a number of subtle differences between the classes used to load and animate each of these formats, especially with the option of embedding the resources or loading them from external files.

MD2—Loading an embedded file

MD2 is the model format used by Quake 2. These models are ideal for use with Away3D because they have a low polygon count and support animations. Let's create an application called `MD2EmbeddedDemo` that demonstrates how a MD2 file can be embedded and loaded.

```
package
{
```

The parsed 3D object will be returned to us as a `Mesh`.

```
import away3d.core.base.Mesh;
```

We will use the static functions provided by the `Cast` class to cast objects between types.

```
import away3d.core.utils.Cast;
```

The class that will load the MD2 files is called `Md2`.

```
import away3d.loaders.Md2;
```

We will apply a `BitmapMaterial` to the 3D object. *Chapter 5, Materials,* covers the `BitmapMaterial` class in more detail.

```
import away3d.materials.BitmapMaterial;
```

The `AnimationData` class contains the functions we will use to animate the 3D object once it is loaded.

```
import away3d.loaders.data.AnimationData;
```

MD2 models can be embedded, but because the ActionScript compiler has no understanding of the MD2 format, they need to be embedded as a raw data file (that is, with a MIME type of `application/octet-stream`).

```
[Embed(source="ogre.md2", mimeType="application/octet-stream")]
protected var MD2Model:Class;
```

By default, the textures for MD2 models are in the PCX format, which is not supported by Away3D. Here we have converted the original PCX image file to a JPG image, which is then embedded. We don't need to specify a MIME type, because the ActionScript compiler understands the format of a JPG image.

```
[Embed(source="ogre.jpg")]
protected var MD2Material:Class;
```

The `Mesh` representing the 3D object is referenced by `md2Mesh` property.

```
protected var md2Mesh:Mesh;
```

The constructor calls the base `Away3DTemplate` class constructor, which will initialize the Away3D engine.

```
public function MD2EmbeddedDemo()
{
    super();
}
```

The `initScene()` function is overridden to load the MD2 file and to add the resulting 3D object to the scene.

```
protected override function initScene():void
{
    super.initScene();
```

First, we create a new `BitmapMaterial` object from the embedded image file.

```
    var modelMaterial:BitmapMaterial =
        new BitmapMaterial(Cast.bitmap(MD2Material));
```

The `parse()` function from the `Md2` class is used to load an embedded MD2 file, which is converted to a `ByteArray` using the `bytearray()` function from the `Cast` class. The `parse()` function will return a `Mesh` object, which is then assigned to the `md2Mesh` property.

```
    md2Mesh = Md2.parse(Cast.bytearray(MD2Model),
        {
```

Models and Animations

We specify the init object parameters necessary to scale, position, and rotate the 3D object within the scene so it will be displayed nicely on the screen. You can learn more about transforming 3D objects like this in *Chapter 3, Moving Objects*.

```
    scale: 0.01,
    z: 100,
    rotationY: -90
  }
);
```

The material is then assigned to the 3D object via the `material` property.

> Unlike the primitive 3D objects we have used previously, materials assigned via the `material` init object parameter will not be applied to the 3D object we are loading using the `Md2` class. The section *The problem with init and Init objects* below explains why this is the case.

```
md2Mesh.material = modelMaterial;
```

The 3D object is added to the scene to make it visible.

```
scene.addChild(md2Mesh);
```

Most MD2 models define a number of animations like stand, run, attack, and jump. These animation names correspond to the actions of the characters in the game Quake 2. While these animation names are common, they are not guaranteed to be included in an MD2 model file. Before we play the desired animation, we first check to see if it is included in the loaded 3D object.

```
var animationData:AnimationData =
    md2Mesh.animationLibrary.getAnimation("stand");
```

If the `animationData` variable is not `null` then the loaded 3D object includes the desired animation.

```
        if (animationData != null)
```

The animation can then be played by calling the `play()` function.

```
        animationData.animator.play();
    }
```

MD2—Loading an external file

The process for loading an external MD2 file is much the same as loading an embedded one. Let's create a call called `MD2ExternalDemo` to load and display an external MD2 file and see how it differs from the `MD2EmbeddedDemo` above.

```
package
{
  import away3d.core.base.Mesh;
```

We need to register a function to be called when the 3D object is loaded, so we can play the initial animation. This function will take a `Loader3DEvent` object as a parameter.

```
  import away3d.events.Loader3DEvent;
```

Instead of returning a `Mesh`, the `Md2` class will instead return a `Loader3D` object, which is used as a placeholder while the 3D object is loaded.

```
  import away3d.loaders.Loader3D;
  import away3d.loaders.Md2;
  import away3d.loaders.data.AnimationData;
```

The `BitmapFileMaterial` class gives us a convenient way to load an external image file and apply it as a material. *Chapter 5, Materials*, covers the `BitmapFileMaterial` class in more detail.

```
  import away3d.materials.BitmapFileMaterial;

  public class MD2ExternalDemo extends Away3DTemplate
  {
    protected var mesh:Mesh;

    public function MD2ExternalDemo()
    {
      super();
    }

    protected override function initScene():void
    {
      super.initScene();
```

When loading an external file, we call the `load()` function from the `Md2` class. The first parameter is the URL of the MD2 file.

[183]

Models and Animations

Due to a bug in the `Loader3D` `loadTextures()` function, the URL supplied to the `load()` function requires a slash, even if the file to be loaded is in the same folder as the SWF file.

The `load()` function will return a `Loader3D` object. This `Loader3D` object is a placeholder, to be displayed while the 3D object is loaded.

```
var placeHolder:Loader3D = Md2.load("./ogre.md2",
  {
    scale: 0.01,
    z: 100,
    rotationY: -90
  }
);
```

When the `Loader3D.LOAD_SUCCESS` event is dispatched, the 3D object has been loaded and parsed, and is ready to be used. We will want to set the initial animation at this point, so we register the `onLoadSuccess()` function to be called when the event is triggered.

```
placeHolder.addEventListener(
  Loader3DEvent.LOAD_SUCCESS,
  onLoadSuccess);
```

The placeholder `Loader3D` object is added to the scene. When the 3D object is loaded, it will be added to the scene and the placeholder 3D object (which is a `Cube` primitive) will be removed.

```
  scene.addChild(placeHolder);
}

  protected function onLoadSuccess(event:Loader3DEvent):void
  {
```

In the `onLoadSuccess()` function, we get a reference to the loaded 3D object.

```
mesh = event.loader.handle as Mesh;
```

The `Md2` class does have the ability to create its own material from the texture information in the MD2 file. Since Flash has no support for the PCX format, which is the default format used by MD2 models, it will attempt to load a JPG image with the same name as the PCX file referenced in the MD2 file. The new extension can be changed from the default of JPG to another image format supported by Flash like PNG or GIF by specifying the `pcxConvert` init object parameter that is supplied to the `Md2` `load()` function.

Chapter 6

However, quite often the texture file referenced by the MD2 file is incorrect, or includes a long path like `quake2/baseq2/players/modelname/texture.pcx`. This unpredictability in texture filenames is best avoided by creating a new `BitmapFileMaterial` instance, passing the URL of the texture file to its constructor, and specifying it at the material to be used by the loaded 3D object via the `material` property.

```
mesh.material = new BitmapFileMaterial("ogre.jpg");
```

We then play the animation called `stand`.

```
var animationData:AnimationData =
  mesh.animationLibrary.getAnimation("stand");
if (animationData != null)
  animationData.animator.play();
      }

    }
}
```

Collada—Loading an embedded file

Loading an embedded Collada model file is quite similar to the process of loading an embedded MD2 file: the model file and the textures are embedded, and a 3D object is created using the `parse()` function from the model loading class (named `Collada` in this case).

```
package
{
   import away3d.containers.ObjectContainer3D;
   import away3d.core.utils.Cast;
```

The `Collada` class will be used to parse the embedded Collada DAE file.

```
   import away3d.loaders.Collada;
   import away3d.loaders.data.AnimationData;
   import away3d.materials.BitmapMaterial;
   import flash.events.Event;

   public class ColladaEmbeddedDemo extends Away3DTemplate
   {
```

Models and Animations

The Collada DAE file is embedded as a raw data file. We could also have specified the MIME type to be `"text/xml"`, since a Collada file is actually an XML file.

```
[Embed(source="beast.dae", mimeType="application/octet-stream")]
protected var ColladaModel:Class;
[Embed(source="beast.jpg")] protected var ColladaMaterial:Class;

public function ColladaEmbeddedDemo()
{
  super();
}

protected override function initScene():void
{
  super.initScene();
  var modelMaterial:BitmapMaterial = new
    BitmapMaterial(Cast.bitmap(ColladaMaterial));
```

Here we use the static `parse()` function from the `Collada` class to create an `ObjectContainer3D` object containing the meshes and animations contained in the model file.

```
  var colladaContainer:ObjectContainer3D =
    Collada.parse(Cast.bytearray(ColladaModel),
```

The models in a Collada file can use a number of separate materials to achieve their final appearance. The Collada file used in this example only references one material, but the logic is still the same. We define an init object parameter called `materials`, and to that we assign another init object that maps Away3D materials to the material names defined in the Collada file. In this example, the single material defined in the Collada file is called `monster`.

```
    {
      materials:
        {
          monster: modelMaterial
        },
```

The 3D object is then rotated, so it will be displayed nicely on the screen.

```
      rotationY: 90
    }
  );
```

The scale of the 3D object is increased to make it easier to see on the screen.

```
colladaContainer.scaleX =
  colladaContainer.scaleY =
  colladaContainer.scaleZ = 20;
scene.addChild(colladaContainer);
```

Here we get a reference to the `AnimationData` object that holds the animation called `default`.

```
var animationData:AnimationData =
  colladaContainer.animationLibrary.getAnimation("default");
```

If the animation exists, we then play it.

```
if (animationData != null)
  animationData.animator.play();
      }

    }
  }
```

Collada—Loading an external file

Loading an external Collada file is much the same as loading an embedded file. The big differences are that we don't need to manually assign any materials, and the animations are played once an event has been dispatched indicating that the model has been loaded.

```
package
{
```

Loading external files is an asynchronous process, and the `Loader3DEvent` class is used by the function registered to the `Loader3DEvent.LOAD_SUCCESS` event that lets us know that the file has been loaded successfully.

```
import away3d.events.Loader3DEvent;
import away3d.loaders.Collada;
```

The `Loader3D` class is used as a placeholder while the Collada file is being loaded.

```
import away3d.loaders.Loader3D;
import away3d.loaders.data.AnimationData;

import flash.events.Event;

public class ColladaExternalDemo extends Away3DTemplate
{
```

Models and Animations

```
public function ColladaExternalDemo()
{
  super();
}
protected override function initScene():void
{
  super.initScene();
```

Here we use the static `load()` function from the `Collada` class. This function takes the URL of the Collada file to be loaded (remember to add a slash to the URL, even for files in the same folder as the SWF file), and returns a `Loader3D` object. We don't need to worry about supplying any information about the materials to be used, as the `Collada` class will create the materials for us by loading the image files referenced in the DAE file.

```
var placeHolder:Loader3D = Collada.load("./beast.dae",
  {
      rotationY: 90
  }
);
```

The `addOnSuccess()` function from the `Loader3D` class provides a short-hand way to register a function to be called when the `Loader3DEvent.LOAD_SUCCESS` event is dispatched.

```
placeHolder.addOnSuccess(onLoadSuccess);
```

The `Loader3D` object is added to the scene, and will display a `Cube` primitive while the Collada file is being loaded.

```
  scene.addChild(placeHolder);
}
```

When the `onLoadSuccess()` function is called, we can scale the 3D object, get access to the default animation data, and then play it if it exists.

```
    protected function onLoadSuccess(event:Loader3DEvent):void
    {
      event.loader.handle.scaleX =
        event.loader.handle.scaleY =
        event.loader.handle.scaleZ = 20;
      var animationData:AnimationData =
        event.loader.handle.animationLibrary.getAnimation(
          "default");
      if (animationData != null)
        animationData.animator.play();
    }
  }
```

AS—Loading a converted model

Models can also be defined in an ActionScript class. You may recall the Sea Turtle "primitive" from *Chapter 2, Creating and Displaying Primitives*, which was an example of a complex model that could be created by instantiating the `SeaTurtle` class.

The Collada DAE and Quake 2 MD2 formats were both demonstrated being loaded from external files and from an embedded resource. Because of the nature of an ActionScript class, loading it from an external file does not make sense, which is why there is only one application shown here demonstrating the use of models stored in an AS file.

For this application, we will use a class called `Ogre`, which has been converted from the MD2 model used in the `MD2ExternalDemo` and `MD2EmbeddedDemo` classes above. The process of creating a class like `Ogre` is explained in the following section *Converting a loaded model to an ActionScript class*.

```
package
{
  import away3d.core.base.Mesh;
  import away3d.core.utils.Cast;
  import away3d.materials.BitmapMaterial;

  public class AS3ModelDemo extends Away3DTemplate
  {
    [Embed(source="ogre.jpg")]
    protected var AS3Material:Class;
    protected var model:Mesh;

    public function AS3ModelDemo()
    {
      super();
    }

    protected override function initScene():void
    {
      super.initScene();
      var modelMaterial:BitmapMaterial =
        new BitmapMaterial(Cast.bitmap(AS3Material));
```

Just like a primitive 3D object, the `Ogre` model is created by instantiating a standard ActionScript class. There is no need to use an intermediary class like `Collada` or `Md2` to load or parse a file.

You will note that we have passed in the `scaling` init object parameter, and then set the material and position directly via the properties exposed by the `Mesh` class. This is because the tool that was used to create this particular AS3 class only reads the `scaling` init object parameter, and does not pass the init object down to the underlying `Mesh` class constructor. This behavior is dependent on the particular way that a modeling application exports an AS3 Away3D model class, so this is not a universal rule.

```
      model = new Ogre(
        {
          scaling: 0.01
        }
      );
      model.material = modelMaterial;
      model.z = 100;
      scene.addChild(model);
    }
  }
}
```

Static models

The 3DS, AWD, KMZ, ASE, or OBJ model formats can all be used to load and display static 3D objects. The following samples presented show you how to load embedded and external files from all of these formats.

3DS—Loading an embedded file

The 3DS model format has been around for over a decade, and is widely supported by 3D authoring applications and 3D engines alike. While many formats claim to offer a "universal" standard, the 3DS format can almost be thought of as a de-facto standard, thanks to its popularity.

```
package
{
  import away3d.containers.ObjectContainer3D;
  import away3d.core.base.Mesh;
  import away3d.core.utils.Cast;
  import away3d.loaders.Max3DS;
  import away3d.materials.BitmapMaterial;

  public class Max3DSEmbeddedDemo extends Away3DTemplate
  {
    [Embed(source="monster.3ds", mimeType="application/octet-stream")]
    protected var MonsterModel:Class;
```

```
[Embed(source="monster.jpg")]
protected var MonsterTexture:Class;

public function Max3DSEmbeddedDemo()
{
  super();
}

protected override function initScene():void
{
  super.initScene();
  var modelMaterial:BitmapMaterial =
    new BitmapMaterial(Cast.bitmap(MonsterTexture));
  var monsterMesh:ObjectContainer3D =
    Max3DS.parse(Cast.bytearray(MonsterModel),
    {
```

When embedding a 3D model file it does not make sense for the Max3DS class to try and load the materials from external image files. Indeed, if the Max3DS class does try to load materials from external images that don't exist an error will be displayed in place of the 3D object that you are trying to load. You can see an example of this error in the image below.

To prevent the Max3DS class from trying to load external image files we set the autoLoadTextures init object parameter to false.

```
      autoLoadTextures: false,
      z: 200
    }
);
```

The parse() function will return a ObjectContainer3D object. The children held by this ObjectContainer3D object represent the 3D objects we have loaded from the 3DS file. We loop through each child, applying the material we created from the embedded texture.

```
    for each (var child:Mesh in monsterMesh.children)
      child.material = modelMaterial;
    scene.addChild(monsterMesh);
    }
  }
}
```

Models and Animations

If the `autoLoadTextures` parameter is not set to `false`, you may see an error as in the following screenshot:

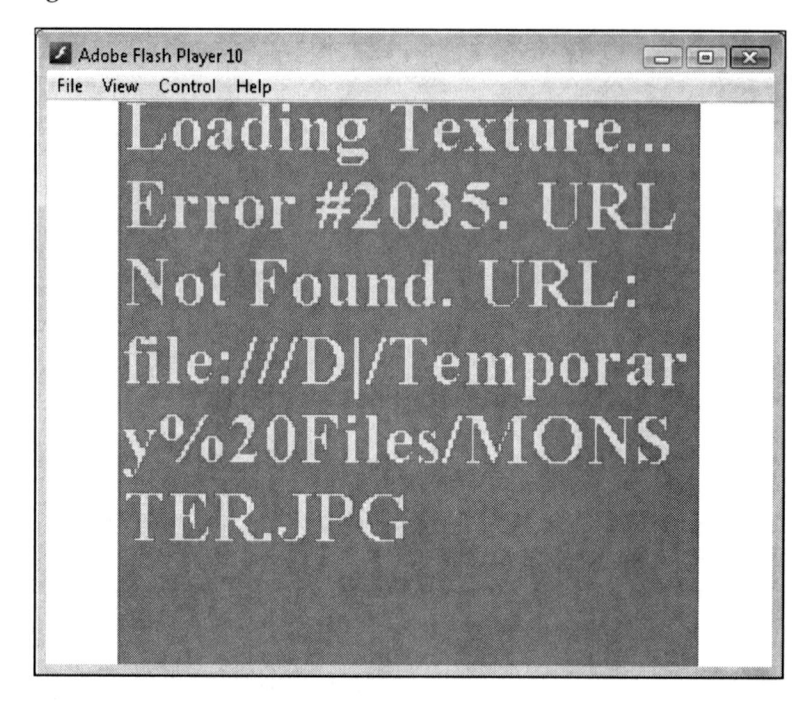

> Loading Texture... Error #2035: URL Not Found. URL: file:///D|/Temporary%20Files/MONSTER.JPG

3DS—Loading an external file

Loading a model from an external 3DS file is very easy. We simply supply the location of the 3DS file to the `Max3DS load()` function, and it will load the model and any materials referenced by the 3DS file.

```
package
{
   import away3d.core.utils.Cast;
   import away3d.loaders.Loader3D;
   import away3d.loaders.Max3DS;

   public class Max3DSExternalDemo extends Away3DTemplate
   {
     public function Max3DSExternalDemo()
     {
       super();
     }

     protected override function initScene():void
     {
       super.initScene();
```

Again, remember to add the slash to the URL.

```
      var monsterMesh:Loader3D = Max3DS.load("./monster.3ds",
        {
          z: 200
        }
      );
      scene.addChild(monsterMesh);
    }
  }
}
```

AWD—Loading an embedded file

The AWD format has been designed specifically for use with Away3D. It is an ASCII-based format, which means it can be viewed in a regular text editor.

```
package
{
  import away3d.core.base.Object3D;
  import away3d.core.utils.Cast;
  import away3d.loaders.AWData;
  import away3d.materials.BitmapMaterial;
  import away3d.core.base.Mesh;
  import away3d.containers.ObjectContainer3D;

  public class AWDEmbeddedDemo extends Away3DTemplate
  {
    [Embed(source="monster.awd", mimeType="application/octet-stream")]
    protected var MonsterModel:Class;
    [Embed(source="monster.jpg")]
    protected var MonsterTexture:Class;

    public function AWDEmbeddedDemo()
    {
      super();
    }

    protected override function initScene():void
    {
      super.initScene();
      var modelMaterial:BitmapMaterial =
        new BitmapMaterial(Cast.bitmap(MonsterTexture));
```

Models and Animations

The `parse()` function will return an `Object3D` object. In this case, this object is actually an instance of the `ObjectContainer3D` class. So we use the `as` statement to cast the returned `Object3D` object to an `ObjectContainer3D` object.

```
var monsterMesh:ObjectContainer3D =
  AWData.parse(Cast.bytearray(MonsterModel),
  {
    z: 200
  }
) as ObjectContainer3D;
```

We use a `for` loop to inspect each of the children of the `ObjectContainer3D` object.

```
for each (var object:Object3D in monsterMesh.children)
{
```

Again we use the `as` statement, but this time we are casting the children of the `ObjectContainer3D` object to a `Mesh` object.

```
var mesh:Mesh = object as Mesh;
```

If the cast was successful (that is, the `mesh` variable is not `null`) then we assign the material created using the embedded resources to the `mesh`.

```
    if (mesh != null)
       mesh.material = modelMaterial;
  }

  scene.addChild(monsterMesh);
    }
  }
}
```

The `AWData` class will attempt to load the materials referenced in the AWD file from external images using the `BitmapFileMaterial` class. There is no option that can be set to stop this behavior, which means that you may see an exception thrown if the SWF does not have the correct permissions to access the file. However this is not a big problem, as only the debug versions of the Adobe Player will display these exceptions, so the vast majority of end users will not see the warning.

The exception you may see will read something like:

SecurityError: Error #2148: SWF file file:///D|/Temporary%20Files/ AWDEmbeddedDemo.swf cannot access local resource file:///D|/ Temporary%20Files/monster.jpg. Only local-with-filesystem and trusted local SWF files may access local resources.

at flash.display::Loader/get content()

at away3d.materials::BitmapFileMaterial/onComplete()[C:\Away3D\away3d\materials\BitmapFileMaterial.as:62]

You can work around this by removing any reference to external image files from the AWD file. Since the AWD format is ASCII-based format, you can open it in a regular text editor.

The following image is of the original AWD file. The text **monster.jpg** has been highlighted on line 7.

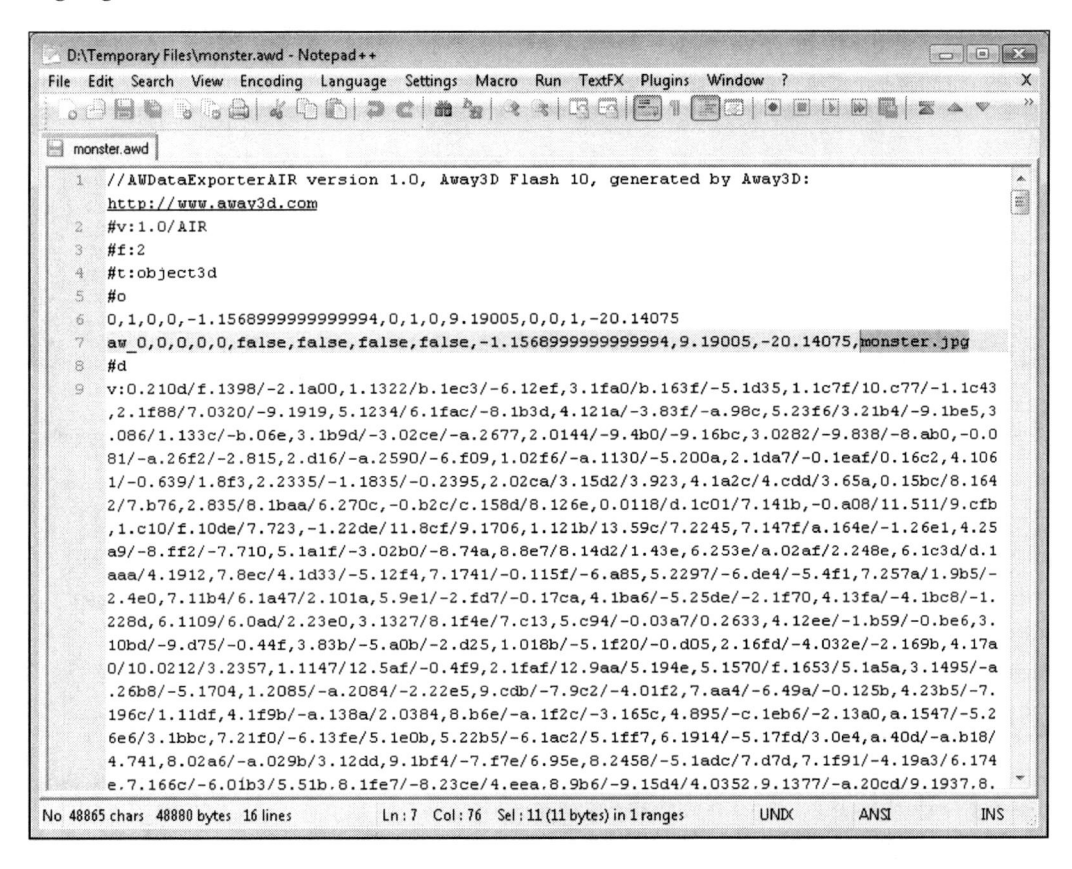

In this next image the text **monster.jpg** has been removed.

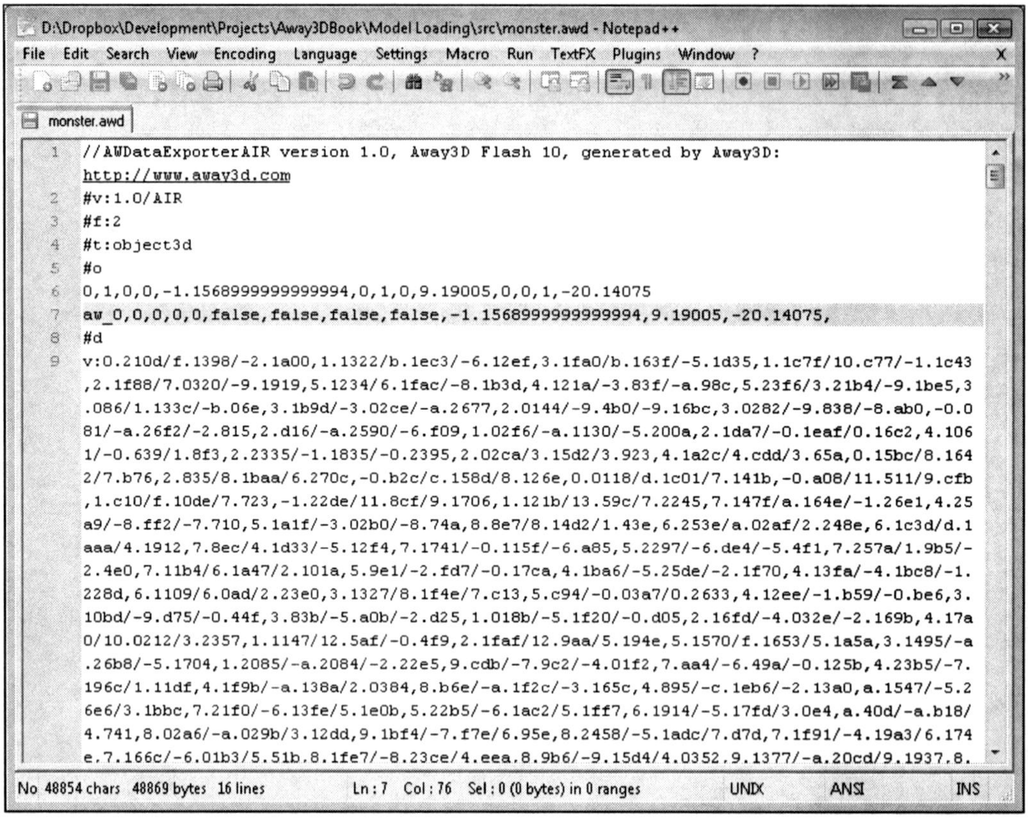

If this new AWD file, with the reference to the JPG file removed, is embedded and loaded, the `AWData` class will not try to load any external image files. This in turn stops an exception from being thrown.

AWD—Loading an external file

When loading an external AWD file, we don't have to worry about the materials like we did with the embedded AWD file. We simply use the `AWData` class to load and apply any textures that are referenced within the AWD file.

```
package
{
  import away3d.loaders.AWData;
  import away3d.loaders.Loader3D;

  public class AWDExternalDemo extends Away3DTemplate
  {
```

```
    public function AWDExternalDemo()
    {
      super();
    }

    protected override function initScene():void
    {
      super.initScene();
```

Make sure you add the slash to the URL.

```
      var monsterMesh:Loader3D = AWData.load("./monster.awd",
        {
          z: 200
        }
      );
      scene.addChild(monsterMesh);
    }
  }
}
```

KMZ

The KMZ format is used by Google Sketch-Up. The Kmz class from the away3d.loaders package should load KMZ files, but due to a bug in Away3D version 3.6 this class cannot be used. Referencing the Kmz class in any way will lead to the following error:

VerifyError: Error #1053: Illegal override of Kmz in away3d.loaders.Kmz.

More information on this bug can be found at http://code.google.com/p/away3d/issues/detail?id=60&can=1&q=kmz.

ASE—Loading an embedded file

The ASE file format is used by 3ds Max. It uses ASCII characters (unlike the binary 3DS format), meaning it is readable if opened using a regular text editor.

Working with an embedded ASE file is quite straightforward. In fact, when loading embedded model files in the other 3D model formats we need to be aware of how textures that are referenced in the file are loaded from external files by default. But with the Ase class, there are no workarounds or special init object parameters to deal with when loading an embedded model file.

```
    package
    {
      import away3d.core.base.Mesh;
      import away3d.core.utils.Cast;
```

Models and Animations

```
import away3d.loaders.Ase;
import away3d.materials.BitmapMaterial;

public class ASEEmbeddedDemo extends Away3DTemplate
{
  [Embed(source="monster.ase", mimeType="application/octet-stream")]
  protected var MonsterModel:Class;
  [Embed(source="monster.jpg")]
  protected var MonsterTexture:Class;

  public function ASEEmbeddedDemo()
  {
    super();
  }

  protected override function initScene():void
  {
    super.initScene();
    var modelMaterial:BitmapMaterial =
      new BitmapMaterial(Cast.bitmap(MonsterTexture));
    var monsterMesh:Mesh =
      Ase.parse(Cast.bytearray(MonsterModel),
      {
        z: 50
      }
    );
    monsterMesh.material = modelMaterial;
    scene.addChild(monsterMesh);
  }
}
```

ASE—Loading an external file

Loading an external ASE file is done in two steps. The first is to load the file in the usual way using the `Ase load()` function.

```
package
{
  import away3d.core.base.Mesh;
  import away3d.events.Loader3DEvent;
  import away3d.loaders.Ase;
  import away3d.loaders.Loader3D;
  import away3d.materials.BitmapFileMaterial;
```

```
public class ASEExternalDemo extends Away3DTemplate
{
  public function ASEExternalDemo()
  {
    super();
  }

  protected override function initScene():void
  {
    super.initScene();
```

Make sure you add the slash to the URL.

```
    var monsterMesh:Loader3D = Ase.load("./monster.ase",
      {
        z: 200
      }
    );
```

The second step is to manually load the materials. The Ase class does not parse any material information from the ASE file format. To accommodate this, the onLoadSuccess() function has been registered through the Loader3D addOnSuccess() function to be called when the Loader3DEvent.LOAD_SUCCESS event is dispatched.

```
    monsterMesh.addOnSuccess(onLoadSuccess);
    scene.addChild(monsterMesh);
  }
```

In the onLoadSuccess() function, we use the BitmapFileMaterial to load an external texture and apply it to the 3D object.

```
  protected function onLoadSuccess(event:Loader3DEvent):void
  {
    (event.loader.handle as Mesh).material =
      new BitmapFileMaterial("monster.jpg");
  }
 }
}
```

OBJ—Loading an embedded file

The OBJ file format was first developed by Wavefront Technologies for its Advanced Visualizer animation package, which has since been incorporated into the Maya 3D modeling application. It is an ASCII-based format, meaning it can be read with a regular text editor. OBJ files are usually partnered with a second MTL file that defines the materials.

```
package
{
  import away3d.core.base.Face;
  import away3d.core.base.Mesh;
  import away3d.core.utils.Cast;
  import away3d.loaders.Obj;
  import away3d.materials.BitmapMaterial;

  public class OBJEmbeddedDemo extends Away3DTemplate
  {
    [Embed(source="monster.obj", mimeType="application/octet-stream")]
    protected var MonsterModel:Class;
    [Embed(source="monster.jpg")]
    protected var MonsterTexture:Class;

    public function OBJEmbeddedDemo()
    {
      super();
    }

    protected override function initScene():void
    {
      super.initScene();
      var modelMaterial:BitmapMaterial =
        new BitmapMaterial(Cast.bitmap(MonsterTexture));
      var monsterMesh:Mesh =
        Obj.parse(Cast.bytearray(MonsterModel),
        {
          z: 200,
```

Setting the `useMtl` init object parameter to `false` is important when using an embedded OBJ model file. If `useMtl` is set to `true`, which it is by default, an attempt will be made to load the MTL file that usually accompanies an OBJ model file. Attempting to load a nonexistent MTL file may result in an error being displayed within the scene (like in the following screenshot), or an exception may be thrown.

```
          useMtl: false
        }
        ) as Mesh;
```

Due to the way the `Obj` class constructs the 3D object from the embedded OBJ file, we need to set the material that is applied to each `Face` in the 3D object rather than assigning a material to the `Mesh material` property.

```
      for each (var face:Face in monsterMesh.faces)
         face.material = modelMaterial;
      scene.addChild(monsterMesh);
    }
  }
}
```

The following image shows an example of the error you may see if the `useMtl` init object parameter is not set to `false`.

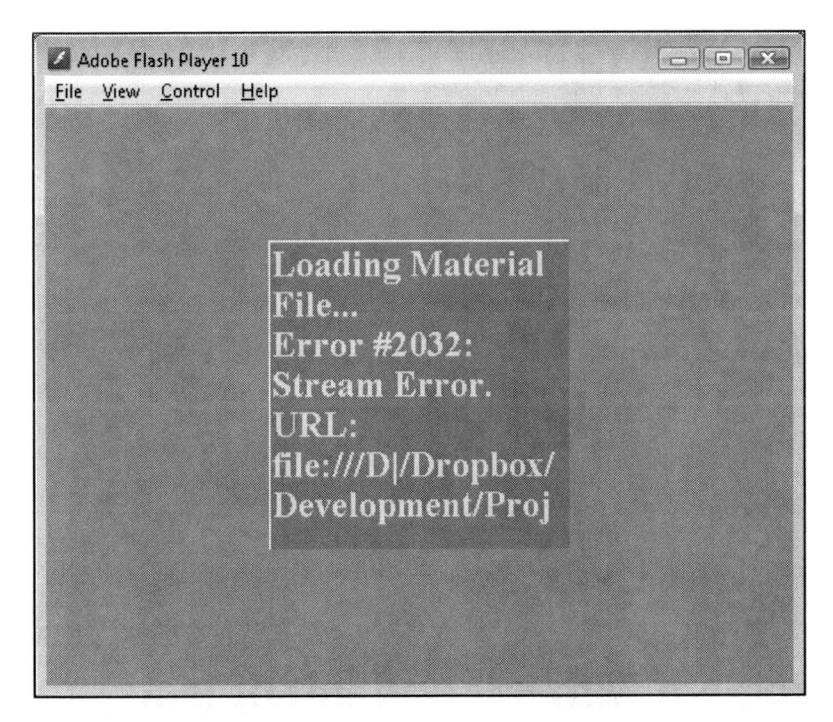

OBJ—Loading an external file

When loading an external OBJ file, the `Obj` class will attempt to load the materials defined in the MTL class with the same name as the OBJ class. Otherwise, loading an external OBJ file is quite straightforward.

Models and Animations

> The Obj class will not parse the MTL file properly if its lines are prefixed with whitespace characters like spaces or tabs. Some exporters, like the one included with 3ds Max, will add these whitespace characters to the MTL file. You can manually remove them using a regular text editor.

```
package
{
  import away3d.loaders.Loader3D;
  import away3d.loaders.Obj;

  public class OBJExternalDemo extends Away3DTemplate
  {
    public function OBJExternalDemo()
    {
      super();
    }

    protected override function initScene():void
    {
      super.initScene();
```

Make sure you add the slash to the URL.

```
      var monsterMesh:Loader3D = Obj.load("./monster.obj",
        {
          z: 200
        }
      );
      scene.addChild(monsterMesh);
    }
  }
}
```

The problem with init and Init objects

We have used the term "init object" quite a bit throughout the book. These init objects are usually created using object literal notation. While they are related to the Init class, they are not the same thing.

Instances of the Init class maintain a reference to an init object, and provide a number of functions that can be used to easily read the properties of the init object. So, an init object (notice the lower case "i") contains a number of properties that define the initial values or settings to be applied to an object. An Init object (with the uppercase "I") is an instance of the Init class that provides a convenient way to read the properties of an init object.

So far we have not had to use the `Init` class directly, but understanding how it works allows us to understand some of the differences between how materials are applied to 3D objects loaded from embedded files and how they were applied to the primitive 3D objects created in *Chapter 2, Creating and Displaying Primitives*. You may have noticed that when using model loading classes (like the `Md2` class) we have applied the material directly via the `Mesh material` property, whereas in *Chapter 2, Creating and Displaying Primitives*, we applied materials of the primitive 3D objects using the `material` init object parameter.

To explain this difference, we first need to know how the `Init` class works. Let's take a look at the `getMaterial()` function provided by the `Init` class.

```
public function getMaterial(name:String):Material
{
    if (init == null)
        return null;

    if (!init.hasOwnProperty(name))
        return null;

    var result:Material = Cast.material(init[name]);

    delete init[name];

    return result;
}
```

The logic used by the `getMaterial()` function is similar to the other "get" functions provided by the `Init` class. It will first check for the existence of the requested property in the init object, referenced by the `init` property. If it does not exist, `null` is returned. If it does exist, the property is cast to a `Material`. Before the material is returned, the init object property that was just accessed is deleted.

Because the init object property is deleted once it is read, calls to the Init class "get" functions in effect *consume* the requested property. This means if two objects share the same init object, the first one to read a specific init object property (via an `Init` object) is the only one to get the value assigned to that property. This consumption of init object properties is important when you see how many classes an init object will pass through. The following list shows a selection of the classes and functions the init object supplied to the `Md2 parse()` function will pass through:

- `Md2.parse`
- `Loader3D.parse`
- `LoaderCube` constructor

- `Loader3D` constructor
- `ObjectContainer3D` constructor
- `Mesh` constructor
- `Object3D` constructor
- `Md2` constructor
- `AbstractParser` constructor and more...

As you can see, the init object you supply to the `Md2 parse()` function changes hands quite a bit, and each time it does there is a chance that a property of that init object will be consumed. This is exactly what happens to the `material` init object property. It is consumed in step 6, where it is used to define the material that will be applied to the `Cube` primitive that is used as a place holder while the MD2 file is downloaded and parsed. The `material` property is then requested a second time in step 9, where it is used to define the material that is applied to the loaded 3D object. Of course, by this time the `material` property has been consumed and is no longer available.

The problem here is that a number of Away3D classes request the same property from an init object, and the order in which they consume these properties is not immediately obvious. In the case of the `Md2` class, the `material` init object property is consumed by the `Mesh` constructor to be applied to the place holder `Cube` primitive, and not the `AbstractParser` constructor, which would apply the material to the loaded 3D object (which is the effect that you may expect when providing the `material` init object parameter).

The workaround to this issue is to simply assign the value to the specified property directly. This is why we have assigned the required material to the `Mesh` `material` property directly in a number of the examples presented in this chapter.

Converting a loaded model to an ActionScript class

The `Mesh` object has a function called `asAS3Class()`, which can be used to dump a 3D object to an ActionScript class.

The following `initScene()` function could be used in the `MD2EmbeddedDemo` from the *MD2 – Embedded File* example. It creates a new `Mesh` object from a MD2 file, and then uses the trace function to output the string returned by the `asAS3Class()` function.

```
protected override function initScene():void
{
  super.initScene();
```

```
    md2Mesh = Md2.parse(Cast.bytearray(MD2Model));
    trace(md2Mesh.asAS3Class("Ogre", "", true, true));
}
```

> The `asAS3Class()` function can output many megabytes of data for complex models. You may find a tool like **Vizzy Flash Tracer** (`http://code.google.com/p/flash-tracer/`) easier to use than your authoring tool when dealing with such large trace dumps.

Converting 3D models into an ActionScript class offers some degree of copy protection by making it harder for your models to be extracted and used by a third party. And because the resulting ActionScript class only includes the data required by Away3D, it can result in smaller model files by stripping some of the extraneous data present in some 3D file formats (although this is not always the case—see *Chapter 13, Performance Tips*, for a more detailed look at the benefits of saving 3D objects as ActionScript classes).

> Animations are not exported when using the `asAS3Class()` function in Away3D version 3.6. This functionality is expected to be included in later versions of Away3D.

Alternatively, you can use a tool like **Prefab** to import a 3D model file and then export an AS class. Prefab is a free tool that runs on the Adobe AIR platform, and can be downloaded from `http://www.closier.nl/prefab/`.

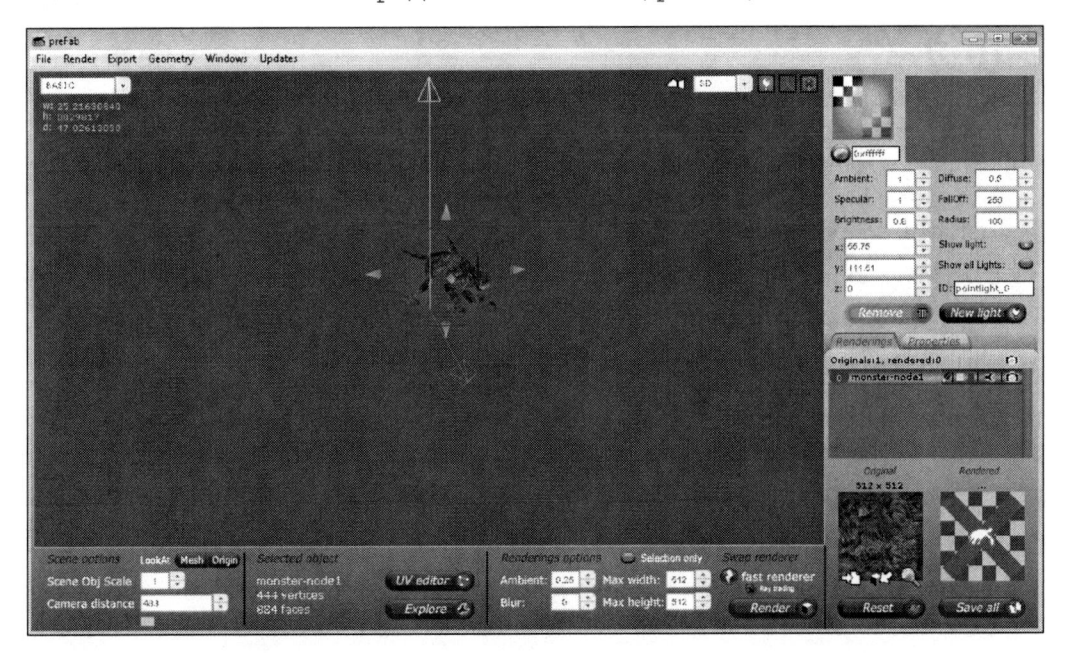

The following instructions show you how to convert a 3D model file into an ActionScript class using Prefab:

1. Click **File | Import 3D** model.
2. Select the 3D model file you wish to import and click on the **OK** button.
3. At this point, you will see a **Geometry integrity report** window. Click on the **Close** button to return to the main window.
4. Select the imported model by clicking on it. When selected, the model should be surrounded by a blue box.
5. Click **Export | Export to Away3D AS3 class**.
6. Select the **Selected Object** and **Only Geometry** options.
7. Type in a name for the class in the **ClassName** textbox.
8. You can leave the **Package** textbox empty, or you can optionally specify the package that the class should reside in.
9. Click on the **Save File** button.
10. Select a location to save the file (you will most likely want to save it in the same location as other source code files) and click on the **Save** button.

> These instructions are valid for Prefab version 1.336. Prefab is an active project that is updated on a regular basis, and so some of these steps may change in later versions.

Summary

While it is possible to create simple 3D objects manually or through the primitive 3D objects supplied with Away3D, it is very common to display 3D models created and exported from 3D authoring applications. We have seen how these 3D models can be exported from a number of 3D modeling applications, such as 3ds Max, Blender, Milkshape, and Sketch-Up.

We have covered the differences in embedding the 3D model files directly into the final SWF file and loading them as external files. Sample applications were presented that demonstrate how the different formats supported by Away3D, which include 3DS, AWD, MD2, Collada, OBJ, ASE, and ActionScript, can be loaded, parsed, and displayed.

Finally, we saw how we can use the functionality in the `Mesh` class to convert a loaded 3D object into an ActionScript class, which provides a degree of copy protection and optimization.

In the next chapter, we will take a look at the various types of cameras and lenses available in Away3D.

7
Cameras

In *Chapter 1, Building Your First Away3D Application*, we briefly touched on the `Camera3D` class. Just like a real life camera, the `Camera3D` class has a number of properties that can be modified, such as focus, zoom, and field of view. In this chapter, we will see how these properties affect the camera, and how they can be used in conjunction with the various lens classes that are included with Away3D.

Away3D also includes a number of additional camera classes that provide an easy way to trail a moving 3D object, always keep a particular 3D object in view, or to view a 3D object from a variety of different angles.

In this chapter, we will cover the following topics:

- The properties of a camera
- The different lens classes that can be used by the camera
- The different camera classes that are available

The properties of a camera

In photography, adjusting the focal length of a camera lens modifies its **angle of view** (also known as **field of view**, or **FOV**). You can see how this works in the following diagram:

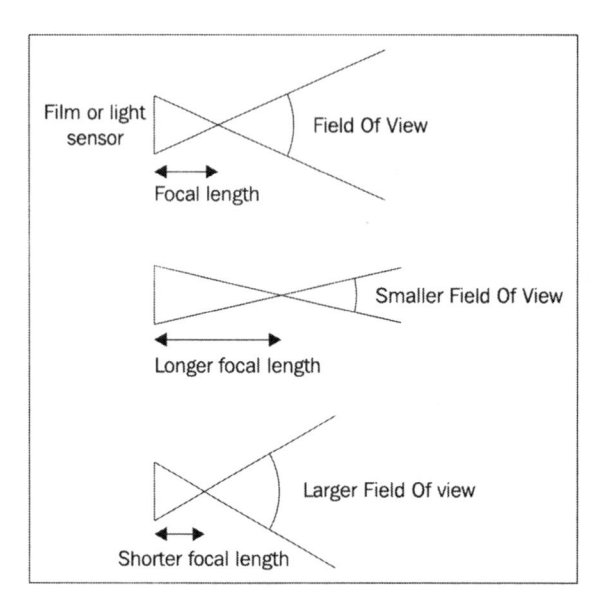

As you can see, a short focal length increases the cameras FOV, while a long focal length decreases it. The greater the FOV, the more of a scene is captured by the camera. Because the physical size of a photograph does not change, this necessarily means that each object in the scene will appear smaller on the photograph. As the FOV decreases, so too does the area of a scene that is captured by the camera, which in turn increases the size of the objects that appear in the photograph.

The `Camera3D` class includes a property called `focus`, which has similar properties to the focal length. As the `focus` property is increased, the FOV (represented by the `fov` property) decreases, reducing the scene's visible area, and enlarging the size on the screen of those 3D objects that are visible. Conversely, decreasing the `focus` property will increase the FOV, which will make more of the scene visible, thus reducing the size on the screen of any visible 3D objects.

The `Camera3D` class also includes a property called `zoom`. As you would imagine, increasing the `zoom` property will "zoom-in" the camera. Zooming in is achieved by reducing the FOV, and this is exactly how the `zoom` property works in the `Camera3D` class too: increasing the `zoom` property will decrease the camera's FOV, while decreasing the `zoom` property will increase the camera's FOV.

The `fov` property itself can be modified directly, and doing so will also modify the `zoom` property accordingly that is, increasing the `fov` property will decrease the `zoom` property, and decreasing the `fov` property will increase the `zoom` property.

> The `zoom` or `focus` properties can be used interchangeably when using the `PerspectiveLens`, `OrthogonalLens`, and `SphericalLens` classes (discussed in the following *Camera lenses* section). The `ZoomFocusLens` class will render the scene differently depending on the values assigned to the `zoom` or `focus` properties, although generally speaking the variation is minor.

The `CameraPropertiesDemo` application, available on the Packt website, allows you to modify the `focus`, `zoom`, and `fov` properties of a camera viewing a scene filled with cubes. This allows you to see the relationship between the three properties on a live `Camera3D` object.

Camera lenses

Just like a real camera, the Away3D camera classes can view the scene through a variety of different lenses. There are four lens classes available in Away3D, each from the `away3d.cameras.lenses` package:

- `ZoomFocusLens`
- `PerspectiveLens`
- `OrthogonalLens`
- `SphericalLens`

Applying an instance of these lens classes to a camera object is as simple as assigning it to the `Camera3D` `lens` property, like so:

```
camera.lens = new SphericalLens();
```

ZoomFocusLens and PerspectiveLens classes

The ZoomFocusLens class is the default class that is assigned to the Camera3D lens property. This lens will render a scene much like your own eyes perceive the real world. While the ZoomFocusLens class will render the scene appropriately in most situations, the class itself is a legacy from earlier code. The PerspectiveLens class will project the scene in a way that is more common amongst modern 3D authoring applications. The difference between the two classes is subtle, but as we will see in *Chapter 8, Mouse Interactivity*, there are occasions where it is necessary to use the PerspectiveLens class.

The following screenshot shows you how a scene will appear when viewed with the ZoomFocusLens and PerspectiveLens classes.

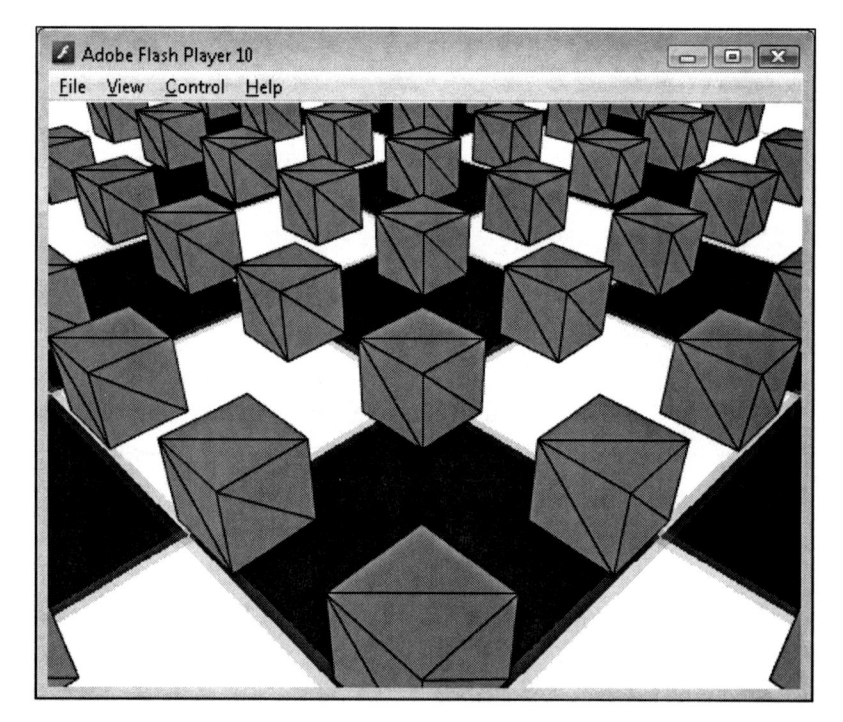

SphericalLens class

The projection method used by the FocusZoomLens and PerspectiveLens classes results in a more distorted view as the FOV increases. You can see this in the following screenshot, which shows a scene viewed through a PerspectiveLens with a large FOV. Notice how the cubes shown at the bottom of the screen have been skewed.

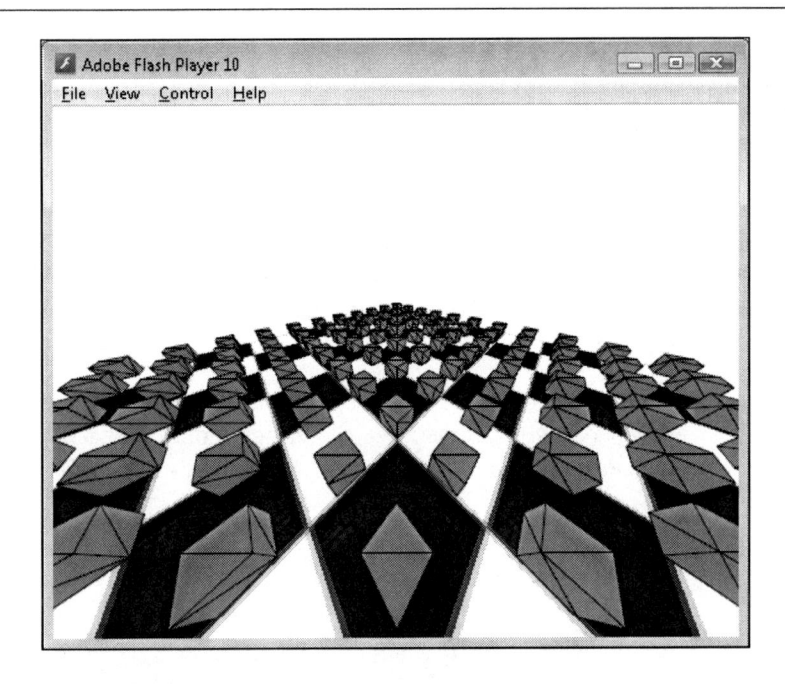

The `SphericalLens` class can be used for situations like this. This class is used to replicate a wide-angle lens, sometimes referred to as a **fish-eye lens**. It views the scene as if it were being reflected in the surface of a glass sphere, and it avoids the distortion as shown in the following screenshot:

OrthogonalLens class

Part of the way the lens classes `ZoomFocusLens`, `PerspectiveLens`, and `SphericalLens` create a 3D perspective is by scaling down 3D objects as they increase in distance from the camera. This effect is similar to how our own eyes perceive the world, but there are situations where this effect is not desirable. **Isometric projection** can be used as an alternative to render 3D objects with a consistent size and maintain the spacing between parallel lines. Isometric projection is used by a number of real-time strategy and adventure games, and also in Computer Aided Design (CAD).

The `OrthogonalLens` class is used in Away3D to render an isometric view. As you can see in the following screenshot, the size of the cubes remain consistent despite their distance from the camera, and all of their parallel edges remain parallel when rendered to the screen.

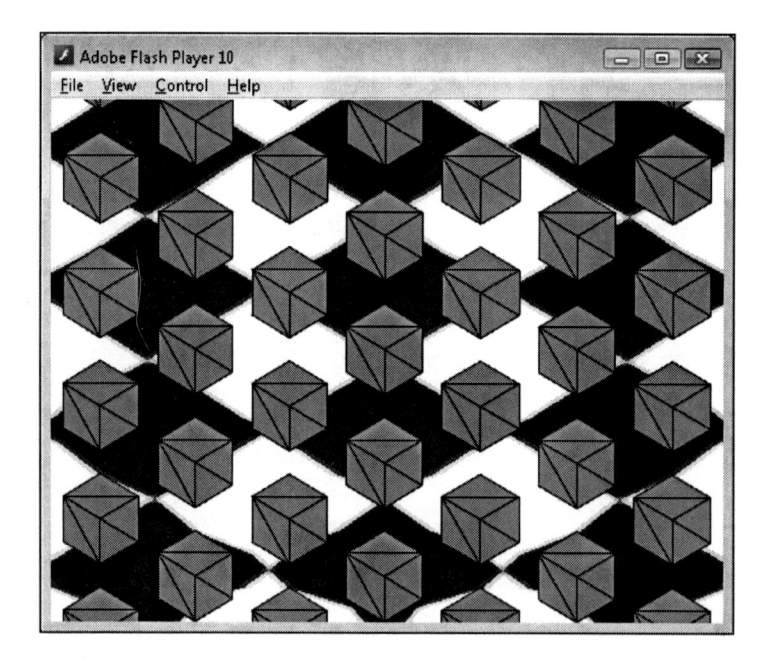

Camera classes

Away3D includes a number of camera classes. We have already used the `Camera3D` class, which is referenced by the `Away3DTemplate` class introduced in *Chapter 1, Building Your First Away3D Application*. The `Camera3D` class can be positioned and transformed within the scene, but it does not have the ability to easily track, follow, or slide around a 3D object. Instead, this functionality is provided by the `TargetCamera3D`, `HoverCamera3D`, and `SpringCam` classes.

Chapter 7

To demonstrate these additional camera classes we will create an application called `CameraDemo`. This application will allow us to use these cameras to view a sphere primitive that can be moved around within the scene in response to keyboard input.

```
package
{
```

The camera classes are found in the `away3d.cameras` package.

```
    import away3d.cameras.HoverCamera3D;
    import away3d.cameras.SpringCam;
    import away3d.cameras.TargetCamera3D;
    import away3d.core.clip.FrustumClipping;
    import away3d.core.render.Renderer;
    import away3d.core.utils.Cast;
    import away3d.materials.BitmapMaterial;
    import away3d.primitives.Plane;
    import away3d.primitives.Sphere;

    import flash.events.Event;
    import flash.events.KeyboardEvent;
    import flash.events.MouseEvent;

    public class CameraDemo extends Away3DTemplate
    {
```

This embedded texture file will be applied to the ground (represented by a plane primitive) to provide a reference point for the moving sphere.

```
        [Embed(source="checkerboard.jpg")]
        protected var CheckerBoardTexture:Class;
```

The `sphere` property will reference the sphere primitive that will be added to the scene.

```
        protected var sphere:Sphere;
```

The three cameras demonstrated by this application (the hover camera, target camera and spring camera) are each referenced by their own similarly named property.

```
        protected var hoverCamera:HoverCamera3D;
        protected var springCamera:SpringCam;
        protected var targetCamera:TargetCamera3D;
```

Cameras

The `lastStageX` and `lastStageY` properties are used to store the position of the mouse during the last frame. This will allow us to find out how far the mouse has moved in any given frame.

```
protected var lastStageX:Number;
protected var lastStageY:Number;
```

The `mouseButtonDown` property will be set to `true` when the mouse button has been pressed, and `false` when it has been released.

```
protected var mouseButtonDown:Boolean;
```

The spring and target cameras are best demonstrated tracking a moving target. These four properties will be `true` when the corresponding arrow keys on the keyboard are pressed, and `false` when they are released. That in turn allows us to move and turn the sphere by a small amount every frame in response to keyboard input.

```
protected var moveForward:Boolean;
protected var moveBackward:Boolean;
protected var turnLeft:Boolean;
protected var turnRight:Boolean;

public function CameraDemo()
{
   super();
}

protected override function initEngine():void
{
   super.initEngine();
```

In this demo, the default renderer can introduce some z-sorting issues between the sphere and the ground plane. Using the Quadtree renderer (which was covered in *Chapter 4, Z-Sorting*) provides a simple fix for this problem.

```
view.renderer = Renderer.CORRECT_Z_ORDER;
```

We can also run into some trouble where the ground plane is culled when it is still visible on the screen. Assigning a new `FrustumClipping` object to the view's `clipping` property ensures that only those parts of the ground plane that are not visible are culled.

```
   view.clipping = new FrustumClipping();
}
```

Chapter 7

The `initScene()` function is used to create a sphere primitive, a plane primitive to represent the ground, and add both 3D objects to the scene. A checkerboard material is applied to the plane primitive, which gives us a point of reference as the sphere primitive is moved around the scene.

```
protected override function initScene():void
{
   super.initScene();
   sphere = new Sphere(
      {
         radius: 10,
         y: 10
      }
   );
   scene.addChild(sphere);

   var plane:Plane = new Plane(
      {
       material: new BitmapMaterial(Cast.bitmap(CheckerBoardTexture)),
         width: 500,
         height: 500
      }
   );
   scene.addChild(plane);
```

The `addHoverCamera()` function is then called, configuring the hover camera as the initial camera.

```
   addHoverCamera();
}
```

The `initListeners()` function contains code to register functions against several different events. For this demo, we need to listen for when keys on the keyboard are pressed (`KeyboardEvent.KEY_DOWN`) and released (`KeyboardEvent.KEY_UP`), when the mouse button is pressed (`MouseEvent.MOUSE_DOWN`) and released (`MouseEvent.MOUSE_UP`), and also for when the mouse is moved (`MouseEvent.MOUSE_MOVE`).

```
   protected override function initListeners():void
{
   super.initListeners();
   stage.addEventListener(
      MouseEvent.MOUSE_DOWN,
      onMouseDown
   );
```

```
            stage.addEventListener(
              MouseEvent.MOUSE_UP,
              onMouseUp
            );
            stage.addEventListener(
              MouseEvent.MOUSE_MOVE,
              onMouseMove
            );
            stage.addEventListener(
              KeyboardEvent.KEY_DOWN,
              onKeyDown
            );
            stage.addEventListener(
              KeyboardEvent.KEY_UP,
              onKeyUp
            );
        }

        protected override function onEnterFrame(event:Event):void
        {
            super.onEnterFrame(event);
```

If the hover camera is the current camera, we need to call its `hover()` function. This will update the position and orientation of the hover camera, moving it towards the target angles that we have given it in response to the movement of the mouse.

```
            if (hoverCamera != null) hoverCamera.hover();
```

Likewise if the spring camera is the current camera, we need to access the `view` property. This does much the same job as the `hover()` function on the hover camera, and will move the camera in response to the movement of the target 3D object it is following.

```
            if (springCamera != null) springCamera.view;
```

Depending on which arrow keys are currently pressed on the keyboard, the sphere will be moved using the `moveForward()` and `moveBackward()` functions, and rotated using the `yaw()` function.

```
            if (moveForward) sphere.moveForward(5);
            else if (moveBackward) sphere.moveBackward(5);
            if (turnLeft) sphere.yaw(-5);
            else if (turnRight) sphere.yaw(5);
        }
```

When the mouse button has been pressed down, the `MouseEvent.MOUSE_DOWN` event will be dispatched, and the `onMouseDown()` function is called.

```
protected function onMouseDown(event:MouseEvent):void
{
```

We set the `mouseButtonDown` property to `true` to indicate that the mouse button is currently pressed.

```
mouseButtonDown = true;
```

We store the current position of the mouse in the `lastStageX` and `lastStageY` properties, which will allow us to calculate how far the mouse has moved next frame.

```
lastStageX = event.stageX;
lastStageY = event.stageY;
}
```

When the mouse button is released the `MouseEvent.MOUSE_UP` event is dispatched, and the `onMouseUp()` function is called.

```
protected function onMouseUp(event:MouseEvent):void
{
```

The `mouseButtonDown` property is set to `false` to indicate that the mouse button has been released.

```
mouseButtonDown = false;
}
```

When a key is pressed on the keyboard, the `KeyboardEvent.KEY_DOWN` event is dispatched, and the `onKeyDown()` function is called. It is here that we set the `moveForward`, `moveBackward`, `turnLeft`, and `turnRight` properties to `true`, if their corresponding arrow key was pressed.

```
protected function onKeyDown(event:KeyboardEvent):void
{
  switch (event.keyCode)
  {
    case 38: // UP ARROW
      moveForward = true;
      break;
    case 40: // DOWN ARROW
      moveBackward = true;
      break;
    case 37: // LEFT ARROW
```

Cameras

```
          turnLeft = true;
          break;
        case 39: // RIGHT ARROW
          turnRight = true;
          break;
    }
}
```

When a key is released on the keyboard, the `KeyboardEvent.KEY_UP` event is dispatched, and the `onKeyUp()` function is called. It is here that we set the `moveForward`, `moveBackward`, `turnLeft`, and `turnRight` properties to `false`, if their corresponding arrow key was released.

```
protected function onKeyUp(event:KeyboardEvent):void
{
    switch (event.keyCode)
    {
      case 38: // UP ARROW
        moveForward = false;
        break;
      case 40: // DOWN ARROW
        moveBackward = false;
        break;
      case 37: // LEFT ARROW
        turnLeft = false;
        break;
      case 39: // RIGHT ARROW
        turnRight = false;
        break;
```

We also watch for the *1*, *2*, or *3* keys on the keyboard being released. In response to these keys being released, we call the `addHoverCamera()`, `addSpringCamera()`, or `addTargetCamera()` functions. Each of these functions initializes a new type of camera through which the scene is viewed.

```
        case 49: // 1
          addHoverCamera();
          break;
        case 50: // 2
          addSpringCamera();
          break;
        case 51: // 3
          addTargetCamera();
          break;
    }
}
```

The remaining code deals with the creation and updating of the three different camera classes.

Target camera

The target camera acts just like the regular camera, with the exception that it will orient itself to always keep a particular 3D object in the centre of its view. Releasing the 3 key on the keyboard will cause the `addTargetCamera()` function to be called, which will create and activate the target camera.

```
protected function addTargetCamera():void
{
```

When a new camera is added to the scene, the references to the other two cameras are set to `null`.

```
hoverCamera = null;
springCamera = null;
```

The target camera is represented by the `TargetCamera3D` class. In the following code, we create a new instance of the `TargetCamera3D` class, supplying an init object to the constructor that defines the target 3D object for the camera, as well as placing the camera 100 units up along the Y-axis, giving it a global position of (0, 100, 0).

The `target` init object parameter is the only one recognized by the `TargetCamera3D` class. However, like all cameras, the `TargetCamera3D` class extends the `Camera3D` class, and init object parameters for the `Camera3D` class can also be passed to the `TargetCamera3D` constructor.

```
targetCamera = new TargetCamera3D(
    {
      target: sphere,
      y: 100
    }
);
```

To view the scene through the new camera, we assign it to the `View3D` camera property.

```
view.camera = targetCamera;
}
```

Cameras

The following table lists the init object parameters recognized by the `TargetCamera3D` class:

Parameter	Data Type	Default Value	Description
target	Object3D	new Object3D()	Defines the 3D object targeted by the camera.

Hover camera

Like the target camera, the hover camera always looks at a target 3D object, but it can also move around it as if it were sliding across the surface of an ellipsoid that surrounds the target. This provides an easy way to view a 3D object from all angles, and by responding to the movement of the mouse can be used to create a natural interface to manipulate how the scene is viewed.

```
protected function addHoverCamera():void
{
   springCamera = null;
   targetCamera = null;
```

The hover camera is represented by the `HoverCamera3D` class. Here, we create a new instance of the class, and supply an init object to define the target 3D object that the camera will always look at, the distance that the camera will be placed from the 3D object, the minimum tilt angle that the camera will be able to use, and the initial target tilt angle. The table below lists all the init object parameters that can be passed to the `HoverCamera3D` constructor.

```
   hoverCamera = new HoverCamera3D(
     {
       target: sphere,
       distance: 100,
       mintiltangle: 5,
       tiltAngle: 45
     }
   );

   view.camera = hoverCamera;
}
```

In this application, the position of the hover camera is controlled using the mouse. We have already seen that the `mouseButtonDown` property is set to `true` or `false` by the `onMouseDown()` and `onMouseUp()` functions in response to the mouse button being pressed or released. Now, when the `onMouseMove()` function is called in response to the `MouseEvent.MOUSE_MOVE` event, we can modify the position of the hover camera.

```
protected function onMouseMove(event:MouseEvent):void
{
```

If the `mouseButtonDown` property is set to `true`, indicating the mouse button is being held down, and the `hoverCamera` property is not `null`, indicating that the hover camera is the current camera, we will use the movement of the mouse to modify the angle of the hover camera.

```
if (mouseButtonDown && hoverCamera != null)
{
```

The angle to pan (which is rotation around the Y-axis) the hover camera by is calculated using the distance the mouse has moved horizontally across the screen. By subtracting the current horizontal position of the mouse (`event.stageX`) from the horizontal position of the mouse from the last frame (`lastStageX`), we can work out how far the mouse has moved during the last frame.

```
var pan:int = (event.stageX - lastStageX);
```

The angle to tilt (which is rotation around the X-axis) the hover camera by is calculated in a similar way, only this time we use the current and last vertical position of the mouse to find its vertical movement over the last frame.

```
var tilt:int = (event.stageY - lastStageY);
```

The hover camera has two properties that define how it should be positioned around the target 3D object. The first is `panAngle`. This property defines the desired angle around the Y-axis that the hover camera should have. The second property, `tiltAngle`, defines the desired angle around the X-axis that the camera should have.

Assigning a value to either of these properties will not immediately jump the camera to a new position. Instead, the camera will incrementally update its position and orientation with each call to the `hover()` function. So by calling the `hover()` function once each frame in the `onEnterFrame()` function, the hover camera will eventually reach the desired position specified by the `panAngle` and `tiltAngle` properties.

```
hoverCamera.panAngle += pan;
hoverCamera.tiltAngle += tilt;
```

The position of the mouse is then stored in the `lastStageX` and `lastStageY` properties.

```
            lastStageX = event.stageX;
            lastStageY = event.stageY;
        }
    }
```

The following table below lists the init object parameters recognized by the `HoverCamera3D` class:

Parameter	Data Type	Default Value	Description
yfactor	Number	2	Fractional difference in distance between the horizontal camera orientation and vertical camera orientation. Higher values mean the camera will be placed further from the target 3D object as the camera moves above or below it.
distance	Number	800	The distance from the camera to the target 3D object when the tiltangle is zero. The yfactor property can be used to change this distance with the vertical movement of the camera.
wrapPanAngle	Boolean	false	Defines whether the value of the pan angle wraps when over 360 degrees or under 0 degrees.
panAngle	Number	0	The desired rotation of the camera around the Y axis, measured in degrees.
tiltAngle	Number	90	The desired rotation of the camera around the X axis, measured in degrees.
minTiltAngle	Number	-90	Minimum bounds for the tiltAngle property.
maxTiltAngle	Number	90	Maximum bounds for the tiltAngle property.
steps	int	8	Fractional step taken each time the hover function is called. Larger values result in the camera moving smaller distances with each call to the hover function.

Spring camera

The spring camera, represented by the `SpringCam` class, provides a camera that will follow a 3D object as it moves around the scene as if it were attached by a spring.

```
protected function addSpringCamera():void
{
   hoverCamera = null;
   targetCamera = null;

   springCamera = new SpringCam();
   springCamera.target = sphere;
   view.camera = springCamera;


 }
  }
 }
```

The `SpringCam` class is unusual in that its initial properties cannot be specified via an init object. The constructor will accept an init object, which is passed to the base `Camera3D` constructor, but all of the properties specific to the `SpringCam` class have to be set individually once a new `SpringCam` object has been created. The following table lists all of the public properties exposed by the `SpringCam` class:

Parameter	Data Type	Default Value	Description
target	Object3D	null	The target 3D object that the camera should follow. If this property is null, the camera will behave like a standard Camera3D.
stiffness	Number	1	The stiffness of the spring, which defines how hard it is to extend. Higher values for this property mean the camera will trail the target at a more fixed distance.
damping	Number	4	Defines the internal friction of the spring, which affects how quickly the spring will snap back. Higher values will reduce how much the camera will bounce. This value should be between 1 and 20.

Cameras

Parameter	Data Type	Default Value	Description
mass	Number	40	The mass of the camera. Higher values will increase the resistance of the camera to the pull of the target 3D object, and give it more momentum when it is moving.
positionOffset	Vector3D	Vector3D(0,5,-50)	The resting position of the camera relative to the position of the target 3D object.
lookOffset	Vector3D	Vector3D (0,2,10)	The position relative to the target 3D object that the camera should look at.

Summary

Away3D includes a number of classes that can be used to change the way the scene is viewed and how the camera interacts with the scene.

The lens classes ZoomFocusLens, PerspectiveLens, SphericalLens, and OrthogonalLens can be used to provide a traditional view of a scene, a wide-angled view, or a view in which objects don't diminish in size as their distance to the camera increases.

The HoverCamera3D, SpringCam, and TargetCamera3D classes provide a convenient way to track moving 3D objects, and also to view them from a variety of different angles.

We also looked at the various properties of a camera, like fov, zoom, and focus, which can be modified to increase or restrict the view of the scene that a camera has.

In the next chapter, we will take a look at how the mouse can be used to interact with the scene, which also provides an example where it is necessary to use the PerspectiveLens class.

8
Mouse Interactivity

Almost every Flash application uses the mouse as the primary means of receiving input from the user. In Flash you respond to mouse events by registering functions against specified mouse events. Away3D follows this same principle, and indeed even uses the same names for mouse events performed on 3D objects as Flash uses for 2D objects. This means that any developer who has used the mouse in a traditional 2D Flash application will have no trouble doing the same in an Away3D application.

We will also see how the position of the mouse on the screen can be projected into a 3D scene, which gives us the ability to create the kind of 3D drag-and-drop interface that is present in many games.

This chapter will cover the following topics:

- The mouse events supported by Away3D
- The difference between the ROLL_OVER/ROLL_OUT and MOUSE_OVER/MOUSE_OUT events
- Projecting the mouse position into the scene

Away3D mouse events

Away3D has support for a number of mouse events relating to 3D objects. All of the events are defined as constant strings in the Mouse3DEvent class. These constants are listed in the following table:

Mouse3DEvent String Constant	Description
MOUSE_MOVE	Dispatched when the mouse cursor is moved across the surface of a 3D object.
MOUSE_OVER	Dispatched when the mouse cursor moves over a new 3D object or face with a new material.

Mouse Interactivity

`Mouse3DEvent` String Constant	Description
MOUSE_OUT	Dispatched when the mouse is moved off a 3D object or face.
MOUSE_DOWN	Dispatched when a mouse button is pressed while the cursor is over a 3D object.
MOUSE_UP	Dispatched when a mouse button is released while the cursor is over a 3D object.
ROLL_OVER	Dispatched when the mouse cursor moves over a 3D object belonging to a group that was not already under the mouse cursor.
ROLL_OUT	Dispatched when the mouse cursor moves off a 3D object.

These events can be dispatched by any object that extends the `Object3D` class, which includes the scene. The view can also dispatch all of these events except for `Mouse3DEvent.ROLL_OVER` and `Mouse3DEvent.ROLL_OUT`.

If you have ever used the Flash mouse events, the Away3D mouse events should look familiar as they mirror those that are available in Flash. Responding to them is also very similar to the way traditional Flash mouse events are handled.

You register an event handler using the `addEventHandler()` function like so:

```
myObject3D.addEventHanlder(
MouseEvent3D.MOUSE_MOVE,
onMouseMove
);
```

The mouse event handler functions look like the following:

```
function onMouseMove(event:MouseEvent3D):void
{
   // do something here
}
```

The `MouseEvent3D` class (from the `away3d.events` package) that is passed to the mouse event handler functions includes some unique properties that allow you to work with mouse events in 3D. These properties are listed in the following table:

Property	Description
screenX	The horizontal coordinate at which the event occurred in view coordinates.
screenY	The vertical coordinate at which the event occurred in view coordinates.
screenZ	The depth coordinate at which the event occurred in view coordinates.

Property	Description
sceneX	The x coordinate at which the event occurred in global scene coordinates.
sceneY	The y coordinate at which the event occurred in global scene coordinates.
sceneZ	The z coordinate at which the event occurred in global scene coordinates.
view	The view object inside which the event took place.
object	The 3D object inside which the event took place.
elementVO	The 3D element inside which the event took place.
material	The material of the 3D element inside which the event took place.
uv	The UV coordinates inside the 3D element where the event took place.
ctrlKey	Indicates whether the *Control* key is active (true) or inactive (false).
shiftKey	Indicates whether the *Shift* key is active (true) or inactive (false).

The difference between ROLL_OVER / ROLL_OUT and MOUSE_OVER / MOUSE_OUT

Away3D supports the Mouse3DEvent.ROLL_OVER / Mouse3DEvent.ROLL_OUT and Mouse3DEvent.MOUSE_OVER / Mouse3DEvent.MOUSE_OUT pair of events. While both pairs of events are triggered when the mouse is moved over an object and then back off, there is a subtle difference between when they are dispatched.

Take the following application. It creates two overlapping spheres, with each added to a container, and uses the trace() function to notify us when the Mouse3DEvent.ROLL_OVER, Mouse3DEvent.ROLL_OUT, Mouse3DEvent.MOUSE_OVER and Mouse3DEvent.MOUSE_OUT events are dispatched by the container.

```
package
{
  import away3d.containers.ObjectContainer3D;
  import away3d.events.MouseEvent3D;
  import away3d.materials.WireColorMaterial;
  import away3d.materials.WireframeMaterial;
  import away3d.primitives.Sphere;

  public class MouseRollMoveEventDemo extends Away3DTemplate
  {
```

Mouse Interactivity

```
public function MouseRollMoveEventDemo()
{
  super();
}
```

In the `initScene()` function we create two spheres that are separated by 100 units along the X-axis. Since these spheres have a default radius of 100 units they will overlap.

```
protected override function initScene():void
{
  super.initScene();
  var sphere1:Sphere = new Sphere(
    {
      x: 50,
      y: 0,
      z: 500
    }
  );

  var sphere2:Sphere = new Sphere(
    {
      x: -50,
      y: 0,
      z: 500
    }
  );
```

The two sphere 3D objects are added as children of a `ObjectContainer3D` object, which in turn is added as a child of the scene.

```
    var container:ObjectContainer3D =
new ObjectContainer3D(sphere1, sphere2);
    scene.addChild(container);
```

We setup event listeners for three events: `MouseEvent3D.MOUSE_OVER`, `MouseEvent3D.MOUSE_OUT`, and `MouseEvent3D.ROLL_OVER`. Three anonymous functions will be called in response to these events, each using the `trace()` function to display a line of text.

```
    container.addEventListener(
      MouseEvent3D.MOUSE_OVER,
      function(event:MouseEvent3D):void
      {
        trace("Container Mouse Over");
      }
```

```
      );
      container.addEventListener(
        MouseEvent3D.MOUSE_OUT,
        function(event:MouseEvent3D):void
        {
          trace("Container Mouse Out");
        }
      );
      container.addEventListener(
        MouseEvent3D.ROLL_OVER,
        function(event:MouseEvent3D):void
        {
          trace("Container Roll Over");
        }
      );
      container.addEventListener(
        MouseEvent3D.ROLL_OUT,
        function(event:MouseEvent3D):void
        {
          trace("Container Roll Out");
        }
      );
    }
  }
}
```

With the application running, the mouse is moved from the empty space surrounding the two spheres onto the one on the left, like in the following image:

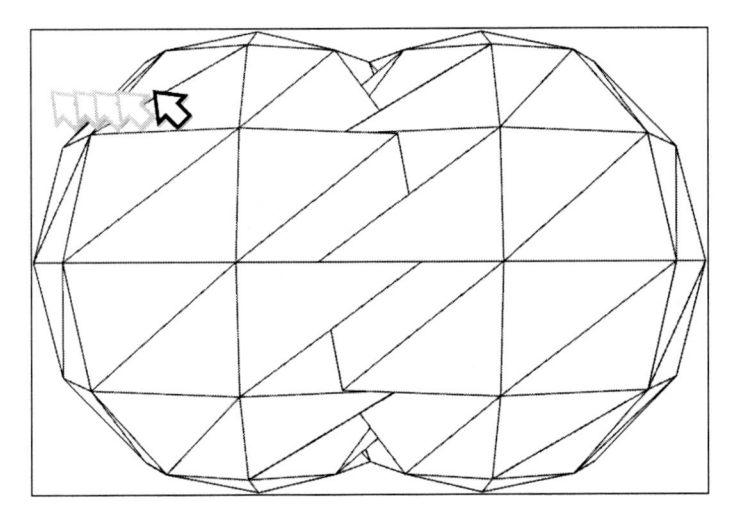

Mouse Interactivity

This produces the following output:

- **Container Mouse Over**
- **Container Roll Over**

Since both the `Mouse3DEvent.ROLL_OVER` and `Mouse3DEvent.MOUSE_OVER` events are triggered when the cursor is moved over a 3D object, you would expect to see this output.

Now the mouse cursor is moved from the left sphere to the right sphere.

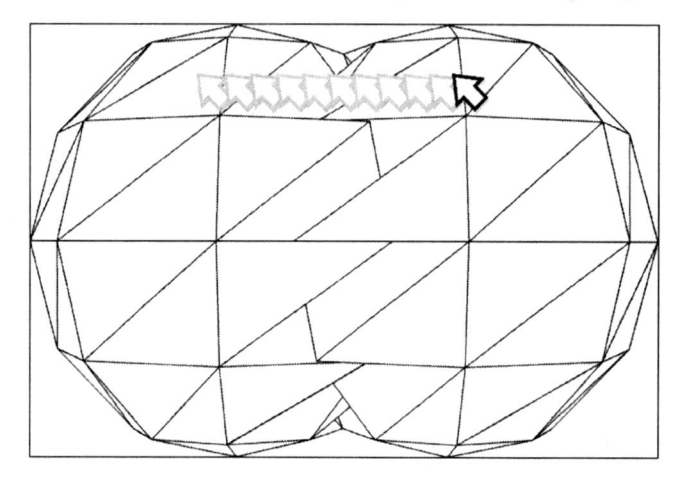

This second movement produces the following output:

- **Container Mouse Out**
- **Container Mouse Over**

When the mouse is moved off the left sphere the `Mouse3DEvent.MOUSE_OUT` event was dispatched. This event then bubbled up to the parent container. Because the two spheres are overlapping, when the mouse cursor moved out of the left sphere, it immediately moved over onto the right sphere. This dispatched the `Mouse3DEvent.MOUSE_OVER` event, which again bubbled up to the parent container.

During this movement the cursor may have moved from one of the containers' child 3D object to the next, but it never passed over empty space in between. In other words, the mouse never moved out of the container. Herein lies the big difference between the two pairs of events. While the `Mouse3DEvent.MOUSE_OVER` and `Mouse3DEvent.MOUSE_OUT` events have bubbled up from the children of the container as the mouse moves over them individually, the `Mouse3DEvent.ROLL_OVER` and `Mouse3DEvent.ROLL_OUT` events will only trigger when the mouse moves over and out of all of the children.

Finally, the mouse moves off the right sphere and back over empty space.

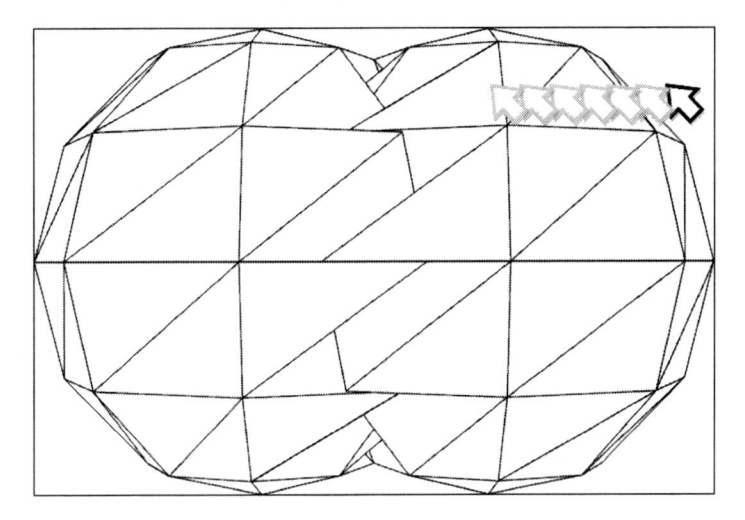

This final movement produces the following output:

Container Mouse Out

Container Roll Out

The Mouse3DEvent.MOUSE_OUT event is triggered because the mouse has moved out of the right sphere. The Mouse3DEvent.ROLL_OUT event is also triggered because the mouse has moved out of all the children contained in the container.

So the Mouse3DEvent.ROLL_OVER event will be dispatched when the mouse moves over any of a container's children, and then the Mouse3DEvent.ROLL_OUT event will be dispatched when the mouse moves off all of the children. On the other hand, the Mouse3DEvent.MOUSE_OVER and Mouse3DEvent.MOUSE_OUT events will be triggered when the mouse moves over and out of each of the individual children.

Projecting the mouse position into the scene

As we have seen, responding to mouse events from 3D objects in Away3D is very easy. We simply specify that a function be called in response to the various events defined in the Mouse3DEvent class, using the same addEventListener() function that is used in regular 2D Flash applications.

Mouse Interactivity

In addition to responding to events in this way, Away3D also allows you to get the position of the mouse cursor within the scene. This position can then be used to construct a ray that extends into the scene, and then intersects a plane. The following image shows how this ray / plane intersection works:

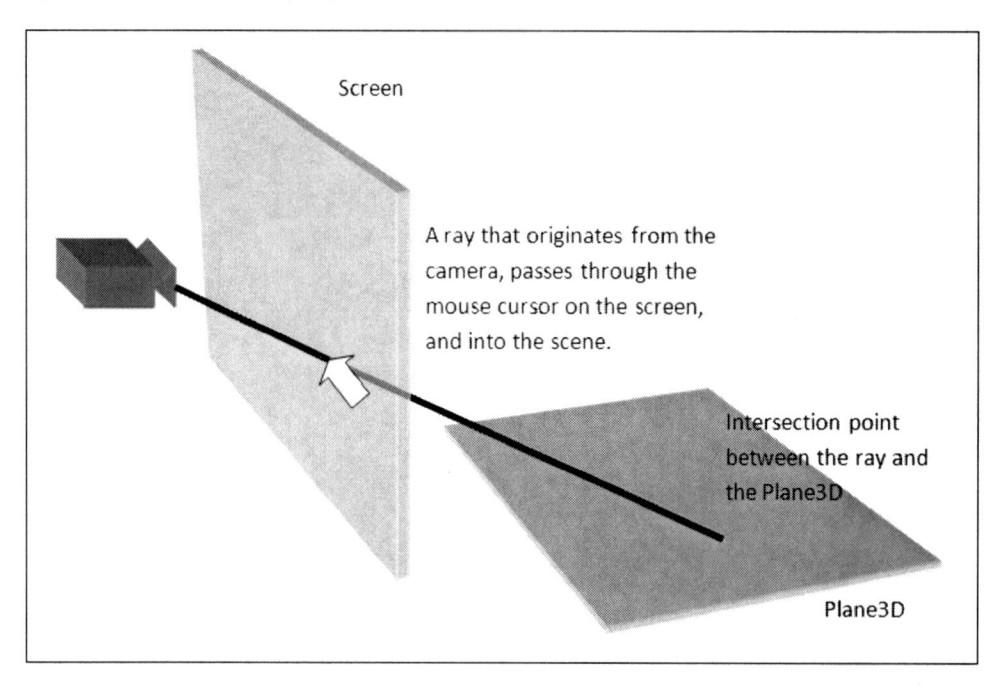

Screen

A ray that originates from the camera, passes through the mouse cursor on the screen, and into the scene.

Intersection point between the ray and the Plane3D

Plane3D

In the following `InteractivityDemo` application we use this ray to find a point on a plane, which is then used to reposition a sphere as if it were being dragged around in the scene. We will also respond to the `MouseEvent3D.MOUSE_OVER`, `MouseEvent3D.MOUSE_OUT`, and `MouseEvent3D.MOUSE_DOWN` events.

```
package
{
    import away3d.cameras.lenses.PerspectiveLens;
    import away3d.core.base.Object3D;
    import away3d.core.geom.Plane3D;
    import away3d.core.render.BasicRenderer;
    import away3d.core.utils.Cast;
    import away3d.events.MouseEvent3D;
    import away3d.materials.BitmapMaterial;
    import away3d.primitives.Plane;
    import away3d.primitives.Sphere;
    import flash.geom.Vector3D;
```

```
import flash.events.Event;
import flash.events.MouseEvent;
import flash.filters.GlowFilter;

public class InteractivityDemo extends Away3DTemplate
{
```

The `checkerboard.jpg` texture is embedded. This will be used for the ground plane 3D object.

```
[Embed(source = "checkerboard.jpg")]
protected var CheckerBoardTexture:Class;
```

The `selectedObject` property will reference the sphere 3D object that is to be moved.

```
protected var selectedObject:Object3D;
```

The `sphere1` and `sphere2` properties will reference the two sphere 3D objects that will be added to the scene.

```
protected var sphere1:Sphere;
protected var sphere2:Sphere;
```

The `groundPlane` property will reference the plane 3D object that will represent the ground.

```
protected var groundPlane:Plane3D;
```

The `throughScreenVector` and `groundPosition` properties will reference the vectors and positions used later in the class while determining the position of the mouse cursor on the ground plane 3D object.

```
protected var throughScreenVector:Vector3D;
protected var groundPosition:Vector3D;

public function InteractivityDemo()
{
  super();
}

protected override function initEngine():void
{
  super.initEngine();
```

Mouse Interactivity

The functions used to project the position of the mouse cursor into the scene and onto a plane only work if the camera is using the perspective lens, which was covered in *Chapter 7, Cameras*. If you use the default lens, which is provided by the `ZoomFocusLens` class, you will find that the mouse cursor's calculated position within the scene doesn't quite line up with the actual position of the mouse cursor.

```
camera.lens = new PerspectiveLens();
```

The scene will contain two spheres, each with `ownCanvas` set to `true`. This is required to apply filters to the individual 3D objects. Away3D has a feature called triangle caching (which is explained in more detail in *Chapter 13, Performance Tips*) which can cause those 3D objects with `ownCanvas` set to `true` to not be sorted correctly as their relative distances to the camera changes. Setting the `forceUpdate` property on the view to `true` disables triangle caching, and fixes these sorting issues.

> Be aware that disabling triangle caching can have a negative effect on performance.

To see the effect that triangle caching can have on the sorting of two or more 3D objects with their `ownCanvas` properties set to `true`, comment out the following line of code. You will notice that one sphere is then always drawn in front of the other, regardless of the position of the spheres within the scene.

```
      view.forceUpdate = true;
}

protected override function initScene():void
{
   super.initScene();
```

The camera is placed 100 units up along the Y-axis, and then tilted down slightly to get a nice view of the scene.

```
      camera.position = new Vector3D(0, 100, 0);
      camera.tilt(20);
```

A bitmap material is created and then assigned to a plane primitive, which is added to the scene to represent the ground.

```
      var planeMaterial:BitmapMaterial =
         new BitmapMaterial(
            Cast.bitmap(CheckerBoardTexture)
         );
      var plane:Plane = new Plane(
         {
```

```
           material: planeMaterial,
           segments: 10,
           width: 1000,
           height: 1000,
           y: -15,
           z: 250
       }
);
```

By setting the `screenZOffset` to `1000`, we are forcing the plane to be drawn beneath the two spheres that will be added next. *Chapter 4, Z-Sorting,* covers the `screenZOffset` property in more detail, as well as a number of additional methods that can be used to adjust the sorting order of 3D objects within the scene.

```
plane.screenZOffset = 1000;
scene.addChild(plane);
```

Now we add two sphere primitives to the scene. The `ownCanvas` init object parameter is set to `true`, which will allow us to use the glow filter to highlight the spheres when they are under the mouse cursor. *Chapter 12, Filters and Postprocessing Effects,* shows you how to use filters in more detail.

```
sphere1 = new Sphere(
    {
       x: -50,
       z: 250,
       radius: 10,
       ownCanvas: true
    }
);
sphere1.ownCanvas = true
scene.addChild(sphere1);

sphere2 = new Sphere(
    {
       x: 50,
       z: 250,
       radius: 10,
       ownCanvas: true
    }
);
scene.addChild(sphere2);
```

Mouse Interactivity

The `Plane3D` class represents an infinite plane. A `Plane3D` *object is not a visible object, and should not to be confused with the* `Plane` *class, which creates a primitive 3D object.*

```
groundPlane = new Plane3D();
```

The `Plane3D` class is initialized from a normal vector (pointing straight up along the Y-axis) and a position that exists anywhere on the plane (the origin, in this case). This creates a plane that lays flat on the X / Z plane.

```
groundPlane.fromNormalAndPoint(
  new Vector3D(0, 1, 0),
  new Vector3D()
);
}

protected override function initListeners():void
{
  super.initListeners();
```

The `onMouseUp()` function is registered against the `MouseEvent.MOUSE_UP` event dispatched by the stage. Note that this is a standard Flash mouse event, and is not dispatched by any Away3D classes.

```
stage.addEventListener(
  MouseEvent.MOUSE_UP,
  onMouseUp
);
```

The three functions `onMouseOver()`, `onMouseOut()`, and `onMouseDown()` are registered with both spheres against the `MouseEvent3D.MOUSE_OVER`, `MouseEvent3D.MOUSE_OUT`, and `MouseEvent3D.MOUSE_DOWN` events. Unlike the event dispatched by the stage above, these three events do represent mouse events within the 3D scene.

```
sphere1.addEventListener(
  MouseEvent3D.MOUSE_OVER,
  onMouseOver
);
sphere1.addEventListener(
  MouseEvent3D.MOUSE_OUT,
  onMouseOut
);
sphere1.addEventListener(
  MouseEvent3D.MOUSE_DOWN,
  onMouseDown
);
```

```
    sphere2.addEventListener(
      MouseEvent3D.MOUSE_OVER,
      onMouseOver
    );
    sphere2.addEventListener(
      MouseEvent3D.MOUSE_OUT,
      onMouseOut
    );
    sphere2.addEventListener(
      MouseEvent3D.MOUSE_DOWN,
      onMouseDown
    );
}
```

> The `addOnMouseMove()`, `addOnMouseDown()`, `addOnMouseUp()`, `addOnMouseOver()`, `addOnMouseOut()`, `addOnRollOver()`, and `addOnRollOut()` functions can be used as a shorthand way of linking functions to events, like:
>
> `sphere1.addOnMouseDown(onMouseDown);`
>
> Likewise, the `removeOnMouseMove()`, `removeOnMouseDown()`, `removeOnMouseUp()`, `removeOnMouseOver()`, `removeOnMouseOut()`, `removeOnRollOver()`, and `removeOnRollOut()` functions can be used to stop a function from responding to an event.

When the mouse has moved over a sphere, we will highlight it by applying the glow filter. This is done by adding an instance of the `GlowFilter` class to an array, which is then assigned to the `filters` property defined by the `Object3D` class. *Chapter 12, Filters and Postprocessing Effects*, goes into these filters in more detail.

```
    protected function onMouseOver(event:MouseEvent3D):void
    {
        event.object.filters = [new GlowFilter()];
    }
```

When the mouse has moved off a sphere the filters are cleared, reverting the sphere back to its default appearance.

```
    protected function onMouseOut(event:MouseEvent3D):void
    {
        event.object.filters = [];
    }
```

Mouse Interactivity

When the mouse is clicked on a sphere it is assigned to the `selectedObject` property, which effectively selects that sphere as the one to be moved.

```
protected function onMouseDown(event:MouseEvent3D):void
{
   selectedObject = event.object;
}
```

When the mouse button is released, the `selectedObject` property is set to `null`, which means that neither of the spheres is selected.

> The spheres are deselected in response to the `MouseEvent.MOUSE_UP` event dispatched by the stage, and not by the `Mouse3DEvent.MOUSE_UP` event dispatched by a 3D object. This was done because releasing the mouse button should deselect the spheres regardless of which Away3D object was under the cursor when the button was released, if any. It is possible that the selected sphere was not under the mouse cursor when the mouse button was released, so if we had registered the `onMouseUp()` function to be called in response to the `MouseEvent3D.MOUSE_UP` event dispatched by the sphere primitives there is a possibility that the sphere would not be deselected as expected.

```
protected function onMouseUp(event:MouseEvent):void
{
   selectedObject = null;
}
```

In the `onEnterFrame()` function we will move the selected sphere to a position under the mouse cursor.

```
protected override function onEnterFrame(event:Event):void
{
   super.onEnterFrame(event);
```

If the `selectedObject` variable is not `null`, indicating that one of the spheres has been selected, we will then move the sphere it references so that it is under the position of the mouse cursor.

```
   if (selectedObject != null)
   {
```

The `Camera3D unproject()` function takes a 2D position on the screen and returns a vector that points from the camera, through the supplied screen position, and out into the scene.

The position of the mouse needs to be supplied relative to the position of the view on the stage. Since the view is situated in the middle of the stage, we have to adjust the mouse coordinates, which are relative to the top-left corner of the stage.

```
throughScreenVector = camera.unproject(
    stage.mouseX - stage.stageWidth / 2,
    stage.mouseY - stage.stageHeight / 2
);
```

> Don't get caught out with the difference between the stage `width`/`height` and `stageWidth`/`stageHeight` properties. The `width` and `height` properties define the area taken up by the children of the stage, while the `stageWidth` and `stageHeight` properties define the actual dimensions of the stage itself. Although it makes little difference when the children of the stage (the `View3D` object in our case) take up all the available space on the stage, it is worth knowing the difference between the two sets of measurements.

To turn this direction vector into a position within the scene we add to it the position of the camera.

```
throughScreenVector =
    throughScreenVector.add(camera.position);
```

The `Plane3D` `getIntersectionLineNumbers()` function takes two points within the scene, and returns the point on the plane where the line defined by these two points intersects it. The position of the camera, and the position of the camera plus the vector of the mouse cursor coordinates projected out into the scene are supplied as the two points to define the line.

```
groundPosition =
    groundPlane.getIntersectionLineNumbers(
        camera.position,
        throughScreenVector
    );
```

The selected sphere is then moved to the intersection point.

```
            selectedObject.position = groundPosition;
        }
      }
    }
}
```

When the application is run, you will see that the sphere under the mouse cursor is highlighted using the glow filter. You can then click and drag the sphere around within the scene. Although a mouse can only be moved in two dimensions, by positioning the spheres on a plane we can provide an intuitive way to move the spheres within a 3D scene.

Summary

Away3D allows you to respond to mouse events on 3D objects using a number of familiar events like MOUSE_UP, MOUSE_DOWN, MOUSE_OVER, MOUSE_OUT, ROLL_OVER, and ROLL_OUT. Functions can be registered to be called in response to these events using the standard addEventListener() function, just as you would do when responding to mouse input in a traditional 2D Flash application, or using one of the shorthand functions that are provided by the Object3D class.

A sample application was presented that demonstrated the subtle distinction between the MOUSE_OVER / MOUSE_OUT and ROLL_OVER / ROLL_OUT events.

Finally, we created an application that demonstrated how to listen for and respond to a number of mouse events. The application also determined the position of the mouse cursor on a plane within the 3D scene, which allowed us to drag-and-drop 3D objects using the mouse.

In the next chapter, we will look at the sprite classes that are available in Away3D, which can be used to create some interesting effects that are not possible with more complex 3D objects.

9
Special Effects with Sprites

In Flash programming, a sprite is usually a graphical object that is added to the stage. All the applications that have been presented in this book have made use of the `Away3DTemplate` class from *Chapter 1, Building Your First Away3D Application*, which extends the Flash `Sprite` class.

Away3D also includes a number of sprite classes. Despite the similar names, the Away3D sprite objects are added to a `Mesh` object and not the Flash stage. Away3D sprites are used to display a texture on a rectangle that is oriented so it always faces the camera.

The three Away3D sprite classes that will be covered in this chapter are:

- `Sprite3D`, which displays a material on a rectangle that is always oriented to face the camera
- `DirectionalSprite`, which displays one of a selection of materials depending on the angle at which it is being viewed
- `DepthOfFieldSprite`, which displays a depth of field effect

Actually, the `Sprite3D` class has already been covered in *Chapter 2, Creating and Displaying Primitives*, but in this chapter we will look at a more practical implementation of the class.

Because they are fairly simple objects, many sprites can be added to the scene while still maintaining a reasonable frame rate. This allows large numbers of sprites to be used to simulate particle effects like smoke or explosions. We will look at how the Stardust particle system library, written by Allen Chou and available from http://code.google.com/p/stardust-particle-engine, can be integrated with Away3D to create 3D particle effects.

Special Effects with Sprites

Using the Sprite3D class

The `Sprite3D` class is the base for all the sprite classes included in Away3D. We saw a basic example of how it can be used in *Chapter 2, Creating and Displaying Primitives*. In the `Sprite3DDemo` class, we will look at a more practical example that uses the `Sprite3D` class to create a scene of rising balloons.

```
package
{
  import away3d.core.base.Mesh;
  import away3d.core.base.Vertex;
  import away3d.core.utils.Cast;
  import away3d.materials.BitmapMaterial;
  import away3d.sprites.Sprite3D;
  import flash.geom.Vector3D;

  import flash.events.Event;
  import flash.utils.getTimer;

  [SWF(backgroundColor=0xFFFFFF)]
  public class Sprite3DDemo extends Away3DTemplate
  {
```

Each balloon will be represented by one of the three textures. Here we embed a blue, a green, and an orange image.

```
    [Embed(source = "blueballoon.png")]
    protected var BlueBalloon:Class;
    [Embed(source = "greenballoon.png")]
    protected var GreenBalloon:Class;
    [Embed(source = "orangeballoon.png")]
    protected var OrangeBalloon:Class;
```

Each `Sprite3D` object will be added to a collection called `balloons`.

```
    protected var balloons:Vector.<Sprite3D> =
  new Vector.<Sprite3D>();
```

The NUMBER_OF_BALLOONS constant defines how many balloons will be added to the scene.

```
    protected static const NUMBER_OF_BALLOONS:int = 1000;

    public function Sprite3DDemo()
    {
      super();
```

```
        }
        protected override function initScene():void
        {
          super.initScene();
```

The position of the camera is set to the origin of the scene.

```
        this.camera.position = new Vector3D();
```

The balloonsTextures collection is filled with three BitmapMaterial objects, one for each of the three embedded textures.

```
        var ballonTextures:Array =
          [
            new BitmapMaterial(
              Cast.bitmap(BlueBalloon),
              {smooth: true}
            ),
            new BitmapMaterial(
              Cast.bitmap(GreenBalloon),
              {smooth: true}
            ),
            new BitmapMaterial(
              Cast.bitmap(OrangeBalloon),
              {smooth: true}
            )
          ];
```

As we saw in *Chapter 2, Creating and Displaying Primitives*, Sprite3D objects need to be added to a Mesh object before they are visible within the scene. Here we create a new Mesh object and add it to the scene.

```
        var mesh:Mesh = new Mesh();
        scene.addChild(mesh);
```

In this for loop, we create the Sprite3D objects that represent the balloons.

```
        var sprite:Sprite3D;
        for (var i:int = 0; i < NUMBER_OF_BALLOONS; ++i)
        {
```

Each Sprite3D object is created using a randomly selected material.

```
          sprite = new Sprite3D(
            ballonTextures[Math.round(Math.random() *
            (ballonTextures.length - 1))]
          );
```

Special Effects with Sprites

The `Sprite3D` object is then randomly positioned in a box that is 1,000 x 1,000 x 2,000 units in size.

```
sprite.x = Math.random() * 1000 - 500;
sprite.y = Math.random() * 1000 - 500;
sprite.z = Math.random() * 2000;
balloons.push(sprite);
```

Finally, to make the `Sprite3D` object visible, we add it to the parent `Mesh` object.

```
      mesh.addSprite(sprite);
   }
}

   protected override function onEnterFrame(event:Event):void
   {
      super.onEnterFrame(event);
```

Every frame we loop through the `Sprite3D` objects and modify their position so they appear to be floating up into space.

```
      for (var i:int = 0; i < NUMBER_OF_BALLOONS; ++i)
      {
```

The position of the `Sprite3D` objects along their X-axis is mapped to a sine wave. This gives them the appearance of swaying gently in the breeze.

```
         balloons[i].x += Math.sin(getTimer() / 1000 + i);
```

The `Sprite3D` objects also rise along the Y-axis. When they reach the top of the imaginary box that contains them, they are dropped down to the bottom of the scene.

```
         if (balloons[i].y >= 500)
            balloons[i].y = -500;
         else
            balloons[i].y += 5;
      }
   }
}
```

When the application is run, you will see an endless sea of balloons rising up into the sky. This simple example shows you the power of sprites. If we were to use a thousand sphere 3D objects to represent the balloons, the application would most likely run at only a few frames per second, but with Sprite3D objects we can create an application that runs quickly and smoothly.

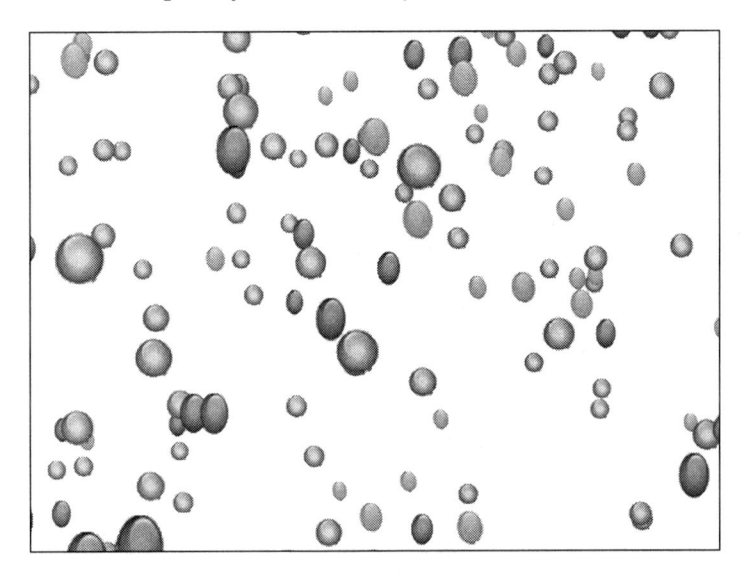

Using the DirectionalSprite class

The DirectionalSprite class provides a way to display one of a selection of materials depending on the relative position of the camera to the sprite. By providing a number of snapshots of a complex 3D object over a range of angles, it is possible to fake the look of a complex 3D object using much less processing power than it would take to render the actual 3D object in real time. This process was popular with a number of older games like Wolfenstein 3D and Doom.

Before we can implement the DirectionalSprite class, we first need a number of images taken or drawn of an object at various angles.

Special Effects with Sprites

Here is a shot taken of a 3D model. In this image, the camera is lying on the positive end of the Z-axis looking back at the 3D object, which is situated at the origin. So the unit vector (a vector with a length of 1 unit) pointing from the 3D object back to the camera is (0, 0, 1). This vector is important, and will be used later on.

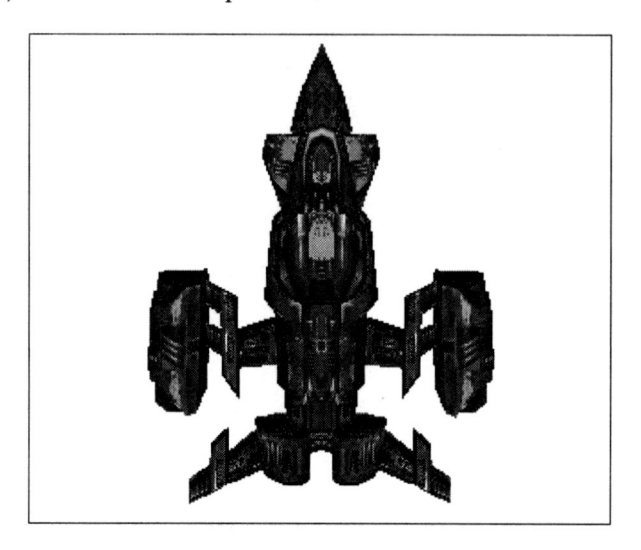

Here is a shot taken from the side of the 3D model. In this image, the camera is lying on the positive end of the X-axis looking at the 3D object at the origin. The unit vector from the 3D object back to the camera for this shot is (1, 0, 0).

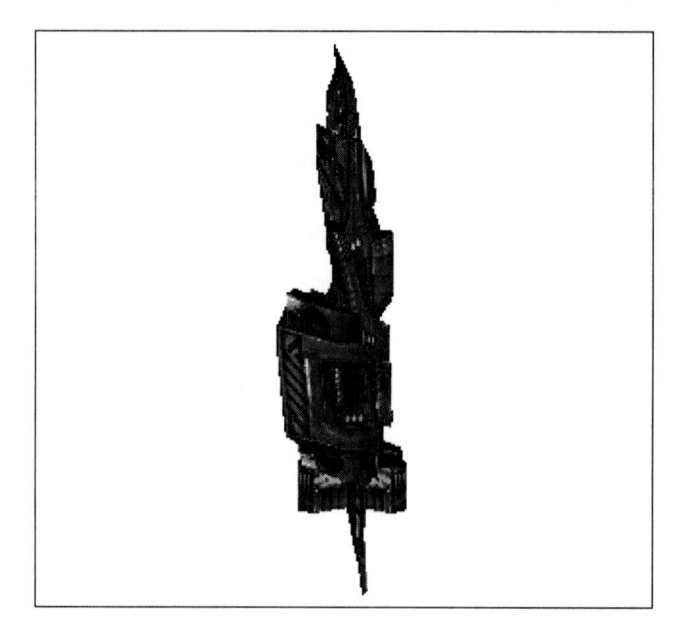

Here are two more shots of the 3D object. They are taken from the opposite sides to the two first shots, so the unit vector from the 3D object back to the camera for these shots is (0, 0, -1) and (0, -1, 0) respectively.

Now that we have some images of the 3D object from different angles, let's create an application called `SimpleDirectionalSpriteDemo` that displays them using a `DirectionalSprite` object.

```
package
{
   import away3d.core.base.Mesh;
   import away3d.core.base.Vertex;
   import away3d.core.utils.Cast;
   import away3d.core.utils.Init;
   import away3d.materials.BitmapMaterial;
   import away3d.sprites.DirectionalSprite;
   import flash.geom.Vector3D;

   import flash.events.Event;

   public class SimpleDirectionalSpriteDemo extends Away3DTemplate
   {
```

[247]

Special Effects with Sprites

The four shots of the 3D object are embedded.

```
[Embed(source = "front.png")]
protected var FrontImage:Class;
[Embed(source = "right.png")]
protected var RightImage:Class;
[Embed(source = "back.png")]
protected var BackImage:Class;
[Embed(source = "left.png")]
protected var LeftImage:Class;

protected var sprite:DirectionalSprite;
protected var parentMesh:Mesh;

public function SimpleDirectionalSpriteDemo()
{
  super();
}

protected override function initScene():void
{
  super.initScene();
```

Here we create a new instance of the `DirectionalSprite` class.

```
sprite = new DirectionalSprite();
```

The `DirectionalSprite` object will display the four images shown previously. Each of these images is added via the `addDirectionalMaterial()` function.

The first parameter defines the direction from the `DirectionalSprite` object to the camera from which the image will be viewed. This is the same direction that was described against the images shown above.

The second parameter is the material that will be displayed. Here, we use a `BitmapMaterial` object that displays one of the embedded images.

```
sprite.addDirectionalMaterial(
  new Vertex(0, 0, 1),
  new BitmapMaterial(
    Cast.bitmap(FrontImage),
    { smooth: true }
  )
);
sprite.addDirectionalMaterial(
  new Vertex(1, 0, 0),
```

```
      new BitmapMaterial(
        Cast.bitmap(RightImage),
        { smooth: true }
      )
    );
    sprite.addDirectionalMaterial(
      new Vertex(0, 0, -1),
      new BitmapMaterial(
        Cast.bitmap(BackImage),
        { smooth: true }
      )
    );
    sprite.addDirectionalMaterial(
      new Vertex( -1, 0, 0),
      new BitmapMaterial(
        Cast.bitmap(LeftImage),
        { smooth: true }
      )
    );
```

To display the DirectionalSprite object, we need to add it to a Mesh object, which we create here.

```
    parentMesh = new Mesh();
```

The DirectionalSprite object is then added to the Mesh object.

```
    parentMesh.addSprite(sprite);
```

Finally, the Mesh object is added to the scene.

```
    scene.addChild(parentMesh);
}
```

In the onEnterFrame() function, we rotate the DirectionalSprite object around its Y-axis, just like we could rotate any other 3D object. It is important to note that rotating the DirectionalSprite object in this way does not actually change its orientation within the scene: all Away3D sprites orient themselves to face the camera at all times. But this rotation does change the material that is displayed by the DirectionalSprite object.

Special Effects with Sprites

To begin with, the `rotationY` property will be 0. This means that the local Z-axis of the `DirectionalSprite` object is pointing down towards the positive end of the global Z-axis. Remember that the `DirectionalSprite` object has been placed in front of the camera. This means that initially the camera is viewing the `DirectionalSprite` object from behind. Thus, the unit vector pointing from the 3D object to the camera is (0, 0, -1).

Looking back to the materials we assigned via the `addDirectionalMaterial()` function, we can see that the image represented by the `BackImage` class is the one that most closely matches the relative position of the camera. This means that when the application is first run, the `DirectionalSprite` object will display the texture showing the 3D object from the back.

Increasing the `rotationY` property has the effect of turning the `DirectionalSprite` object to the right. When the rotation property approaches 90 degrees, the `DirectionalSprite` object will display the `RightImage` texture because the relative angle between the camera and the `DirectionalSprite` object will be smallest when compared with the angle defined for the `RightImage` texture.

As the `rotationY` property increases even more, the `DirectionalSprite` object will display the `FrontImage` and `LeftImage` textures, before going back to display the `BackImage` texture.

```
protected override function onEnterFrame(event:Event):void
{
   super.onEnterFrame(event);
   parentMesh.rotationY += 5;
}
   }
}
```

While this application only shows four images, you can use many more images to achieve smoother transition between angles. The `DirectionalSpriteDemo` application available on the Packt website uses 72 images to show the 3D object from angles 5 degrees apart. This produces quite a smooth appearance as the `DirectionalSprite` object is rotated, and does so at a high frame rate. However, while the `DirectionalSprite` class can use many individual images to display highly detailed 3D objects while maintaining a high frame rate, quite often the memory required by the individual images is much greater than if you were to add a 3D object to the scene directly.

Chapter 9

Using the DepthOfFieldSprite class

In photography, the **depth of field** refers to the area in front of the camera that appears sharp and in focus. This effect is quite often used to emphasize a portion of a scene, while de-emphasizing the foreground and background.

When rendering a scene in Away3D, there is no depth of field; the entire scene is in perfect focus. However, the effect can be approximated by using the `DepthOfFieldSprite` class, which will precalculate a number of increasingly blurry images from the material that is supplied to the `DepthOfFieldSprite` constructor and store them in a shared cache. One of these images will then be displayed by the sprite at runtime depending on the distance of the `DepthOfFieldSprite` object to the camera.

```
package
{
   import away3d.containers.ObjectContainer3D;
   import away3d.core.base.Mesh;
   import away3d.core.utils.Cast;
   import away3d.core.utils.DofCache;
   import away3d.materials.BitmapMaterial;
   import away3d.sprites.DepthOfFieldSprite;

   import flash.display.BitmapData;
   import flash.events.Event;

   public class DepthOfFieldSpriteDemo extends Away3DTemplate
   {
```

We embed an image file, which will be used as the base texture for the `DepthOfFieldSprite` objects.

```
      [Embed(source="blackdot.png")]
   protected var BlackDot:Class;
```

The container `Mesh` into which we will be adding the `DepthOfFieldSprite` objects is referenced by the `container` property.

```
      protected var container:Mesh;

      public function DepthOfFieldSpriteDemo ()
      {
        super();
      }
```

Special Effects with Sprites

The `DofCache` class includes a number of properties that define the appearance of the `DepthOfFieldSprite` class. These have been defined in the `initEngine()` function.

```
protected override function initEngine():void
{
  super.initEngine();
```

The `aperture` property is used to approximate the effect of a camera's aperture. Larger values for the `aperture` property increase the depth of field, meaning that `DepthOfFieldSprite` objects remain relatively sharp over a large area in front of the camera. Smaller values will lead to `DepthOfFieldSprite` objects appearing sharp within a smaller area.

```
DofCache.aperture = 50;
```

The `doflevels` property defines how many discreet levels of blurriness will be precalculated and cached for a given bitmap image. One of these cached images will then be displayed by a `DepthOfFieldSprite` object at runtime, depending on its position relative to the camera. Larger values for the `doflevels` property result in a smoother transition from one cached image to the next. However, this increased visual quality requires more memory to accommodate the additional cached images and takes more time while the images are precalculated.

```
DofCache.doflevels = 32;
```

The `maxblur` property defines the maximum blurriness to apply to a `DepthOfFieldSprite` object. Larger values for the `maxblur` property will result in more pronounced distinction between those `DepthOfFieldSprite` objects that are in the depth of field and those that are not.

```
DofCache.maxblur = 50;
```

The `focus` property defines the distance in front of the camera where `DepthOfFieldSprite` objects are considered to be in focus.

```
DofCache.focus = 2000;
```

Setting the `usedof` property to `true` will allow `DepthOfFieldSprite` objects to display the depth of field effect. Otherwise, they would behave like a regular `Sprite3D` object.

```
DofCache.usedof = true;
}
```

> Each of the properties defined in the `DofCache` class, with the exception of `usedof`, has an equivalent property in the `Camera3D` class. The `enableDof()` function from the `Camera3D` class copies these properties from the `Camera3D` class to the `DofCache` class, and sets the `usedof` property to `true`.
>
> The reason why we have set the values directly on the `DofCache` class, instead of using those in the `Camera3D` class, is because the camera's focus will quite often be different to the value used to calculate the depth of field effect. If you remember from *Chapter 7, Cameras*, setting the camera's focus to 2,000 would decrease the camera's field of view, which would have the undesired effect of providing a very narrow view of the scene.
>
> To get the effect we are after, the values that affect the depth of field effect are set directly on the `DofCache` class, and the camera is left alone.

In the `initScene()` function, we create a number of `DepthOfFieldSprite` objects and add them to the scene.

```
protected override function initScene():void
{
    super.initScene();
```

Here we define a reference to a `BitmapMaterial` object that will be supplied to the `DepthOfFieldSprite` constructor.

> It would be possible to create the `DepthOfFieldSprite` objects with their own reference to a `BitmapMaterial` object with the following code:
>
> ```
> var sprite: DepthOfFieldSprite =
>     new DepthOfFieldSprite(
>     new BitmapMaterial(Cast.bitmap(BlackDot))
>     )
>     );
> ```
>
> However, doing so increases the amount of time it takes to initialize the application. Supplying a common material object to the `DepthOfFieldSprite` constructor avoids this issue.

```
var blackDotBitmap:BitmapMaterial =
    new BitmapMaterial(Cast.bitmap(BlackDot));
```

Special Effects with Sprites

The container `Mesh` that will hold the `DepthOfFieldSprite` objects is created, positioned, and added to the scene.

```
container = new Mesh({z: 1000});
scene.addChild(container);
```

Now we create the `DepthOfFieldSprite` objects, and randomly place them in a 1,000 x 1,000 x 1,000 unit area. Because the `DepthOfFieldSprite` objects are children of the `Mesh` object created above, their global range along the Z-axis will be from 500 to 1,500, while their ranges on the X and Y axes will both be from -500 to 500.

```
var sprite:DepthOfFieldSprite;
for (var i:int = 0; i < 250; ++i)
{
   sprite = new DepthOfFieldSprite(blackDotBitmap);
   sprite.x = Math.random() * 1000 - 500;
   sprite.y = Math.random() * 1000 - 500;
   sprite.z = Math.random() * 1000 - 500

   container.addSprite(sprite);
}
```

In the `onEnterFrame()` function, the container is rotated around the Y-axis. This, in turn, rotates the children `DepthOfFieldSprite` objects, modifying their distance to the camera, and thus showing off the depth of field effect.

```
protected override function onEnterFrame(event:Event):void
{
   super.onEnterFrame(event);
   container.rotationY += 1;
}
   }
}
```

As you can see from the following screenshot, those `DepthOfFieldSprite` objects that lay within the depth of field are drawn as sharp black dots. As the `DepthOfFieldSprite` objects move progressively further outside the depth of field, they become increasingly blurred.

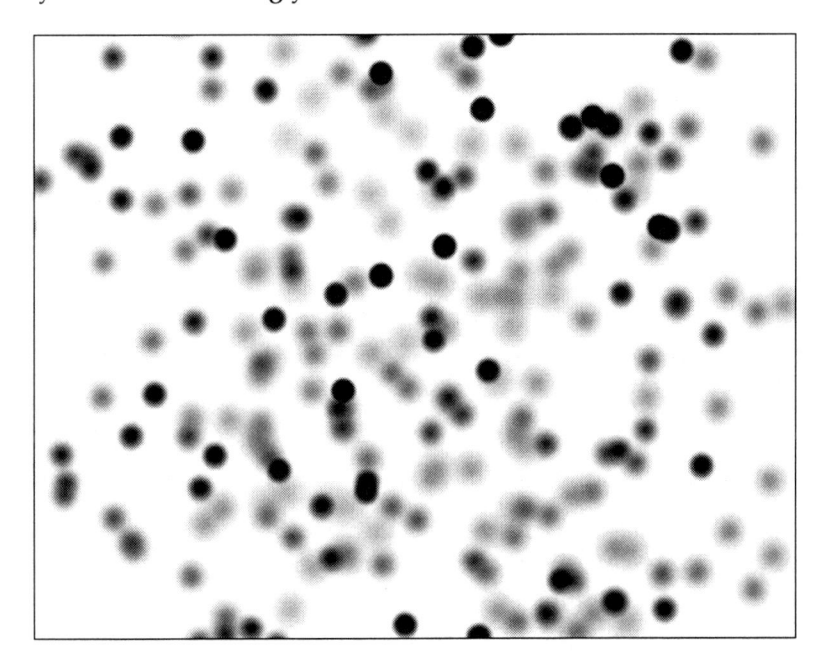

Using a particle system

In the preceding examples, we have manually created and transformed the sprite objects. In the `Sprite3D` demo, we created an effect that looked like a field of rising balloons, and in the `DepthOfFieldSpriteDemo` demo we created an effect that looked like a collection of particles suspended in a clear, rotating liquid. We could create an almost endless variety of effects, like smoke, fire, water, firework, in much the same way, but defining the properties of each of these effects individually every time would be time consuming. This is where a **particle system** comes in handy. A particle system provides a collection of common classes that allow you to quickly build up effects using particles (or sprites, as is the case with Away3D).

Special Effects with Sprites

> Generally speaking, the term particle and sprite can be used interchangeably. Technically, in the context of Away3D's integration with Stardust, a sprite is an Away3D sprite object, while a particle is an object managed by Stardust that is used to display a sprite.

Away3D does not include a particle system, but there are a number of particle system libraries available that can be integrated with Away3D. Flint, which can be downloaded from `http://flintparticles.org/`, is a particle system that natively supports Away3D. Flint includes a number of demos that show how it can be used with Away3D.

Stardust, which can be downloaded from `http://code.google.com/p/stardust-particle-engine/`, is another particle system with support for Flash 3D engines. At the time of writing, Stardust version 1.2.163 does not have any native support for Away3D, but it is fairly easy to integrate the two libraries.

The following code uses Stardust version 1.2.163, which relies on the CJsignals library that can be downloaded from `http://code.google.com/p/cjsignals/`.

We need to create two classes to integrate Stardust and Away3D. The first is an initializer class. The purpose of this class is to provide a way to construct new Away3D sprite objects by calling the constructor of an Away3D sprite class with some specified arguments. In essence, this initializer class provides a flexible mechanism by which new sprite objects can be created at runtime.

Creating the Away3D Stardust initializer

We will create this initializer class in the `stardust.initializers` package, which is in keeping with the format used by the Stardust library itself.

```
package stardust.initializers
{
   import away3d.sprites.Sprite3D;

   import idv.cjcat.stardust.common.particles.Particle;
   import idv.cjcat.stardust.common.utils.construct;
   import idv.cjcat.stardust.threeD.initializers.Initializer3D;
```

We will call this class `Away3DParticle`, to indicate that it initializes an Away3D sprite to be attached to a Stardust particle. We extend the Stardust `Initializer3D` class, which will allow this class to initialize a 3D Stardust particle.

```
   public class Away3DParticle extends Initializer3D
   {
```

The `_constructorParams` collection will hold the values that will be passed to the `Sprite3D` constructor.

```
private var _constructorParams:Array;
```

The constructor takes an `Array` and assigns it to the `_constructorParams` property.

```
public function Away3DParticle(constructorParams:Array = null)
{
   this.constructorParams = constructorParams;
}
```

A pair of `get()` and `set()` functions are defined to allow the constructor parameters to be retrieved and set after the `Away3DParticle` object has been created.

```
public function get constructorParams():Array { return _constructorParams; }
public function set constructorParams(value:Array):void
{
   if (!value) value = [];
   _constructorParams = value;
}
```

The `initialize()` function is called by the Stardust library to attach a new Away3D sprite to a particle.

```
override public function initialize(particle:Particle):void
{
```

The `construct()` function, provided by the Stardust library, provides a way to pass an arbitrary number of parameters to the constructor of a given class, which is the `Sprite3D` class in this case. The resulting `Sprite3D` object is then assigned to the Stardust particle object's `target` property. This allows us to retrieve a reference to the `Sprite3D` object from the Stardust particle object later on.

```
      particle.target = construct(Sprite3D, _constructorParams);
   }
  }
 }
```

Creating the Away3D Stardust particle renderer

The second class we need to create is the particle renderer. This class provides a way for the Stardust library to add and remove sprites from the scene, as well as transfer the properties of the Stardust particles (like position, rotation, and scale) to the Away3D sprites that will be visually representing them.

We will create this particle renderer class in the `stardust.renderers` package. Again, this is in keeping with the format used by the Stardust library itself.

```
package stardust.renderers
{
   import away3d.core.base.Mesh;
   import away3d.sprites.Sprite3D;
   import idv.cjcat.stardust.common.emitters.Emitter;
   import idv.cjcat.stardust.common.particles.ParticleCollection;

   import idv.cjcat.stardust.common.events.EmitterEvent;
   import idv.cjcat.stardust.common.particles.ParticleIterator;
   import idv.cjcat.stardust.common.renderers.Renderer;
   import idv.cjcat.stardust.common.xml.XMLBuilder;
   import idv.cjcat.stardust.threeD.particles.Particle3D;
```

The class is called `Away3DParticleRenderer`, to indicate that it is used to render Away3D particles. We extend the Stardust `Renderer` class, which provides the functions used by the Stardust library to manage its particles.

```
   public class Away3DParticleRenderer extends Renderer
   {
```

The `particleContainer` property will maintain a reference to the parent `Mesh` object that will hold our `Sprite3D` objects.

```
      private var particleContainer:Mesh;
```

The constructor takes a `Mesh` parameter, and assigns it to the `particleContainer` property.

```
      public function Away3DParticleRenderer(particleContainer:Mesh = null)
      {
        super();
        this.particleContainer = particleContainer;
      }
```

The `render()` function is used to transfer the properties of the Stardust particles to the Away3D sprites that represent them.

```
      protected override function render(emitter:Emitter, particles:
    ParticleCollection, time:Number):void
        {
```

Here we loop over all the particles provided by the `particles` parameter.

```
            var particle:Particle3D;
            var iter:ParticleIterator =
              particles.particles.getIterator();
            while (particle = Particle3D(iter.particle))
            {
```

If you look back at the `Away3DParticle initialize()` function, you will see that we assigned the `Sprite3D` objects to the `target` property of the Stardust particle object. Here we do the reverse, using the `target` property to get access to the `Sprite3D` object.

```
                var p:Sprite3D = particle.target as Sprite3D;
```

The Stardust `Particle3D` class maintains its own set of properties, which are used to define the appearance of the particle. However, the Stardust particle itself is not visible; it simply holds the properties that define how the particle should appear. It is the job of the particle renderer class to map the properties of the Stardust particle to the object that is being used to represent the particle on the screen. In our case, the object that is being used to represent the particle on the screen is a `Sprite3D`. Here we take the position and scale of the Stardust particle and assign those values to the `Sprite3D` object.

> The `Particle3D` class includes some additional properties, like color, mask, and alpha, that we have not applied to the `Sprite3D` object.

```
                p.x = particle.x;
                p.y = particle.y;
                p.z = particle.z;
                p.scaling = particle.scale;


                iter.next();
            }
        }
```

Special Effects with Sprites

> It would also be possible to map the rotation of the Stardust particle like so:
>
> p.rotation = particle.rotationZ;
>
> However, there is a bug in Away3D 3.6 that causes sprites to be rotated incorrectly. This issue has been fixed in the version of Away3D available from the SVN repository.

The particlesAdded() function is used to add the Sprite3D objects attached to Stardust particles to the parent Mesh object, referenced by the particleContainer property.

```
protected override function particlesAdded(emitter:Emitter,
particles:ParticleCollection):void
{
  if (!particleContainer) return;
  var particle:Particle3D;
  var iter:ParticleIterator =
    particles.particles.getIterator();
  while (particle = Particle3D(iter.particle))
  {
    var p:Sprite3D = particle.target as Sprite3D;
    particleContainer.addSprite(p);
    iter.next();
  }
}
```

The particlesRemoved() function is used to remove the Sprite3D objects attached to Stardust particles from the parent Mesh object.

```
protected override function particlesRemoved(emitter:Emitter,
particles:ParticleCollection):void
{
  if (!particleContainer) return;
  var particle:Particle3D;
  var iter:ParticleIterator =
    particles.particles.getIterator();
  while (particle = Particle3D(iter.particle))
  {
    var p:Sprite3D = particle.target as Sprite3D;
    particleContainer.removeSprite(p);
    iter.next();
  }
}
```

The `getXMLTagName()` function should return the name of the class. This function is used by the Stardust library to load particle effects from an XML file.

```
    //XML

    public override function getXMLTagName():String
    {
      return "Away3DParticleRenderer";
    }

    //end of XML
  }
}
```

Creating the Stardust emitter

Now that we have created the classes that will allow Away3D to be used with Stardust, we can create a simple emitter. An emitter combines initializers, which define the initial properties of a particle, and actions, which define how a particle will be modified over time. The Stardust library comes with a large selection of initializers and actions, which allow us to create some interesting effects with a minimum of code.

```
    package
    {
      import away3d.core.utils.Cast;
      import away3d.materials.BitmapMaterial;

      import idv.cjcat.stardust.common.actions.Age;
      import idv.cjcat.stardust.common.actions.DeathLife;
      import idv.cjcat.stardust.common.actions.ScaleCurve;
      import idv.cjcat.stardust.common.clocks.SteadyClock;
      import idv.cjcat.stardust.common.initializers.Life;
      import idv.cjcat.stardust.common.math.UniformRandom;
      import idv.cjcat.stardust.threeD.actions.Damping3D;
      import idv.cjcat.stardust.threeD.actions.Move3D;
      import idv.cjcat.stardust.threeD.actions.Spin3D;
      import idv.cjcat.stardust.threeD.emitters.Emitter3D;
      import idv.cjcat.stardust.threeD.fields.UniformField3D;
      import idv.cjcat.stardust.threeD.initializers.Omega3D;
      import idv.cjcat.stardust.threeD.initializers.Position3D;
      import idv.cjcat.stardust.threeD.initializers.Rotation3D;
      import idv.cjcat.stardust.threeD.initializers.Velocity3D;
```

Special Effects with Sprites

```
import idv.cjcat.stardust.threeD.zones.SinglePoint3D;
import idv.cjcat.stardust.threeD.zones.SphereShell;

import stardust.initializers.Away3DParticle;
```

The emitter class, called `StarDustSparksEmitter`, extends the Stardust `Emitter3D` class. This will allow us to define a 3D particle system.

```
public class StarDustSparksEmitter extends Emitter3D
{
```

The Away3D `Sprite3D` objects will display a `BitmapMaterial` that displays the embedded `star.png` image as a texture.

```
[Embed(source="star.png")]
protected var Star:Class;

public function StarDustSparksEmitter()
{
```

The base `Emitter3D` class constructor takes a clock object as a parameter. This clock object defines how many particles will be created per frame. Here we have used the `SteadyClock` class. By passing in `0.3` to the `ticksPerCall` constructor parameter, we have given this emitter a 30 percent chance of creating a new particle every frame.

```
super(new SteadyClock(0.3));
```

Now we define the initial properties of the particles. This is done by passing initializer classes to the emitter using the `addInitializer()` function.

First up, we use the `Away3DParticle` initializer, which we created above, to assign a `Sprite3D` object to each new particle. We have passed in an `Array` that contains a new `BitmapMaterial` object as the first parameter of the `Away3DParticle` constructor. This `BitmapMaterial` object will then be passed to the `Sprite3D` constructor as new `Sprite3D` objects are created by the `Away3DParticle` `initialize()` function. The second object in the `Array` is an init object, which sets the `smooth` init object parameter to `true`. This init object will be passed as the second parameter to the `Sprite3D` constructor.

```
addInitializer(
  new Away3DParticle(
    [
      new BitmapMaterial(Cast.bitmap(Star),
        {smooth: true})
    ]
  )
);
```

The `Life` initializer uses the `UniformRandom` class to set the initial lifespan of each new particle to between 10 and 50 frames.

```
addInitializer(new Life(new UniformRandom(50, 10)));
```

The `Position3D` initializer uses the `SinglePoint3D` class to set the initial position of each new particle to (0, 0, 2500).

```
addInitializer(
    new Position3D(new SinglePoint3D(0, 0, 2500)));
```

The `Velocity3D` initializer uses the `SphereShell` class to define the initial velocity of the new particles. This velocity is defined as a vector pointing from the origin to a random point on a sphere centered on the origin (defined by the first three parameters passed to the `SphereShell` constructor) that is between 30 and 40 units in radius (defined by the last two parameters passed to the `SphereShell` constructor). You can see in the following image how some of these random vectors might be created:

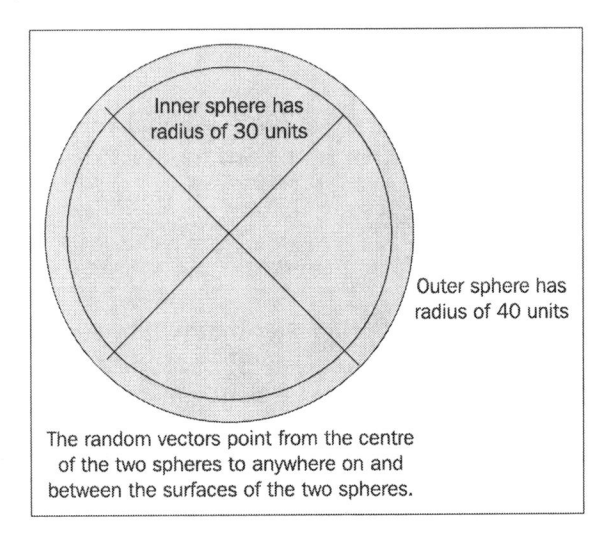

Inner sphere has radius of 30 units

Outer sphere has radius of 40 units

The random vectors point from the centre of the two spheres to anywhere on and between the surfaces of the two spheres.

```
addInitializer(
    new Velocity3D(new SphereShell(0, 0, 0, 30, 40)));
```

Special Effects with Sprites

The `Rotation3D` initializer is used here to set the initial rotation of the new particles to between 0 and 180 degrees around the Z-axis. Because of a bug in Away3D 3.6, the `Sprite3D` objects won't actually be rotated. However, if you use the version of Away3D from the SVN repository, and include the line of code motioned in the tip for the `Away3DParticleRenderer render()` function, you can implement rotations for `Sprite3D` objects.

> Because a `Sprite3D` object is always oriented to face the camera, rotating the particles around the X and Y axes won't have any effect.

```
addInitializer(
  new Rotation3D(
  null,
  null,
  new UniformRandom(0, 180)
  )
);
```

Finally, we use the `Omega3D` initializer to set the rotational velocity of the new particles to between 0 and 5 degrees per frame around the Z-axis.

```
addInitializer(
   new Omega3D(null, null, new UniformRandom(0, 5))
);
```

Now that we have defined the initial properties that will be assigned to new particles, we need to define how the particles will be modified over time. New action classes are added to the emitter using the `addAction()` function.

The `Age` action will decrease the life of each particle by one each frame.

```
addAction(new Age());
```

The `DeathLife` action will remove a particle from the system when its age reaches zero.

```
addAction(new DeathLife());
```

The `Move3D` action will move a particle according to its velocity in three dimensions each frame.

```
addAction(new Move3D());
```

The `Spin3D` action will rotate a particle according to its rotational velocity each frame.

```
addAction(new Spin3D());
```

The `Damping3D` action will reduce the velocity of the particles by the supplied fraction each frame. By supplying 0.05 to the `Damping3D` constructor, we will decrease the velocity of each particle by 5 percent each frame.

```
addAction(new Damping3D(0.05));
```

The `ScaleCurve` action is used to scale the particle from nothing up to its native size, and then back down to nothing. Because we have supplied 0 to the first `ScaleCurve` constructor parameter, the particles will not be scaled up, and instead will be created at their native size. Setting the second parameter to 10 indicates that the particles will scale down to nothing over the last 10 frames of their life.

```
          addAction(new ScaleCurve(0, 10));
        }
      }
    }
```

Putting it all together

With the emitter created, we can now initialize the Away3D engine, the Away3D particle renderer, and the emitter itself. This is done by a class called `StarDustDemo`.

```
package
{
  import away3d.core.base.Mesh;
  import flash.geom.Vector3D;

  import flash.events.Event;

  import idv.cjcat.stardust.threeD.emitters.Emitter3D;

  import stardust.renderers.Away3DParticleRenderer;
```

We create a new class that extends the `Away3DTemplate` class, just as we have done for all the other applications presented in this book so far.

```
  public class StarDustDemo extends Away3DTemplate
  {
```

The emitter will be referenced by the `emitter` property.

```
protected var emitter:Emitter3D;

public function StarDustDemo()
{
   super();
}

protected override function initScene():void
{
   super.initScene();
```

The position of the camera is set to the origin of the scene.

```
this.camera.position = new Vector3D();
```

We need to create a new instance of the emitter class.

```
emitter = new StarDustSparksEmitter();
```

We also need to create a new instance of the Away3D particle renderer class. We pass in the `scene` property to the `Away3DParticleRenderer` constructor. This means that all the new `Sprite3D` objects will be directly added to the scene.

```
var renderer:Away3DParticleRenderer =
   new Away3DParticleRenderer(this.scene);
```

The emitter is then added to the Away3D particle renderer.

```
renderer.addEmitter(emitter);
}

protected override function onEnterFrame(event:Event):void
{
   super.onEnterFrame(event);
```

To update the particle system, we need to call the emitter's `step()` function. This will update the particle effect by one frame.

```
emitter.step();
      }
   }
}
```

Although we had to do some work creating the classes that glue the Stardust library to the Away3D engine, once that was done we could create a reasonably complicated particle effect (including movement, rotation, and scaling) with just a dozen or so lines of code (if you exclude the boilerplate code for the import statements and the class and function declarations). This is why a library like Stardust is so useful.

You can see the final result of the `StarDustDemo` application in the following screenshot:

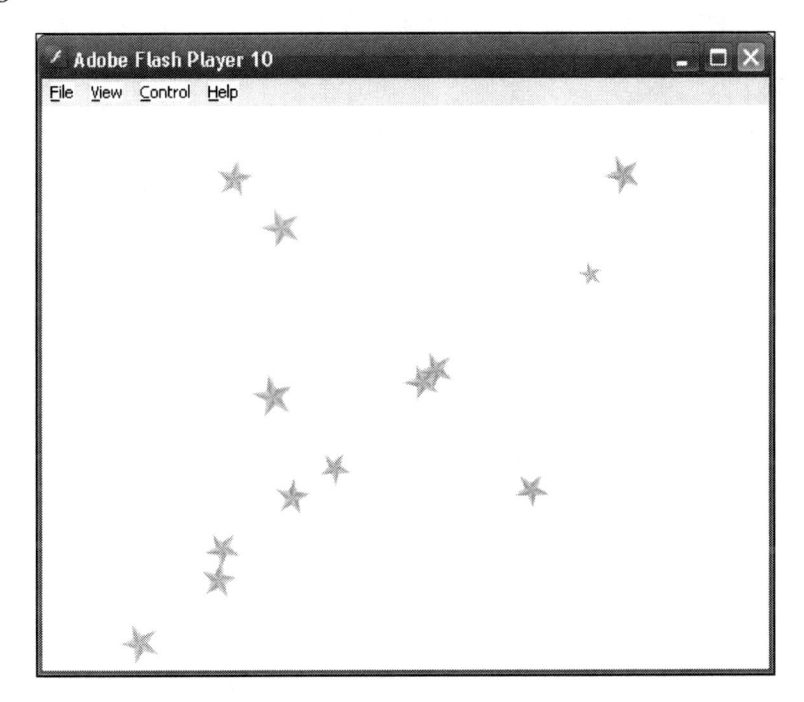

Summary

Away3D includes three sprite classes:

- `Sprite3D`
- `DepthOfFieldSprite`
- `DirectionalSprite`

The `Sprite3D` class is used to display a static image that is oriented to always face the camera. The `DepthOfFieldSprite` class is used to approximate the depth of field effect that is seen in photography. And the `DirectionalSprite` class is used to display one of a number of images depending on the orientation of the sprite in relation to the camera, using a technique that was popular in older games like Doom.

Thanks to their simple geometry, numerous Away3D sprites can be added to the scene at any given time while maintaining a high frame rate. We can take advantage of this to create some interesting visual effects, either by using the various sprite classes on their own, or by using them in conjunction with a particle system like Flint or Stardust. Stardust does not integrate with Away3D natively, but we have seen how to create two classes, `Away3DParticle` and `Away3DParticleRenderer`, that let us display a Stardust particle system using Away3D `Sprite3D` objects.

In the next chapter, we will look at how Away3D can be used to create and display 3D text.

10
Creating 3D Text

Away3D includes a number of ways to programmatically create 3D objects. We saw in *Chapter 2, Creating and Displaying Primitives*, how to create a 3D object from the ground up using the base elements, such as vertices and triangle faces, or by using the primitive 3D object classes.

A relatively recent addition to Away3D is the ability to create a 3D object from a font, which allows us to easily add 3D text into a scene. This ability is provided by an external library called **swfvector**, which is contained in the `wumedia` package. More information about the swfvector library can be found at `http://code.google.com/p/swfvector/`. This library was not developed as part of the Away3D engine, but has been integrated since version 2.4 and 3.4, to enable Away3D to provide a way to create and display text 3D objects within the scene.

Away3D also includes the ability to warp a text 3D object by aligning it to a path made up of both straight and curved sections. This chapter will present a sample application that can warp 3D text, as well as some handy tips on debugging this alignment process.

In this chapter, we will look at:

- Embedding fonts into an application
- Creating a text 3D object
- Applying materials to the 3D text
- Giving the 3D text some depth
- Warping the 3D text along a path

Creating 3D Text

Embedding fonts

Creating a text 3D object in Away3D requires a source SWF file with an embedded font. To accommodate this, we will create a very simple application using the `Fonts` class below. This class embeds a single true-type font called Vera Sans from the `Vera.ttf` file.

When compiled, the resulting SWF file can then be referenced by our Away3D application, allowing the embedded font file to be accessed.

> When embedding fonts using the Flex 4 SDK, you may need to set the embedAsCFF property to `false`, like:
>
> `[Embed(mimeType="application/x-font", source="Vera.ttf", fontName="Vera Sans", embedAsCFF=false)]`
>
> This is due to the new way fonts can be embedded with the latest versions of the Flex SDK. You can find more information on the embedAsCFF property at http://help.adobe.com/en_US/flex/using/WS2db454920e96a9e51e63e3d11c0bf6320a-7fea.html

```
package
{
  import flash.display.Sprite;

  public class Fonts extends Sprite
  {
    [Embed(mimeType="application/x-font", source="Vera.ttf", fontName="Vera Sans")]
    public var VeraSans:Class;
  }
}
```

> The font used here is Bitstream Vera, which can be freely distributed, and can be obtained from http://www.gnome.org/fonts/. However, not all fonts can be freely redistributed, so be mindful of the copyright or license restrictions that may be imposed by a particular font.

Displaying text in the scene

Text 3D objects are represented by the `TextField3D` class, from the `away3d.primitives` package. Creating a text 3D object requires two steps:

1. Extracting the fonts that were embedded inside a separate SWF file.
2. Creating a new `TextField3D` object.

Let's create an application called `FontDemo` that creates a 3D textfield and adds it to the scene.

```
package
{
```

We import the `TextField3D` class, making it available within our application.

```
    import away3d.primitives.TextField3D;
```

The `VectorText` class will be used to extract the fonts from the embedded SWF file.

```
    import wumedia.vector.VectorText;

public class FontDemo extends Away3DTemplate
{
```

The `Fonts.SWF` file was created by compiling the `Fonts` class above. We want to embed this SWF file as raw data, so we specify the MIME type to be `application/octet-stream`.

```
    [Embed(source="Fonts.swf", mimeType="application/octet-stream")]
      protected var Fonts:Class;

    public function FontDemo()
    {
      super();
    }

    protected override function initEngine():void
    {
      super.initEngine();
```

Creating 3D Text

Before any `TextField3D` objects can be created we need to extract the fonts from the embedded SWF file. This is done by calling the static `extractFonts()` function in the `VectorText` class, and passing a new instance of the embedded SWF file. Because we specified the MIME type of the embedded file to be `application/octet-stream`, a new instance of the class is created as a `ByteArray`.

```
        VectorText.extractFont(new Fonts());
      }

      protected override function initScene():void
      {
        super.initScene();
        this.camera.z = 0;
```

Here we create the new instance of the `TextField3D` class. The first parameter is the font name, which corresponds to the font name included in the embedded SWF file. The `TextField3D` constructor also takes an `init` object, whose parameters are listed in the next table.

```
        var text:TextField3D = new TextField3D("Vera Sans",
          {
            text: "Away3D Essentials",
            align: VectorText.CENTER,
            z: 300
          }
        );
        scene.addChild(text);
      }
    }
  }
```

The following table shows you the `init` object parameters accepted by the `TextField3D` constructor.

Parameter	Type	Default Value	Description
size	int	20	The font size in pixels.
leading	int	20	Determines the amount of space between lines in a paragraph.
letterSpacing	int	0	Determines the amount of space between each character.
text	String	""	The text to display.

Parameter	Type	Default Value	Description
width	int	500	The width of the drawing area. If the text is greater than this number then we start wrapping to the next line. To disable wrapping set the textWidth property to Number.POSITIVE_INFINITY.
align	String	"TL" or VectorText.TOP_LEFT	Defines the alignment of the text. The VectorText class defines a number of constants that can be assigned to the align property. These are TOP_LEFT_CENTER, TOP_LEFT, TOP_RIGHT, BOTTOM_LEFT, BOTTOM_LEFT_CENTER, BOTTOM_RIGHT, LEFT, LEFT_CENTER, RIGHT, TOP, BOTTOM, and CENTER.

When the application is run, the scene will contain a single 3D object that has been created to spell out the words "Away3D Essentials" and formatted using the supplied font. At this point, the text 3D object can be transformed and interacted with, just like other 3D object.

3D Text materials

If you remember from *Chapter 2, Creating and Displaying Primitives*, bitmap materials are applied to the surface of a 3D object according to their UV coordinates. The default UV coordinates defined by a TextField3D object generally do not allow bitmap materials to be applied in a useful manner. However, simple colored materials like WireframeMaterial, WireColorMaterial, and ColorMaterial can be applied to a TextField3D object.

Extruding 3D text

By default, a text 3D object has no depth (although it is visible from both sides). One of the extrusion classes (which are covered in more detail in *Chapter 11, Extrusions and Modifiers*) called TextExtrusion can be used to create an additional 3D object that uses the shape of a text 3D object and extends it into a third dimension. When combined, the TextExtrusion and TextField3D objects can be used to create the appearance of a solid block of text. The FontExtrusionDemo class in the following code snippet gives an example of this process:

```
package
{
  import away3d.containers.ObjectContainer3D;
  import away3d.extrusions.TextExtrusion;
  import away3d.primitives.TextField3D;

  import flash.events.Event;

  import wumedia.vector.VectorText;

  public class FontExtrusionDemo extends Away3DTemplate
  {
    [Embed(source="Fonts.swf", mimeType="application/octet-stream")]
    protected var Fonts:Class;
```

The TextField3D 3D object and the extrusion 3D object are both added as children of a ObjectContainer3D object, referenced by the container property.

```
    protected var container:ObjectContainer3D;
```

The text property will reference the TextField3D object used to display the 3D text.

```
    protected var text:TextField3D;
```

The extrusion property will reference the TextExtrusion object used to give the 3D text some depth.

```
    protected var extrusion:TextExtrusion;

    public function FontExtrusionDemo()
    {
      super();
    }

    protected override function initEngine():void
    {
```

Chapter 10

```
      super.initEngine();
      this.camera.z = 0;
      VectorText.extractFont(new Fonts());
    }

    protected override function initScene():void
    {
      super.initScene();

      text = new TextField3D("Vera Sans",
        {
          text: "Away3D Essentials",
          align: VectorText.CENTER
        }
      );
```

The `TextExtrusion` constructor takes a reference to the `TextField3D` object (or any other `Mesh` object). It also accepts an `init` object, which we have used to specify the depth of the 3D text, and to make both sides of the extruded mesh visible.

```
      extrusion = new TextExtrusion(text,
        {
          depth: 10,
          bothsides:true
        }
      );
```

The `ObjectContainer3D` object is created, supplying the `TextField3D` and `TextExtrusion` 3D objects that were created above as children. The initial position of the `ObjectContainer3D` object is set to 300 units down the positive end of the Z-axis.

```
      container = new ObjectContainer3D(text, extrusion,
        {
          z: 300
        }
      );
```

The container is then added as a child of the scene.

```
      scene.addChild(container);
    }

    protected override function onEnterFrame(event:Event):void
    {
      super.onEnterFrame(event);
```

[275]

Creating 3D Text

The container is slowly rotated around its Y-axis by modifying the `rotationY` property in every frame. In previous examples, we have simply incremented the rotation property, without any regard for when the value became larger than 360 degrees. After all, rotating a 3D object by 180 or 540 degrees has the same overall effect. But in this case, we do want to keep the value of the `rotationY` property between 0 and 360 so we can easily test to see if the rotation is within a given range. To do this, we use the mod (%) operator.

```
container.rotationY =
    (container.rotationY + 1) % 360;
```

Z-sorting issues can rise due to the fact that the `TextExtrusion` and `TextField3D` objects are so closely aligned. This issue results in parts of the `TextField3D` or `TextExturude` 3D objects showing through where it is obvious that they should be hidden.

To solve this problem, we can use one of the procedures detailed in *Chapter 4, Z-Sorting*, to force the sorting order of 3D objects. Here we are assigning a positive value to the `TextField3D screenZOffset` property to force it to be drawn behind the `TextExturude` object, when the container has been rotated between 90 and 270 degrees around the Y-axis. When the container is rotated like this, the `TextField3D` object is at the back of the scene. Otherwise, the `TextField3D` is drawn in front by assigning a negative value to the `screenZOffset` property.

```
        if (container.rotationY > 90 &&
            container.rotationY < 270)
          text.screenZOffset = 10;
        else
          text.screenZOffset = -10;
      }
    }
  }
```

The result of the `FontExtrusionDemo` application is shown in the following image:

Warping 3D text

Away3D can not only create text 3D objects, it can also warp them by aligning them to arbitrary paths made up of straight lines or curves. This can be used to create some interesting effects, like wrapping text around another 3D object. The following `TextWarpingDemo` class demonstrates how to align a 3D text object to a wave-like curve, a path made up of two straight lines, and a simple, single curve.

```
package
{
```

The `Path` and `PathCommand` classes are used to define the path that the text will align itself to.

```
    import away3d.core.geom.Path;
    import away3d.core.geom.PathCommand;
    import away3d.materials.ColorMaterial;
```

The `PathAlignModifier` class is responsible for transforming a 3D object to align it to a given path.

```
    import away3d.modifiers.PathAlignModifier;
    import away3d.primitives.TextField3D;
    import flash.geom.Vector3D;
    import flash.events.KeyboardEvent;

    import wumedia.vector.VectorText;

    public class TextWarpingDemo extends Away3DTemplate
    {
      [Embed(source="Fonts.swf", mimeType="application/octet-stream")]
      protected var Fonts:Class;
      protected var text:TextField3D;

      public function TextWarpingDemo()
      {
        super();
      }

      protected override function initEngine():void
      {
        super.initEngine();
        VectorText.extractFont(new Fonts());
      }
```

Creating 3D Text

```
protected override function initScene():void
{
  super.initScene();
  this.camera.z = 0;
  followLine();
}

protected override function initListeners():void
{
  super.initListeners();
  stage.addEventListener(
    KeyboardEvent.KEY_UP,
    onKeyUp
    );
}

protected function onKeyUp(event:KeyboardEvent):void
{
  switch (event.keyCode)
  {
    case 49:  // 1
      followContinuousCurve();
      break;
    case 50: // 2
      followLine();
      break;
    case 51: // 3
      followCurve();
      break;
  }
}
```

The `setupText()` function will remove an existing text 3D object (if one exists) and recreate it each time we align it to a new path when the `followContinuousCurve()`, `followLine()`, and `followCurve()` functions are called.

```
protected function setupText():void
{
  if (text != null)
  {
    scene.removeChild(text);
  }
```

Chapter 10

You will notice that we have added a few extra spaces in the string we want to display as a 3D object. This is simply to allow the text to align nicely around the right angle we will add in the straight line path created in the `followLine()` function.

```
text = new TextField3D("Vera Sans",
  {
    text: "Away3D    Essentials",
    size: 15,
    material: new ColorMaterial(0)
  }
);
scene.addChild(text);
}
```

The next three functions are used to align the 3D text object to various paths. The `followContinuousCurve()` function will create a wave-like path to align the text 3D object.

```
protected function followContinuousCurve():void
{
```

We call the `setupText()` function to create our text 3D object.

```
setupText();
```

Next, we create a new `Path` object. It is this object that will contain the points that define the path that our text 3D object will align itself to.

```
var path:Path = new Path();
```

Here we have used the `continousCurve()` function to define a curve with four points, supplied as an array of `Vector3D` objects. We have defined a curve that starts at (-75, -50, 300), moves up towards (-25, 50, 300), then moves down towards (25, -50, 300), and finally moves towards the last point at (75, 0, 300).

```
path.continuousCurve(
  [
    new Vector3D(-100, -50, 300),
    new Vector3D(-25, 50, 300),
    new Vector3D(25, -50, 300),
    new Vector3D(100, 0, 300)
  ]
);
```

Creating 3D Text

This creates a path that looks like the following image:

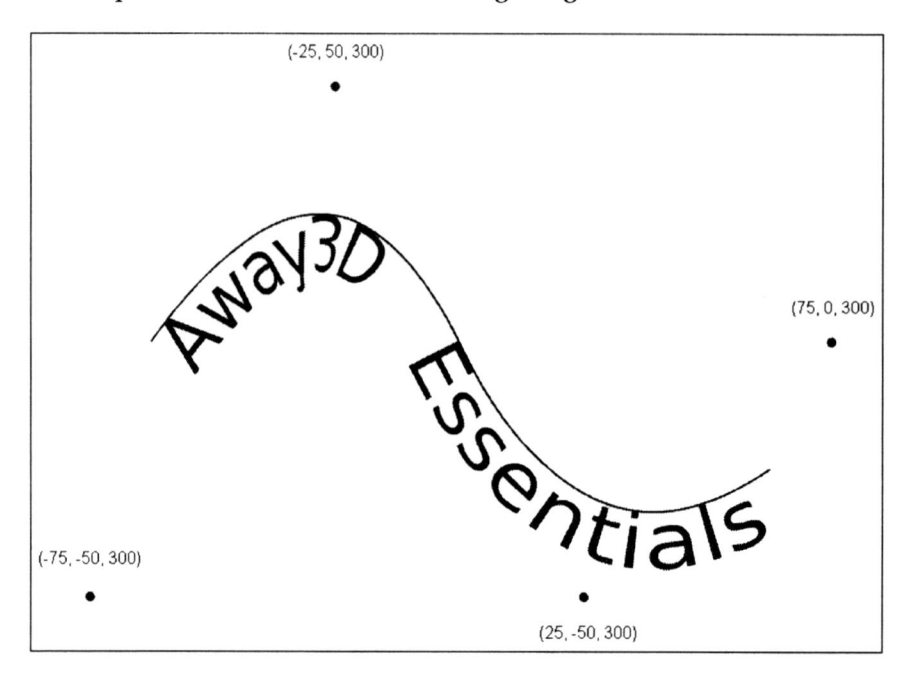

(-25, 50, 300)

(75, 0, 300)

(-75, -50, 300)

(25, -50, 300)

> Due to the way the curve is calculated, it starts half way in between the first and second points and finishes half way between the last and the second last points. You can confirm this for yourself by adding the following code after the call to the continuousCurve() function:
>
> ```
> scene.addChild(new Sphere({x: -75, y: -50, z: 300, radius: 1, material: new ColorMaterial(0)}));
> scene.addChild(new Sphere({x: -25, y: 50, z: 300, radius: 1, material: new ColorMaterial(0)}));
> scene.addChild(new Sphere({x: 25, y: -50, z: 300, radius: 1, material: new ColorMaterial(0)}));
> scene.addChild(new Sphere({x: 75, y: 0, z: 300, radius: 1, material: new ColorMaterial(0)}));
> path.debugPath(scene);
> path.showAnchors = false;
> ```

> The sphere 3D objects are positioned in the scene using the same locations as the points we supplied to the `continuousCurve()` function. Calling the `debugPath()` function will then create a `PathDebug` object, which will visually display the path. You will see that the start and end points of the curve lie inbetween the points we supplied to the `continuousCurve()` function.
>
> We have also set the `showAnchors` property to `false`. When set to `true` (which is the default) the `PathDebug` object will add a number of sphere 3D objects to show the points that make up the path, much like we have just done manually. However, these spheres have a radius of 50 units, which would unfortunately completely fill up a scene like this. To work around this, you can modify the `PathDebug` class file, located in the `away3d.core.geom` package, to change the size of these debug spheres.
>
> The first line of the `addAnchor()` function looks like this (it is line 72 of the `PathDebug.as` file):
>
> ```
> var sphere:Sphere = new Sphere({material:mat,
> radius:50, segmentsH:2, segmentsW:2 });
> ```
>
> Simply change the `radius` init object parameter to something like 5 instead of 50.

We create a new `PathAlignModifier` object, which will be used to modify our text 3D object so it is aligned to our path. The constructor takes the 3D object that is to be modified, and the path that it will be aligned to.

```
var aligner:PathAlignModifier =
    new PathAlignModifier(text, path);
```

The `execute()` function will then make the required changes to the text 3D object.

```
    aligner.execute();
}
```

The `followLine()` function is used to align the text 3D object along a path made up of a number of straight lines.

```
protected function followLine():void
{
   setupText();
   var path:Path = new Path();
```

Above, we used the `continuousCurve()` function from the `Path` class to create our path. Creating a path with straight lines is a little different. For this, we add a number of `PathCommands` objects to the `array` property of the `Path` class.

Creating 3D Text

The first parameter we supply to the `PathCommand` constructor is the type of command that we are defining. Since we are defining a straight line, we use the `PathCommand.LINE` constant.

The second parameter is the starting point of the line.

The third parameter is a control point. This is used when defining a curve, but has no relevance when defining a straight line, so we leave it as `null`.

The fourth parameter is the end point of the line.

We `push()` two new `PathCommand` objects on to the `array` property of the `Path` class with the following code snippet:

```
path.array.push(
  new PathCommand(
    PathCommand.LINE,
    new Vector3D(-75, -35, 300),
    null,
    new Vector3D(-75, 35, 300)
  )
);
path.array.push(
  new PathCommand(
    PathCommand.LINE,
    new Vector3D(-75, 35, 300),
    null,
    new Vector3D(75, 35, 300)
  )
);
```

This will define a path that looks like the following image:

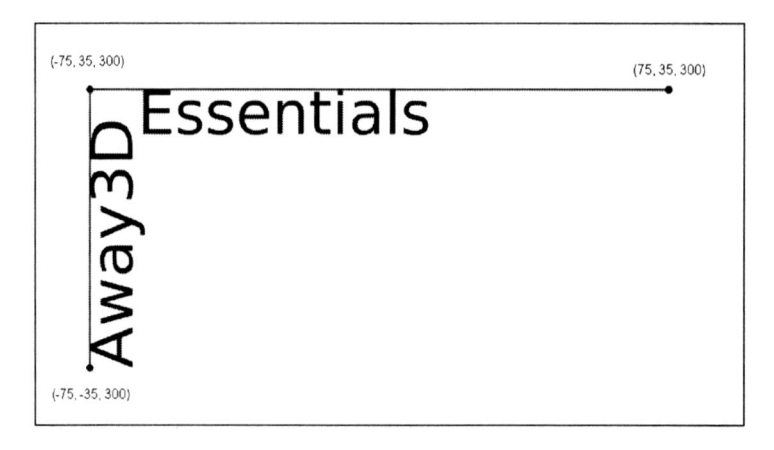

[282]

> Even though it makes no sense to have a modifier point when defining a straight line, you will find that the `PathDebug` class expects the modifier points not to be `null`. If you were to call the `debugPath()` function on the `Path` object with the straight line path we have defined above, you would see an error because the `PathDebug` object tries to read a `null` modifier point object. The easiest way to visually debug a straight line path is to use either the start or end point as a modifier point. In the following code, we have defined the same path as we did previously, with the exception that the start and modifier points are the same:
>
> ```
> path.array.push(
>   new PathCommand(
>     PathCommand.LINE,
>     new Vector3D(-75, -35, 300),
>     new Vector3D(-75, -35, 300),
>     new Vector3D(-75,  35, 300)
>   )
> );
> path.array.push(
>   new PathCommand(
>     PathCommand.LINE,
>     new Vector3D(-75, 35, 300),
>     new Vector3D(-75, 35, 300),
>     new Vector3D( 75, 35, 300)
>   )
> );
> ```

Again we create a new `PathAlignModifier` object, supplying the text 3D object and the `Path` that it should be aligned to, and then call the `execute()` function to make the changes.

```
    var aligner:PathAlignModifier =
      new PathAlignModifier(text, path);
    aligner.execute();
}
```

The `followCurve()` function will create a single curve to align the text 3D object.

```
protected function followCurve():void
{
  setupText();

  var path:Path = new Path();
```

Creating 3D Text

Just like with the straight line path we created above, the curve is defined by adding a `PathCommand` object to the `array` property of the `Path` class. We specify the type of the `PathCommand` using the `PathCommand.CURVE` constant, and then define the curve using a start, modifier, and end point.

```
path.array.push(
  new PathCommand(
    PathCommand.CURVE,
    new Vector3D(-75, -45, 300),
    new Vector3D(0, 50, 300),
    new Vector3D(75, 0, 300)
  )
);
```

This will define a curve that looks the like the following image:

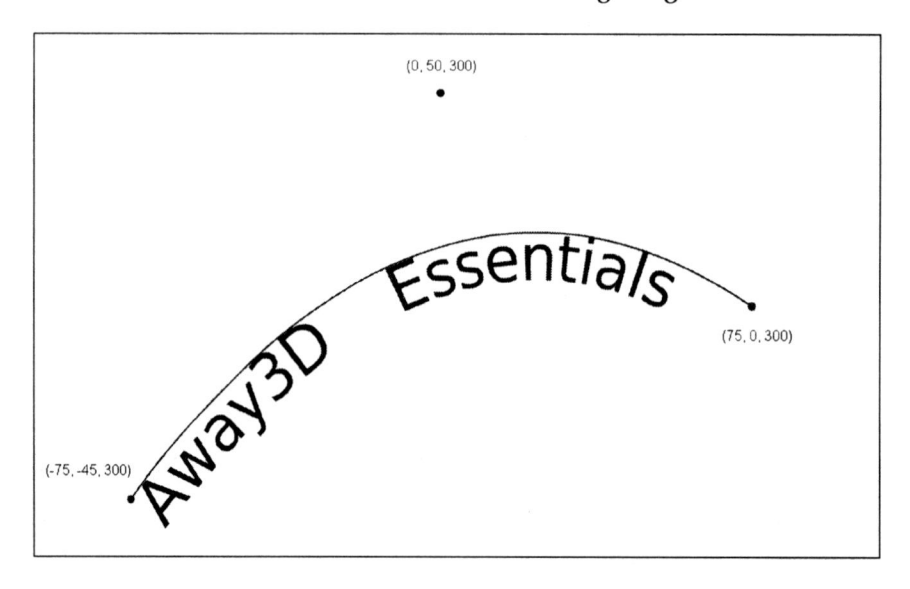

Again, we create a new `PathAlignModifier` object, and call it's `execute()` function.

```
      var aligner:PathAlignModifier =
        new PathAlignModifier(text, path);
      aligner.execute();
    }
  }
}
```

When the application is run you can press the 1, 2, and 3 keys on the keyboard to see the results of warping a text 3D object along the three different types of paths.

Summary

It is possible in Away3D to create text 3D objects and then manipulate them in a variety of ways. This chapter covered how to embed a true-type font file in a SWF that could then be used by the swfvector library. We then looked at a simple application that created a flat text 3D object within the scene.

These text 3D objects can be warped in a variety of interesting ways by aligning them to a path. A sample application was presented that aligned a text 3D object to a variety of paths made with both curves and straight lines.

We also saw how to give the 3D text object some depth with one of the many extrusion classes available in Away3D. In the next chapter, we will look at more of these modifier classes, and how they can be used to programmatically create additional custom 3D objects.

11
Extrusions and Modifiers

As we have seen, there are many ways to create a 3D object in Away3D. *Chapter 2, Creating and Displaying Primitives*, covered the creation of a 3D object from its base components. That same chapter also covered a number of primitive 3D objects available in the `away3d.primitives` package. Then in *Chapter 6, Models and Animations*, we looked at how 3D objects are created by loading external model files. Finally, in *Chapter 10, Creating 3D Text*, we saw how text 3D objects can be created.

In addition to these methods, Away3D also has the ability to create and manipulate 3D objects programmatically using classes from the `away3d.extrusions` and `away3d.modifiers` packages. In fact, we have already seen one of these classes, `TextExtrusion`, at work in *Chapter 10, Creating 3D Text*, where it was used to give depth to a flat text 3D object.

Although creating objects in this manner is not as flexible as creating them in a 3D modeling application, it is possible to create a wide variety of 3D shapes using just a few lines of code.

This chapter will cover the following topics:

- Creating a flag with the `PathExtrusion` class
- Creating walls with the `LinearExtrusion` class
- Creating a vase with the `LatheExtrusion` class
- Creating terrain with the `SkinExtrusion` or `Elevation` and `HeightMapModifier` classes
- Skimming the surface of a terrain 3D object with the `ElevationReader` class

Extrusions and Modifiers

Creating a flag with the PathExtrusion class

The `PathExtrusion` class, from the `away3d.extrusions` package, can be used to extend a cross section along a path. This cross section is known as a **profile**, and is defined as an array of `Vector3D` objects. In practice, it works much the same way as the `TextExtrusion` class that was introduced in *Chapter 10, Creating 3D Text*, by adding depth to an initial flat surface. But whereas the `TextExtrusion` class will extend a flat text 3D object perpendicular to the surface of the text, the `PathExtrusion` class can extend a surface along the length of a `Path` object, which can be a series of straight lines or a Bezier curve. This makes the `PathExtrusion` class ideal for creating 3D objects like ribbons and flags.

To demonstrate the `PathExtrusion` class, we will create an application called `PathExtrusionDemo`, which will create a simple flag 3D object.

```
package
{
   import away3d.core.geom.Path;
   import away3d.core.utils.Cast;
   import away3d.extrusions.PathExtrusion;
   import away3d.materials.BitmapMaterial;
   import flash.geom.Vector3D;

   public class PathExtrusionDemo extends Away3DTemplate
   {
     [Embed(source="away3dlogo.jpg")]
     protected var Away3DLogo:Class;

     public function PathExtrusionDemo()
     {
       super();
     }

     protected override function initScene():void
     {
       super.initScene();
```

To get a good view of the flag 3D object we will be creating, the camera is positioned along the Y and Z axes, and then we use the `lookAt()` function to orient the camera so that it is looking back at the scene's origin.

```
       camera.position = new Vector3D(0, 500, 500);
       camera.lookAt(new Vector3D(0, 0, 0));
```

Here we create a new `Path` object. If you recall from *Chapter 10, Creating 3D Text*, a path contains a number of `PathSegment` objects, which in turn are defined by three positions in space: the beginning, a control point, and the end. In this example, we are creating a `Path` object that will contain two `PathSegment` objects. The first `PathSegment` object is defined by the first three `Vector3D` objects in the array supplied to the `Path` constructor, and the second `PathSegment` object is defined by the last three `Vector3D` objects in the array. The resulting `Path` object looks like the following image:

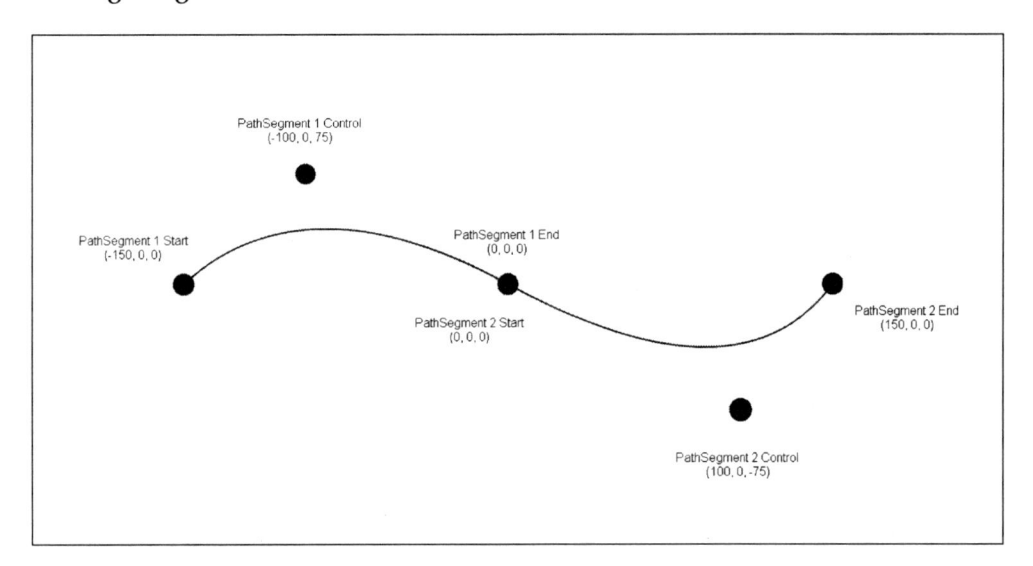

```
var path:Path = new Path(
    [
        new Vector3D(-150, 0, 0),
        new Vector3D(-100, 0, 75),
        new Vector3D(0, 0, 0),
        new Vector3D(0, 0, 0),
        new Vector3D(100, 0, -75),
        new Vector3D(150, 0, 0)
    ]
);
```

The cross section, or profile, is defined as an array of `Vector3D` objects. In this case, the profile is simply a vertical line 200 units in height.

```
var profile : Array =
    [
        new Vector3D(0, -100, 0),
        new Vector3D(0, 100, 0)
    ];
```

Extrusions and Modifiers

We then use the `Path` object and profile to create a new `PathExtrusion` object. The `subdivision` init object parameter is used to define the detail of the resulting 3D object, with higher values resulting in the final 3D object being constructed using more triangle faces, which produces a smoother appearance.

```
var extrusion:PathExtrusion = new PathExtrusion(
  path,
  profile,
  null,
  null,
  {
    material: new BitmapMaterial(Cast.bitmap(Away3DLogo)),
    bothsides: true,
    subdivision: 10
  }
);
```

The resulting `PathExtrusion` object is then added to the scene.

```
    scene.addChild(extrusion);
  }

 }
}
```

The following screenshot shows the output of this application:

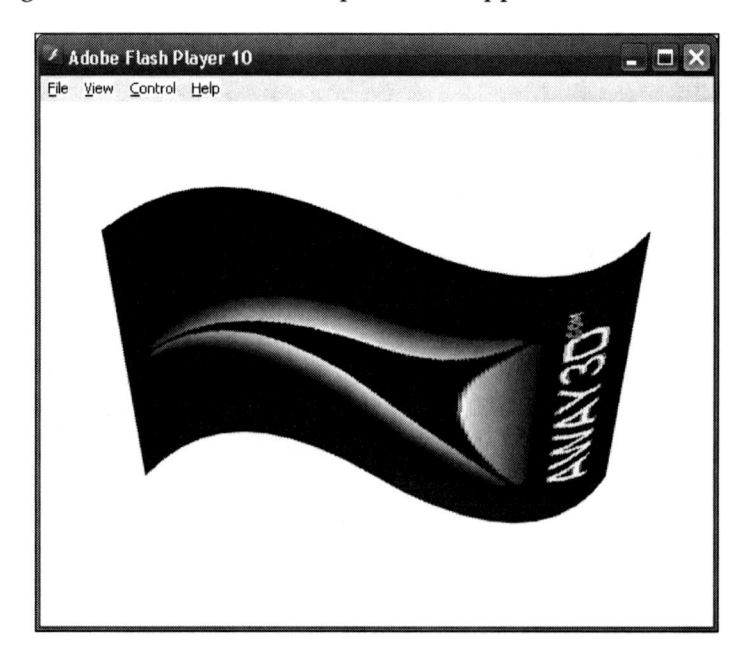

Chapter 11

Creating walls with the LinearExtrusion class

The `LinearExtrusion` class is used to create solid rectangular 3D objects from a profile made up of one or more straight lines. This is useful for creating walls where a number of lines are used to define the "floor plan" of a structure. In the following `LinearExtrusionDemo` application, we will use the `LinearExtrusion` class to build a 3D object that could represent the walls in an L-shaped house.

```
package
{
   import away3d.extrusions.LinearExtrusion;
   import flash.events.Event;
   import flash.geom.Vector3D;

   public class LinearExtrusionDemo extends Away3DTemplate
   {
      protected var walls:LinearExtrusion;

      public function LinearExtrusionDemo()
      {
         super();
      }

      protected override function initScene():void
      {
         super.initScene();

         camera.position = new Vector3D(1000, 750, 1000);
         camera.lookAt(new Vector3D(0, 0, 0));
```

[291]

Extrusions and Modifiers

The `wallPoints` array is a collection of points that define a number of connected lines. These lines define the base outline of the walls that will make up our 3D object. The end point of the last line is used as the starting point of the next line. The points used in the following code define a profile that looks like the following image:

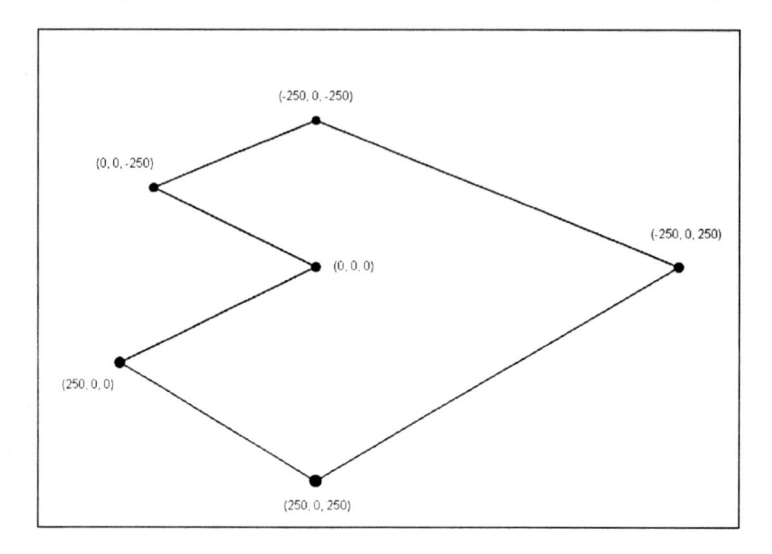

```
var wallPoints:Array =
    [
        new Vector3D( -250, 0, -250),
        new Vector3D( 0, 0, -250),
        new Vector3D(0, 0, 0),
        new Vector3D(250, 0, 0),
        new Vector3D(250, 0, 250),
        new Vector3D(-250, 0, 250),
        new Vector3D( -250, 0, -250)
    ];
```

Here we create a new `LinearExtrusion` object. The `offset` init object parameter defines the height of the walls, while the `thickness` parameter defines their width. The `recenter` parameter is used to ensure that the origin of the resulting 3D object is at its center.

```
walls = new LinearExtrusion(
    wallPoints,
    {
        thickness:10,
        offset: 150,
        recenter:true
```

```
            }
        );

        scene.addChild(walls);
    }
  }
}
```

The following screenshot shows the output of this application:

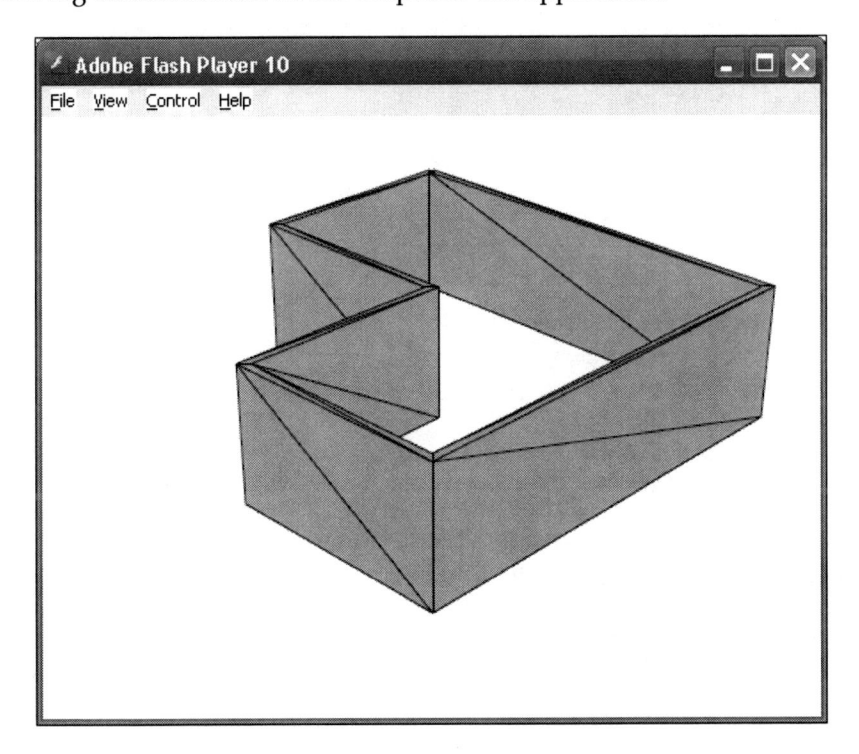

Creating a vase with the LatheExtrusion class

Lathing is a process used by carpenters that involves carving a piece of wood as it is spun around by a machine called a lathe. Lathing can be used to create objects like bowls, vases, posts, or any other object whose profile does not change as it spins around a central axis. Such objects are said to have **axial symmetry**.

Extrusions and Modifiers

These 3D objects can be created in Away3D using the `LatheExtrusion` class, which will take a profile and rotate it around an axis (the Y axis by default) to produce a solid 3D object. The following `LatheExtrusionDemo` will use the `LatheExtrusion` class to create a simple vase 3D object.

```
package
{
  import away3d.extrusions.LatheExtrusion;
  import flash.geom.Vector3D;

  public class LatheExtrusionDemo extends Away3DTemplate
  {
    protected var vase:LatheExtrusion;

    public function LatheExtrusionDemo()
    {
      super();
    }

    protected override function initScene():void
    {
      super.initScene();

      camera.position = new Vector3D(0, 500, 500);
      camera.lookAt(new Vector3D(0, 0, 0));
```

Here is the profile that will be passed to the `LatheExtrusion` class. You will notice that the x coordinates of the points that make up the profile are all positive, and do not cross over the Y axis (remember that the Y axis is the default axis around which the profile will be rotated). This ensures that the profile does not intersect itself as it is rotated. It is generally a good idea to ensure that the profile supplied to the `LatheExtrusion` class does not cross the axis around which it will be rotated.

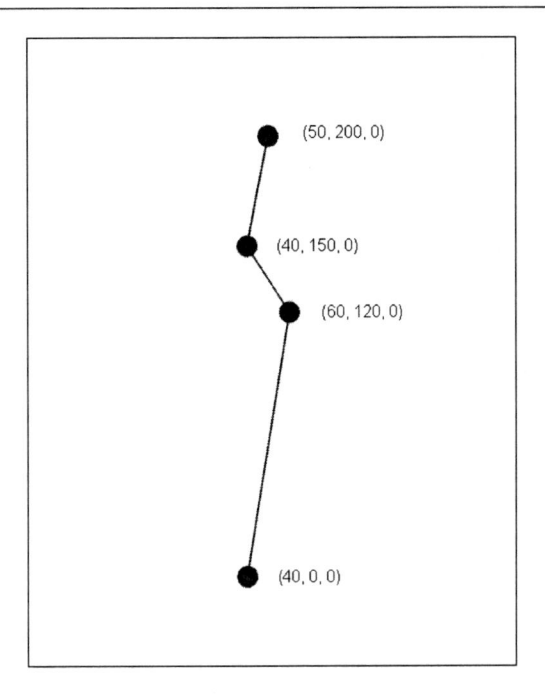

Just as with the `LinearExtrusion` class, the profile is defined as an array of `Vector3D` objects.

```
var profile : Array = [
    new Vector3D(50, 200, 0),
    new Vector3D(40, 150, 0),
    new Vector3D(60, 120, 0),
    new Vector3D(40, 0, 0)
];
```

We then create a new instance of the `LatheExtrusion` class. The `centerMesh` init object parameter is used in much the same way as the `recenter` init object parameter described for the `LinearExtrusion` class.

We also need to set the `flip` init object parameter to `true` to orient the triangle faces that make up the resulting 3D object so that they are visible from our camera's point-of-view. If we left the `flip` parameter at its default value of `false`, we would end up looking straight through the outside edge of the vase.

Extrusions and Modifiers

> The code documentation for the `LatheExtrusion` constructor actually lists `recenter` as a valid init object parameter. This is incorrect. The `LatheExtrusion` constructor will not process the `recenter` init object parameter.

```
      vase = new LatheExtrusion(
        profile,
        {
          subdivision: 12,
          centerMesh: true,
          thickness: 10,
          flip: true
        }
      );
      scene.addChild(vase);
    }
  }
}
```

The following screenshot shows the output of this application:

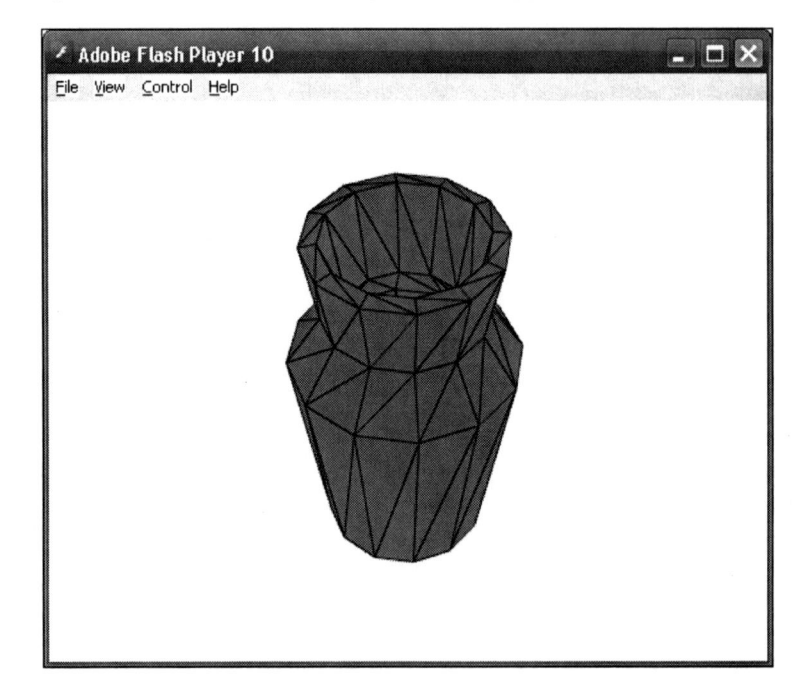

Creating terrain with the SkinExtrusion class

Unlike the preceding extrusion classes, the SkinExtrusion class does not extend a profile by creating additional dimensions. Instead, it takes an array of individual points and uses them to define the vertices of a 3D object that can be added to the scene. On the surface there does not seem to be a great deal of benefit to using the SkinExtrusion class over manually creating a mesh, like we did in *Chapter 2, Creating and Displaying Primitives*. In practice however, the points used by the SkinExtrusion class are generated by another class called Elevation. The Elevation class, in turn, takes an image, called a **height map**, the individual pixel colors of which are used to plot the heights of a collection of points over a plane.

You can see how this works in the following image. The black and white plane is textured with the same height map used to plot the height of the red points above it. You will notice that the points occupy a higher position over the brighter areas of the height map.

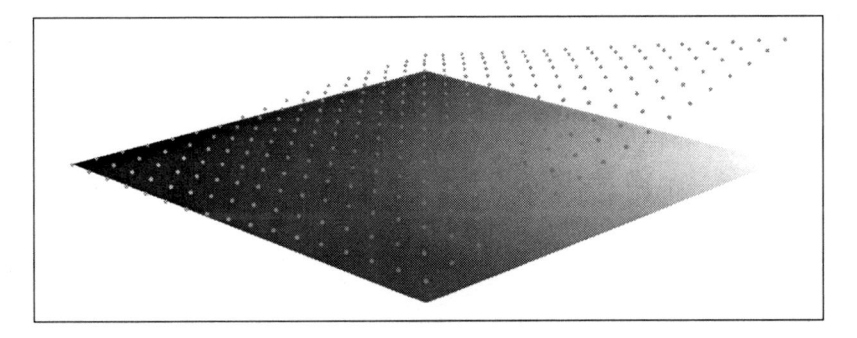

In the SkinExtrusionDemo application, we will use the height map (on the left side of the following image) and texture (on the right side) to create a 3D object that looks like an outdoor terrain.

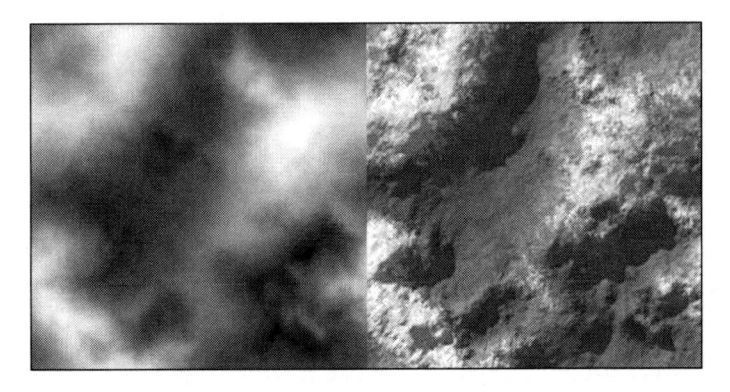

Extrusions and Modifiers

> You can use the free T2 application from `http://www.toymaker.info/html/texgen.html` to create realistic textures from a height map.

```
package
{
  import away3d.core.utils.Cast;
  import away3d.extrusions.Elevation;
  import away3d.extrusions.SkinExtrude;
  import away3d.materials.BitmapMaterial;
  import flash.geom.Vector3D;

  public class SkinExtrusionDemo extends Away3DTemplate
  {
```

The height map and the texture image files are embedded for easy access.

```
    [Embed(source="heightmap.jpg")]
    protected var Heightmap:Class;

    [Embed(source="terrain.jpg")]
    protected var Terrain:Class;

    protected var extrude:SkinExtrude;

    public function SkinExtrusionDemo()
    {
      super();
    }

    protected override function initScene():void
    {
      super.initScene();

      camera.position = new Vector3D(400, 200, 400);
      camera.lookAt(new Vector3D(0, 0, 0));

      var terrainMaterial:BitmapMaterial =
        new BitmapMaterial(Cast.bitmap(Terrain));
```

Before we can use the `SkinExtrusion` class, we first need to create an instance of the `Elevation` class.

```
      var elevation:Elevation = new Elevation();
```

Chapter 11

We then use the `generate()` function to create the multidimensional array of `Vector3D` objects that will be used by the `SkinExtrusion` class. The second through to the sixth parameters passed to the `generate()` function are the same as the default values defined by the function.

The first parameter specifies the `BitmapData` object that represents the height map.

The second parameter defines the color channel that will be read to determine the height of the resulting points. We supply the string `"r"` to indicate that we are reading the red colour of the pixels.

> Since our height map is a gray scale image, where the red, green, and blue color values are all the same for any given pixel, it would make no difference which color channel the `generate()` function reads from.

The third and fourth parameters define how many samples will be read from the height map along the width and height of the height map, respectively. Higher values here result in a more detailed 3D object.

The fifth and sixth parameters define the scale of the plane over which the points will be positioned. The default is 1, which means the plane will have the same dimensions as the height map.

For the seventh parameter, we have not used the default parameter value. It is used to scale the height of the terrain, whose points by default have a maximum height of 255 units. The default value for the scale is 1, but since we have supplied a scale value of 0.25, our terrain 3D object will have a maximum height of one quarter of the default.

```
var verticies:Array =
  elevation.generate(
    Cast.bitmap(Heightmap),
    "r",
    16,
    16,
    1,
    1,
    0.25
  );
```

We now use this array to generate a new `SkinExtrude` 3D object.

Extrusions and Modifiers

The `coverall` init object parameter is set to `true` to ensure that any material applied to it covers the entire resulting 3D object. Like the `LinearExtrusuion` class, the `recenter` parameter will adjust the positions of the vertices that make up the 3D object so the origin of the mesh is at its center. This recentering process also takes the height of the 3D object into account, meaning that when `recenter` is `true`, the highest point of the 3D object will be above the local origin of the 3D object, and the lowest point will be below it. You can see the local origin of the recentered `SkinExtrude` 3D object by the position of the black dot in the following image:

If `recenter` was `false`, as it is by default, the origin of the mesh would be at one of the corners, and all of its vertices would be above the origin. In the following image, the black dot shows the local origin of a `SkinExtrude` 3D object that has not been recentered.

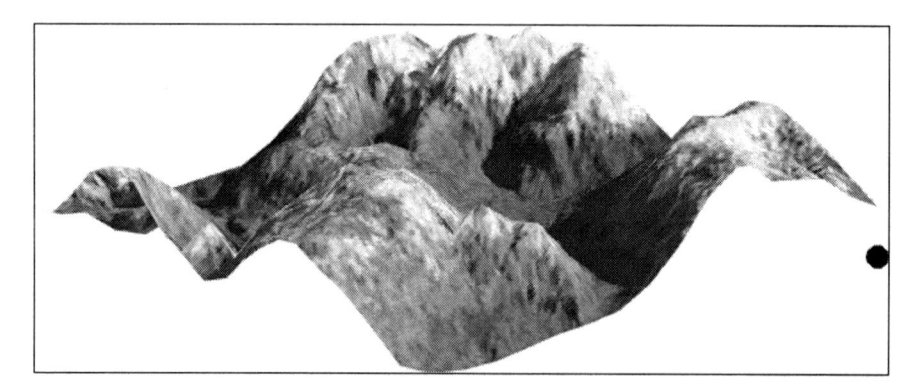

```
extrude = new SkinExtrude(verticies,
    {
        coverall: true,
        material: terrainMaterial,
        recenter: true,
```

```
                    bothsides: true
                }
            );
```

The points returned by the `generate()` function lie over a plane whose edges are parallel to the X / Y axes. When these points are passed to the `SkinExtrude` class, you will in effect create a 3D object that looks like a bumpy vertical wall. By rotating the 3D object by 90 degrees around the X axis, we will orient it so it looks like it represents the ground.

```
            extrude.rotationX = 90;
```

Setting the `recenter` property to `true` will reposition the 3D object. Here we simply set its position back to the origin of the scene.

```
            extrude.x = extrude.y = extrude.z = 0;

            scene.addChild(extrude);
        }
    }
}
```

The following screenshot shows the result of this application:

Extrusions and Modifiers

Reading the height of a terrain surface with the ElevationReader class

When using a 3D object created with the `SkinExtrusion` class, it is very common to need to find the height of the surface at a given point. For example, you may want to ensure that a 3D object representing a car is positioned so that it appears above a `SkinExtrusion` 3D object, simulating the car driving across some terrain. The `ElevationReader` class can be used for this purpose. When it is created with the same height map supplied to an `Elevation` object, the `getLevel()` function returns the corresponding height of points returned by the `Elevation` `generate()` function. This value can then be used to position 3D objects relative to a `SkinExtrusion` 3D object.

The following `ElevationReaderDemo` application shares much of its code with the `SkinExtrusionDemo` application. Some additional code has been introduced to create a `ElevationReader` object, which we use to modify the height of a sphere as it moves randomly across the surface of a `SkinExtrusion` 3D object.

```
package
{
    import away3d.core.utils.Cast;
    import away3d.extrusions.Elevation;
    import away3d.extrusions.ElevationReader;
    import away3d.extrusions.SkinExtrude;
    import away3d.materials.BitmapMaterial;
    import away3d.primitives.Sphere;
    import com.greensock.TweenLite;
    import flash.events.Event;
    import flash.geom.Vector3D;

    public class ElevationReaderDemo extends Away3DTemplate
    {
      [Embed(source="heightmap.jpg")]
      protected var Heightmap:Class;

      [Embed(source="terrain.jpg")]
      protected var Terrain:Class;

      protected var extrude:SkinExtrude;
      protected var sphere:Sphere;
      protected var elevationreader:ElevationReader;
```

```
    public function ElevationReaderDemo()
    {
      super();
    }

    protected override function initScene():void
    {
      super.initScene();

      camera.position = new Vector3D(400, 200, 400);
      camera.lookAt(new Vector3D(0, 0, 0));

      var terrainMaterial:BitmapMaterial =
        new BitmapMaterial(Cast.bitmap(Terrain));

      var elevation:Elevation = new Elevation();
      var verticies:Array =
        elevation.generate(
          Cast.bitmap(Heightmap),
          "r",
          16,
          16,
          1,
          1,
          0.25
        );

      extrude = new SkinExtrude(verticies,
        {
          coverall: true,
          material: terrainMaterial,
          recenter:true,
          bothsides: true
        }
      );

      extrude.rotationX = 90;
      extrude.x = extrude.y = extrude.z = 0;

      scene.addChild(extrude);
```

The process of creating an `ElevationReader` object is very similar to creating an `Elevation` object. First a new instance of the `ElevationReader` class is instantiated.

```
    elevationreader = new ElevationReader();
```

We then call the `traceLevels()` function, supplying exactly the same parameters we supplied to the `Elevation generate()` function. It is important that the parameters passed to the `generate()` and `traceLevels()` functions are the same, because this ensures that the values returned by the `getLevel()` function below are consistent with the height of the `SkinExtrude` 3D object.

```
elevationreader.traceLevels(
  Cast.bitmap(Heightmap),
  "r",
  16,
  16,
  1,
  1,
  0.25
);
```

We then create a sphere that we will move randomly across the surface of the terrain.

```
sphere = new Sphere({radius: 10});

scene.addChild(sphere);
```

Finally, we call the `moveSphere()` function to kick off the tweening operation.

```
    moveSphere();
}

override protected function onEnterFrame(event:Event):void
{
  super.onEnterFrame(event);
```

Every frame we adjust the height of the sphere to match the height of the terrain, which is determined by calling the `getLevel()` function.

We supply the position of the sphere along the X and Z axes as the first two parameters. This may seem confusing at first when you consider that these parameters are actually called x and y. The reason we supply the spheres position on the Z axis to the y parameter is because the `SkinExtrude` 3D object was rotated 90 degrees around the X axis. Unfortunately, the `ElevationReader` class does not have the same ability to be rotated, which means we need to manually translate the movement of the sphere along the Z axis in world space into vertical movement along the Y axis in the local space of the `ElevationReader`.

The third parameter is used to apply an offset to the height returned by the `getLevel()` function.

If you look back at the code used to create the `SkinExtrude` 3D object, you will notice that the `recenter` init object parameter is set to `true`. This has the effect of setting the origin of the `SkinExtrude` 3D object to its center, as opposed to one of its corners. This also means that the lowest point of the `SkinExtrude` 3D object (that is, the points that relate to the darkest areas on the corresponding height map) will be below this centre point, while the highest point will be above the centre.

We don't need to adjust for the centering of the `SkinExtrude` 3D object when supplying the `x` and `y` parameters to the `getLevel()` function, as these values are assumed to be centered. However, the value returned by the `getLevel()` function is always positive—it does not take into account the effect that the centering has on the relative height of the `SkinExtrude` 3D object. This is why we calculate the `offset` by first subtracting 255 * 0.25 * 0.5, which will adjust the returned value so it relates to the actual minimum height of the matching `SkinExtrude` 3D object (remember that the maximum height of the `SkinExtrude` 3D object is 255 units, which we scaled by 0.25, and then centered it, which dropped the position of the terrain by half its height). We then add the radius of the sphere to ensure the bottom of the sphere is above the `SkinExtrude` 3D object.

> If the `SkinExtrude` `recenter` init object parameter was set to `false`, we would need to adjust the values supplied to the `x` and `y` parameters like so (where 128 is half the width and depth of the terrain):
> ```
> sphere.y = elevationreader.getLevel(
>     sphere.x + 128,
>     -sphere.z + 128,
>     sphere.radius
> );
> ```

```
        sphere.y = elevationreader.getLevel(
          sphere.x,
          -sphere.z,
          -255 * 0.25 * 0.5 + sphere.radius
        );
    }
```

The `moveSphere()` function is used to set up a recursive tweening operation that will move the sphere to a random position over the terrain.

```
        protected function moveSphere():void
        {
          TweenLite.to(sphere, 2,
            {
              x: Math.random() * 256 - 128,
              z: Math.random() * 256 - 128,
```

Extrusions and Modifiers

By setting the `onComplete` parameter to recursively call the `moveSphere()` function, we are ensuring that the sphere will continuously move to random points.

```
            onComplete: moveSphere
        }
    );
    }
  }
}
```

When this application is run, you will see that the sphere remains above the terrain as it moves across its surface.

HeightMapModifier

We have seen how a height map can be used to modify the height of a planar surface with the `SkinExtrusion` / `Elevation` classes. The `HeightMapModifier` class uses the same principle, but instead of being limited to modifying the height of a planar surface, it can be used to modify the surface height of any 3D object, be it a flat 3D object like a plane, a solid 3D object like a sphere, or a complex 3D object loaded from an external model file. It does this by repositioning the vertices of a 3D object along their **normal vector** (a normal vector is simply a vector that is perpendicular to a surface).

Take a look at the following height map:

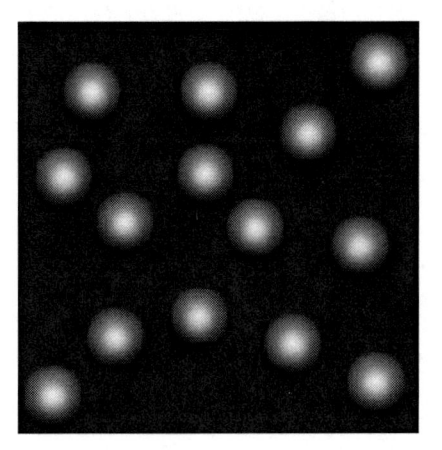

The `HeightMapModifierDemo` application will apply this height map to a sphere to create what could be a cratered moon or asteroid.

```
package
{
   import away3d.core.utils.Cast;
   import away3d.materials.utils.HeightMapDataChannel;
   import away3d.modifiers.HeightMapModifier;
   import away3d.primitives.Plane;
   import away3d.primitives.Sphere;
   import flash.geom.Vector3D;

   public class HeightMapModifierDemo extends Away3DTemplate
   {
      [Embed(source="sphere.jpg")]
      protected var SphereTex:Class;

      protected var sphere:Sphere;

      public function HeightMapModifierDemo()
      {
         super();
      }

      protected override function initScene():void
      {
         super.initScene();
```

[307]

Extrusions and Modifiers

```
        camera.position = new Vector3D(0, 0, 500);
        camera.lookAt(new Vector3D(0, 0, 0));

        sphere = new Sphere(
          {
            segmentsW: 32,
            segmentsH: 32
          }
        );

        scene.addChild(sphere);
```

To apply the height map to our sphere 3D object, we first need to create a new instance of the `HeightMapModifier` class. We supply the 3D object that we will be modifying, the height map, the color channel to read from the height map, and the maximum distance to vary the surface of the 3D object by.

> There is some inconsistency between the types used to define a color channel. We saw previously that the `Elevation` and `ElevationReader` classes take a string to define a color channel. The `HeightMapModifier` class is a little different, taking instead a unit. Here we use one of the constant values defined in the `HeightMapDataChannel` class to specify that the `HeightMapModifier` class should read the red color channel.

```
        var modifier:HeightMapModifier = new HeightMapModifier(
          sphere,
          Cast.bitmap(SphereTex),
          HeightMapDataChannel.RED,
          16
        );
```

The `execute()` function will then actually modify our sphere 3D object.

```
        modifier.execute();
      }
    }
}
```

The following screenshot shows the end result:

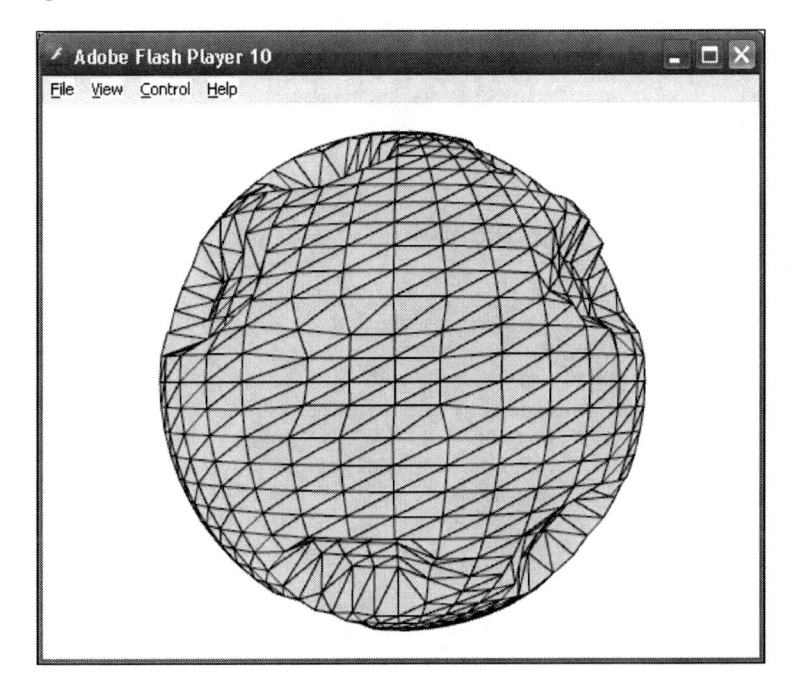

You may notice that the `HeightMapModifier` class will use a height map in the opposite manner to the `Elevation` class. The brighter areas in a height map used by the `HeightMapModifier` class will actually result in a depression when applied to a 3D object, instead of an increased height as is the case with the `Elevation` class. The simple way around this is to supply a value of `-1` to the `scale` parameter in the `HeightMapModifier` constructor, like so:

```
var modifier:HeightMapModifier = new HeightMapModifier(
  sphere,
  Cast.bitmap(SphereTex),
  HeightMapDataChannel.RED,
  16,
  -1
);
```

This change reverses the sign of the values read from the height map (that is, positive values become negative), and produces the following result:

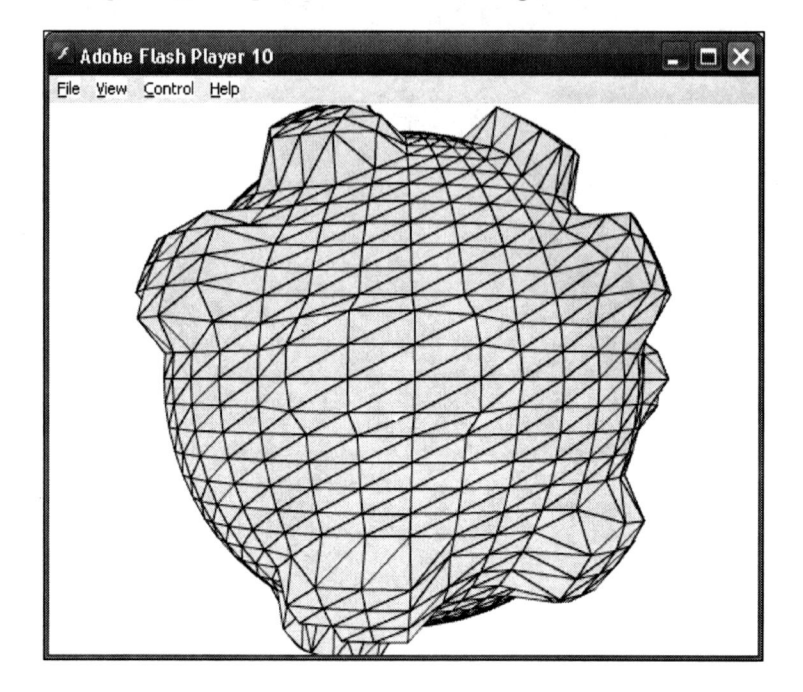

Summary

The extrusion and modifier classes in Away3D can be used to quickly create complex 3D objects to represent objects like terrain, walls, flags, ribbons, and more. The `PathExtrusion`, `LinearExtrusion`, and `LatheExtrusion` classes will extend a base profile along a path or around an axis, while the `SkinExtrusion` class can be used in conjunction with the `Elevation` class to create a 3D object from a height map.

We also looked at the `ElevationReader` class, which provides a convenient way to determine the height of a `SkinExtrusion` 3D object. A sample application was shown that used the `ElevationReader` class to move a sphere over the surface or a `SkinExtrusion` 3D object.

Finally, we covered the `HightMapModifier` class, which will use a height map to apply a deformation to any 3D object.

In the next chapter, we will take a look at how to add visual effects to an Away3D application, using both the Flash filter classes, and those that are included as part of Away3D.

12
Filters and Postprocessing Effects

Away3D supports a number of methods for displaying effects. As a Flash developer, you are probably already familiar with the standard Flash filter classes from the flash.filters package. Away3D supports the use of these classes, and they can be applied to individual 3D objects, or the entire view, to display effects like a blur effect, glow effect, and drop shadows. And thanks to the new functionality provided by the latest version of Flash, filters can also be applied using Pixel Bender shaders and the ShaderFilter class.

In addition to the filter classes provided by Flash, Away3D includes a FogFilter class. This class can be used to apply a fog-like effect to the scene, while also offering some performance benefits.

Finally, we will see how to make use of the BitmapSession class and the various functions available in Flash to manipulate bitmap images to create a custom effect.

This chapter covers the following topics:

- Applying the Flash filter classes to individual 3D objects, and the entire view
- Applying Pixel Bender shaders using the ShaderFilter class
- Using the FogFilter class
- An example of how to use the BitmapSession class can be used to create a custom effect

Filters and Postprocessing Effects

Flash and Away3D filters

Both Away3D and Flash define classes called filters that can be used to apply visual effects. Despite both being referred to by the same name, there are significant differences between the two.

The Flash filters

Since Flash Player 8 developers have had access to a number of standard filters that can be applied to `DisplayObject` objects via their `filters` property, and the introduction of Pixel Bender in Flash Player 10 allows an almost unlimited variety of filters to be created and applied using the `ShaderFilter` class.

Because each 3D object within an Away3D scene is eventually displayed on the screen by an object that extends the `DisplayObject` class, the standard Flash filters can be applied to them. This allows for some interesting effects to be created with very little code.

Applying filters

The standard Flash filters can be applied to any individual 3D object whose `ownCanvas` property is set to `true`. The `ownCanvas` property was covered in *Chapter 4, Z-Sorting*, where it was used to draw a 3D object into its own canvas for the purposes of forcing its sorted depth within the scene. This canvas, as we noted previously, extends the `DisplayObject` class, which means it can have a Flash filter applied to it. In this way, we can selectively apply the Flash filter effects to individual 3D objects of our choosing.

The Flash filter effects can also be applied to all visible 3D objects at once by assigning them to the `View3D` object.

Let's create an application called `OwnCanvasDemo` to demonstrate how filters can be applied to individual and all 3D objects.

```
package
{
    import away3d.containers.ObjectContainer3D;
    import away3d.core.base.Mesh;
    import away3d.core.utils.Cast;
    import away3d.loaders.Max3DS;
    import away3d.materials.BitmapMaterial;
    import flash.display.BitmapDataChannel;
    import flash.display.Shader;
    import flash.events.Event;
    import flash.events.KeyboardEvent;
```

The classes imported from the `flash.filters` package will be used to apply the various effects that this application will demonstrate.

```
import flash.filters.BitmapFilterQuality;
import flash.filters.BlurFilter;
import flash.filters.DisplacementMapFilter;
import flash.filters.DisplacementMapFilterMode;
import flash.filters.GlowFilter;
import flash.filters.ShaderFilter;
import flash.geom.Point;
import flash.text.TextField;

public class OwnCanvasDemo extends Away3DTemplate
{
```

PBJ files are compiled Pixel Bender shaders. The cross-stitch shader used in this example was downloaded from the **Adobe Pixel Bender Exchange** (http://www.adobe.com/cfusion/exchange/index.cfm?event=productHome&exc=26), which is a website run by Adobe that provides a number of Pixel Bender shaders. Here we have embedded the `crosstitch.pbj` file as a raw data file.

```
[Embed(source="crossstitch.pbj", mimeType="application/octet-stream")]
protected var PixelBenderShader:Class;
```

We also embedded a number of other files, including a 3DS model file and two texture image files.

```
[Embed(source="ship.3ds", mimeType="application/octet-stream")]
protected var ShipModel:Class;
[Embed(source="ship.jpg")]
protected var ShipTexture:Class;
[Embed(source="displacementmap.jpg")]
protected var DisplacementMap:Class;
```

The `filterText` property will be used to reference a `TextField` object, which will be used to display the name of the currently applied filter.

```
protected var filterText:TextField;
```

Filters and Postprocessing Effects

We will create two 3D objects: one will have the filters applied to it, while the other will be an unmodified control. This allows a 3D object that has a filter applied to it to be easily compared with the original 3D object.

```
protected var shipModel:ObjectContainer3D;
protected var shipModel2:ObjectContainer3D;

public function OwnCanvasDemo()
{
   super();
}
```

The `TextField` object referenced by the `filterText` property is initialized in the `initUI()` function.

```
protected override function initUI():void
{
   super.initUI();
   filterText = new TextField();
   filterText.x = 10;
   filterText.y = 10;
   filterText.width = 300;
   this.addChild(filterText);
}

protected override function initListeners():void
{
   super.initListeners();
   stage.addEventListener(KeyboardEvent.KEY_UP, onKeyUp);
}
```

The `initScene()` function is used to create and display two 3D objects. The process of loading a 3D object from an external model file is described in more detail in *Chapter 6, Models and Animations*.

```
protected override function initScene():void
{
   super.initScene();
   this.camera.z = 0;
   var shipMaterial:BitmapMaterial =
     new BitmapMaterial(Cast.bitmap(ShipTexture));
   shipModel = Max3DS.parse(Cast.bytearray(ShipModel),
     {
        scale: 0.15,
        z: 500,
        x: 75,
        autoLoadTextures: false,
```

By setting the `ownCanvas` init object parameter to `true`, we are in fact giving this 3D object its own Render Session object to be drawn into. This will allow us to apply filters to this individual 3D object, without affecting other 3D objects in the scene.

```
            ownCanvas: true
        }
    );
    for each (var child:Mesh in shipModel.children)
      child.material = shipMaterial;
    scene.addChild(shipModel);
```

A second 3D object is created. As this 3D object will not have any filters applied to it, we do not need to set the `ownCanvas` init object parameter.

```
    shipModel2 = Max3DS.parse(Cast.bytearray(ShipModel),
        {
           scale: 0.15,
           z: 500,
           x: -75,
           autoLoadTextures: false
        }
    );
    for each (child in shipModel2.children)
      child.material = shipMaterial;
    scene.addChild(shipModel2);
```

Calling the `clearFilters()` function will start the application with no filters applied.

```
    clearFilters();
}
```

The `onKeyUp()` function is called when a key on the keyboard is released. We will use it to apply the various filters that this application demonstrates.

```
    protected function onKeyUp(event:KeyboardEvent):void
    {
      switch (event.keyCode)
      {
        case 49: // 1
          clearFilters();
          break;
        case 50: // 2
          applyBlurFilter();
          break;
        case 51: // 3
```

Filters and Postprocessing Effects

```
                applyDisplacementMapFilter();
                break;
            case 52: // 4
                applyGlowFilter();
                break;
            case 53: // 5
                applyShaderFilter();
                break;
            case 54: // 6
                applyViewBlurFilter();
                break;
        }
    }
```

The `onEnterFrame()` function is used to rotate each of the 3D objects around within the scene.

```
    protected override function onEnterFrame(event:Event):void
    {
        super.onEnterFrame(event);
        shipModel.rotationX = shipModel2.rotationX += 2;
        shipModel.rotationY = shipModel2.rotationY += 1;
    }
```

The `clearFilters()` function assigns an empty array to the `filters` property, which is defined by the `Object3D` class, on both the view and the 3D object referenced by the `shipModel` variable. This has the effect of removing any filters that may have been applied.

> Despite having the same name, the `filters` property defined by the `Object3D` class is not the same as the `filters` property defined by the `DisplayObject` class (the `Object3D` class does not extend the `DisplayObject` class). However, the two properties can be used in much the same way. When the `ownCanvas` property for a 3D object is set to `true`, the array supplied to the `filters` property will be eventually applied to the `filters` property of the Render Session object used to draw that 3D object to the screen, making the result of the filter(s) (or lack thereof) visible on the screen.

```
    protected function clearFilters():void
    {
        filterText.text = "None";
        shipModel.filters = [];
        view.session.filters = [];
    }
```

Applying the BlurFilter

The `applyBlurFilter()` function is used to blur the 3D object using the `BlurFilter` class. The `BlurFilter` class can be used to create the appearance of 3D object that is out of focus or obscured by fog.

```
protected function applyBlurFilter():void
{
```

The `TextField` object is updated to reflect the filter that is currently being applied.

```
filterText.text = "BlurFilter";
```

A new instance of the `BlurFilter` class is assigned to an array, which in turn is assigned to the 3D objects `filters` property.

The first two parameters passed to the `BlurFilter` constructor, `blurX` and `blurY`, define the amount of horizontal and vertical blur respectively.

The third parameter, `quality`, is used to define how many times the blur effect is applied. The `BitmapFilterQuality` class defines three constant values, `LOW`, `MEDIUM`, and `HIGH`, although you can directly supply an int value up to 15. The lower the value, the faster the effect will be rendered.

> The array assigned to the `filters` property can contain more than one Flash filter object, allowing for effects to be combined.

```
shipModel.filters = [
  new BlurFilter(
    4,
    4,
    BitmapFilterQuality.LOW)
  ];
}
```

The following image shows a 3D space ship object with a blue filter applied to it:

Filters and Postprocessing Effects

Applying the DisplacementMapFilter

The `applyDisplacementMapFilter()` function applies an array with a new `DisplacementMapFilter` object to the `filters` property. The `DisplacementMapFilter` class is used to warp the appearance of a 3D object using a **displacement map,** which is simply an image whose color values are used to offset the position of the pixels in the original image (or in our case the 2D rendering of a 3D object) that it is applied to. This effect can be used to create a rippling effect like a 3D object being under water or behind textured glass.

The first parameter supplied to the `DisplacementMapFilter` constructor, `mapBitmap`, is set to a `BitmapData` object created from one of the embedded images.

The second parameter, `mapPoint`, is the location on the filtered image at which the top-left corner of the displacement filter will be applied. You can use this if you only want to apply the filter to part of an image, but in our case we want to apply the effect to the whole image, so we supply a new `Point` object, which has the default coordinates of (0, 0).

The third and fourth parameters, `componentX` and `componentY`, define which color channel of the displacement map image affects the X and Y position of pixels respectively. We have used the red channel, but since our displacement map is a gray-scale image, where the red, green, and blue color channels are all equal, the actual choice of color channel here would make no difference to the end result.

The fifth and sixth parameters, `scaleX` and `scaleY`, define the multiplier value, which specifies how strong the X and Y axis displacement is, respectively.

The seventh parameter, `mode`, determines what the Flash Player should do in any empty spaces created by pixels being shifted away. The `DisplacementMapFilterMode` class defines several options that can be used here.

`IGNORE`	Will display the original pixels.
`WARP` (the default)	Will wrap the pixels around from the other side of the image.
`CLAMP` (used in this example)	Uses the nearest shifted pixel.
`COLOR`	Fills in the space with a specific color.

```
protected function applyDisplacementMapFilter():void
{
  filterText.text = "DisplacementMapFilter";
  shipModel.filters = [
    new DisplacementMapFilter(
      Cast.bitmap(DisplacementMap),
```

```
                new Point(),
                BitmapDataChannel.RED,
                BitmapDataChannel.RED,
                15,
                15,
                DisplacementMapFilterMode.CLAMP)
        ];
    }
```

The following image shows a 3D object with the `DisplacementMapFilter` class applied to it:

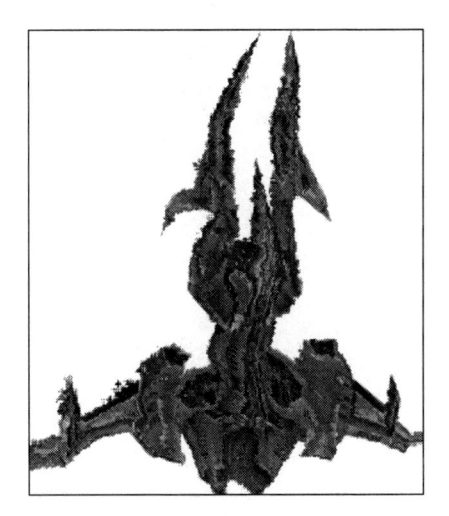

Applying the GlowFilter

The `applyGlowFilter()` function is used to apply a new instance of the `GlowFilter` class, which surrounds the 3D object with a soft glow. This effect is great for highlighting a selection, or to create a halo-like effect.

The first parameter supplied to the `GlowFilter` constructor, `color`, defines the color of the glow effect.

The second parameter, `alpha`, defines the transparency of the glow color.

The third and fourth parameters, `blurX` and `blurY`, define the amount of horizontal and vertical glow, respectively.

```
        protected function applyGlowFilter():void
        {
          filterText.text = "GlowFilter";
          shipModel.filters = [
```

Filters and Postprocessing Effects

```
            new GlowFilter((
               0x4488FF,
               1,
               12,
               12)
         ];
      }
```

The following image shows a 3D object with the `GlowFilter` class applied to it:

Applying Pixel Bender shaders

Pixel Bender excels when used to create filter-like effects, and can be used to create a huge variety of effects in addition to the handful of filters included in the `flash.filters` package. The `applyShaderFilter()` applies a cross-stitch shader obtained from the Adobe Pixel Bender Exchange as a filter.

> We have already seen Pixel Bender in action with some of the materials covered in *Chapter 5, Materials,* with classes like `Dot3BitmapMaterialF10`, `PhongPBMaterial`, and `FresnelPBMaterial`. Pixel Bender materials and shaders are features that rely on Flash Player 10.

```
   protected function applyShaderFilter():void
   {
      filterText.text = "ShaderFilter";
```

In order to apply a Pixel Bender shader as a filter, we need to create a `Shader` object. The `Shader` constructor takes a new instance of the class representing the embedded PBJ file.

```
var shader:Shader = new Shader(new PixelBenderShader());
```

This `Shader` object is then passed to the constructor of a new `ShaderFilter` object.

```
var shaderFilter:ShaderFilter = new ShaderFilter(shader);
```

The `ShaderFilter` class allows us to use Pixel Bender shaders in the same manner as the filter classes shown previously by assigning it to an array passed to the `filters` property.

```
        shipModel.filters = [shaderFilter];
    }
```

The following image shows the effect of the cross-stick shader applied to a 3D object:

Applying filters to the view

Filters can also be applied to the entire view instead of individual 3D objects. When a filter is applied to the view all 3D objects will be affected, regardless of whether or not their `ownCanvas` property is set to `true`.

Filters and Postprocessing Effects

Here we assign a `BlurFilter` to the `View3D` object, using the same method of passing an array to the `filters` property. The end result of this action will be that both the 3D objects appear blurred.

```
      protected function applyViewBlurFilter():void
      {
        clearFilters();
        filterText.text = "View BlurFilter";
        view.session.filters = [new BlurFilter()];
      }
    }
  }
}
```

Away3D filters

The filters included with Away3D perform such tasks as sorting the 3D objects in the scene, removing those mesh elements that are further than a specified distance from the camera, or retaining only a specified number of mesh elements. In addition, the `FogFilter` class can be used to apply a fog-like effect to the scene, shading 3D objects with an increasingly opaque color the further they are from the camera. It does this by subdividing the scene and then shading each face of a 3D object depending on which subdivision they fall in. The following image illustrates a fog filter with seven such subdivisions:

Chapter 12

The fog filter offers a performance benefit as well, as the mesh elements that fall behind the last segment are not rendered.

The following `Away3DFilterDemo` class demonstrates how the `FogFilter` class can be used by applying it to a scene containing a number of cubes that are rotated around the Y-axis. This rotation moves the individual cubes through the fog effect created by the `FogFilter` class.

```
package
{
   import away3d.containers.ObjectContainer3D;
   import away3d.core.filter.FogFilter;
   import away3d.core.render.BasicRenderer;
   import away3d.materials.ColorMaterial;
   import away3d.primitives.Cube;
   import flash.events.Event;

   public class Away3DFilterDemo extends Away3DTemplate
   {
      protected var container:ObjectContainer3D;

      public function Away3DFilterDemo()
      {
         super();
      }

      protected override function initScene():void
      {
         super.initScene();
         this.camera.z = 0;
```

A `Container3D` object is created. This will be used as the parent container of the cubes that make up the scene.

```
         container = new ObjectContainer3D(
            {
               z: 200
            }
         );
         scene.addChild(container);
```

Filters and Postprocessing Effects

The scene will be made up of a number of cubes lined up in a 6 x 6 x 6 grid, for a total of 216 cubes. Each cube is added as a child of the ObjectContainer3D object created previously.

```
for (var primitveX:int = -50; primitveX <= 50; primitveX += 20)
{
  for (var primitveY:int = -50; primitveY <= 50; primitveY += 20)
  {
    for (var primitveZ:int = -50; primitveZ <= 50; primitveZ += 20)
    {
      container.addChild(
        new Cube(
          {
            x: primitveX,
            y: primitveY,
            z: primitveZ,
            width: 10,
            height: 10,
            depth: 10
          }
        )
      );
    }
  }
}
```

Here we create a new instance of the FogFilter class.

```
var fogFilter:FogFilter = new FogFilter(
{
```

The FogFilter class uses a ColorMaterial class to generate the fog effect. Here we have created a new instance of the ColorMaterial class that will display a white color, which means the FogFilter will create a white-fog effect.

```
material: new ColorMaterial(0xFFFFFF),
```

The minZ parameter defines how far from the camera the fog effect starts.

```
minZ: 125,
```

The `maxZ` parameter defines how far from the camera the mesh element in a 3D object can be before it is completely obscured by the fog (and therefore not rendered at all).

```
maxZ: 175,
```

The `subdivisions` parameter defines how many discrete layers there are to the fog effect. Larger values for this parameter produce a smoother appearance at the expense of using more memory.

```
            subdivions: 5
        }
    );
```

Despite being included in all the renderers available in Away3D (*Chapter 4, Z-Sorting*, explains renderers in more detail), the `filters` property is not a part of the base `Renderer` class that all the rendering classes implement. So to get access to the `filters` property, we need to cast the `View3D` renderer property to either the `BasicRenderer` or `QuadrantRenderer` type. Then we can assign the `FogFilter` class to the `filters` property as part of an array.

> The `BasicRenderer` will always append a new `ZSortFilter` object, used to sort the 3D objects in the scene, to any array assigned to the `filters` property. The `QuadrantRenderer` does not append any of its default filters to the supplied array. So when assigning filters to a `QuadrantRenderer` object, it is best to add them one at a time to the existing array, like so:
>
> `(view.renderer as QuadrantRenderer).filters.push(fogFilter);`

```
        (view.renderer as BasicRenderer).filters = [fogFilter];
    }
```

The container is rotated around its Y-axis. This will rotate its children in and out of the fog, providing an effective demonstration of the effect provided by the `FogFilter` class.

```
        protected override function onEnterFrame(event:Event):void
        {
            super.onEnterFrame(event);
            ++container.rotationY;
        }
    }
}
```

In the following image, you can see how the shading applied to the mesh elements that make up the cubes increases as the distance between them and the camera increases.

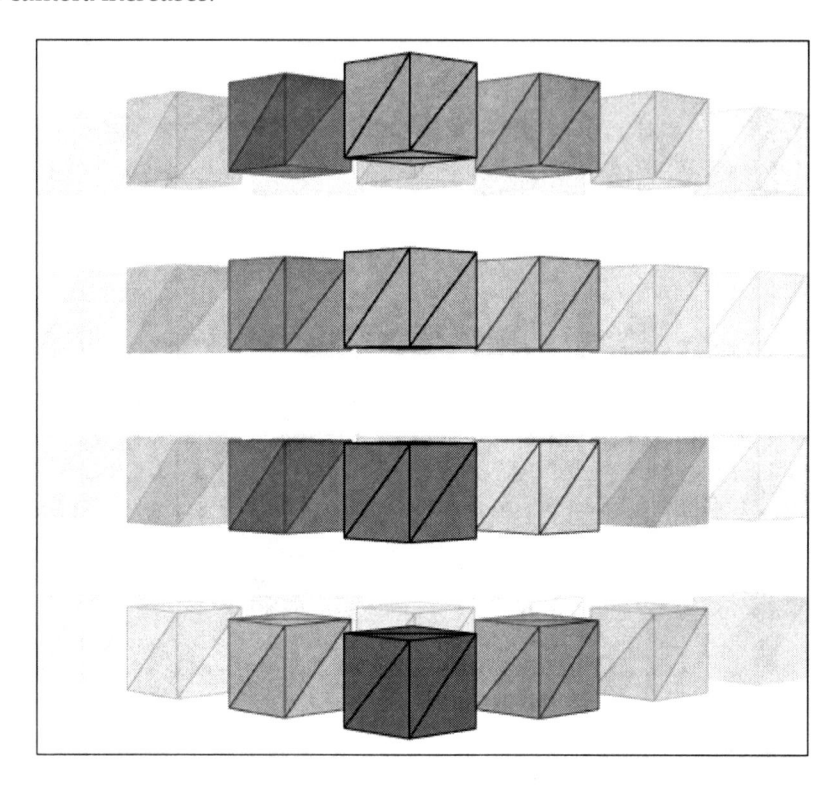

Render Sessions

By default, each mesh element is drawn to a single Render Session object. The default Render Session object used by the view and the scene is represented by the `SpriteSession` class. Because each 3D object will share its parent's Render Session by default, this also means that each 3D object also uses the scene's `SpriteSession` object as well.

Away3D also includes a `BitmapSession` class, which provides easy access to the underlying bitmap data used to draw the Render Session to the screen. This bitmap data can be accessed and modified to create some interesting effects.

Postprocessing with the BitmapRenderSession

To demonstrate the use of the `BitmapSession` class, we will create an application where we replace the default `SpriteSession` object used by the view with a new `BitmapSession` object. Since we can get access to the `BitmapData` object used by the `BitmapSession` class to display the final result, we can use the various drawing routines provided by the `BitmapData` class to create some interesting effects.

The PostProcessingDemo application shown below will use the following process to create a smoky effect that appears to rise off the 3D objects in the scene:

1. A copy of the last frame is transferred to a buffer.
2. The buffer is translated slightly up along the Y-axis.
3. The color of the pixels in the buffer are modified to be slightly more transparent, and to fade into a blue-gray color.
4. The new frame is rendered.
5. The new frame is drawn on top of the buffer.
6. The buffer is drawn to the screen.
7. Go back to step 1.

```
package
{
    import away3d.containers.ObjectContainer3D;
    import away3d.core.base.Mesh;
    import away3d.core.session.BitmapSession;
    import away3d.core.utils.Cast;
    import away3d.events.ViewEvent;
    import away3d.loaders.Max3DS;
    import away3d.materials.BitmapMaterial;
    import flash.display.BitmapData;
    import flash.events.Event;
    import flash.filters.BitmapFilterQuality;
    import flash.filters.BlurFilter;
    import flash.geom.ColorTransform;
    import flash.geom.Matrix;
    import flash.geom.Point;

    public class PostProcessingDemo extends Away3DTemplate
    {
        [Embed(source="ship.3ds", mimeType="application/octet-stream")]
        protected var ShipModel:Class;
        [Embed(source="ship.jpg")]
        protected var ShipTexture:Class;

        protected var shipModel:ObjectContainer3D;
```

Filters and Postprocessing Effects

The effect relies on the image from the last frame being carried across between frames to be used as the background for the next frame. The `buffer` variable will be used to reference the `BitmapData` object that contains the processed copy of the last frame.

```
protected var buffer:BitmapData;
```

To use the `BitmapSession` class, we need to create a new instance of it. The `BitmapSession` constructor takes a single parameter that defines the scale. We have supplied a value of 1, which means that the `BitmapSession` uses the same resolution as the view.

```
protected var bitmapSession:BitmapSession =
   new BitmapSession(1);
```

The smoke effect will be smoothed using an instance of the `BlurFilter` class.

```
protected var blur:BlurFilter = new BlurFilter();
```

The `ColorTransform` class can be used to modify the color and transparency of the individual pixels that make up an image. The following `ColorTransform` object will increase the transparency of a color (or, more accurately, make the color less opaque) while adding 1 to the red channel, 3 to the green channel, and 10 to the blue channel. Modifying the color channels in this way will eventually result in a blue-gray color.

```
protected var fade:ColorTransform =
   new ColorTransform(1, 1, 1, .99, 1, 3, 10, 0);
```

A number of the drawing routines used below require a `Point` object set to (0, 0). It is always best to try and avoid creating new objects where possible, so we define a new instance of the `Point` class here. If no parameters are specified for the `Point` constructor it will default to the position (0, 0).

```
protected var point:Point = new Point();
```

For each frame, the pixels from the last frame will be translated up the screen. Note that we are working with the Flash 2D coordinate system here. This means that moving pixels up the screen involves decreasing their Y coordinates. The following matrix constructor specifies the default values for all the parameters except the sixth, which defines the translation along the Y-axis.

```
protected var matrix:Matrix = new Matrix(1, 0, 0, 1, 0, -1);

public function PostProcessingDemo()
{
   super();
}
```

```
        protected override function initEngine():void
        {
            super.initEngine();
```

For the `BitmapSession` object we created to be used by the view, it has to be assigned to the `View3D session` property.

```
            view.session = bitmapRenderSession;
        }

        protected override function initScene():void
        {
            super.initScene();
            this.camera.z = 0;
            var shipMaterial:BitmapMaterial =
                new BitmapMaterial(Cast.bitmap(ShipTexture));
            shipModel = Max3DS.parse(Cast.bytearray(ShipModel),
                {
                    autoLoadTextures: false,
                    scale: 0.2,
                    z: 500
                }
            );
            for each (var child:Mesh in shipModel.children)
                child.material = shipMaterial;
            scene.addChild(shipModel);
        }

        protected override function initListeners():void
        {
            super.initListeners();
```

The second half of the effect is processed once the current frame has been rendered (that is, after the `onEnterFrame()` function has been called). For this, we register the `onRenderComplete()` function to be called when the `ViewEvent.RENDER_COMPLETE` event is dispatched. We could also have achieved the same result by performing the postprocessing once we had called the `Away3DTemplate onEnterFrame()` function (by calling `super.onEnterFrame()`)

```
            view.addEventListener(
                ViewEvent.RENDER_COMPLETE,
                onRenderComplete
            );
        }

        override protected function onEnterFrame(event:Event):void
        {
```

Filters and Postprocessing Effects

The first half of the effect is processed before the current frame is rendered. Normally in the `onEnterFrame()` function, we start by immediately calling the `onEnterFrame()` function from the base class. In this case though we want to get access to the last frame that was rendered before the view clears the screen and renders the next frame. So we don't call `super.onEnterFrame(event)` right away.

We start by rotating the 3D object in the scene.

```
shipModel.rotationX += 2;
shipModel.rotationY += 1;
```

The first half of the effect involves taking the bitmap data from the last frame and drawing it to a buffer using a slight vertical offset and color transformation.

We need to get a copy of the bitmap data from the last frame rendered. This is done using the `BitmapSession.getBitmapData()` function, which takes the current view object as a parameter.

```
var bitmapSessionData:BitmapData =
   bitmapSession.getBitmapData(view);
```

If this is the first time a frame has been rendered (that is, `buffer` is `null`), the buffer is created to be the same size as the `BitmapSession` bitmap data by supplying `bitmapSessionData.width` and `bitmapSessionData.height` as the first two parameters of the `BitmapData` constructor.

```
if (buffer == null)
{
  buffer = new BitmapData(
    bitmapSessionData.width,
    bitmapSessionData.height,
    true,
    0);
}
```

The buffer content is cleared by drawing a blank rectangle over the buffer.

```
buffer.fillRect(buffer.rect, 0);
```

The contents of the current frame is copied to the buffer using the `BitmapData` `draw()` function.

The first parameter, `source`, is the data source to copy from, which is set to the `BitmapData` object we retrieved from the `BitmapSession` and assigned to the `bitmapSessionData` variable.

The second parameter, `matrix`, is a matrix that can be used to transform the source data as it is copied. The `matrix` object supplied here translates the individual pixels up the screen by one.

The third parameter, `colorTransform`, is a `ColorTransform` object. The `fade` variable references a `ColorTransform` object that will convert the pixels to a blue color and decrease their alpha component, which has the effect of making them more transparent.

```
buffer.draw(bitmapSessionData, matrix, fade);
```

Finally, we use the `BlurFilter` object, referenced by the `blur` variable, to apply a blur effect to the buffer. This is done using the `BitmapData applyFilter()` function.

The first parameter, `sourceBitmapData`, is the bitmap data source to apply the effect to. We have supplied the buffer itself.

The second parameter, `sourceRect`, defines the area within the bitmap data source to use as the input. We want to apply the effect to the whole image, so we supply the buffers `rect` property.

The third parameter, `destPoint`, defines the point within the destination image that corresponds to the upper-left corner of the source rectangle. This will always be the point (0, 0). For this we use the default `Point` object we created earlier.

The fourth parameter, `filter`, defines the filter object that you use to perform the filtering operation. We have supplied the previously created `BlurFilter` object referenced by the `blur` variable.

```
buffer.applyFilter(buffer, buffer.rect, point, blur);
```

Now that we have captured and modified the last frame, we can go on to render the next frame.

```
        super.onEnterFrame(event);
    }
```

The second half of the effect is processed once the current frame has been rendered.

```
protected function onRenderComplete(event:ViewEvent):void
{
```

Once again we need to get a reference to the bitmap data of the `BitmapSession` object.

```
    var bitmapSessionData:BitmapData =
      bitmapSession.getBitmapData(view);
```

Filters and Postprocessing Effects

This bitmap data is copied, or cloned, into a new `BitmapData` object that is assigned to the `postProcess` variable.

```
var postProcess:BitmapData = bitmapSessionData.clone();
```

The current frame is drawn on top of the processed copy of the last frame.

```
buffer.draw(postProcess);
```

This combined image is then drawn back into the `BitmapSession`, causing it to be drawn onto the screen.

```
        bitmapSessionData.copyPixels(buffer, buffer.rect, point);
    }
  }
}
```

The following image shows the final effect:

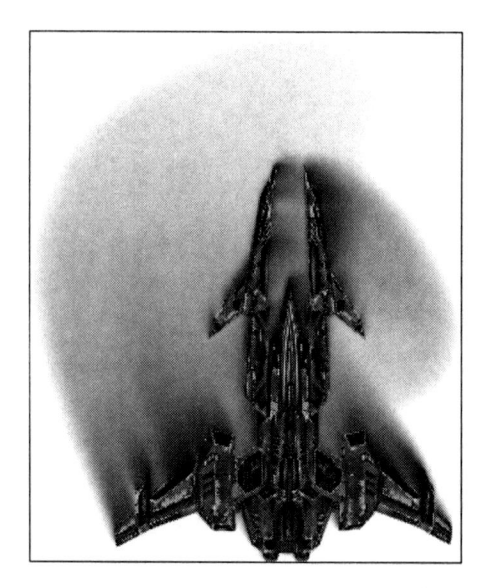

Summary

In this chapter, we looked at the various methods by which a developer can add effects to an Away3D application. We saw how the Flash filter classes from the `flash.filter` package can be applied to an individual 3D object, or the entire view. Example applications were presented that demonstrated the `BlurFilter`, `DisplacementMapFilter`, and `GlowFilter` classes, as well as a sample Pixel Bender shader, applied using the `ShaderFilter` class.

In addition, we saw how the `FogFilter` class could be used to apply a fog-like effect to the scene.

Finally, we looked at how the bitmap data exposed by the `BitmapSession` class can be used to create some interesting custom effects, like the smoky effect shown in the sample application.

We touched briefly on the performance benefits that can be achieved using the `FogFilter` class. In the next chapter, we will take a deeper look at the techniques that are available to get the maximum performance out of an Away3D application.

13
Performance Tips

The Flash platform has evolved over many years to provide an incredibly rich and engaging experience that can take advantage of the latest hardware that is available. The ActionScript Virtual Machine 2 (AVM2) introduced with Flash Player 9 offers a number of performance improvements over the AVM1 used by previous versions of the Flash Player, and technologies like Pixel Bender, introduced with Flash Player 10, provides developers with an even greater level of performance and flexibility. Away3D will quite often take advantage of these features transparently, but there are still a number of techniques that can be employed to increase the speed and responsiveness of an Away3D application.

This chapter will demonstrate a number of these techniques, including:

- Determining the current frame rate
- Setting the maximum frame rate
- Setting the stage quality
- Modifying the size and scaling of the viewport
- Triangle caching
- Level Of Detail (LOD) 3D objects
- The Away3D filter classes
- 3D model loading performance

Determining the current frame rate

When we talk about the performance of an Away3D application, almost always we are referring to the number of **frames per second** (**FPS**) that are being rendered. This is also referred to as the **frame rate**. Higher frame rates result in a more fluid and visually-appealing experience for the end user. Although it is possible to visually determine if an application has an acceptable frame rate, it can also be useful to get a more objective measurement. Fortunately, Away3D has this functionality built in.

Performance Tips

By default, when it is constructed, the `View3D` class will create an instance of the `Stats` class, which is in the `away3d.core.stats` package. This `Stats` object can be accessed via the `statsPanel` property from the `View3D` class. You can display the output of the `Stats` object on the screen using the **Away3D project stats** option in the context (or right-click) menu of an Away3D application.

> To see the **Away3D Project stats** option in the context menu you will need to click on a visible 3D object. If you click on the empty space around the 3D objects in the scene, you will see the standard Flash context menu.

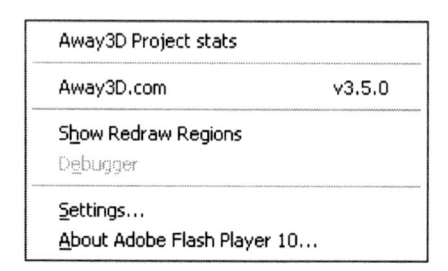

```
Away3D Project stats
Away3D.com                          v3.5.0
Show Redraw Regions
Debugger
Settings...
About Adobe Flash Player 10...
```

This will display a window similar to the following screenshot:

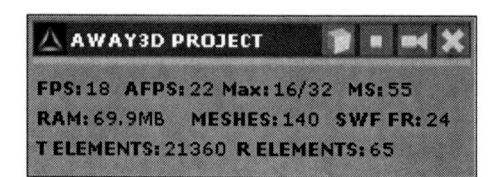

```
AWAY3D PROJECT
FPS:18  AFPS:22  Max:16/32  MS:55
RAM:69.9MB   MESHES:140  SWF FR:24
T ELEMENTS:21360  R ELEMENTS:65
```

This window provides a number of useful measurements:

- FPS, which measures the current frames per second
- AFPS, which measures the average number of frames per second
- Max, which measures the maximum peak value of the frames per second
- MS, which measures the time it took to render the last frame in milliseconds
- RAM, which measures how much memory the application is using
- MESHES, which measures the number of 3D objects in the scene
- SWF FR, which measures the maximum frame rate of the Flash application
- T ELEMENTS, which measures the total number of individual elements that make up the 3D objects in the scene
- R ELEMENTS, which measures the number of individual elements that make up the 3D objects that are being rendered to the screen

These values come in very handy when trying to quantify the performance of an Away3D application.

Setting the maximum frame rate

Recent versions of Flash default to a maximum frame rate of 24 frames per second. This is usually fine for animations, but changing the maximum frame rate for a game may allow you to achieve a more fluid end result. The easiest way to do this is to use the SWF frameRate meta tag, which is a line of code added before the Away3DTemplate class introduced in *Chapter 1, Building Your First Away3D Application*.

```
[SWF(frameRate=100)]
public class Away3DTemplate extends Sprite
{
   // class definition goes here
}
```

> The SWF FR measurement displayed by the Away3D Stats object reflects the maximum frame rate defined by the frameRate meta tag.

Note that setting the maximum frame rate using the frameRate meta tag does not mean that your application will always run at a higher frame rate, just that it can run at a higher frame rate. A slow PC will still run an Away3D application at a low frame rate even if the maximum frame rate has been set to a high value.

You also need to be aware that any calculations performed in the onEnterFrame() function, such as transforming a 3D object, can be dependent on the frame rate of the application. In the following code, we rotate a 3D object by 1 degree around the X-axis every frame. This kind of transformation has been common throughout the examples provided in this book.

```
override protected function onEnterFrame(event:Event):void
{
   super.onEnterFrame(event);
   shipModel.rotationX += 1;
}
```

If the frame rate is 30 FPS, the 3D object will rotate around the X-axis by 30 degrees every second. If the frame rate is 90 FPS, the 3D object will rotate around the X-axis by 90 degrees every second. If your application requires these kinds of transformations to be performed consistently regardless of the frame rate, you can use a tweening library like the one demonstrated in *Chapter 3, Moving Objects*.

Setting Flash quality to low

You may have noticed that Flash offers a number of quality settings in its context menu. This quality setting can be set to one of the four options, which are defined in the `StageQuality` class from the `flash.display` package. As described by the Flash API documentation, these settings are:

- `StageQuality.LOW`: Low rendering quality. Graphics are not anti-aliased, and bitmaps are not smoothed, but runtime still use mip-mapping.
- `StageQuality.MEDIUM`: Medium rendering quality. Graphics are anti-aliased using a 2 x 2 pixel grid, bitmap smoothing is dependent on the `Bitmap.smoothing` setting. Runtimes use mip-mapping. This setting is suitable for movies that do not contain text.
- `StageQuality.HIGH`: High rendering quality. Graphics are anti-aliased using a 4 x 4 pixel grid, and bitmap smoothing is dependent on the `Bitmap.smoothing` setting. Runtimes use mip-mapping. This is the default rendering quality setting that Flash Player uses.
- `StageQuality.BEST`: Very high rendering quality. Graphics are anti-aliased using a 4 x 4 pixel grid. If `Bitmap.smoothing` is `true` the runtime uses a high-quality downscale algorithm that produces fewer artifacts.

> **Mip-mapping** refers to the use of mip-maps, which are precomputed smaller versions of an original bitmap. They are used instead of the original bitmap when the original is scaled down by more than 50 %. This bitmap scaling may occur when a 3D object with a bitmap material is itself scaled down, or off in the distance within the scene.

The quality setting is defined by assigning one of these values to the `quality` property on the stage object:

```
stage.quality = StageQuality.LOW;
```

> A number of demos that are supplied with Away3D set the stage quality by using the SWF quality metatag, like so:
>
> `[SWF(quality="LOW")]`
>
> The Flex compiler does not support setting the stage quality in this way. Although this code will not raise any errors during compilation, the stage quality will remain at the default value of `StageQuality.HIGH`.
>
> You can find more information on the metatags supported by the Flex compiler at http://livedocs.adobe.com/flex/3/html/help.html?content=metadata_3.html.

Setting the stage quality to low will improve the performance of your Away3D application. The increase is felt most in applications that display a large number of 3D objects, like `DOFSpriteDemo` application from *Chapter 9, Special Effects with Sprites*.

The downside to setting the stage quality to low is that it affects all the objects on the stage, not just those drawn by Away3D. The low stage quality is particularly noticeable when rendering text, so the visual quality of controls like textfields and buttons can be significantly degraded.

> Using the medium-quality setting offers a good compromise between speed and visual quality.

Reducing the size of the viewport

The fewer pixels that are drawn to the screen, the faster the rendering process will be. The area that the view will draw into can be defined by assigning a `ClippingRectangle` object to the `clipping` property on the `View3D` class.

To use the `RectangleClipping` class you first need to import it from the `away3d.core.clip` package. You can then define the area that Away3D will draw into by supplying the `minX`, `maxX`, `minY`, and `maxY` init object parameters to the `RectangleClipping` constructor like so:

```
view.clipping = new RectangleClipping(
  {
    minX: -100,
    maxX: 100,
    minY: -100,
    maxY: 100
  }
);
```

The preceding code will limit the output of the view to an area 200 x 200 units in size.

Performance Tips

The `ViewportClippingDemo` application, which can be found on the Packt website, allows you to modify the size of the clipping rectangle at runtime using the arrow up and arrow down keys. You can see the difference that the clipping rectangle makes in the following image. On the left, the clipping rectangle is set to the full area of the stage. On the right, the clipping rectangle has been reduced.

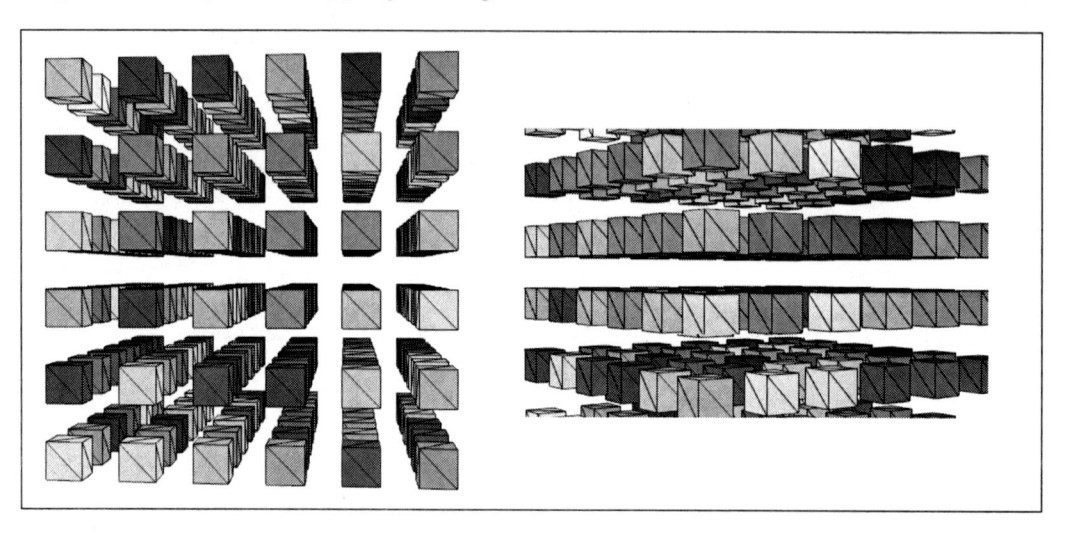

Scaling the viewport output

Another way to reduce the number of pixels rendered by Away3D is to assign a `BitmapSession` object to the `session` property in the `View3D` class. The `Number` passed to the `BitmapSession` constructor defines the internal scale of the bitmap that the scene will be rendered into. The default scale is 2, which will create an internal bitmap whose width and height are half that of the view. This means that the final size of the internal bitmap is one quarter of the size of the view, and thus only a quarter of the number of pixels need to be rendered.

To use the `BitmapSession` class, it first needs to be imported from the `away3d.core.session` package. A new `BitmapSession` object can then be assigned to the `session` property in the `View3D` class:

```
view.session = new BitmapSession(2);
```

The internal bitmap is scaled up to fill the stage when it is drawn. So unlike clipping the viewport, using the `BitmapSession` class allows your application to be displayed using the entire area available to it. However, this does result in a pixilated look. You can see this pixelation in the following images. The `BitmapSession` object used to render the image on the left has a scaling of 1, while the `BitmapSession` object used to render the image on the right has a scaling of 2.

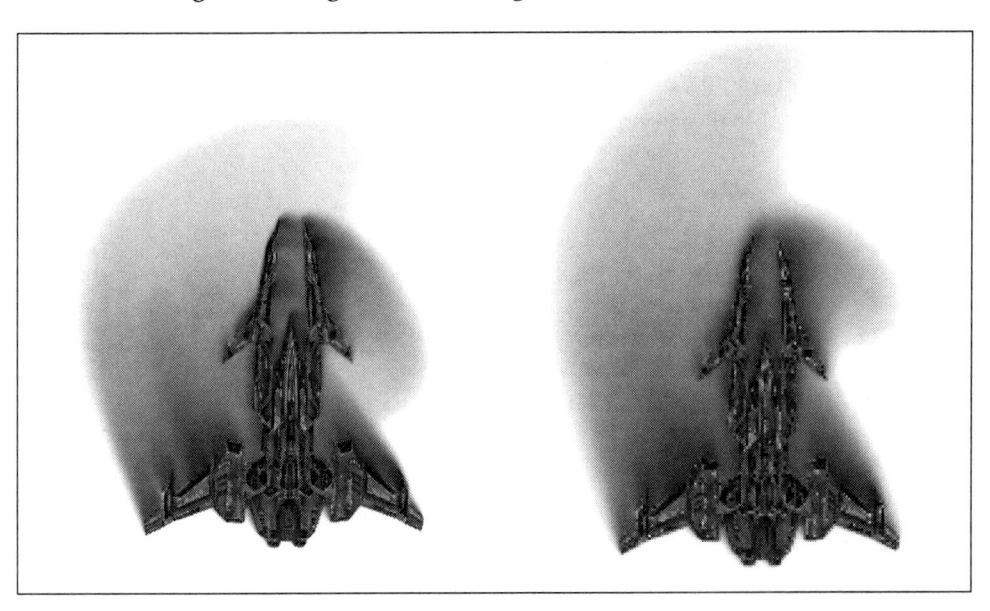

Triangle caching

Away3D includes a feature called triangle caching, which is enabled by default. Triangle caching removes the need for 3D objects to be re-rendered if the appearance of the canvas they are rendered into has not been modified during the last frame.

By default, all 3D objects are rendered into one common canvas. In this scenario, the triangle caching system will only provide some benefit if none of the 3D objects in the scene are modified. While this results in a massive speed boost for static 3D scenes, the ability to draw a static scene at a high frame rate is actually not all that helpful—you could just as easily display a static image instead. Thankfully, triangle caching can also be separately enabled for an individual 3D object by setting its `ownCanvas` property to `true`, or enabled for a group of 3D objects by adding them as children of an `ObjectConatiner3D` object that has its `ownCanvas` property set to `true`. In this way, the 3D objects that are re-rendered each frame can be limited to those individual 3D objects that are modified, or to the children of a container where one of those children was modified. In all cases though, modifying the camera will cause each 3D object to be re-rendered.

Performance Tips

Triangle caching is most useful when the camera is static and only a small number of 3D objects need to be modified for a given frame. The `TriangleCachingDemo` application demonstrates this by adding 75 complex 3D objects to a scene. Each of these 3D objects has its `ownCanvas` property set to `true`, enabling the triangle caching to be applied to each 3D object individually. Each 3D object also responds to the `MouseEvent3D.MOUSE_OVER` and `MouseEevent3D.MOUSE_OUT` events to animate it when it is under the mouse cursor. With a maximum of one 3D object being modified at any one time, and therefore a maximum of one 3D object being re-rendered every frame, triangle caching allows the application to run at a much higher frame rate than would be possible if every 3D object was re-rendered for every frame.

```
package
{
  import away3d.containers.ObjectContainer3D;
  import away3d.core.base.Mesh;
  import away3d.core.utils.Cast;
  import away3d.events.MouseEvent3D;
  import away3d.loaders.Max3DS;
  import away3d.materials.BitmapMaterial;

  import flash.events.Event;
  import flash.filters.GlowFilter;
  import flash.utils.getTimer;

  public class TriangleCachingDemo extends Away3DTemplate
  {
    [Embed(source="ship.3ds", mimeType="application/octet-stream")]
    protected var ShipModel:Class;
    [Embed(source="ship.jpg")]
    protected var ShipTexture:Class;

    protected static const MESH_SCALE:Number = 0.02;
    protected static const SCALE_FACTOR:Number = Math.PI / 1000;
    protected var selectedMesh:ObjectContainer3D;

    public function TriangleCachingDemo()
    {
      super();
    }

    protected override function initScene():void
    {
      super.initScene();
      this.camera.z = 0;
```

The initial 3D model is loaded and textured from the embedded files. We will use this as a template for all the 3D objects that will be added to the scene.

```
var shipMaterial:BitmapMaterial =
  new BitmapMaterial(Cast.bitmap(ShipTexture));
var shipModel:ObjectContainer3D =
  Max3DS.parse(Cast.bytearray(ShipModel),
    {
      autoLoadTextures: false,
      scale: MESH_SCALE,
      rotationY: 180,
```

For the triangle caching system to work we need to set the `ownCanvas` property to `true`.

```
      ownCanvas: true
    }
  );
for each (var child:Mesh in shipModel.children)
  child.material = shipMaterial;
```

Here we use three `for` loops, each used to calculate either the x, y, or z position of the individual 3D objects that will be added to the scene.

```
var meshClone:ObjectContainer3D
for (var xPos:int = -40; xPos <= 40; xPos += 20)
{
  for (var yPos:int = -40; yPos <= 40 ; yPos += 20)
  {
    for (var zPos:int = 100; zPos <= 180 ; zPos += 40)
    {
```

We then clone the template 3D object. This saves us the time it takes to parse the 3D model file (which, as we will see later on, can be quite significant). It also saves some memory, as each of the cloned 3D objects references the geometry of the template 3D object, instead of maintaining their own copy of that data.

```
      meshClone = shipModel.clone() as ObjectContainer3D;
```

The cloned 3D object is then repositioned and added to the scene.

```
      meshClone.x = xPos;
      meshClone.y = yPos;
      meshClone.z = zPos;
      scene.addChild(meshClone);
```

Performance Tips

Each cloned 3D object is set to respond to the `MouseEvent3D.MOUSE_OVER` and `MouseEvent3D.MOUSE_OUT` events.

```
            meshClone.addEventListener(
               MouseEvent3D.MOUSE_OVER,
               onMouseOver
            );
            meshClone.addEventListener(
               MouseEvent3D.MOUSE_OUT,
               onMouseOut
            );
         }
      }
   }
}

      protected function onMouseOver(event:MouseEvent3D):void
      {
```

We set the `selectedMesh` property to reflect the currently selected 3D object when the mouse is over it.

```
         selectedMesh = event.target as ObjectContainer3D;
```

The `GlowFilter` class is used to visually indicate which 3D object is selected.

```
         selectedMesh.filters = [new GlowFilter()];
      }

      protected function onMouseOut(event:MouseEvent3D):void
      {
```

When the mouse has been moved off a 3D object, the `selectedMesh` property is set to `null` to reflect the fact that no 3D object is currently selected.

```
         selectedMesh = null;
         var mesh:ObjectContainer3D =
            event.target as ObjectContainer3D;
```

The `filters` property of the 3D object is set to an empty array, clearing the `GlowFilter` object that was assigned to in the `onMouseOver()` function.

```
         mesh.filters = [];
```

The scale of the 3D object is set back to its default.

```
    mesh.scale(MESH_SCALE);
}

protected override function onEnterFrame(event:Event):void
{
  super.onEnterFrame(event);
  if (selectedMesh != null)
  {
```

If there is a 3D object under the mouse pointer, we use some simple math to bounce its scale between 1 and 2. This demonstrates how individual 3D objects can be transformed or animated, while triangle caching is used on the remaining static 3D object to maintain a high frame rate.

```
    var betweenNegOneAndOne:Number =
       Math.sin(getTimer() * SCALE_FACTOR);
    var betweenZeroAndOne:Number =
       (betweenNegOneAndOne + 1) / 2;
    var betweenOneAndTwo:Number =
       betweenZeroAndOne + 1;
    selectedMesh.scale(betweenOneAndTwo * MESH_SCALE);
     }
   }
  }
}
```

Level of detail models

Level of detail is a technique that is used to display simpler models with a lower polygon count when they are off in the background, while displaying higher quality models with larger polygon counts when they are closer to the camera. Sacrificing the quality of those 3D objects in the background can produce a significant performance boost, and because distant 3D objects are smaller when drawn on the screen quite often there is no noticeable drop in visual quality.

The `LODObject` class, from the `away3d.containers` package, is a container that will display its child 3D objects only when they fall within a certain perspective value range. This perspective value is calculated with the formula:

```
perspective value = camera zoom / (1 + distance from camera / camera focus)
```

Performance Tips

A number of LODObject objects can be used as a group to implement the level of detail technique. As an example, let's take three sphere primitives, each constructed with a different number of polygons:

```
var sphere0:Sphere = new Sphere(
    {
       radius:50,
       segmentsW: 4,
       segmentsH:3
    }
);
var sphere1:Sphere = new Sphere(
    {
       radius:50,
       segmentsW: 10,
       segmentsH:8
    }
);
var sphere2:Sphere = new Sphere(
    {
       radius:50,
       segmentsW: 16,
       segmentsH:12
    }
);
```

Each of these spheres is then added as a child of a new LODObject object. The minp init object parameter defines the minimum end of the perspective value range that the children of the LODObject object will be visible at. The maximum end of the range is defined up to (but not including) the value supplied via the maxp parameter.

```
var lodObject0:LODObject = new LODObject(
    {
       minp:0,
       maxp:0.25
    },
    sphere0
);
var lodObject1:LODObject = new LODObject(
    {
       minp:0.25,
       maxp:0.5
    },
    sphere1
);
```

```
var lodObject2:LODObject = new LODObject(
  {
    minp:0.5,
    maxp:1
  },
  sphere2
);
```

To use these three `LODObject` objects as a group, they can be added as children of a standard `ObjectContainer3D` object:

```
var container:ObjectContainer3D =
  new ObjectContainer3D(lodObject0, lodObject1, lodObject2);
```

When the container is added to the scene, one of these three spheres will then be visible as the distance between the `ObjectContainer3D` object (and its children `LODObject` objects) and the camera changes. To work out at what distance the spheres are visible, the preceding formula can be rewritten as:

```
distance from camera = (1 / perspective value * camera zoom - 1) *
camera focus
```

Using the default values for the cameras zoom (10) and focus (100) properties, we can work out that the `sphere0` 3D object will be visible when it is greater than 3,900 units from the camera. The `sphere1` 3D object will be visible when it is between 3,900 and 1,900 units from the camera. And the `sphere2` 3D object will be visible when it is up to 1,900 units from the camera.

When the application is run, the following images will appear depending on the distance from the camera to the container that holds the `LODObject` objects:

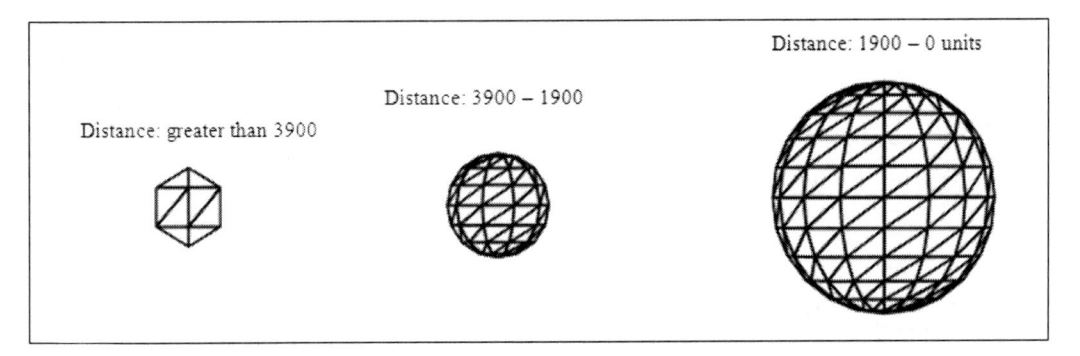

Performance Tips

Away3D filters

In *Chapter 12, Filters and Postprocessing Effects*, we saw how the `FogFilter` class could be used to add a fog effect to the scene. It was also noted that those 3D objects that were behind the last layer of fog were not rendered at all, providing an increase in performance.

Two additional filters are also included in the `away3d.core.filter` package: `MaxPolyFilter` and `ZDepthFilter`. Neither adds a visual effect to the scene, but they can both be used to reduce the number of mesh elements that get drawn to the screen.

Both filters can be applied like the `FogFilter` class from *Chapter 12, Filters and Postprocessing Effects*, by assigning them to the `filters` property available on both the `BasicRenderer` and `QuadrantRenderer` classes. Or they can be passed into either the `BasicRenderer` or `QuadrantRenderer` constructors, with the resulting render class then assigned to the `renderer` property from the `View3D` class.

ZDepthFilter

The `ZDepthFilter` class defines a maximum z depth for mesh elements. Those that lie beyond that maximum depth are not drawn to the screen. This provides the same performance benefits as the `FogFilter` class, but without the fog effect.

The `ZDepthFilter` constructor takes one parameter, `maxZ`, which defines the distance from the camera after which mesh elements are culled. In the following example, a new instance of the `ZDepthFilter` class has been created that will cull all mesh elements that are more than 200 units away from the camera.

```
var zDepthFilter:ZDepthFilter = new ZDepthFilter(200);
view.renderer = new BasicRenderer(zDepthFilter);
```

> In Away3D 3.6, there is a bug in the `ZDepthFilter` class that prevents it from working correctly. By using the `FrustumClipping` class, from the `away3d.core.clip` package, you can achieve the same visual effect as the `ZDepthFilter` class, but there is no performance benefit.
>
> ```
> view.clipping = new FrustumClipping({maxZ:200});
> ```

MaxPolyFilter

The `MaxPolyFilter` filter will only allow a set number of mesh elements to be drawn to the screen. It does this by retaining only the specified number of mesh elements from the collection that would be drawn to the screen. Since this collection is sorted by depth, this has the effect of discarding those mesh elements that represented the furthest 3D objects in the scene.

The `ZDepthFilter` constructor takes one parameter, `maxP`, which defines how many mesh elements will be rendered. The following code creates a new instance of the `MaxPolyFilter` class that will draw only the closest 500 mesh elements.

```
var maxPolyFilter:MaxPolyFilter = new MaxPolyFilter(500);
view.renderer = new BasicRenderer(maxPolyFilter);
```

> The value assigned to the `maxP` property relates directly to the R ELEMENTS value displayed by the stats panel.

Offscreen rendering

There are many instances where a 3D application will display a great number of similar 3D objects. A school of fish, a crowd of people or a city block could easily be created by drawing a handful of individual 3D objects many times over.

Offscreen rendering can speed up these types of scenes considerably. Consider the city scene in the following screenshot:

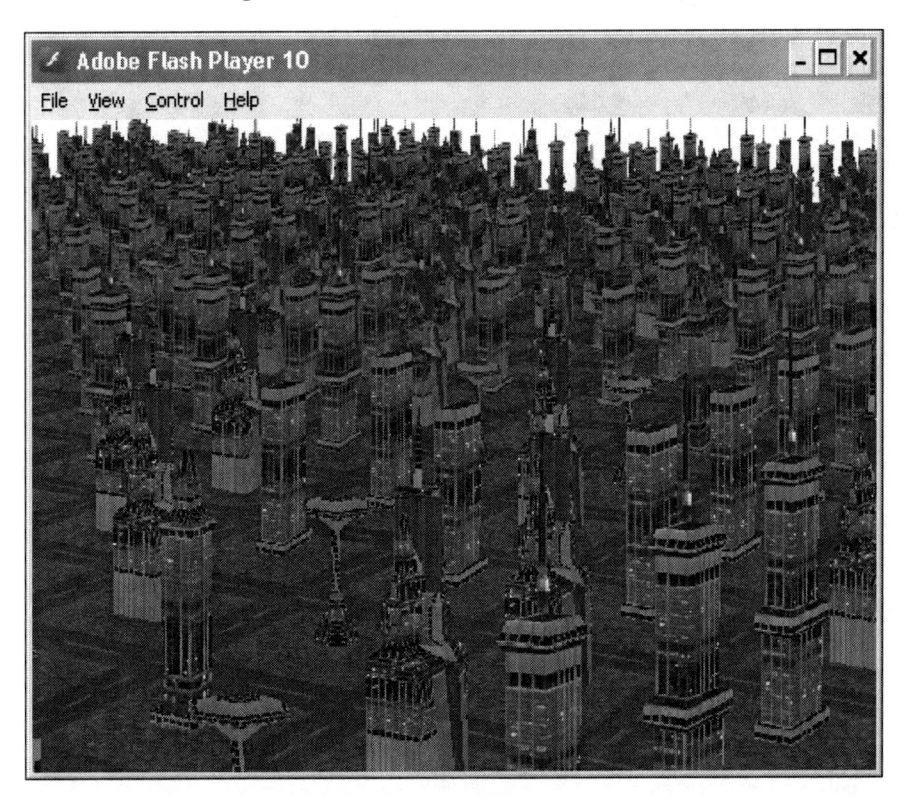

Performance Tips

Even though the scene is made up of hundreds of buildings, each building is displayed using one of five different models. Since each building is situated on a single plane, meaning each is being viewed from roughly the same angle, offscreen rendering can be employed in this situation to provide a performance boost.

The idea behind offscreen rendering is that a 3D object is rendered by a view that has not been added to the stage, and is therefore not visible (or "offscreen"). The image of the rendered 3D object is then displayed by a number of Sprite3D objects within the visible scene. Rendering a single 3D object and displaying the result on multiple Sprite3D objects is much faster than rendering the original 3D object multiple times.

To demonstrate how offscreen rendering is implemented in Away3D, we will create an application called OffscreenRenderingDemo.

```
package
{
    import away3d.cameras.HoverCamera3D;
    import away3d.containers.ObjectContainer3D;
    import away3d.containers.View3D;
    import away3d.core.base.Mesh;
    import away3d.core.clip.RectangleClipping;
    import away3d.core.session.BitmapSession;
    import away3d.core.utils.Cast;
    import away3d.loaders.Max3DS;
    import away3d.materials.BitmapMaterial;
    import away3d.primitives.Plane;
    import away3d.sprites.Sprite3D;

    import flash.display.BitmapData;
    import flash.display.StageQuality;
    import flash.events.Event;
    import flash.events.MouseEvent;

    [SWF(backgroundColor="#FFFFFF")]
    public class OffscreenRenderingDemo extends Away3DTemplate
    {
```

The textures that will be applied to the buildings and the ground plane are embedded.

```
        [Embed(source="building.jpg")]
        protected var BildingTexture:Class;
        [Embed(source="ground.jpg")]
        protected var GroundTexture:Class;
```

As are the 3DS files that hold the models for our buildings.

```
    [Embed(source="building1.3ds", mimeType="application/octet-
stream")]
    protected var Building1:Class;
    [Embed(source="building2.3ds", mimeType="application/octet-
stream")]
    protected var Building2:Class;
    [Embed(source="building3.3ds", mimeType="application/octet-
stream")]
    protected var Building3:Class;
    [Embed(source="building4.3ds", mimeType="application/octet-
stream")]
    protected var Building4:Class;
    [Embed(source="building5.3ds", mimeType="application/octet-
stream")]
    protected var Building5:Class;
```

Each building will be added to its own view. The `buildingViews` collection will hold references to these offscreen views.

```
    protected var buildingViews:Vector.<View3D> =
      new Vector.<View3D>();
```

Each of the five views will be used to create a `BitmapMaterial` object, which will later be displayed on a `Sprite3D` object. The `billboardMaterials` collection will hold references to these materials.

```
    protected var billboardMaterials:Vector.<BitmapMaterial> =
      new Vector.<BitmapMaterial>();
```

The `mouseButtonDown`, `lastStageX`, and `lastStageY` properties are used to rotate the hover camera. *Chapter 7, Cameras*, covers the hover camera in more detail.

```
    protected var mouseButtonDown:Boolean = false;
    protected var lastStageX:Number = 0;
    protected var lastStageY:Number = 0;

    public function OffscreenRenderingDemo()
    {
      super();
    }
```

Performance Tips

The `initEngine()` function is used to set the stage quality to low, create a hover camera, and to create a number of offscreen views by calling the `buildOffscreenView()` function.

```
protected override function initEngine():void
{
  super.initEngine();
  stage.quality = StageQuality.LOW;
  view.camera = new HoverCamera3D(
    {
      distance: 1500,
      yfactor:1,
      tiltAngle: 15
    }
  );

  for (var i:int = 0; i < 5; ++i)
    buildingViews.push(buildOffscreenView());
}
```

The `buildOffscreenView()` function is where the offscreen views are created.

```
protected function buildOffscreenView():View3D
{
```

Creating an offscreen view is no different to a regular view. Both are represented by the `View3D` class.

```
var buildingView:View3D = new View3D();
```

Even though we don't actually add the offscreen view to the stage, we still need to position it as if it were a visible view.

```
buildingView.x = stage.stageWidth / 2;
buildingView.y = stage.stageHeight / 2;
```

In order to take the output of the view and display it as a material, we need to use the `BitmapSession` class. Using the bitmap data that the `BitmapSession` renders to as the source bitmap data for a `BitmapMaterial` class, we can take the offscreen rendering of a 3D object and display it on a `Sprite3D` object within the visible scene.

```
buildingView.session = new BitmapSession(1);
```

Using the `RectangleClipping` class is very important, as it reduces the number of pixels that have to be drawn by the `Sprite3D` objects. The demo would work, for the most part, if there was no clipping done for the offscreen views, because the space around the 3D objects they render would be transparent. However, drawing even completely transparent pixels back in the onscreen view has a performance cost, so it is better to limit the number of pixels that the offscreen views render.

```
buildingView.clipping =
   new RectangleClipping(
      {
         minX:-35,
         maxX:35,
         minY: -175,
         maxY: 175
      }
   );
```

The offscreen view also gets a hover camera. As the hover camera rotates around in the onscreen view, it will also rotate around in the offscreen views. This matches the angles of both cameras, so the offscreen view of the 3D objects approximates how they would be seen if they had been added directly to the onscreen view.

```
buildingView.camera =
   new HoverCamera3D(
      {
         distance:1500,
         yfactor:1,
         tiltAngle: 15
      }
   );
```

We return the new view, so it can be added to the `buildingViews` collection by the `initObject()` function.

Importantly, we have not added these offscreen views to the display list. This means that they will not be visible.

```
      return buildingView;
}
```

Performance Tips

In order to move the hover camera around, we need to listen to a number of mouse events. Again all of this code is explained in *Chapter 7, Cameras*.

```
protected override function initListeners():void
{
  super.initListeners();
  stage.addEventListener(
    MouseEvent.MOUSE_DOWN,
    mouseDown
    );
  stage.addEventListener(
    MouseEvent.MOUSE_UP,
    mouseUp
  );
  stage.addEventListener(
    MouseEvent.MOUSE_MOVE,
    mouseMove
  );
}

protected override function onEnterFrame(event:Event):void
{
  super.onEnterFrame(event);
```

The position of the hover camera from the on screen view is updated.

```
(view.camera as HoverCamera3D).hover();

for each (var offscreenView:View3D in buildingViews)
{
```

The position of the hover cameras from each of the offscreen views are also updated to match the orientation of the hover camera in the onscreen view.

```
(offscreenView.camera as HoverCamera3D).hover();
```

We also need to render each of the offscreen views.

```
offscreenView.render();
  }
}

protected override function initScene():void
{
  super.initScene();
```

Each of the building 3D objects will share the same material, which we create here from the embedded texture.

```
var buildingMaterial:BitmapMaterial =
    new BitmapMaterial(Cast.bitmap(BildingTexture));
```

Each of the building 3D models is then loaded. Loading models from a model file is covered in more detail in *Chapter 6, Models and Animations*.

```
var building1:ObjectContainer3D =
  Max3DS.parse(
    Building1,
    {
      autoLoadTextures: false,
      y: -200
    }
  );
var building2:ObjectContainer3D =
  Max3DS.parse(
    Building2,
    {
      autoLoadTextures: false,
      y: -200
    }
  );
var building3:ObjectContainer3D =
Max3DS.parse(
  Building3,
  {
    autoLoadTextures: false,
    y: -200
  }
);
var building4:ObjectContainer3D =
  Max3DS.parse(
    Building4,
    {
      autoLoadTextures: false,
      y: -200
    }
  );
var building5:ObjectContainer3D =
  Max3DS.parse(
    Building5,
```

Performance Tips

```
    {
        autoLoadTextures: false,
        y: -200
    }
);

    for each (var container:ObjectContainer3D in [building1,
building2, building3, building4, building5])
        for each (var child:Mesh in container.children)
            child.material = buildingMaterial;
```

These building 3D objects are then added to one of the offscreen scenes.

```
buildingViews[0].scene.addChild(building1);
buildingViews[1].scene.addChild(building2);
buildingViews[2].scene.addChild(building3);
buildingViews[3].scene.addChild(building4);
buildingViews[4].scene.addChild(building5);
```

This application will display each of the buildings in the scene as a `Sprite3D` object added to a `Mesh` object. Here we create a new `Mesh` object and add it to the onscreen scene.

```
var sceneMesh:Mesh = new Mesh();
scene.addChild(sceneMesh);
```

We loop over each of the five offscreen views.

```
var view:View3D;
var bitmap:BitmapData;
for (var i:int = 0; i < 5; ++i)
{
```

We get a reference to the offscreen view from the `buildingViews` collection.

```
view = buildingViews[i];
```

We then get a reference to the `BitmapData` object that the views `BitmapSession` draws in to.

```
bitmap = (view.session as BitmapSession).getBitmapData(view);
```

Finally, we create a new `BitmapMaterial` object, supplying the `BitmapData` reference we obtained above. This new `BitmapMaterial` object is then stored in the `billboardMaterials` collection.

Now, because the view and the `BitmapMaterial` objects both reference the same `BitmapData` object, when the offscreen views render a frame it is automatically reflected in the corresponding `BitmapMaterial` object, and thus also shown by any `Sprite3D` object displaying the `BitmapMaterial` object as a material.

```
      billboardMaterials.push(
        new BitmapMaterial(bitmap)
      );
    }
```

We add a plane primitive to the scene, which will represent the ground. Notice that we have used the `screenZOffset` init object parameter to ensure that the ground is always drawn beneath the `Mesh` that contains the building `Sprite3D` objects. The `screenZOffset` init object parameter is covered in *Chapter 4, Z-Sorting*.

```
      scene.addChild(
        new Plane(
          {
            material: new BitmapMaterial(Cast.bitmap(GroundTexture)),
            width: 8000,
            height: 8000,
            x: -66,
            z: 66,
            y: -130,
            segments: 20,
            screenZOffset: 1000
          }
        )
      );
```

This is what everything has been working up to: creating the `Sprite3D` objects that will display the output of the offscreen views. We use a nested `for` loop to create 1,600 billboards in a grid on the X/Z plane.

```
      var randomMaterial:BitmapMaterial;
      var sprite:Sprite3D;
      for (var xPos:int = -4000; xPos < 4000; xPos += 200)
      {
        for (var zPos:int = -4000; zPos < 4000; zPos += 200)
        {
```

Performance Tips

Each billboard will display a random `BitmapMaterial` object from the `billboardMaterials` collection.

```
randomMaterial =
  billboardMaterials[
    Math.round(Math.random() * 4)
  ];
```

We then create a new `Sprite3D` object, supplying the randomly selected material, and then positioning it within the grid.

```
sprite = new Sprite3D(randomMaterial);
sprite.x = xPos;
sprite.y = 0;
sprite.z = zPos;
```

The `Sprite3D` object is then added to the `Mesh` object, which will make it visible within the scene.

```
      sceneMesh.addSprite(sprite);
    }
  }
}
```

The `mouseDown()` and `mouseUp()` functions are used to set the properties that control how the hover cameras are moved.

```
protected function mouseDown(event:MouseEvent):void
{
  this.mouseButtonDown = true;
  this.lastStageX = event.stageX;
  this.lastStageY = event.stageY;
}

protected function mouseUp(event:MouseEvent):void
{
  this.mouseButtonDown = false;
}
```

The tilt and pan angles of the offscreen and onscreen hover cameras are all updated to reflect any mouse movement over the last frame.

```
protected function mouseMove(event:MouseEvent):void
{
  if (this.mouseButtonDown)
  {
```

[358]

```
                var pan:int = (event.stageX - lastStageX);
                var tilt:int = (event.stageY - lastStageY);

                (view.camera as HoverCamera3D).panAngle += pan;
                (view.camera as HoverCamera3D).tiltAngle += tilt;

                for each (var offscreenView:View3D in buildingViews)
                {
                   (offscreenView.camera as HoverCamera3D).panAngle += pan;
                   (offscreenView.camera as HoverCamera3D).tiltAngle += tilt;
                }

                this.lastStageX = event.stageX;
                this.lastStageY = event.stageY;
            }
        }

    }
}
```

The end result is a mesh with 1,600 Sprite3D elements. Each Sprite3D displays the output of one of five offscreen views, while each offscreen view is rendering a single building 3D object. This creates a scene that would be impossible to render at a reasonable frame rate if each building 3D object has been added to the scene individually.

Offscreen rendering actually achieves a similar result to the DirectionalSprite class, which you can read about in *Chapter 9, Special Effects with Sprites*. There are three main benefits to using offscreen rendering:

1. Each model rendered offscreen can be viewed from any angle, not just the discreet angles defined by a DirectionalSprite object.
2. The collective size of the hundreds of images it takes to render a DirectionalSprite object from all angles can often far outweigh the size of a single off screen 3D model and its textures.
3. It is often easier to work with a single 3D object than to pre-render all the images required by a DirectionalSprite object.

Performance Tips

Model formats

Away3D can load 3D models from a variety of formats. The decision on which format to use in your published application is sometimes determined by the features that each format provides. If you require bones animation, you may choose to use the Collada format, while the Quake2 **MD2** format supports vertex animation. However, for static models any of the formats can be used.

Differences in these formats can lead to significant differences in the time it takes them to be loaded and parsed, as well as factors such as model complexity, animation, UV data, and external materials. When your choice of model format is not dictated by their functionality, these differences can have a significant impact on your applications' loading times. Under certain circumstances, one model format may load as much as ten times faster than another.

Take a look at the following graph. The values represent the average time it took to load a common sphere from seven different model formats supported by Away3D, using the **3DS** format as a baseline. The sphere was made up of 3,970 triangles, did not include any animation or bones, was not textured, and contained no UV data. The models were embedded into the SWF, removing any variation that may have arisen from loading the files externally across the network.

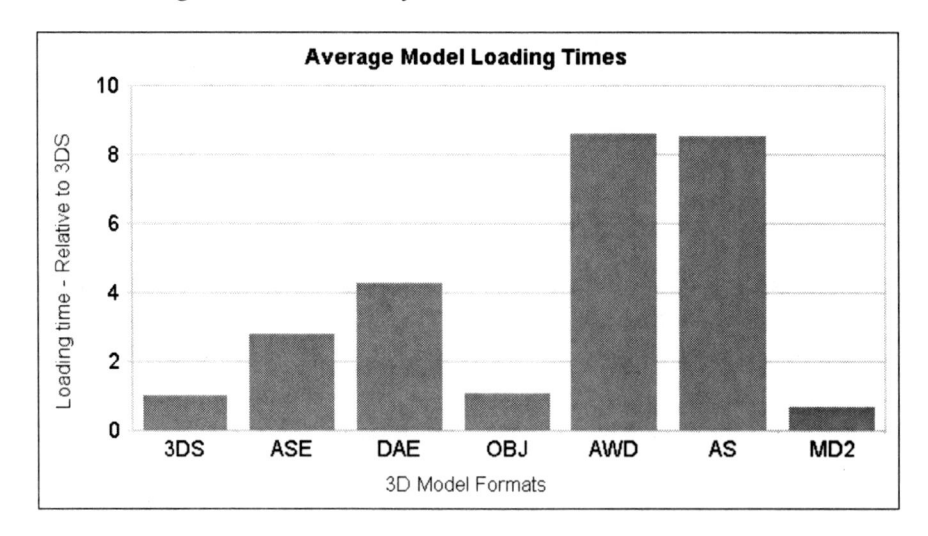

As you can see, the time it took to load this sample 3D model varies quite significantly. The **MD2**, **3DS**, and **OBJ** formats all load relatively quickly, while the **ASE**, **DAE**, **AWD**, and **AS** formats take significantly more time.

Now, take a look at the graph for loading times for a more complex sphere that is made up of 7,922 triangles (again without any textures, bones, animations, or UV data). Again, the values are relative to the time it takes to load the **3DS** model. The **MD2** format was not included because it is limited to 4,092 triangles.

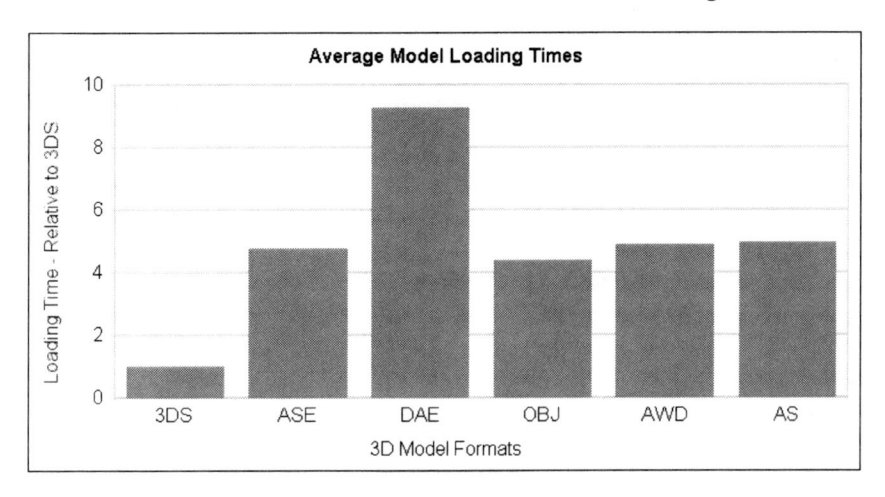

Average Model Loading Times

The situation here is different, with **3DS** clearly being the fastest format to load.

What is important to take from these graphs are not the specific numbers themselves, but the fact that under different circumstances some model formats can load significantly faster than the others. Finding the best model format does have to be done on a case by case basis, but it is worth doing as there is a huge potential to reduce the time it takes to load 3D model files.

The following `ModelLoadingSpeedTest` application is an example of how the loading times of different formats can be measured. It loads a number of 3D models in different formats five times each in random order, and displays the averaged loading times on the screen. It is a quick way to judge which formats will perform the best.

```
package
{
    import away3d.loaders.AWData;
    import away3d.loaders.Ase;
    import away3d.loaders.Collada;
    import away3d.loaders.Max3DS;
    import away3d.loaders.Md2;
    import away3d.loaders.Obj;
    import away3d.materials.WireColorMaterial;
```

Performance Tips

```
import flash.events.Event;
import flash.text.TextField;
import flash.utils.getTimer;

public class ModelLoadingSpeedTest extends Away3DTemplate
{
```

Sample models saved in the various formats are embedded. When using this class to test your own 3D models, you will have to update the `src` parameter to reflect the names of your 3D model files.

```
    [Embed(source="TestSphere.3ds", mimeType="application/octet-stream")]
    protected var TestModel3DS:Class;
    [Embed(source="TestSphere.ase", mimeType="application/octet-stream")]
    protected var TestModelASE:Class;
    [Embed(source="TestSphere.dae", mimeType="application/octet-stream")]
    protected var TestModelDAE:Class;
    [Embed(source="TestSphere.obj", mimeType="application/octet-stream")]
    protected var TestModelOBJ:Class;
    [Embed(source="TestSphere.awd", mimeType="application/octet-stream")]
    protected var TestModelAWD:Class;
    [Embed(source="TestSphere.md2", mimeType="application/octet-stream")]
    protected var TestModelMD2:Class;
```

The following six `Array` objects are used to hold the loading times for the various 3D model formats we are testing.

```
    protected var ThreeD3LoadTimes:Array = new Array();
    protected var MD2LoadTimes:Array = new Array();
    protected var ASELoadTimes:Array = new Array();
    protected var DAELoadTimes:Array = new Array();
    protected var OBJLoadTimes:Array = new Array();
    protected var AWDLoadTimes:Array = new Array();
    protected var ASLoadTimes:Array = new Array();
```

Each embedded 3D model will be loaded, and the loading process timed, by a separate function. These functions will be added to the `functionCalls` collection, which we will then use to randomly select the next model loading operation.

```
    protected var functionCalls:Array = new Array();
```

The `TextField` object referenced by the `results` property will be used to display the status of the application, and the results when the test is completed.

```
protected var results:TextField;

public function ModelLoadingSpeedTest()
{
   super();
```

Each of the six functions used to load a 3D model is added to the `functionCalls` collection five times. This means that each of these functions will be called five times each, allowing us to get an average loading time for each of the 3D model formats.

```
for (var i:int = 0; i < 5; ++i)
{
   functionCalls.push(load3DS);
   functionCalls.push(loadASE);
   functionCalls.push(loadOBJ);
   functionCalls.push(loadDAE);
   functionCalls.push(loadAWD);
   functionCalls.push(loadAS);
   functionCalls.push(loadMD2);
}
}

protected override function initUI():void
{
   super.initUI();
   results = new TextField();
   results.x = 10;
   results.y = 10;
   results.width = 300;
   addChild(results);
}

protected override function onEnterFrame(event:Event):void
{
   super.onEnterFrame(event);
```

As we call each of the functions, they are removed from the `functionCalls` collection. If the `functionCalls` collection has no more elements, we don't need to do any more processing.

```
if (functionCalls.length != 0)
{
```

Performance Tips

The status text on the screen is updated to show how many function calls remain.

```
results.text =
  functionCalls.length +
  " model loading operations remaining";
```

Here we get a reference to and remove a random function from the `functionCalls` collection.

```
var randomPos:int =
  Math.round(
    Math.random() * (functionCalls.length - 1)
  );
var func:Function = functionCalls[randomPos];
functionCalls.splice(randomPos, 1);
```

The function is then called, which will record the time it takes to load a 3D model.

```
func();
```

If there are no more functions left in the `functionCalls` collection we have run through all the tests, we can now display the results.

```
if (functionCalls.length == 0)
{
```

The average loading time is calculated for each of the different 3D model formats.

```
var avg3DS:Number =
  getAverage(ThreeD3LoadTimes);
var avgASE:Number = getAverage(ASELoadTimes);
var avgDAE:Number = getAverage(DAELoadTimes);
var avgOBJ:Number = getAverage(OBJLoadTimes);
var avgAWD:Number = getAverage(AWDLoadTimes);
var avgAS:Number = getAverage(ASLoadTimes);
var avgMD2:Number = getAverage(MD2LoadTimes);
```

The results are then displayed on the screen.

```
results.text =
  "MD2: " +
  avgMD2.toPrecision(4) +
  " seconds\n" +
  "3DS: " +
  avg3DS.toPrecision(4) +
  " seconds\n" +
  "ASE: " +
```

```
              avgASE.toPrecision(4) + "
              seconds\n" +
              "DAE: " +
              avgDAE.toPrecision(4) +
              " seconds\n" +
              "OBJ: " +
              avgOBJ.toPrecision(4) +
              " seconds\n" +
              "AWD: " +
              avgAWD.toPrecision(4) +
              " seconds\n" +
              "AS: " +
              avgAS.toPrecision(4) +
              " seconds";
        }
    }
}
```

The `getAverage()` function simply returns the average value of an `Array` containing a collection of `Number`.

```
        protected function getAverage(array:Array):Number
        {
          var average:Number = 0;
          for each (var time:Number in array)
            average += time;
          return average / array.length;
        }
```

Each of the six functions below are used to load a 3D model of a particular format. You can get more information on loading 3D models in *Chapter 6, Models and Animations*.

```
        protected function loadMD2():void
        {
```

We make a note of the current time before the 3D model is loaded. The value returned by the `getTimer()` function is in milliseconds.

```
            var start:int = getTimer();
```

The 3D model is loaded.

```
            Md2.parse(TestModelMD2);
```

Performance Tips

We make a note of the current time after the 3D model is loaded.

```
var stop:int = getTimer();
```

The time it took to load the 3D model is calculated in seconds.

```
var time:Number = (stop - start) / 1000;
```

This loading time is then stored in the appropriate `Array` object.

```
MD2LoadTimes.push(time);
}
```

All the following functions use the same logic as the `loadMD2()` function described above to store the time it takes to load a 3D object from a given model format.

```
protected function load3DS():void
{
  var start:int = getTimer();
  Max3DS.parse(
    TestModel3DS,
    {
      autoLoadTextures: false
    }
  );
  var stop:int = getTimer();
  var time:Number = (stop - start) / 1000;
  ThreeD3LoadTimes.push(time);
}

protected function loadASE():void
{
  var start:int = getTimer();
  Ase.parse(TestModelASE, {scaling: 1});
  var stop:int = getTimer();
  var time:Number = (stop - start) / 1000;
  ASELoadTimes.push(time);
}

protected function loadDAE():void
{
  var start:int = getTimer();
  Collada.parse(TestModelDAE);
  var stop:int = getTimer();
  var time:Number = (stop - start) / 1000;
```

```
      DAELoadTimes.push(time);
    }

    protected function loadOBJ():void
    {
      var start:int = getTimer();
      Obj.parse(
        TestModelOBJ,
        {
          useMtl:false,
          material: new WireColorMaterial()
        }
      );
      var stop:int = getTimer();
      var time:Number = (stop - start) / 1000;
      OBJLoadTimes.push(time);
    }

    protected function loadAWD():void
    {
      var start:int = getTimer();
      AWData.parse(TestModelAWD, {});
      var stop:int = getTimer();
      var time:Number = (stop - start) / 1000;
      AWDLoadTimes.push(time);
    }

    protected function loadAS():void
    {
      var start:int = getTimer();
      new TestSphere();
      var stop:int = getTimer();
      var time:Number = (stop - start) / 1000;
      ASLoadTimes.push(time);
    }

  }
}
```

Another issue to consider is the size of the 3D model files. The test sphere model used in the first loading test ranged in size from 55 KB for the **MD2** file all the way up to 1.47 MB for the **ASE** file. That means the **ASE** file would take over 20 times as long to download once the application was launched if it were not embedded in the **SWF** file.

Summary

Optimizing your Away3D application can be the difference between a slow and frustrating or rewarding experience for the end user. In this chapter, we looked at how the performance of an Away3D application can be easily monitored using the included `Stats` class. A number of techniques were then presented that can be employed to trade off visual accuracy with performance, such as reducing the stage quality, using filters to reduce the number of elements that are rendered to the screen, reducing the resolution of the rendered output, and reducing the screen area that is drawn to.

A sample application was presented that demonstrated how offscreen rendering can be used to create detailed scenes that would not be possible to create with standard 3D objects alone.

The `LODObject` class was covered, which can be used to increase performance by rendering lower detail 3D models when further back in the scene.

Finally, we saw how the various 3D model formats supported by Away3D can affect an application's loading performance.

Index

Symbols

_constructorParams collection 257
_constructorParams property 257
_index init object parameter, AnimatedBitmapMaterial class 147
3D formats, Away3D
 3DS Max 174
 3DS MAX Ascii 174
 ActionScript 174
 Away3D 174
 Collada 174
 Google Earth 174
 Quake II 174
 Wavefront 174
3D modeling applications
 3ds Max 173
 about 173
 Blender 173
 Milkshape 173
 Sketch-Up 173
3D models
 animated models 180
 exporting 174
 exporting, from 3ds Max 175
 exporting, from MilkShape 176
 exporting, from Sketch-Up 176, 177
 loading 179
 MD2 180
 static models 190
3D object
 scaling 88
 transforming 71
3D object, scaling
 scale() function 88
 scale init object parameter 88
 scaleX property 88
 scaleY property 88
 scaleZ property 88
3D object rotation
 movePivot() function 86
 pitch() function 87
 roll() function 87
 scenePivotPoint property 87
 yaw() function 87
3ds Max
 3D models, exporting from 175
3DS model format
 about 190
 embedded file, loading 190-192
 external file, loading 192, 193
3D text
 creating 269
 extruding 274
 warping 277-284
3D text, creating
 3D text, extruding 274-276
 3D text, warping 277-284
 3D text materials 273
 fonts, embedding 270
 text, displaying in scene 271-273
3D text materials 273

A

AbstractParser constructor 204
AbstractPrimitive class 45
ActionScript Virtual Machine 2 (AVM2) 335
addAction() function 264
addChild() function 44, 73
addDirectionalMaterial() function 248
addEventHandler() function 226
addEventListener() function 231
addHoverCamera() function 215, 218

addInitializer() function 262
additional renderers, Away3D
  about 108
  CORRECT_Z_ORDER renderer 108
  INTERSECTING_OBJECTS renderer 112
addOnMouseDown() function 237
addOnMouseMove() function 237
addOnMouseOut() function 237
addOnMouseOver() function 237
addOnMouseUp() function 237
addOnRollOut() function 237
addOnRollOver() function 237
addOnSuccess() function 188
addSpringCamera() function 218
addTargetCamera() function 218, 219
Adobe Flash Builder
  Away3DTemplate, adding 21, 22
  empty project, creating 10
  Flex SDK, using 13-15
  SphereDemo, running 28
Adobe Flash CS4
  about 11, 12
  Away3DTemplate, adding 23, 24
  empty project, creating 11, 12
  Flex SDK, using 17
  SphereDemo, running 28
Adobe Flex Builder
  about 10
  Away3DTemplate, adding 21, 22
  empty project, creating 10
  Flex SDK, using 13-15
  SphereDemo, running 28
Adobe Pixel Bender Exchange 313
AFPS 336
alpha init object parameter, ShadingColor-
    Material class 157
alpha init object parameter, WireColorMate-
    rial class 139
ambient init object parameter, Shading-
    ColorMaterial class 156
AmbientLight3D class 122
AnimatedBitmapMaterial material
  about 146, 147
  init object parameters 147
animated materials
  about 145
  AnimatedBitmapMaterial 146

Interactive MovieMaterial 148
MovieMaterial material 145
AnimationData class 180
AnimationData object 187
animationData variable 182
aperture property 252
applyBlurFilter() function 317
applyDisplacementMapFilter() function 318
applyGlowFilter() function 319
applyShaderFilter() function 320
applyWireColorMaterial() function 133, 139
applyWireframeMaterial() function 120
AS
  converted model, loading 189
asAS3Class() function 204
Ase class 199
ASE file format
  about 197
  embedded file, loading 197
  external file, loading 198, 200
Ase load() function 198
autoLoadTextures parameter 192
autoplay init object parameter, Animated-
    BitmapMaterial class 147
autosave attribute
  camera lenses 209
autoUpdate init object parameter, Movie-
    Material class 146
Away3D
  3D formats 174
  3D text, creating 269
  additional renderers 108
  colors 119
  downloading 8
  empty project, creating 10
  Flash quality, setting to low 338
  frame rate, determining 335-337
  global coordinate system 71
  level of detail models 345, 347
  lights 122
  local coordinate system 71
  materials 117, 122
  maximum frame rate, setting 337
  model formats 360
  mouse events 225
  objects, positioning in 3D scene 25
  offscreen rendering 349, 350

[370]

)painter's algorithm 100
parent coordinate system 71-74
scene, sorting 100-103
sorting order, adjusting 103
source, downloading using SVN 9
source ZIP file, downloading 8, 9
sprite classes 241
textures, loading from external resources 168
triangle caching 341-345
viewport output, scaling 340, 341
viewport size, reducing 339, 340
z-sorting 107
Away3D. Flint
about 256
URL 256
away3d.lights package 122
Away3DFilterDemo class 323
Away3D Filters 322-326
Away3D filters
about 348
MaxPolyFilter 348
ZDepthFilter 348
Away3DParticle initialize() function 259, 262
Away3DParticleRenderer class 258
Away3DParticleRenderer render() function 264
Away3D Stardust initializer
creating 256, 257
Away3D Stardust particle renderer
creating 258-260
Away3DTemplate
adding, to Adobe Flash Builder 21, 22
adding, to Adobe Flash CS4 23, 24
adding, to Adobe Flex Builder 21, 22
adding, to FlashDevelop 22, 23
extending 26, 27
running 21
Away3DTemplate class 18, 128, 179, 265, 337
Away3DTemplate constructor 26, 179
AWData class 194
AWD format
about 193
embedded file, loading 193-196
external file, loading 196, 197

axial symmetry 294
axTiltAngle parameter, HoverCamera3D class 222

B

base elements, 3D object
segments 38
Sprite3D 35-37
basic materials
about 137
ColorMaterial 140
WireColorMaterial 137, 138
WireframeMaterial 139
BASIC property 108
BasicRenderer 325
BitmapData applyFilter() function 331
BitmapData draw() function 330
BitmapData object 141 299
BitmapFileMaterial class 41, 183
BitmapFileMaterial material
about 169
init object parameters 169
BitmapMaterial class 94, 180
BitmapMaterial material
about 141
init object parameters 142
BitmapMaterial object 181
bitmap materials
about 141
BitmapMaterial material 141
TransformBitmapMaterial material 143
BitmapRenderSession
postprocessing, with 327-332
BitmapSession.getBitmapData() function 330
BitmapSession class 326
BitmapSession constructor 340
bitmapSessionData variable 331
BitmapSession object 340
Blender
3D models, exporting from 177
blendMode init object parameter, BitmapMaterial class 142
blendMode init object parameter, EnviroColorMaterial class 154

BlurFilter
  applying 317
BlurFilter class 317
bounce property 130
buffer variable 328
buildOffscreenView() function 352
bytearray() function 181

C

**cache init object parameter, ShadingColor-
    Material class** 157
camera
  properties 208
Camera3D class
  focus property 208
  fov property 209
  zoom property 209
Camera3D unproject() function 238
camera classes
  about 212-214
  hover camera 220
  spring camera 223
  target camera 219
CameraDemo 213
camera lenses
  about 209
  OrthogonalLens 212
  PerspectiveLens 210
  SphericalLens 210
  ZoomFocusLens 210
Cast class 94, 142
centerMesh init object parameter 295
**checkPolicyFile init object parameter, Bit-
    mapFileMaterial** 169
CJsignals library
  downloading 256
clearFilters() function 315, 316
clipping property 339
ClippingRectangle object 339
Collada
  about 174
  embedded file, loading 185, 186
  external file, loading 187, 188
Collada class 185
Collada exporters 178, 179
ColladaMax plugin
  about 175
  downloading 175
  installing 175
ColorMaterial material
  about 140, 141
  init object parameters 141
colors
  about 119
  defining 119
  defining, by integer 119
  defining, by string 120
ColorTransform class 328
**colorTransform init object parameter, Bit-
    mapMaterial class** 143
composite materials
  about 149
  DepthBitmapMaterial 149, 151
  EnviroBitmapMaterial 151, 152
  EnviroColorMaterial 153
cone class
  about 46
  init object parameters 47
construct() function 257
Container3D object 323
continousCurve() function 279
CORRECT_Z_ORDER renderer 108
Cube class
  about 47
  init object parameters 48
CubeMaterialsData constructor 49
CubFaces class 128
CubicEnvMapPBMaterial material
  about 167, 168
  init object parameters 168
currentPrimitive property 41, 130
Cylinder class
  about 51
  init object parameters 51

D

Damping3D action 265
DeathLife action 264
**debug init object parameter, BitmapMate-
    rial class** 142
**debug init object parameter, ColorMaterial
    class** 141

debugPath() function 281
DepthBitmapMaterial material
  about 149, 151
  init object parameters 151
DepthOfFieldSprite class
  about 251
  aperture property 252
  doflevels property 252
  focus property 252
  implementing 251-255
  maxblur property 252
DepthOfFieldSpriteDemo demo 255
depth sorting 100
destPoint parameter 331
diffuse init object parameter, ShadingColor-
    Material class 156
DirectionalLight3D class 122
directionalLight property 130
DirectionalSprite class
  about 245
  implementing 245-250
DirectionalSprite object 248, 249
displacement map 318
DisplacementMapFilter
  applying 318
DisplacementMapFilter constructor 318
DisplacementMapFilter object 318
DisplayObject class 312
DisplayObject object 312
distance parameter, HoverCamera3D class
    222
doflevels property 252
Dot3BitmapMaterialF10 material
  about 122, 161, 162
  init object parameters 162
Dot3BitmapMaterial material
  about 122, 160
  init object parameters 161

E

EarthDiffuse class 128, 141
Elevation class 297
Elevation generate() function 302
ElevationReader class 302
emitter property 266
empty project
  creating 10

creating, in Adobe Flash CS4 11, 12
creating, in Adobe Flex Builder 10
creating, in FlashDevelop 10, 11
EnviroBitmapMaterial material
  about 151, 152
  init object parameters 152
EnviroColorMaterial material
  about 153
  init object parameters 153
enviroMap init object parameter, EnviroBit-
    mapMaterial class 152
enviroMap init object parameter, Enviro-
    ColorMaterial class 154
environment mapping, shading techniques
    125
envMapAlpha init object parameter, Cubi-
    cEnvMapPBMaterial 168
envMapAlpha init object parameter, Fres-
    nelPBMaterial 166
execute() function 281-284, 308
extractFonts() function 272

F

faces init object parameter, CubicEnv-
    MapPBMaterial 168
faces init object parameter, FresnelPBMate-
    rial 166
FFmpeg
  about 147
  downloading 147
Fighter class 95
filters property 312, 344
filterText property 313
fish-eye lens 211
flag
  creating, PathExtrusion class used 288-290
Flash API documentation, settings
  Bitmap.smoothing setting 338
  StageQuality.BEST 338
  StageQuality.HIGH 338
  StageQuality.LOW 338
  StageQuality.MEDIUM 338
FlashDevelop
  about 10, 11
  Away3DTemplate, adding 22, 23
  empty project, creating 10, 11

Flex SDK, using 15, 16
SphereDemo, running 28
Flash filters
 about 312
 applying 312-316
 applying, to the view 321
 BlurFilter, applying 317
 DisplacementMapFilter, applying 318, 319
 GlowFilter, applying 319, 320
 Pixel Bender Shaders, applying 320, 321
Flash platform 335
Flash Player 10
 about 7
 downloading 8
 overview 7
Flash quality
 setting, to low 338
Flash Sprite class 18
flat shading, shading techniques 126
Flex SDK
 about 13
 downloading 13
 using, in Adobe Flash Builder 13, 14
 using, in Adobe Flash CS4 17
 using, in Adobe Flex Builder 13, 14
 using, in FlashDevelop 15, 16
flip parameter 295
focus property 252
FogFilter class 322
followContinuousCurve() function 278, 279
followCurve() function 278, 283
followLine() function 278-281
FontDemo application
 creating 271
Fonts.SWF file 271
Fonts class 271
FPS 336
frameCount property 130
frame rate
 determining 335, 336
frameRate meta tag 337
frames per second (FPS) 335
FresnelPBMaterial material
 about 165, 166
 init object parameters 166
FrustumClipping object 214

G

generate() function 299
geodesic sphere
 about 52
 comparing, with regular sphere primitive 53
GeodesicSphere class
 about 52
 init object parameters 54
get() function 257
getAverage() function 365
getLevel() function 302
getMaterial() function 203
getXMLTagName() function 261
global coordinate system. *See also* world space 72
globalProjection init object parameter, TransformBitmapMaterial class 144
gloss init object parameter, PhongMultiPassMaterial 165
gloss init object parameter, PhongPBMaterial 164
GlowFilter
 applying 319
GlowFilter class 237, 319, 344
GlowFilter constructor 319
grid plane 54
GridPlane class
 about 55
 the init object parameters 55
groundPlane property 233
groundPosition property 233

H

height map 297
HeightMapModifier class 306
HeightMapModifierDemo application
 about 307
 applying 307-310
hover() function 216, 221
hover camera 220
HoverCamera3D class
 about 220
 init object parameters 222
hoverCamera property 221

I

initCone() function 47
initCube() function 48, 131
initCylinder() function 51
initDirectionalLight() function 132
initEngine() function 19, 41, 108, 352
initGeodesicSphere() function 53
initGridPlane() function 55
initial application
  creating 18-20
initialize() function 257
initLineSegment() function 56
initListeners() function 19, 134, 215
initObject() function 353
init object parameters
  align 273
  back 46
  bothsides 46
  leading 272
  letterSpacing 272
  material 46
  outline 46
  size 272
  text 272
  width 273
init object parameters, AnimatedBitmapMaterial class
  _index 147
  autoplay 147
  loop 147
  movie 147
init object parameters, BitmapFileMaterial
  checkPolicyFile 169
  url 169
init object parameters, BitmapMaterial material
  bitmap 142
  blendMode 142
  color 143
  colorTransform 143
  debug 142
  repeat 142
  showNormals 143
  smooth 142
  wireColor 142

init object parameters, ColorMaterial material
  color 141
  debug 141
init object parameters, cone class
  height 47
  openEnded 47
  radius 47
  segmentsH 47
  segmentsW 47
  yUp 47
init object parameters, Cube class
  cubeMaterials 49
  depth 48
  faces 49
  flip 48
  height 48
  mappingType 48
  segmentsD 48
  segmentsH 48
  segmentsW 48
  width 48
init object parameters, CubicEnvMapPBMaterial
  bitmap 168
  envMapAlpha 168
  faces 168
  normalMap 168
  targetModel 168
init object parameters, Cylinder class
  height 51
  openEnded 52
  radius 51
  segmentsH 52
  segmentsW 51
  yUp 52
init object parameters, DepthBitmapMaterial class
  bitmap 151
  maxColor 151
  maxZ 151
  minColor 151
  minZ 151
init object parameters, Dot3BitmapMaterial class
  bitmap 161
  normalMap 161

shininess 161
specular 161
init object parameters, Dot3BitmapMaterialF10
  bitmap 162
  normalMap 162
  shininess 162
  specular 162
init object parameters, EnviroBitmapMaterial class
  bitmap 152
  enviroMap 152
  mode 152
  reflectiveness 152
init object parameters, EnviroColorMaterial class
  blendMode 154
  color 154
  enviroMap 154
  mode 154
  reflectiveness 154
  smooth 154
init object parameters, FresnelPBMaterial
  bitmap 166
  envMapAlpha 166
  faces 166
  innerRefraction 166
  normalMap 166
  outerRefraction 166
  refractionStrength 166
  targetModel 166
init object parameters, GeodesicSphere class
  fractures 54
  radius 54
init object parameters, HoverCamera3D class
  distance 222
  maxTiltAngle 222
  minTiltAngle 222
  panAngle 222
  steps 222
  tiltAngle 222
  wrapPanAngle 222
  yfactor 222
init object parameters, LineSegment class
  edge 56
  end 57
  segments 57
  start 57
init object parameters, MovieMaterial class
  autoUpdate 146
  interactive 146
  lockH 146
  lockW 146
  movie 146
  transparent 146
init object parameters, PhongBitmapMaterial class
  bitmap 158
  shininess 158
  specular 158
init object parameters, PhongColorMaterial class
  color 159
  shininess 159
  specular 159
init object parameters, PhongMovieMaterial class
  movie 160
  shininess 160
  specular 160
init object parameters, PhongMultiPassMaterial
  bitmap 165
  gloss 165
  normalMap 165
  specular 165
  specularMap 165
  targetModel 165
init object parameters, PhongPBMaterial
  bitmap 164
  gloss 164
  normalMap 164
  specular 164
  specularMap 164
  targetModel 164
init object parameters, Plane class
  height 58
  segments 58
  segmentsH 58
  segmentsW 58
  width 58
  yUp 58

init object parameters, RegularPolygon class
  radius 59
  sides 59
  subdivision 59
  yUp 59
init object parameters, RoundedCube class
  cubeMaterials 60
  cubicmapping 60
  depth 60
  faces 60
  height 60
  radius 60
  subdivision 60
  width 60
init object parameters, ShadingColorMaterial class
  alpha 157
  ambient 156
  cache 157
  color 156
  diffuse 156
  specular 157
init object parameters, Sphere class
  radius 65
  segmentsH 65
  segmentsW 65
  yUp 65
init object parameters, TargetCamera3D class
  target 220
init object parameters, Torus class
  radius 67
  segmentsR 67
  segmentsT 67
  tube 67
  yUp 67
init object parameters, TransformBitmapMaterial class
  bitmap 144
  globalProjection 144
  offsetX 144
  offsetY 144
  projectionVector 144
  rotation 144
  scaleX 144
  scaleY 144
  throughProjection 144
  transform 144
init object parameters, Triangle class
  edge 68
  yUp 68
init object parameters, WhiteShadingBitmapMaterial class
  bitmap 155
  shininess 155
init object parameters, WireColorMaterial material
  alpha 139
  color 139
  wirecolor 139
init objects
  issues 202-204
initPlane() function 57, 131
initPointLight() function 132
initRegularPolygon() function 58
initRoundedCube() function 60
initScene() function 21, 41, 42, 73, 95, 133, 179, 215, 228, 314
initSeaTurtle() function 61, 63
initSkybox() function 62, 63
initSkybox6() function 63
initSphere() function 64, 131, 138
initTorus() function 67, 131
initTriangle() function 68
initTrident() function 69
initUI() function 19, 21, 133, 314
innerRefraction init object parameter, FresnelPBMaterial 166
interactive init object parameter, MovieMaterial class 146
Interactive MovieMaterial material 148
INTERSECTING_OBJECTS property 108
INTERSECTING_OBJECTS renderer 112
isometric projection 212

K

kernels 121
keyCode property 135
Kmz class 197
KMZ format 197

L

LatheExtrusion class 293
level of detail 345, 347

Life initializer 263
light materials
  about 154
  Dot3BitmapMaterial 160
  PhongBitmapMaterial 157
  PhongColorMaterial 158
  PhongMovieMaterial 159
  ShadingColorMaterial 155
  WhiteShadingBitmapMaterial 154
lights
  about 122
  ambient lights 122
  directional lights 122
  point lights 122
LinearExtrusion class 291
LineSegment class
  about 56
  init object parameters 56
load() function 179, 183, 184
loaded model
  converting, to ActionScript class 204-206
Loader3D.parse 203
Loader3D class 187
Loader3D constructor 204
Loader3DEvent object 183
Loader3D object 184
LoaderCube constructor 203
loadMD2() function 366
loadTextures() function 184
LocalAxisMovement 75
local coordinate system. See local space
local space 75-77
lockH init object parameter, MovieMaterial class 146
lockW init object parameter, MovieMaterial class 146
LODObject class 345
lookAt() function 288
lookOffset property, SpringCam class 224
loop init object parameter, AnimatedBitmapMaterial class 147

M

mappingType init object parameter 49
mass property, SpringCam class 224

materials
  about 117
  animated materials 145
  applying 127-137
  basic materials 137
  bitmap materials 141
  composite materials 149
  Dot3BitmapMaterial 122
  Dot3BitmapMaterialF10 122
  light materials 154
  PhongBitmapMaterial 122
  PhongColorMaterial 122
  PhongMovieMaterial 122
  PhongMultiPassMaterial 122
  PhongPBMaterial 122
  Pixel Bender materials 161
  resource management 118
  ShadingColorMaterial 122
  shading techniques 123
  WhiteShadingBitmapMaterial 122
MaterialsDemo applyColorMaterial() function 120
MaterialsDemo applyWireColorMaterial() function 120
MaterialsDemo class 120, 127
matrices 89
Max 336
Max3DS class 191
maxblur property 252
maxColor init object parameter, DepthBitmapMaterial class 151
maxColor parameter 150
maximum frame rate
  setting 337
MaxPolyFilter 348
maxZ init object parameter, DepthBitmapMaterial class 151
maxZ parameter 149, 325
MD2
  about 180
  embedded file, loading 180-182
  external file, loading 183, 184
Md2 constructor 204
MD2EmbeddedDemo 180
Md2 parse() function 204
measurements
  AFPS 336

FPS 336
Max 336
MESHES 336
MS 336
RAM 336
R ELEMENTS 336
SWF FR 336
T ELEMENTS 336
Mesh constructor 204
MESHES 336
Mesh material property 138
MilkShape
  3D models, exporting from 176
minColor init object parameter, DepthBitmapMaterial class 151
minColor parameter 149
minTiltAngle parameter, HoverCamera3D class 222
minZ init object parameter, DepthBitmapMaterial class 151
minZ parameter 149, 324
Mip-mapping 338
mode init object parameter, EnviroBitmapMaterial class 152
mode init object parameter, EnviroColorMaterial class 154
model formats, Away3D
  about 360
  Collada format 360
  graphical representation 360, 361
  loading time, measuring 361-367
  Quake2 MD2 format 360
  selecting 360
monster 186
Mouse3DEvent.MOUSE_OVER event 230
Mouse3DEvent.ROLL_OVER event 231
Mouse3DEvent string constant
  MOUSE_DOWN 226
  MOUSE_MOVE 225
  MOUSE_OUT 226
  MOUSE_OVER 225
  MOUSE_UP 226
  ROLL_OUT 226
  ROLL_OVER 226
mouseButtonDown property 221
MouseEevent3D.MOUSE_OUT event 342
MouseEvent3D.MOUSE_OVER event 342

MouseEvent3D class
  properties 226
mouse events, Away3D 225
mouse position
  projecting, into scene 231-240
Move3D action 264
moveBackward() function 216
moveForward() function 77, 216
movePivot() function 86
moveSphere() function 304, 305
movie init object parameter, AnimatedBitmapMaterial class 147
movie init object parameter, MovieMaterial class 146
movie init object parameter, PhongMovieMaterial class 160
MovieMaterial material
  about 145
  init object parameters 146
MS 336

N

nesting
  about 92
  example 93, 94
NestingDemo class 94
newMaterial variable 138
normalMap init object parameter, CubicEnvMapPBMaterial 168
normalMap init object parameter, Dot3BitmapMaterial class 161
normalMap init object parameter, Dot3BitmapMaterialF10 162
normalMap init object parameter, FresnelPBMaterial 166
normalMap init object parameter, PhongMultiPassMaterial 165
normalMap init object parameter, PhongPBMaterial 164
normal mapping, shading techniques
  about 124, 125
  benefits 124

O

Object3D class 18, 316
Object3D constructor 204

[379]

ObjectConatiner3D object 341
ObjectContainer3D class 73
ObjectContainer3D constructor 204
ObjectContainer3D object 186, 324
objects
  positioning, in 3D scene 25
OBJ file format
  about 200
  embedded file, loading 200
  external file, loading 201, 202
offscreen rendering
  about 349, 350
  demonstrating 350
  employing 350
  implementing 350-359
OffscreenRenderingDemo
  creating 350
offset init object parameter 292
offsetX init object parameter, TransformBit-mapMaterial class 144
offsetY init object parameter, TransformBit-mapMaterial class 144
Ogre 189
Omega3D initializer 264
onComplete parameter 306
onEnterFrame() function 20, 42, 89, 97, 134, 149, 221, 238, 316, 329, 330, 337
onKeyDown() function 217
onKeyUp() function 42, 134, 315
onLoadSuccess() function 184, 188, 199
onMouseDown() function 217, 236
onMouseOut() function 236
onMouseOver() function 236, 344
onMouseUp() function 236
onRenderComplete() function 329
OpenCollada exporter
  about 178
  URL 178
OrthogonalLens class 212
outerRefraction init object parameter, FresnelPBMaterial 166
OwnCanvasDemo 312
ownCanvas property 312, 341 106

P

painter's algorithm 100
panAngle 221

panAngle parameter, HoverCamera3D class 222
parameters, SkyBox6 class
  material 64
parameters, Skybox class
  back 63
  down 63
  front 63
  left 63
  right 63
  up 63
parameters, Trident class
  len 69
  showLetters 69
parameters, WireframeMaterial material
  thickness 140
  wireAlpha 140
  wirecolor 140
parent coordinate system. *See also* parent space 73, 74
parse() function 181
Particle3D class 259
particleContainer property 258
particlesRemoved() function 260
particle system
  about 255
  Away3D Stardust initializer, creating 256, 257
  Away3D Stardust particle renderer, creating 258-260
  implementing 255, 256
  Stardust emitter, creating 261-265
PathAlignModifier class 277
PathAlignModifier object 283, 284
Path class 277
PathCommand.LINE constant 282
PathCommand class 277
PathCommand constructor 282
PathCommands objects 281
Path constructor 289
PathDebug object 281
PathExtrusion class
  about 288
  demonstrating 288
Path object 289
PathSegment objects 289
PerspectiveLens class 210

PhongBitmapMaterial material
  about 122, 157
  init object parameters 158
PhongColorMaterial material
  about 122, 158
  init object parameters 159
PhongMovieMaterial material
  about 122, 159
  init object parameters 160
PhongMultiPassMaterial material
  about 122, 164
  init object parameters 164
PhongPBMaterial material
  about 122, 162, 163
  init object parameters 164
phong shading, shading techniques 126
pitch() function 87
Pixel Bender 121, 335
Pixel Bender materials
  about 161
  CubicEnvMapPBMaterial 167, 168
  Dot3BitmapMaterialF10 161, 162
  FresnelPBMaterial 165, 166
  PhongMultiPassMaterial 164
  PhongPBMaterial 162, 164
Pixel Bender Shaders
  applying 320
  implementing 121
Plane3D class 236
Plane3D getIntersectionLineNumbers()
  function 239
Plane class
  about 57
  init object parameters 58
PointLight3D class 122
pointLight property 130
Position3D initializer 263
positionOffset property, SpringCam class 224
position property
  coordinate systems 78
Prefab
  about 205
  download link 205
primitive 3D objects
  common init object properties 45
  cone 46, 47

creating 39-44
cube 47, 49
cylinder 51
geodesic sphere 52, 53
grid plane 54, 55
LineSegment 56
plane 57
RegularPolygon 58
RoundedCube 59
sea turtle 60
skybox 62, 63
skybox6 63
sphere 64
torus 66
triangle 67
trident 68
PrimitivesDemo class 40
profile 288
projectionVector init object parameter,
  TransformBitmapMaterial class 144
properties, MouseEvent3D class
  ctrlKey 227
  elementVO 227
  material 227
  object 227
  sceneX 227
  sceneY 227
  sceneZ 227
  screenX 226
  screenY 226
  screenZ 226
  shiftKey 227
  uv 227
  view 227
public properties, SpringCam class
  damping 223
  lookOffset 224
  mass 224
  positionOffset 224
  stiffness 223
  target 223
pushback property 104
pushfront property 103

Q

QuadrantRenderer 325

[381]

R

RAM 336
recenter init object parameter 295
recenter parameter 292
RectangleClipping class 339
RectangleClipping constructor 339
reflectiveness init object parameter, Enviro-BitmapMaterial class 152
reflectiveness init object parameter, Enviro-ColorMaterial class 154
refractionStrength init object parameter, FresnelPBMaterial 166
RegularPolygon class
  about 58
  init object parameters 59
R ELEMENTS 336
removeCurrentPrimitive() function 43, 44
removeLights() function 132
removeOnMouseDown() function 237
removeOnMouseMove() function 237
removeOnMouseOut() function 237
removeOnMouseOver() function 237
removeOnMouseUp() function 237
removeOnRollOut() function 237
removeOnRollOver() function 237
removePrimitive() function 130
render() function 259
Render class 108
Renderer class 108
renderer init object parameter 108
RenderersDemo application 109, 110
RenderersPerformanceDemo application 112, 113, 115
Render Session object 326
repeat init object parameter, BitmapMaterial class 142
resource management
  about 118
  embedded resources 118
  external resources 118
roll() function 87
ROLL_OVER / ROLL_OUT
  MOUSE_OVER / MOUSE_OUT, diffentiating between 227-231
Rotation3D initializer 264
rotation init object parameter, TransformBitmapMaterial class 144
rotation property
  coordinate systems 78
rotationX property 71
rotationY property 71
rotationZ property 71
RoundedCube class
  about 59
  init object parameters 60

S

ScaleCurve action 265
scale property
  coordinate systems 79
scaleX init object parameter, TransformBitmapMaterial class 144
scaleY init object parameter, TransformBitmapMaterial class 144
scene
  sorting 100-103
Scene3D class 73
scenePivotPoint property 87
screenZOffset init object parameter 357
screenZOffset property 104, 105
SeaTurtle class 95, 189 61
segments 38
selectedMesh property 344
selectedObject property 233, 238
selectedObject variable 238
set() function 257
setupText() function 278
ShaderFilter class 312
shaders 121
ShadingColorMaterial material
  about 122, 155
  init object parameters 156
shading techniques
  about 123
  environment mapping 125
  flat shading 126
  normal mapping 124, 125
  phong shading 126
  texture mapping 123
shininess init object parameter, Dot3BitmapMaterial class 161

shininess init object parameter, Dot3BitmapMaterialF10 162
shininess init object parameter, PhongBitmapMaterial class 158
shininess init object parameter, PhongColorMaterial class 159
shininess init object parameter, PhongMovieMaterial class 160
shininess init object parameter, WhiteShadingBitmapMaterial class 155
showAnchors property 281
showNormals init object parameter, BitmapMaterial class 143
SinglePoint3D class 263
Sketch-Up
  3D models, exporting from 176
SkinExtrude 3D object 300
SkinExtrusion 3D object 302
SkinExtrusion class 297
SkinExtrusionDemo application 297
Skybox6 class
  about 63
  parameters 64
Skybox class
  about 62, 63
  parameters 63
smooth init object parameter, BitmapMaterial class 142
smooth init object parameter, EnviroColorMaterial class 154
sorting order
  adjusting 103
  ownCanvas property 106
  pushback property 104
  pushfront property 103
  screenZOffset property 104, 105
sourceBitmapData parameter 331
source parameter 128
sourceRect parameter 331
specular init object parameter, Dot3BitmapMaterial class 161
specular init object parameter, Dot3BitmapMaterialF10 162
specular init object parameter, PhongBitmapMaterial class 158
specular init object parameter, PhongColorMaterial class 159

specular init object parameter, PhongMovieMaterial class 160
specular init object parameter, PhongMultiPassMaterial 165
specular init object parameter, PhongPBMaterial 164
specular init object parameter, ShadingColorMaterial class 157
specularMap init object parameter, PhongMultiPassMaterial 165
specularMap init object parameter, PhongPBMaterial 164
Sphere 3D object 27
Sphere class
  about 64
  init object parameters 65
Sphere class constructor 72
SphereDemo
  running 28
  running, in Adobe Flash Builder 28
  running, in Adobe Flash CS4 28
  running, in Adobe Flex Builder 28
  running, in FlashDevelop 28
SphereDemo class 26
SphereDemo constructor 26
SphereShell class 263
SphericalLens class 210, 211
Spin3D action 265
SpringCam class
  about 223
  public properties 223
spring camera 223
Sprite3D 35-37
Sprite3D class
  about 242
  example 242-244
  implementing 242
Sprite3DDemo class 242
Sprite3D object 257
sprite classes
  about 241
  DepthOfFieldSprite 241
  DirectionalSprite 241
  Sprite3D 241
SpriteSession class 326
Stardust
  about 256

URL 256
stardust.initializers package 256
StarDustDemo 265
Stardust emitter
  creating 261-265
Stardust Initializer3D class 256
StarDustSparksEmitter class 262
static models
  3DS 190
  ASE 197
  AWD 193
  KMZ 197
  OBJ 200
Stats object 336
statsPanel property 336
SteadyClock class 262
step() function 266
steps parameter, HoverCamera3D class 222
stiffness property, SpringCam class 223
subdivisions parameter 325
SWF FR 336
SWF frameRate meta tag 337
swfvector 269

T

T2 application 298
target camera 219
TargetCamera3D class
  about 219
  init object parameters 220
target init object parameter 219
targetModel init object parameter, CubicEnvMapPBMaterial 168
targetModel init object parameter, FresnelPBMaterial 166
targetModel init object parameter, PhongMultiPassMaterial 165
targetModel init object parameter, PhongPBMaterial 164
target property, SpringCam class 223
T ELEMENTS 336
terrain
  creating, with SkinExtrusion class 297-301
terrain surface height
  reading, with ElevationReader Class 302-306

TextExtrusion class 288
TextField3D class 271
TextField3D constructor 272
TextField object 134, 314
TextField text property 138
TextureLoader class 127
TextureLoader object 170
TextureLoadQueue addItem() function 170
TextureLoadQueue class 127
  about 169
  using, for loading multiple external resources 169, 171
texture mapping, shading techniques 123
textures
  about 117
  BitmapFileMaterial 169
  differentiating, with materials 117
  loading, from external resources 168
  loading, TextureLoadQueue used 169, 170
TextWarpingDemo class 277
the init object parameters, GridPlane class
  height 55
  segments 55
  segmentsH 55
  segmentsW 55
  width 55
  yUp 55
thickness init object parameter, WireframeMaterial class 140
throughProjection init object parameter, TransformBitmapMaterial class 144
throughScreenVector property 233
ticksPerCall constructor parameter 262
tiltAngle parameter, HoverCamera3D class 222
TortoiseSVN
  about 9
  downloading 9
  installing 9, 10
Torus class
  about 66
  init object parameters 67
trace() function 228
traceLevels() function 304
TransformBitmapMaterial material
  about 143
  init object parameters 144

transform init object parameter, Transform-BitmapMaterial class 144
transform matrix 89
transform property
  coordinate systems 79
transparent init object parameter, MovieMaterial class 146
triangle caching 341-344
TriangleCachingDemo application 342
Triangle class
  about 67
  init object parameters 68
Trident class
  about 68
  parameters 69
tweening
  about 89
  example application 90, 91
TweeningDemo 90
TweenLite
  about 89
  downloading 89
TweenLite class 90
tweenToRandomPosition() function 91

U

UniformRandom class 263
url init object parameter, BitmapFileMaterial 169
UV coordinates 38, 39

V

vase
  creating, with LatheExtrusion class 293, 294, 295
Vector3D objects 289
VectorText class 271
Velocity3D initializer 263
View3D class 336
View3D constructor 108
View3D renderer property 325 109
ViewportClippingDemo application 340
viewport output
  scaling 340

viewport size
  reducing 339
Vizzy Flash Tracer 205

W

wallPoints array 292
walls
  creating, with LinearExtrusion class 291, 292
WhiteShadingBitmapMaterial material
  about 122, 154
  init object parameters 155
wireAlpha init object parameter, WireframeMaterial class 140
wirecolor init object parameter 119
wireColor init object parameter, BitmapMaterial class 142
wirecolor init object parameter, WireColorMaterial class 139
wirecolor init object parameter, WireframeMaterial class 140
WireColorMaterial material
  about 117, 137
  applying 137
  init object parameters 139
WireframeMaterial material
  about 139
  parameters 140
world space 72
wrapPanAngle parameter, HoverCamera3D class 222
wumedia package 269

Y

yaw() function 87
yfactor parameter, HoverCamera3D class 222

Z

z-Sorting 100
z-sorting 107
z depth 100
ZDepthFilter 348
ZoomFocusLens class 210

Thank you for buying
Away3D 3.6 Essentials

About Packt Publishing

Packt, pronounced 'packed', published its first book "*Mastering phpMyAdmin for Effective MySQL Management*" in April 2004 and subsequently continued to specialize in publishing highly focused books on specific technologies and solutions.

Our books and publications share the experiences of your fellow IT professionals in adapting and customizing today's systems, applications, and frameworks. Our solution based books give you the knowledge and power to customize the software and technologies you're using to get the job done. Packt books are more specific and less general than the IT books you have seen in the past. Our unique business model allows us to bring you more focused information, giving you more of what you need to know, and less of what you don't.

Packt is a modern, yet unique publishing company, which focuses on producing quality, cutting-edge books for communities of developers, administrators, and newbies alike. For more information, please visit our website: www.packtpub.com.

About Packt Open Source

In 2010, Packt launched two new brands, Packt Open Source and Packt Enterprise, in order to continue its focus on specialization. This book is part of the Packt Open Source brand, home to books published on software built around Open Source licences, and offering information to anybody from advanced developers to budding web designers. The Open Source brand also runs Packt's Open Source Royalty Scheme, by which Packt gives a royalty to each Open Source project about whose software a book is sold.

Writing for Packt

We welcome all inquiries from people who are interested in authoring. Book proposals should be sent to author@packtpub.com. If your book idea is still at an early stage and you would like to discuss it first before writing a formal book proposal, contact us; one of our commissioning editors will get in touch with you.

We're not just looking for published authors; if you have strong technical skills but no writing experience, our experienced editors can help you develop a writing career, or simply get some additional reward for your expertise.

Unity 3D Game Development by Example Beginner's Guide

ISBN: 978-1-849690-54-6 Paperback: 384 pages

A seat-of-your-pants manual for building fun, groovy little games quickly

1. Build fun games using the free Unity 3D game engine even if you've never coded before
2. Learn how to "skin" projects to make totally different games from the same file – more games, less effort!
3. Deploy your games to the Internet so that your friends and family can play them
4. Packed with ideas, inspiration, and advice for your own game design and development

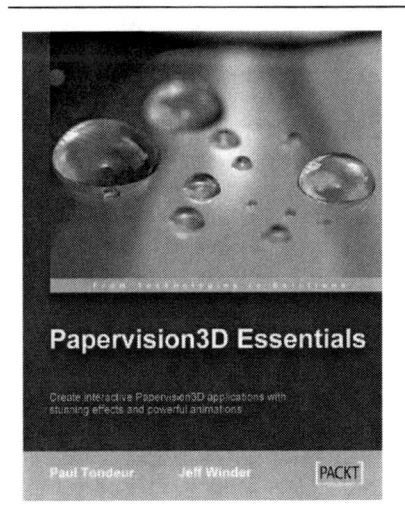

Papervision3D Essentials

ISBN: 978-1-847195-72-2 Paperback: 428 pages

Create interactive Papervision 3D applications with stunning effects and powerful animations

1. Build stunning, interactive Papervision3D applications from scratch
2. Export and import 3D models from Autodesk 3ds Max, SketchUp and Blender to Papervision3D
3. In-depth coverage of important 3D concepts with demo applications, screenshots and example code.
4. Step-by-step guide for beginners and professionals with tips and tricks based on the authors' practical experience

Please check **www.PacktPub.com** for information on our titles

CPSIA information can be obtained at www.ICGtesting.com
Printed in the USA
238602LV00003B/5/P